BRITISH CINEMA
AND
THATCHERISM

BRITISH CINEMA
AND
THATCHERISM

Fires were started

Edited by

Lester Friedman

UCL
PRESS

© 1993 by the Regents of the University of Minnesota

First published in 1993 in Great Britain by UCL Press

UCL Press Limited
University College London
Gower Street
London WC1E 6BT

The name of University College London (UCL) is a registered
trade mark used by UCL Press with the consent of the owner.

ISBN: 1-85728-072-5 HB
ISBN: 1-85728-073-3 PB

A CIP catalogue record for this book is available from the British Library.

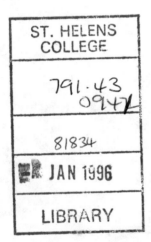
Typeset in Century Old Style.
Printed in the United States of America on acid-free paper

For Delia
With great affection and respect

Being a film producer in England in 1985 is bewildering. Continuous requests from journalists across Europe for interviews suggest that they know something you don't. Their view of someone producing films in London as someone at the centre of a dynamic surge of creative energy is far indeed from the actual experience; an experience of scarcity, deviousness and stark pessimism. During the press conference . . . at the Berlin Film Festival this year, I was asked what structures existed to allow the making of films to such professional standards yet without obvious commercial intent. The answer was a description of a system that soon will have no provision for the art of cinema to the extent that this differs from the commerce of the cinema; of a country in which people whose work would be valued by industry and government in any other European country are often left unable to work at all; and of the most backward official attitude to independent cinema anywhere in Europe.

—Peter Sainsbury, producer

For fifty years public policy (as expressed principally in government legislation) has taken the direction of measures to shore up the British component of what was seen in cinemas (and also on TV). The means adopted have been trade measures (quotas, levies, occasional subsidies), operating under a cultural cover: the business was worth supporting because the product was artistic and part of national culture. It is time to do away with this humbug and look more closely at what the national culture is and what part British films, new or old, have to play in it. By its lumpen-monetarist approach to this industry, the Conservative Government has swept away some of the humbug. But the effect will be purely negative if the elimination of an industrial policy for the cinema is not used as an opportunity to promote a cultural policy in its place.

—Geoffrey Nowell-Smith

Contents

Preface

Like many film teachers in their mid-forties, I have little formal training in cinema studies. Instead, I came to film via Saturday matinees and double features, combining a love of movies with graduate studies in literary history, theory, and criticism. My academic concentration was on the British Romantic Era, and though I wanted to write my doctoral dissertation on film and literature, my adviser sagely warned me that such a topic would squash my chances for a job in any reputable English department. That was "popular culture," he said dismissively, adding that it might draw students to English classes but was clearly not suitable for serious and rigorous study. So, accepting his advice, I wrote on the works of Milton and Shelley, a choice designed to set me firmly on the traditional academic path of literary studies. But I was not quite through with film. I taught it via crossover electives with titles like "Literature and Film" or "The Novel and the Film." I even published an article on *Frankenstein* in a collection about film adaptations of English novels, combining my knowledge of the nineteenth century and of film. With a sympathetic colleague, I contemplated an anthology about film and literature, one tentatively titled to mimic the phrase uttered so repetitively by our students: "No, but I saw the movie."

British films, in particular, filled my need for a wide variety of literary adaptations that my English department colleagues might consider acceptable. After all, such movies were based on serious works of literature, and those cultured British accents were highly valued in academic enclaves. But how disappointing most of these films really were, neither matching the power of their sources nor working as a pure cinematic experience. Their slow and ponderous pace, as well as stodgy fidelity to detail, proved no match for their

American counterparts: the bawdy humor of *The Graduate*, the frenetic pacing of *Bonnie and Clyde*, or the cynical heroism of *The Wild Bunch*. Seeing Olivier in *Hamlet* or *Henry V* proved of little interest to my students, and David Lean's meticulous mise-en-scène provided small recompense for having to read *Oliver Twist* or *Great Expectations*. Even the more modern films left them cold, say *Loneliness of the Long Distance Runner* or *Look Back in Anger*. They did respond a bit better to *Tom Jones*, though I always suspected that the cleavage, not the cinematic style, engaged them. So, after a few years of struggling to connect literature and cinema, of teaching first-rate films of second-rate novels or second-rate films of first-rate literature, I simply gave up and taught them as essentially separate entities, each with its own unique assets and limitations. I rarely included British movies in my film classes; I'd had enough of that restrained solemnity and boring camera work to last me a lifetime.

I recite this brief history of my academic life to recount how many of us now teaching film first encountered British cinema and to understand, perhaps, one reason it has excited so little scholarly and commercial interest over the years. Except for the brief flurry of attention during the late fifties and early sixties, the so-called Free Cinema movement, and an even briefer fixation with the "Swinging London" of the later sixties, both audiences and academics basically ignored the British cinema. Such, however, was not the case with British film during the Thatcher era. On the commercial level, both *Chariots of Fire* (1981) and *Gandhi* (1983) swept the Oscar competition, prompting verification of scriptwriter Collin Welland's exuberant declaration: "The British are coming!" Such a cry found equal validation in the government-backed declaration of 1985 as the "Year of the British Film," a self-promotional gimmick that drew further attention to British movies. Yet beneath all the hype was some real, some significant, substance. British filmmakers from all segments of the industry turned out picture after picture that demanded attention. They struggled with the social and economic upheavals that characterized the Thatcher years, creating a cinema that made the world take notice.

Thatcherism

"Mrs. Thatcher has resigned from No. 10. Thank God!" So read the scrawled message that greeted harried commuters at the Bethnal Green subway stop in the East End, a working-class section of London. Yet to her staunch allies, Margaret Thatcher's precipitous fall from power was, as one newspaper reported, a case where "the termites have finally felled the oak." Clearly, few in her own country, in Europe, or for that matter around the world, took a neutral position about Great Britain's first woman prime minister, the so-called Iron Lady who won three election victories and dominated British politics for a turbulent eleven-year reign (1979-90). During this period, Thatcher often turned events in her favor, from the brief but successful war with Argentina over the Falkland Islands (April 1962), to the rancorous victory over the National Union of Mineworkers (March 1984), to the narrow escape from an IRA bombing (October 1984). Starting on February 11, 1975, when she defeated Edward Heath to gain the leadership of the (then in opposition) Conservative party, until November 22, 1990, when she resigned after failing to gain enough votes to continue her leadership of that same party, Margaret Thatcher radically changed the face of Great Britain, offering the citizens of her country a combination of economic, political, social, and ideological principles that so completely broke with the post–World War II consensus as to totally restructure British daily life. After all, how many other prime ministers became an -ism during their own lifetimes?

The most prominent component of Thatcherism remains its economic policies. She deplored what she contemptuously labeled "the Nanny State" and consistently sought ways to eliminate what she deemed as governmental "interference" within the economic sphere. "We should not expect the state," she told the electorate in 1980, "to appear in the guise of an extravagant good fairy at every christening, a loquacious companion at every stage of life's journey, the unknown mourner at every funeral" (*Newsweek*, December 3, 1990, 30). To accomplish this, Thatcher set up programs that favored the individual over the collective state: promoting thrift, eliminating Keynesian deficit financing, curtailing subsidies to ailing industries, selling council houses to sitting tenants, ignoring union demands, defending "sound" money policies, privatizing $57 billion worth of state-owned industries, lifting foreign-exchange controls, encouraging free-market economics (Biddiss, 2; Finer, 129). Using such slogans as "Roll Back the Frontiers of the State" and "Set the People Free," the Thatcher-led Conservatives united the disgruntled middle and upper classes against the working and lower classes to assault and ultimately dismantle the institutional and governmental policies that dominated postwar Great Britain. As Rudolf Klein characterizes it, "For the first time since 1945 Britain actually had a Government which took pride in stressing how little it could do, instead of emphasizing how much it would do" (quoted in Biddiss, 7).

Socially, Thatcher defined her philosophy as incorporating decidedly "Victorian" values. The daughter of a small-town greengrocer from Grantham, Thatcher's personal beliefs spring from her traditional background: self-reliance, family discipline, self-control, patriotism, individual duty (Gould and Anderson, 42). "She has presented herself as the champion of those keenest to exercise personal responsibility, to exhibit self-reliance and initiative, to maintain the traditional structure and role of the family, and to recognize the demands of duty as well as the allure of entitlements" (Biddiss, 2). This form of "competitive self-interest" was enthusiastically welcomed by the economic community, a segment of British society well suited to her particular brand of social Darwinism. From the Left, however, her positions were characterized far less as gentility as patriarchalism, racism, and imperialist nostalgia (Hall and Jacques, 11). Such beliefs also underline the two major political blunders that finally ended her career: (1) the hated Poll Tax, which reduced the tax burden on large property owners and placed it on lower and middle class citizens, and (2) her stubborn refusal to bring Great Britain harmoniously into the European Community (EC) integration.

On this side of the Atlantic, Thatcher captured the public imagination as no British politician has since Winston Churchill. Much of this stems from her close personal relationship and political affinity with the popular Ronald Reagan, a man with whom she shared a commitment to curbing the role of government and establishing the power of free enterprise. His first state dinner, for example, was for her, as was his last. At home, Labour party members often criticized Thatcher for her obsession with America, charging that she should seek closer ties with the European Community rather than with the United States; yet, she never wavered from her position as America's staunchest ally throughout her entire time in office. In his book *Reagan and Thatcher*, Goeffrey Smith talks about how much these two leaders had in common, from their modest upbringing in archetypal small towns, to their initial status as political outsiders viewed as ideological extremists, to their similar economic, domestic, and foreign policy philosophies. Reagan, of course, fully supported Thatcher during the Falklands war, providing much-needed military and political support; she vigorously defended his attack of Libya, allowing U.S. bombers to refuel on British air bases before taking their revenge on Colonel Qaddafi. Her deep bond to America lasted beyond Reagan's term in office: one of her last official acts as prime minister was to deploy fourteen thousand British troops to Saudi Arabia.

How, then, to capture Thatcherism in a few brief catch phrases? David Marquand spells out four basic dimensions: (1) Thatcherism is a sort of British Gaullism that grew out of a pervading sense of despair and national decline; (2) Thatcherism rests upon an economic foundation that rejects Keynesian theory and supports a free-market economy; (3) Thatcherism embodies a conservative Toryism that stresses patriotism and British traditions; (4) Thatcherism is style as well as substance, a charismatic populism where "the leader knows instinctively what the populace feel and want" (Marquand, 160-66). Year after year during the 1980s, movies from Great

Britain engaged the attention of the world, a diverse series of pictures prov-
ing an intimate, often quite uncomfortable, look into the modern British consciousness molded by Thatcher and her policies. Many of these films directly
attacked the Thatcher government, seeing her free-market philosophy as a
callous disregard for everyone but the entrepreneurial buccaneers who plun-
dered the economy; others portrayed the strains of living in a society torn
apart by racial hatred and domestic poverty. Some rejected the constraints
of formal narrative structures to explore the intricacies of form and shape, of
time and space. Yet all these texts, in one form or another, spring from a
distinct period in British history, one dominated by the powerful rhetoric, decisive actions, and pervasive ideology of Margaret Thatcher.

Methodological Assumptions about Authorship

This anthology attempts to situate a group of texts within a stream of cultural, historical, and ideological factors. But to write about directors as we
do will no doubt strike some as naive, since filmmaking is obviously a collab-
orative effort that depends on many people, technologies, situations, and
conditions beyond the conscious control of so-called auteurs. Yet, those involved in filmmaking know that almost all production crews function via a hierarchy, one in which anyone may contribute but where one person (often
the director) must ultimately decide what is and what is not included in the
final work. Within the scholarly community, some will immediately dismiss
this approach as ignoring the main thrust of contemporary film theory. We
live in a world dominated by poststructuralist thought, one in which Roland
Barthes declares the death of the author and Jacques Derrida rejects individual consciousness as the source of meaning. Deconstruction, reader-
response criticism, Marxism, reception theory, semiotics, structuralism,
psychoanalytic theory, phenomenology, negative hermeneutics, and other
contemporary modes of critical thought either downgrade or totally eliminate the traditionally dominant role of the author in the making and meaning
of a text. As Bill Nichols summarizes the writings of poststructuralist think-
ers, the author basically "becomes a fictitious unity masking the patterns of
regulation and control that characterize the systems or codes of which the
subject is only an expression" (Nichols, 8). Here any idea of the author as
self-expressive personality free from social and aesthetic restraints virtually
disappears, because one can think and communicate only through various
culture-bound systems and codes. Obliterating the person, the text, in effect, creates the author's identity.

Clearly, elements of poststructuralist thought are quite liberating, particularly in regard to some basic authorial and critical issues. Conceiving of the

text as composed of unlimited, even contradictory, "meanings," rather than restricting it to one or two master themes officially sanctioned by critical consensus, opens works to a healthy abundance of diverse approaches. By thus freeing readers from the impossible task of searching for what the author "truly means," modern theorists encourage a range of possible responses, thereby fostering a play of irreconcilable differences that rub against the grain of any particular text. Such a process exposes the cracks and fissures in texts previously seen as unified. "The object of the critic," argues Catherine Belsey, "is to seek not the unity of the work, but the multiplicity and diversity of its possible meanings" (Belsey, 104). Insistence on the inherent ideological position of all criticism forces reconsideration of previous judgments as accepted absolutes, understanding them instead as subjective points of view about a particular artwork rather than objective truths. Thus, modern theorists force us to recognize that every critic's evaluations rest on a partly conscious, partly unconscious system of particular beliefs and values about human beings and artistry.

These poststructuralist positions necessarily force authors to relinquish their traditional authority over the text, since their interpretations stand as no more "correct" than those of other readers. Once the work is completed, therefore, the author becomes simply another commentator about its meaning. We need not feel constrained by the boundaries of an artist's personal understanding, or to cite D. H. Lawrence's famous dictum: "Never trust the artist. Trust the tale." A clear-cut example here would be Shakespeare; obviously, he never studied Freud, yet his works possess powerful psychological insights that make them relevant to our own time. To limit ourselves to discussing only what a sixteenth-century, bourgeois Englishman meant his plays to be about (assuming we could discover what that was) would drastically simplify the dramas, perhaps confining their value to historical artifact. But by analyzing Shakespeare's plays via a terminology, a belief system if you will, that the author could never know, modern critics make the works more understandable, more meaningful, to a generation obsessed with psychoanalysis. Thus, every age "discovers" what elements in a work of art relate most to its own needs and desires. Such is the case in the cinema, as well as in the other arts, so we should not be surprised to find filmmakers shocked by interpretations of their own movies.

But even poststructuralist theories must still account for something constructed by someone, even if that someone was determined and constrained by certain systems and codes. Authors are, indeed, social constructions; they must be understood as existing with specific elements of time, style, attitude, form, and meaning. But even shifting an author's voice from dominant to equal among other readers of the text should not totally eliminate him or her from the ensuing discourse. John Caughie suggests that discussions about authorship serve to tie a piece to outside social and historical forces by examining how the author's "place within a particular social history is written into the text" (Caughie, 2-3). Paul Giles goes even further when he warns us that "a critic in the 1980s should not neglect Shakespeare's modes and institutions of production, but . . . not treat Shakespeare's plays as being equivalent to those of Thomas Kyd, for whom the modes of production are very similar" (Giles, 2). For Pam Cook, the modern assault on the artist as sole creator has transformed, not destroyed, auteurism, "from a way of accounting for the whole of cinema into a critical methodology which poses questions for film study and cultural practices in general" (Cook, 114). Thus, a notion of authorship helps to establish a text's cultural, social, and historical context, but does not limit its relevance to a particular time and place. By analyzing these films produced by British directors during a distinct period, the writers in this anthology situate these texts into an amalgam of cultural, social, institutional, and historical conditions.

Construction and Organization

This anthology is divided into two major sections. The first portion, "Cultural Contexts and Cinematic Constructions," establishes the background for the films made during the Thatcher era that will be discussed subsequently. It makes readers dig into the soil that nourishes these movies. So, for example, Leonard Quart's essay explores the politics of Margaret Thatcher, analyzing her policies and elaborating on the films that responded to her philosophy. Peter Wollen, concerned more with cinematic than political history, compares the films made during the 1980s with those made during that Free Cinema period, paying particular attention to how modernism shaped the films of Derek Jarman and Peter Greenaway. Turning his attention to the British image culture, Thomas Elsaesser scrutinizes the relationships between a "social imaginary" of Britain and the projection of a "national imaginary"—the relation of Britishness to a national cinema. Paying more attention to the interconnections between television and film during the 1980s, Paul Giles probes Channel Four's contribution to British filmmaking during the decade, specifically how television affected the aesthetics of British films during this era.

One particular area that consistently attracted the attention of directors and screenwriters during the Thatcher years was the continued violence in Northern Ireland; Brian McIlroy contextualizes a series of these films, demonstrating how mainstream filmmakers became more assertive and aggressive in their presentation of these "problems" over the course of the decade.

Like Thomas Elsaesser, Andrew Higson sees British films as commodities for consumption in the international image market, though here he focuses on the cycle of quality costume dramas called "heritage films." For him, these pictures depict an ambivalence of nostalgia, one that ostensibly criticizes but emotionally embraces the past. The last essay in this section, Mary Desjardins's discussion of motherhood during the Thatcher era, shows how the positioning of mothers within specific narratives represents the British culture coming to terms with feminism, particularly during a time when both their queen and their prime minister were women. Taken as a whole, then, the essays in this first section provide an industrial, psychological, political, social, and ideological context for this era of dramatic and dynamic changes in British life.

The essays in Part 2 of this anthology, "Filmmakers during the Thatcher Era," elaborate upon the works of a representative sample of directors during this period, ranging from works by established artists to new moviemakers who came to prominence in this decade. So, for example, Manthia Diawara and Antonia Lant investigate two types of collectives, each one defined by a particular ideological agenda: films made by black collectives (Ceddo, Black Audio, Sankofa) and women's independent collectives (Leeds Animation Workshop) during the 1980s. Both demonstrate how the contours of independent British film production in the 1980s, which appeared rather narrow from the vantage point of the United States, were actually aesthetically varied and thematically diverse. Next, Barry Grant and Jim Leach investigate the 1980s work of two directors prominent before the Thatcher era, Ken Russell and Nicolas Roeg. Each writer finds new and interesting changes during this time. For Grant, Russell's films during this period aptly demonstrate both the values of British tradition and a disdain for them that mirrors the tensions inherent in Thatcherism itself. Leach, using Roeg's films to explore the homogenizing effect of American cultural power during the 1980s, places Roeg's British perspective on American culture within the context of the ideology of Thatcherism.

Susan Barber, too, looks at a director whose career began before Thatcher became prime minister, but whose reputation rose dramatically during her reign: Stephen Frears. She positions his films as reactions to and critiques of the dynamics of Thatcherism—specifically with respect to race, class, and gender—as she charts Frears's increasing disillusionment with the Thatcher administration. Tony Williams also sees the work of a far different type of director, Terence Davies, as challenging the hegemony of Thatcherism, this time the officially sanctioned family institution. Williams charts Davies' pictorialization of how this reactionary authoritarianism has caused misery for those outside the family norm. In a similar manner, Michael Walsh elaborates on Peter Greenaway's productions during the 1980s, seeing him as an allegorist whose features comment indirectly but decisively on the postimperial Britain of Margaret Thatcher. Finally, Chris Lippard and Guy Johnson examine how issues of health and illness, which have long preoccupied British filmmakers, become metaphors for contagion during the 1980s; in particular, the films of Derek Jarman use sickness as a position of power from which to dissolve narrative and threaten established power.

Taken as a whole, then, this collection of essays establishes the unique relationship between the era of Margaret Thatcher and the diverse group of filmmakers who invigorated the British cinema during her time of power. Perhaps the only common element connecting these directors is their revulsion, to one degree or another, for the ideology of Thatcherism, though their methods of expressing that distaste cover the spectrum of aesthetic options. Some of the most potent political opposition to the Thatcher government, therefore, appeared in the movie theaters rather than in the House of Commons. Ironically, of course, one might argue that a less commanding and infuriating figure than Margaret Thatcher, even one proposing similar policies, would have failed to rouse the ire of Britain's filmmakers to such a fever pitch. So, in a truly paradoxical manner, the intense and unwavering hatred of Margaret Thatcher provided the spark necessary to force Britain's best visual artists to new creative heights and, in so doing, to ignite a moribund industry. More importantly for those not intimately connected to the British culture, these pictures bear little resemblance to the tastefully tedious adaptations that so many of us associate with the British cinema. They forcefully demonstrate how filmmakers, though not legislators of the world, can at least offer a viable alternative to officially sanctioned versions of the truth, while at the same time creating bold and serious works that reach far beyond the confines of geography and petty politics.

Works Cited

Belsey, Catherine. 1980. *Critical Practice*. London: Methuen.
Biddiss, Michael. 1987. "Thatcherism: Concept and Interpretations." In *Thatcherism*, edited by Minogue and Biddiss, 1-20.
Caughie, John, ed. 1981. *Theories in Authorship: A Reader*. London: Routledge and Kegan Paul.
Cook, Pam, ed. 1985. *The Cinema Book*. New York: Pantheon.
Finer, S. E. 1987. "Thatcherism and British Political History." In *Thatcherism*, edited by Minogue and Biddiss, 127-40.
Giles, Paul. 1991. "The Cinema of Catholicism: John Ford and Robert Altman." In *Unspeakable Images: Ethnicity in American Cinema*, edited by Lester D. Friedman. Champaign: University of Illinois Press, 140-66.
Gould, Julius, and Digby Anderson. "Thatcherism and British Society," in *Thatcherism*, edited by Minogue and Biddiss, 38-54.
Hall, Stuart, and Martin Jacques, eds. 1983. *The Politics of Thatcherism*. London: Lawrence and Wishart.

Marquand, David. 1988. "The Paradoxes of Thatcherism." In *Thatcherism*, edited by Skidelsky, 159-72.

Minogue, Kenneth, and Michael Biddiss, eds. 1987. *Thatcherism: Personality and Politics*. New York: St. Martin's Press.

Nichols, Bill, ed. 1985. *Movies and Methods: An Anthology*. Berkeley: University of California Press.

Skidelsky, Robert, ed. 1988. *Thatcherism*. London: Basil Blackwell.

Smith, Geoffrey. 1991. *Reagan and Thatcher*. New York: Norton.

Acknowledgments

Anthologies are curious hybrids: not quite collaborations, they nonetheless represent the shared intellectual and emotional energy between editor and contributor. Along with their energy, these writers also brought their receptive attitudes, wry wits, and understanding patience to this project. Never did I suffer from the slings of annoyance or the arrows of outrageous egos. I quickly grew to appreciate these generous habits of the mind as this project devoured my summer, especially as contributors previously known only through their work became friends whose voices I immediately recognized. My phone bill reflects our long conversations, many of which ranged well beyond their particular essay or my specific comments. I thank all the contributors to this anthology for their unflagging enthusiasm, dedication, and commitment to this project; they made a potentially difficult and draining process into an enjoyable and rewarding experience.

My wife Carolyn, as usual, provided me with much-needed doses of love and support during particularly stressful moments, as did my parents, Eva and Eugene Friedman. For assistance at the SUNY Health Science Center, I gratefully thank John Bernard Henry, president, and Donald Goodman, dean and provost, both of whom create an atmosphere in which diverse ideas can flourish. Sharon Osika-Michaels, part of the Liberal Arts and Sciences Division, provided expert secretarial services far beyond routine typing and proofreading. At Syracuse University, I continually benefit from the intellectual stimulation of my colleague, Owen Shapiro, and from the expert research skills of Denise Stevens at the E. S. Bird Library. Janaki Bakhle, acquisitions editor at the University of Minnesota Press, provided critical insight and enthusiastic support for this project from inception to completion, ably assisted by Robert Mosimann. This book also benefited from the sharp copyediting skills of Anne Running.

One person deserves special mention for helping me complete this anthology: Michael Nelson, a graduate film major in the Art Media Studies Department at Syracuse University. Mike was an integral part of this project from start to finish. He read and commented on all the early essay drafts, gave valuable structural suggestions, and performed necessary research tasks. Every teacher should be fortunate enough to find such a student.

I wish to thank the following sources, which supplied stills for this book: United Artists, Miramax, Academy of Motion Picture Arts and Sciences, Orion, Jerry Ohlinger's Movie Material Store, Samuel Goldwyn Company, British Film Institute, Warner Brothers, Leeds Animation Workshop, Cannon Releasing Corporation, Hemdale, and Cineaste.

One

The Empire Strikes Out: An American Perspective on the British Film Industry

Lester D. Friedman

> A typical nineteenth-century Punch cartoon would show two
> people sitting at a table, with up to eight lines of dialogue under
> the drawing. Cartoons nowadays have quite a different emphasis
> and consequently more impact. Much of what is described as
> British cinema is still in the Victorian cartoon age.
>
> — Simon Perry, producer

The British cinema industry has both benefited and suffered from sharing an ostensibly common language with its powerful American competitor. Over the years, the government made sporadic attempts to support its fledgling film industry: the first Cinematograph Films Act (1927), which outlawed block booking and imposed a compulsory quota of British films; the new Films Act (1938), which upped the quotas and regulated labor conditions; the National Film Finance Corporation (1949), which supported independent productions; and the Eady Levy (1950), which added a tax to ticket sales and used the revenues to subsidize production costs. In spite of these and other measures to spur British productions, American films dominated the British film market from the early days of the cinema until the present time. Many English filmmakers found America's post–World War II position of overwhelming box-office superiority particularly galling, claiming that Hollywood "exploited wartime disruptions to establish an unfair advantage" (Murphy, 47). In addition, the Hollywood tradition of block booking, a practice that gave foreign distributors first-rate films only if they also agreed to purchase lesser productions, left little room for homegrown products in British theaters. Finally, American studios routinely established joint projects with British production companies, thereby avoiding the government sanctions imposed on foreign films. As Alan Sapper, general secretary of the Association of Cinematograph, Television and Allied Technicians, noted:

> British film production levels rely mainly on American finance and on its
> ability to service national and international and cable operations. No reliance
> can be put on this boom period continuing for more than a year or so — if

1

the dollar/pound exchange rate deteriorates, as far as America is
concerned, so will our film production level. (quoted in Roddick, 16)

Hollywood, then, effectively colonialized Britain's native markets and, except for some relatively brief periods, the British failed to mount any effective challenge to this foreign domination of its film industry.

In addition to circumventing government policies and dominating movie
houses, the American film industry also damaged its British counterpart by
enticing the best on- and offscreen talent to work in the United States. Thus,
the rich coffers and worldwide distribution networks of Hollywood's sprawl-
ing studios eventually lured performers such as Charlie Chaplin, Richard
Burton, Sean Connery, David Niven, Robert Donat, Daniel Day Lewis,
Michael Caine, Jeremy Irons, Vanessa Redgrave, Malcolm McDowell, Julie
Christie, Cary Grant, Albert Finney, Alec Guinness, Dirk Bogarde, Lau-
rence Olivier, Peter O'Toole, Rex Harrison, Leslie Howard, Charles Laugh-
ton, Vivian Leigh, James Mason, and Peter Sellers to work in sunny Califor-
nia. Similarly, world-class directors such as Alfred Hitchcock, Richard
Attenborough, Clive Donner, Stephen Frears, Alan Parker, Ridley Scott, Alexander Korda, Michael Caton-Jones, Michael Apted, Terry Gilliam, Ronald
Neame, Carol Reed, Victor Saville, John Schlesinger, Peter Yates, Michael
Winner, Neil Jordan, Hugh Hudson, Ken Russell, John Boorman, and Tony
Scott all vacated Great Britain for the technical expertise, larger budgets,
and stronger world presence of the Hollywood feature film business. Some
nationalists castigated these performers and filmmakers for deserting their
homeland and thus impoverishing their native cinema. Yet can we really
blame them for seeking a niche within the American industry that regularly
churned out products, rather than banking their careers on the fitful British
industry?

The British movie business also suffers from attacks by native scholars
and commentators, a process Charles Barr labels "cultural self-laceration":

> This critical work has had a consistently greater prestige internationally
> than British cinema itself, and the very prestige of this tradition has, with a
> certain irony, helped to keep the prestige of British films at a low level, as a
> result of the consistent way in which the most progressive and interesting
> elements in this criticism have—at least until recently—been actively
> hostile, or at best indifferent, to the work of a commercial mainstream of
> the British cinema. (Barr, 7)

British critics who penned influential books or essays usually drew upon
American rather than British films, using American not British directors to
support their theories. So, for example, when Peter Wollen writes his
groundbreaking *Signs and Meaning in the Cinema*, he focuses on John Ford

and Orson Welles and Sergei Eisenstein; when Robin Wood investigates the cinema in a series of significant books, he explores the works of Arthur Penn and Howard Hawks and Ingmar Bergman; when Laura Mulvey expounds on her influential theory of pleasure and spectatorship, she cites examples from the American films of Hitchcock and von Sternberg. Wood seemingly spoke for a generation of British critics when, in 1974, he said, "My own reluctance to confront the British cinema is simply attributable to my sense that its achievement is so limited and so much less interesting than that of other countries" (Barr, 3). By emphasizing American rather than British products, these writers drew attention away from their native cinema and made Hollywood films even more dominant.

One can imagine how participants in a moviemaking industry competing directly with American products quickly understand the process described above as a perversely circular entrapment: American movies are financed better so they draw international talent, therefore they are distributed more widely, therefore they fill more local theaters and squeeze out native productions, therefore they are reviewed more often, therefore more people hear about them, therefore more people go to see them, therefore they make more money, therefore American films are better funded. . . . Putting it more simply, producer Leon Clore once remarked, "If the United States spoke Spanish, we would have a film industry" (Roddick, 5). Of course, others propose a far simpler reason to account for Hollywood's defeat of Great Britain's film industry: British films are simply not very good. François Truffaut summed up this attitude most succinctly when he claimed, in his 1966 book about Hitchcock, that there was "a certain incompatibility between the terms 'cinema' and 'Britain.' " Satyajit Ray expanded on this concept, claiming:

I do not think the British are temperamentally equipped to make the best use of the movie camera. The camera forces one to face facts, to probe, to reveal, to get close to people and things; while the British nature inclines to the opposite; to stay aloof, to cloak harsh truths with innuendoes. You cannot make great films if you suffer from constricting habits of this sort. What is more, the placidity and monotony of habit patterns that mark the British way of life are the exact opposite of what constitutes the real meat for the cinema. (Barr, 9)

As previously noted, British critics never effectively countered these types of assertions. In fact, by using their talents and insights to illuminate mainly American films, while basically ignoring the products of their own culture, they implicitly concurred with statements like those made by Truffaut and Ray.

We have already seen that the British film industry suffers because its actors and directors blend in so easily with their Hollywood counterparts. In Hollywood, few British directors need an interpreter on the set, and cultured British accents endow performers with an aura of stylish sophistication. In addition, British television programs as diverse as "The Benny Hill Show," "EastEnders," and "Masterpiece Theatre" remain a staple of public and cable television networks, retaining a reasonably large and loyal American viewership. Finally, the oft-cited "special" relationship between Great Britian and the United States—evidenced in England's important role in American history, the popularity of British rock music and fashion, and most recently the close connection between Margaret Thatcher and Ronald Reagan—does much to erase the natural proclivity of most Americans to distrust anything "foreign." Looking at these factors from the British film community's perspective, we might naturally assume that the absence of any language barriers, which allows this effortless access to American productions, would provide some positive trade-offs that compensate for the considerable damage it causes. In other words, how does a common language benefit the British movie business? For example, a similar language should allow British films to penetrate far deeper into American markets than do other non-U.S. productions. So, we might assume, British films could find audiences beyond the usual urban areas designed for foreign film distribution; they could reach viewers in less sophisticated locales, those sites traditionally inhospitable to movie subtitles, dubbed dialogue, and foreign environments.

Such has not been the case. While American film-goers welcome British directors and performers, British films rarely achieve popular acclaim and monetary rewards. Only a small percentage of British films, such as *The Private Life of Henry VIII* (1933) and *Chariots of Fire* (1981), ever match the financial levels attained by even moderately successful American pictures in the United States. The few times British companies did challenge the Americans on their home turf, notably Alexander Korda during the 1930s and J. Arthur Rank following World War II, they put few dents in the domestic market. Other than the occasional British blockbuster, typically a coproduction between local companies and American backers/studios, British films in America fared most successfully on the so-called art-house circuit, which catered to "a small but increasingly important middle-class audience which looked askance at the commercial vulgarity of Hollywood" (Murphy, 62). When we rightfully ignore essentialist statements like those of Truffaut and Ray that locate the problem of British films inherently within native character, and instead peer within the rigidly structured British society and film history, we quickly discover an interesting paradox: the same components

that buttress the British cinema simultaneously hinder its widespread acceptance among American audiences. These fundamental ingredients include
the British literary history, theatrical tradition, preoccupation with class issues, and emphasis on the documentary.

The magisterial tradition of literary excellence represents the brightest
jewel in Great Britain's cultural crown. Surely no American college or university, no matter how committed to critical theory or contemporary voices,
would dare eliminate classes in Shakespeare or Milton or Shelley. Certainly
no high-school student would graduate without at least some cursory exposure to a Bronte novel, a Shaw play, or a Browning poem. Most Americans
initially encounter these literary works within an academic environment of
enthusiastic teachers insistent on communicating the beauty of Wordsworth's
verse or the bleakness of Hardy's vision. Often, therefore, we associate
British literary works with serious contemplation, solemn veneration, and
portentous meanings. Of course, teachers desperately trying to reach their
students often incorporate film adaptations of classic British works into their
curricula, hoping to capture the imagination of a generation weaned on MTV
and far more attuned to cinematic rather than literary stimuli. Yet the inclu-
sion of such "Trojan horses" designed to lure students into appreciating
great examples of British literature reduces these films to just another
dreary homework assignment and eliminates the pleasures associated with
an evening at the flicks. Such reverence and weightiness, in fact, strikes
most students as stuffy, as far removed from the scent of buttered popcorn
and taste of stale Kit Kats.

The number of literary adaptations, particularly novels, within the British
film industry's yearly output ranges from about 5 percent to about 26 percent
(McFarlane, 121). Yet, at least in part because of potential educational markets, film adaptations of literary works represent the greatest proportion of
British films exported to the United States for residual rental purposes. Relatively few of these traditionally "tasteful" adaptations display any sense of
intellectual boldness or cinematic creativity. (Exceptions that spring to mind
are the works of Alfred Hitchcock, Michael Powell and Emeric Pressburger,
and Ken Russell, adaptations that rarely find their way into literature class-
rooms.) Instead, they genuflect reverently to the original source material,
rarely daring to venture very far beyond the most stolid of approaches:

> British adaptations have exhibited a decorous, dogged fidelity to their
> sources, content to render through careful attention to their *mise-en-scène*
> the social values and emotional insight of those sources rather than
> subjecting them to critical scrutiny or, indeed, to robust exploitation. . . .
> The standard British film version of the novel has been a prime example of

those pervasive qualities of "good taste, characterised by restraint,
understatement, and sophistication" which Alan Lovell identified as the
British cinema's "negative reactions" to the more dangerous and flamboyant
and vigorous aspects of Hollywood. (McFarlane, 120-21)

Though American cinema, too, often cannibalizes literary works, most
American filmmakers view their source material simply as a blueprint, usually feeling quite free to invent or eliminate characters, drastically alter locales, and totally transform endings — all done in the name of making elements "cinematic." Such mutations, when successful, delight mainstream
audiences who care little about fidelity to literary materials. So while the
British literary legacy provided its film industry with a seemingly limitless
source of subjects and stories, the obsession with faithfully recreating the
written work on the screen fostered a tentative cinema, one concerned
more with accuracy than with audaciousness.

Like its literary heritage, the British theatrical tradition also shackled its
film industry. In America during the cinema's so-called Golden Age, the respective centers for movies and plays remained a continent apart from each
other: film production occurred predominately in California, and theater, in
New York City. In Great Britain, however, performers working in the theatrical center of London could easily and quickly reach nearby studios like Ealing, Denham, Shepperton, and Elstree, so they frequently made movies
during the day and appeared in plays during the evening. In addition, British
films drew upon established playwrights from Shakespeare to Shaw, from
John Osborne to Joe Orton, as source material, usually treating them as rev-
erentially as they did British literature:

One senses . . . signs of retreat, to the cinema as a transcription system
for significant stage productions; to theatrical films as prestige cultural
packages, precisely aimed at British art house and selected foreign markets
(particularly in America). . . . [T]heatrical material became something to
lean on, not something to mould for a specific cinematic purpose. (Brown,
162, 159)

Perhaps even more important, as Julian Petley aptly observes, "British acting has been dominated by the theatrical tradition, yielding performances
that, by comparison with Hollywood, are wordy and stagey" (Petley, 111). A
common denominator among the newest crop of British actors — such as
Jonathan Pryce, Ben Kingsley, and Bob Hoskins — remains their theatrical
backgrounds. Petley, like many other critics, bemoans this tendency as "an
important aspect of the persistence of the primarily *literary* tradition of British culture, one which tends to result, in terms of cinema, in an excess of
theatrical or literary adaptations or, in the case of original screenplays,

scriptwriter's films" (Petley, 121). So while the British theatrical tradition, which afforded a wealth of source material, also provided a steady flow of well-trained performers, their histrionic style and allegiance to the theater inhibited, perhaps even intimidated, British filmmakers, encouraging them to concentrate on the word rather than on the image.

As the British film industry remained tethered to these literary and theatrical traditions, so it never shook free from a preoccupation with class consciousness, positioning this issue as informing all aspects of public and private daily life. This hierarchical stratification of British life reaches into every niche of society and creates a caste system far beyond the understanding of most Americans. Listen, for instance, to Hanif Kureishi, a Pakistani novelist and the screenwriter of *My Beautiful Laundrette* and *Sammy and Rosie Get Laid*, as he delineates its intimate connection with racism:

> Racism goes hand-in-hand with class inequality. Among other things, racism is a kind of snobbery, a desire to see oneself as superior culturally and economically, and a desire to actively experience and enjoy that superiority by hostility or violence. And when that superiority of class and culture is unsure or is not acknowledged by the Other . . . but is in doubt, as with the British working class and the Pakistanis in England, then it has to be demonstrated physically. Everyone knows where they stand then—the class inequality is displayed, just as any other snob demonstrates superiority by exhibiting wealth or learning or ancestry. (Kureishi, 29)

Such a class-bound conception finds little resonance in the cultural consciousness of the United States. Instead, our daily lives and artistic texts constantly reverberate, either overtly or covertly, with issues revolving about race.

But, for the most part, our country prides itself precisely on being classless; indeed, our cherished national myths enshrine what one can do, not who you are or where you came from before that moment. The archetypal American hero remains the rugged loner who fights for personal rights and individual freedoms, not the union organizer who battles for a better hourly wage or the factory worker who struggles against the bosses. So in American society, to speak quite generally and perhaps naively, people define themselves more by race, or religion, or even ethnic groupings than by longstanding class stratifications, as they so often do in Great Britain. Not surprisingly, our films reflect these classless ideals and individual initiatives: the musical rewards the talented; the detective film highlights the cynical seeker of truth; the Western mythologizes the solitary defender of law and order; the gangster film rewards (and then destroys) the cunning criminal; the horror movie fears and pities the deformed monster. The point, however, is to defeat evil individuals, not to question, reform, or destroy the basic system that spawned them. In essence, then, traditional American films see evil-doers as an aberration of a basically healthy society. They remain outside that society, intrinsically different from the mainstream and rarely signifying some internal social flaw that must be altered by fact or deed. Once they are dispatched, life returns to normal.

As opposed to this American vision of the one versus the many, the British cinema depicts a persistent vision of irreconcilable binary opposites: of working class and management, of capitalism and socialism, of the lower and upper classes engaged in a ceaseless war against each other. These stark class-bound juxtapositions set off far too many internal alarms for most American viewers and, of course, the foregrounding of economic issues risks raising the biggest bogeyman of them all: the specter of communism. Ironically, the working-class American finds little that is more threatening than communism, seeing its economic tenets as fundamentally anti-American. British films that attack the capitalistic system, seeing class issues as embedded within economic inequities, strike many American viewers as strident and offensive. Yet even British directors committed to the American film industry explore class issues within movies ostensibly about far different matters. Take, for example, Ridley Scott's surprisingly powerful summer bombshell, *Thelma and Louise* (1991). Most American directors could never equal Scott's sensitivity to the social position of these two women, seeing them as fatally constrained by their class in society as well as by their gender. Yet most American viewers ignore the class issues and focus solely on the feminist concerns, willing to challenge long-held gender stereotypes but not deeply felt social beliefs. So while issues of class provided British movie-makers with a master theme, such concerns tended to characterize their films as mainly localized and essentially parochial.

American viewers uncomfortable with, or simply uninterested in, this continual emphasis on class distinctions also have little experience with the mode of filmmaking that profoundly shaped the British film industry: the documentary. When was the last time you saw a nonfiction film in a movie theater? How many times a week do you curl up on the couch to watch a documentary on television? Americans simply don't watch documentaries. In fact, only a handful have been released commercially over the years: *Roger and Me, Truth or Dare, Hearts and Minds, Harlan Country*. Probably few reading this introduction have seen all four of these works. Even the scholarly establishment takes relatively little notice of documentaries, other than an occasional paper about Frederick Wiseman or the Maysal Brothers. With the exception of works about pioneering director Robert Flaherty, American film historians take equally sparse notice of documentary filmmaking. Take, for instance, Gerald Mast's classic study of world cinema, *A Short History of the Movies*. Out of some 565 pages, Mast devotes 37 (including 2 about Flaherty and 2 about the role of documentary in English cinema) to examples of documentaries throughout the evolution of the film, a number equal to the time he spends on French director Jean Renoir alone and less than half the space he allots to D. W. Griffith. One could easily imagine that a habitual American filmgoer, say one who averages a film every other week or so, would never have seen a documentary film outside of high-school health class.

This type of filmmaking, however, received far wider distribution and critical attention in Great Britain than in the United States, particularly during the Second World War. Even more significantly, as Alan Lovell claims, "the importance of the documentary movement lies not in the quality of individual films, but in the impact it had in general on the British cinema" (quoted in Higson, 72). That impact was aesthetic, thematic, and stylistic. So, for example, the British film industry's commitment to realism as opposed to fantasy (even British fantasy films seem somehow realistic) springs from this source, as does its concern during the 1960s with exploring the lives of working-class men and its preference for black-and-white cinematography. John Grierson, a seminal figure in the development of the British cinema, envisioned film as having primarily a social responsibility, unlike Hollywood movies, which functioned essentially as entertainment:

Thus at the heart of the documentary idea is a powerful differentiation between "realism" and "escapism": between a serious, committed, engaged cinema, and mass entertainment. Further, this logic posits the "realist" cinema, with its foundations in the documentary film movement, as the key point of reference in the call for an indigenous "British" cinema. (Higson, 74)

Finally, of course, this documentary tradition found an institutionalized form in British television, as John Reith (the British television industry's equivalent to John Grierson) incorporated the dogma of public service broadcasting into the consciousness of the British public. " 'Actuality' and 'documentary' are terms as synonymous with Britain," says Paul Swann, "as neorealism is with Italy and the New Wave with France. Interestingly, all these were attempts to respond to the colonial control of the American film in their respective countries" (Swann, 1). No British director could possibly escape the influence of Great Britain's documentary-realist tradition, a powerful ideological and aesthetic force that shaped directors' visions of the role and the responsibility of both the filmmaker and his or her film. So while the Brit-

ish documentary movement provided the commercial cinema with a particular form and focus, its aesthetics often rendered such films drably pedes-
trian and unable to compete with their flashy American counterparts.

The films of the Thatcher era covered in this anthology come out of these
forceful traditions of a literary and theatrical heritage, of a class consciousness and documentary aesthetic, that dominate the evolution of British cinema. Yet, they deal with these legacies in some strikingly unique ways.
Stephen Frears, for example, forges a new compromise with his literary
sources, remaining faithful to the essential ideals of a piece but clearly adding
his own vision to the work. Terence Davies makes excellent use of the documentary heritage, while simultaneously subverting the patriarchial oppressiveness of British society. Peter Greenaway and Derek Jarman bring a
painter's eye to the modern British cinema, valuing visual details over narrative traditions. The independent collectives of blacks and of women shed
increasing light on the connections between a class-bound society and the
infusion of racism and sexism. But we should not see works by such directors as implicitly rejecting the strengths of previous eras. Rather, they manage to incorporate a decidedly British vision of the world without sinking into
parochial specificity:

> Our job in the UK is to set about defining "British" pictures in the broadest
> possible terms. Our cinema can and must reflect a genuine *creative*
> perspective. It must reflect the desire to see Britain and the world through
> British eyes and attitudes, and to *communicate* what we see in an
> entertaining and comprehensive manner to our audiences around the world.
> (David Puttnam, quoted in Roddick, 49)

Producer David Puttnam's quote argues for a vital British film industry that
vigorously competes in the international market. Other insiders during the
Thatcher era clearly understood that, rather than a lasting renaissance, this
period should best be regarded, in director Christopher Petit's phrase, as "a
brief revival in production" (Roddick, 22).

Whether part of a profound renaissance or a brief production revival,
these pictures, often fueled by their creators' disgust with the current state
of British life, rank with the best movies made during the 1980s in any country in the world. British films of this period could not help being political (in
the broadest sense of that word), as they charted the inexorably downward
spiral of their homeland; but the best of them saw far beyond the passing
concerns of partisan politics. Surely many of Margaret Thatcher's policies
made these filmmakers' worst fears flesh. She attacked their deepest beliefs
and laid waste their industry. As creators of movies, their weapon was the
camera, not the rifle, and their bunker became the editing room. Though

driven by their hatred of the present government, these visual artists still managed to tease the permanent out of the momentary. They instinctively understood that Mrs. Thatcher's ideology, her creation and re-creation of past and present history, must be matched by an alternative vision that offered a different version of this era. Such a vision need not even be overtly political. It simply needed to observe with care and caution. To do that, these filmmakers reconfigured the British cinematic tradition. The resulting series of unique and significant films found a receptive international audience more concerned with cinematic style and thematic insights than with parochial politics. Yet, even from this close historical vantage point, we can recognize the power of their images and appreciate the depth of their imagination. Their pictures defined a turbulent era, revived the moribund British cinema, and froze a crucial moment in British culture.

Works Cited

Auty, Marty, and Nick Roddick, eds. 1985. *British Cinema Now*. London: British Film Institute.

Barr, Charles. 1986. "Introduction: Amnesia and Schizophrenia." In *All Our Yesterdays*, edited by Barr, 1-29.

———, ed. 1986. *All Our Yesterdays: 90 Years of British Cinema*. London: British Film Institute.

Brown, Geoff. 1986. " 'Sister of the Stage': British Film and British Theatre." In *All Our Yesterdays*, edited by Barr, 143-67.

Higson, Andrew. 1986. "Britain's Outstanding Contribution to the Film: The Documentary-Realist Tradition." In *All Our Yesterdays*, edited by Barr, 72-97.

Hill, John. 1986. *Sex, Class and Realism: British Cinema, 1956-1963*. London: BFI Publishing.

Kureishi, Hanif. 1986. *My Beautiful Laundrette and The Rainbow Sign*. London: Faber and Faber.

McFarlane, Brian. 1986. "A Literary Cinema? British Films and British Novels." In *All Our Yesterdays*, edited by Barr, 120-42.

Mast, Gerald. 1986. *A Short History of the Movies*. 4th ed. New York: Macmillan.

Murphy, Robert. 1986. "Under the Shadow of Hollywood." In *All Our Yesterdays*, edited by Barr, 47-71.

Petley, Julian. 1985. "Reaching for the Stars." In *British Cinema Now*, edited by Auty and Roddick, 111-22.

Roddick, Nick. 1985. "If the United States Spoke Spanish, We Would Have a Film Industry. . . ." In *British Cinema Now*, edited by Auty and Roddick, 3-18.

Swann, Paul. 1989. *The British Documentary Movement, 1926-1946*. Cambridge: Cambridge University Press.

Part I

Cultural Contexts and Cinematic Constructions

Two

The Religion of the Market: Thatcherite Politics and the British Film of the 1980s

Leonard Quart

In the late fifties and early sixties, films like Karel Reisz's *Saturday Night and Sunday Morning* (1960), Tony Richardson's *Loneliness of the Long Distance Runner* (1962), and Lindsay Anderson's *This Sporting Life* (1963) ushered in a "New Wave" in British cinema that resurrected, in a more psychological and less socially oriented form, the realistic tradition of John Grierson and Humphrey Jennings. This film revival paralleled a literary one — the revolt of the so-called Angry Young Men. Writers like John Braine, John Osborne, and Colin Wilson wrote novels, plays, and essays with working-class characters at their center, creating a literature that noisily thumbed its nose at conventional class snobbery and the genteel values of polite, restrained behavior. These writings, though much more politically conservative than they first appeared, attacked the philistinism and materialism of British society rather than the oppressiveness and inequity of its social institutions. The films, in turn, also focused on working-class characters, locales, and concerns, a rarity in British cinema of the time, using psychological rather than documentary realism as a formal strategy. In fact, the films explored the consciousness and desires of their working-class protagonists and their ambivalent feelings about their own community, rather than the social texture and structure of that community itself. Films like *This Sporting Life* never expressed a hint of commitment to any specific political agenda or ideology (though Anderson and Reisz leaned to the left). Instead, they projected a broad social awareness and general sense of political responsibility conveyed, most incisively by Anderson's attack on traditional English cinema as "snobbish, anti-intelligent, emotionally inhibited, wilfully blind to the conditions and

15

problems of the present, dedicated to an out-of-date national ideal" (McFarlane, 137).

These realist films appeared during a boom period of full employment and increased productivity, a time when England perceived itself to be an affluent society where unequal income distribution was beginning to disappear as a social problem and issue. Despite the growing prosperity, however, income and class inequalities continued to exist, but the political debates of the period usually avoided dealing with these unpleasant social and economic facts. The Tories had controlled the government since 1951, espousing economic policies in the late fifties that differed little from those of Labour party leader Hugh Gaitskill. Both parties shared a political commitment to welfare capitalism and Cold War ideology. In turn, the New Wave films expressed a social vision, more a moral and cultural critique than an overtly political one. The films' protagonists, like factory worker Arthur Seaton (Albert Finney) in *Saturday Night and Sunday Morning*, instinctively rebelled against the tedium and constraints of domestic life and work, his philosophy tersely summed up in a line like "don't let the bastards grind you down." Seaton, however, neither contemplated nor embraced any alternative political or social ideology. He valued sexuality and spontaneity, defied convention, and remained as alienated from his own working-class community as he was from the larger political and social system. Thus the emphasis of the New Wave films remained firmly on the autonomy and integrity of the individual versus social forces: the unseeing borstal staff in *The Loneliness of the Long Distance Runner*; the manipulative, callous rugby team owners in *This Sporting Life*; the insidious, stultifying consumer and television culture that threatened the spirit and soul running through almost all the films.

As invigorating and exciting as it was, the New Wave failed to sustain a renaissance in English cinema. Directors like Karel Reisz, Tony Richardson, and John Schlesinger (*A Kind of Loving*, 1962) went on to careers in Hollywood, each directing only a couple more films in England; to this date, Lindsay Anderson has directed only five feature films in his home country. The next two decades saw formally imaginative, socially illuminating, and psychologically penetrating films by directors like Nicolas Roeg, Ken Loach, Tony Garnett, and Joseph Losey, but the vast body of British cinema remained mired in uninspired mediocrity and predictability. It wasn't until the Thatcher era, 1979-90, that genuine signs of an English film resurgence could again be seen. Margaret Thatcher took power during a time of profound economic trouble, government impotence, and declining national prestige. In dealing with these problems, she helped construct a much different social and political world than the one promoted in the fifties by the centrist consensual politics of Prime Minister Harold Macmillan. The accompanying film renaissance stands as one of the more positive by-products of the Thatcher ethos, though in an almost totally oppositional and critical manner.

Margaret Thatcher's father shaped her political personality. Alfred Roberts, a petty bourgeois Methodist grocer and self-made man turned small-town politician, lived by such values as self-help, moral virtue, and public duty. In her own way, his daughter closely adhered to these values during her years as prime minister. Given this background, she was strongly attracted to the monetarist economic theories (an imposition of stringent controls of the money supply) of American New Right economist Milton Friedman. Though strict monetarism was abandoned during her first term, she continually displayed an almost religious commitment to the idea of the market playing the central role in the society; in a sense, she extended the economic values of the grocery store to the society at large. Thatcher vowed to reduce the regulatory role of government and bureaucracy, attacking welfare state dependency by reducing social spending, services (transportation, education, and health), and taxes. She also aided the wealthy by easing the capital gains tax and cutting the top tax rate on earned income from 83 percent to 40 percent. She privatized public companies like British Airways, vehemently criticized socialism, espoused an ethic of individual self-sufficiency, and promoted the avaricious pursuit of personal profit as a moral virtue. Her social perspective helped purge traditional British guilt feelings about material gain, "which inflicted alike egalitarian socialists who had no money and paternalist conservatives born with plenty of it" (Young, 256).

Thatcher was an extremely overbearing, vindictive, and energetic politician who acted out of a sense of moral rectitude and certitude; she never exhibited a tinge of self-doubt about her political principles and moral ends. For eleven years (as the longest serving prime minister in this century) and through three victorious elections, she totally dominated and radically transformed the political and social life of Great Britain. Many of the changes Thatcher wrought in British political life remain deeply set in the country's cultural matrix. Thatcher operated as an ideological, autocratic politician who polarized opponents and tolerated no dissent from her cabinet colleagues, invoking both hostility and devotion from members of her own party, rather than seeking to mute conflict and create a political consensus. Though never really liked by the British public because of her abrasive and unsympathetic personality, she did gain their grudging respect.

Thatcher recreated the Tory party by taking power out of the hands of the squirearchy and aristocracy—cautious, paternalistic, socially concerned politicians like the Carringtons, the Pyms, and the Whitelaws—who stood for

moderation and compromise. Primarily men of the upper class whose politics were shaped under the aegis of Macmillan, they were committed to government spending and Keynesian economics. Their policies remained dedicated to the idea of "one nation" rather than to Thatcher's neo-Darwinian
notion of the social good being derived from the conflict of self-interested
groups. After the first few difficult years, with unemployment rising to three
million and the collapse of industrial production, she constructed an inclu-
sive, populist version of the Tory party. Furthermore, she guided the Tories
as their appeal extended to the rising lower-middle class, the skilled working
class, and even manual laborers—deeply encroaching on traditional Labour
party loyalty by leading the nation to a jingoistic, flag-waving "victory" in the
Falklands and by promoting the expansion of share ownership and the sale of
council flats to tenants (turning one million families into homeowners).
Thatcher envisioned people's social class position more as a situation to be
changed and overcome rather than as a historically fixed state. She was,
however, no egalitarian; for example, she opposed redistributive programs,
seeing little need to soften the gap between the wealthy and the impoverished or to cushion the social and economic pain of those who failed in the
painful struggle for economic success. At the same time, she opposed any
class, racial, or ethnic constraints on economic mobility. Advocating the creation of a mythic meritocracy, she garnered her greatest political support
from members of the self-made middle class. And though class still continues to play a prime role in British life, Thatcher did leave a legacy of a less
calcified, more fluid class system.

Thatcher found her prime political villains in the trade unions, whose
commitment to collective rights and blanket protections stood in direct conflict with her belief in the unrestricted play of free markets. Because of their
inflationary wage claims and their destructive strikes during the Callaghan
years (the late seventies), they provided Thatcher with an unpopular enemy,
one she treated in a contemptuous manner matched by no other postwar
prime minister. Building upon her election mandate, she succeeded in passing a series of antiunion laws: the ending of the closed shop, the banning of
political strikes and secondary and mass picketing, and the use of the secret
ballot for the election of union leaders and the approval of strikes. With the
bloody collapse of the ill-conceived coal miners' strike of 1984-85, Thatcher
won the nation's admiration for the strength she demonstrated in defeating
her perfect foil—left-wing, rhetoric-spouting, uncompromising miners'
union leader Arthur Scargill. Her defeat of the miners led to growing worker
disenchantment with unions and, coupled with a rise in unemployment in the
declining manufacturing industries, to a loss of about one-fourth of the coun-

try's union membership. Thus, Thatcher profoundly reduced the power of unions. Strikes became rare and when attempted were usually unsuccessful.

She did not face much stronger opposition from either the Labour party or the centrist Liberals-SDP (Social Democratic party) Alliance. In fact, both opposition parties stumbled about in confusion, unable to define a political course that would strike a popular spark. The Labour party, especially, was beset with factionalism and a penchant for self-destructive politics. The party leadership had to deal with continual political onslaughts from its far left. It also carried the burden of a seemingly outmoded ideological legacy that granted Thatcher a great deal of political immunity during her time in office. This immunity allowed Thatcher, despite her antistatist position on issues involving economic regulation, to strengthen the central government at the expense of local government. She abolished the left-wing Greater London Council, reduced local council power over education and housing, and placed stricter controls over all local expenditure. Government intrusion upon freedom of the press (and other media) also greatly increased, since she viewed national security as superseding the right to publish and broadcast. Clearly inherent in the Thatcher ethos was a strongly authoritarian, antilibertarian strain that viewed freedom as primarily economic rather than political in nature.

During Thatcher's last term in office, she began to lose her instinct for gauging the popular mood. Her political support rapidly diminished, and she lagged behind the Labour party in the polls. By 1990 the boom of the eighties had ended in a trade deficit, double-digit inflation, and continuing unemployment. Similarly, she presided over declining manufacturing output, labor productivity, and business investment. Thatcher compounded these unfavorable economic statistics by passing an extremely unpopular poll tax. This regressive head tax fell equally on all adults eighteen to sixty-five. Introduced in Scotland on April 1, 1989, it went into effect in England and Wales in 1990. The poll tax replaced the somewhat more progressive local property tax ("the rates") and was supposed to spread the cost of local government services like roads, policing, and schools to everybody who lived in an area— council flat renters as well as property owners. Thatcher viewed the tax as the "flagship" of her third term, but the law aroused the rage of both rural and inner city inhabitants, who saw the tax as totally inequitable. Millions of people refused to pay. A massive London protest demonstration was organized, ultimately turning into one of the most violent central London riots in decades. Freed by this dramatic shift in public mood, her own party, fearing the loss of seats, forced her unwilling resignation in November 1990. She was replaced by a very different sort of politician—her own handpicked suc-

reading) practically

cessor, the more pragmatic and centrist, less ideological and abrasive John Major. Since leaving office, Thatcher has been a politically disruptive force for the Tories, continually sniping at Major's actions. In fact, she became sufficiently alienated from the party to announce her unwillingness to seek a parliamentary seat in the next election.

Still, despite her abrupt fall from grace and the ephemeral quality of her economic revolution, Thatcher left an indelible mark on British politics and society. She cut the economic power of the state while expanding the political power of the central government. She helped create an England where the rich got richer while the poor became more impoverished (with 20 percent of the people living under the poverty line), reversing a forty-year pattern where incomes were gradually growing more equal. By 1988 the best-off tenth of the population enjoyed nearly nine times more income than the worst-off tenth, though real wages did go up for the majority of those who worked.

Thatcher promoted an individualist ethos and an entrepreneurial culture where the acquistion of wealth and the consumption of goods became the prime values, while the ethic of social responsibility and mutual aid began to unravel. It was now more stylish "to consume rather than care" (Young, 537). England became a more morally callous country of striking social contrasts: a decaying industrial North where mining villages and steel towns (Labour party bastions) began to wither away, and a booming South dominated by immense office and residential construction projects (e.g., London's Canary Wharf) and high-tech and financial industries. The Labour party had almost no seats in the South, except for the inner London area, while Scotland and the North returned vast Labour majorities. Amid the rising standard of living, an embittered, visible underclass began to develop; the number of homeless rose to one million (150,000 under the age of twenty-five); burglary, car thievery, and vandalism greatly increased; and the country held the dubious distinction of having the highest per capita prison population within the European Community. Still the yuppification of southern England bloomed. Building cranes, glass office buildings, bistros, boutiques, and smartly dressed investment bankers shared the London streets with scabrous homeless men living in cardboard villages and doorways on the Strand. Computer executives strolled past adolescent runaways (the weekly welfare benefits for the under-twenty-five unemployed young were severely cut) begging dolefully outside tube stations and on the steps of the National Theatre.

Thatcher entered office attacking the permissive society and trumpeting traditional bourgeois values like respectability, family, and nation—and a strain of Thatcherism promoted a repressive agenda on law and order, abortion, and homosexuality. But despite Thatcher's ritualistic deference to the prime significance of the family, her economic policies subverted many of those same values. In the England of the eighties, acquisitive individualism and aggressive self-interest thrived, not Victorian domestic virtues. This belief in unlimited economic growth superseded the preservation of the past. However, Thatcherite entrepreneurial adventurousness and risk-taking produced some positive effects, turning England into an economically competitive force in Europe. Thatcher revived an almost congenitally sick and sluggish economy by promoting the development of modern business methods and technologies, attracting foreign investment, weeding out failing businesses, and ending factory overmannning (*Economist*, 17-20). Until the economic recession in 1990–91, the Thatcher years saw the growth of a more efficient and productive economy, which in 1988 was "still growing at 4 per cent after seven years' continuous expansion" (Young, 532). British society became Americanized: much more efficient, hedonistic, cash-obsessed, and competitive. It was now dominated by a driven New Class, one utterly removed from the more moribund, communally oriented working class and the complacently paternalistic upper-class cultures that traditionally dominated British life.

Thatcher's success changed the parameters of political debate and tactics. It forced Labour to transform itself into a centrist, European-style Social Democratic party, so that it could become politically competitive again. Under the leadership of Neil Kinnock, who replaced Michael Foot after the 1983 election debacle, the party modernized itself. Kinnock, an intellectually uninspired but politically adept Welshman, made the party more media and public relations conscious. With the help of Shadow Cabinet members like Roy Hattersley, Gerald Kaufman, Bryan Gould, and John Smith, he forced Labour to reevaluate many of its past political positions. Faced with a diminishing industrial working class, the party expanded its electoral appeal to a wider range of social interest groups, including small business people, consumers, and environmentalists. It began this process by moving away from its anachronistic commitment to public ownership—repudiating clause four of the party's constitution (which calls for nationalization of the basic industries) and pushing the left wing to the periphery of the party. Ultimately, Labour purged the Trotskyist Militant Tendency altogether, muting the power of grass-roots activists and militantly class-conscious union leaders. Party leadership now rests firmly in the hands of pragmatic members of the House of Commons, whose politics revolve around what is socially possible rather than ideologically pure.

Because Labour's union base no longer carries the same political weight, the party now advocates greater collaboration between government and industry. It also grants management the freedom to strengthen their companies. Labour has even moved toward an ideological acceptance of the free market, except that it seeks to make it work more efficiently and with greater responsiveness to social needs and the public interest. It essentially accepts privatization of industry, but wants to reverse some of the destructive consequences of Thatcher's policy of business deregulation; for example, strengthening the system of environmental regulation and establishing compulsory licensing in the construction industry. Almost magically, the traditional class-based Labour antagonism to business and management has begun to disappear. The party has dropped a number of other articles of its faith, including unilateralism and opposition to the European Community. It went so far as to support the Gulf War—quieting, even politically strong-arming in the name of a unified party, Labour M.P.'s with deep reservations about the Allied military intervention. Labour is also more concerned about issues involving individual rights, and consumer and feminist concerns, than in the past. It understands that it must appeal to a greater variety of social interest groups, and that individuals are often members of more than one interest group—their political commitments being more fluid now than when class loyalty was the primary way of defining one's politics.

Thatcher (with the unplanned help of events in Eastern Europe and the former Soviet Union) probably killed off socialism as a viable political alternative in Britain, but she never destroyed the British public's support for the NHS (National Health Service) and other prime institutions of the welfare state. People may have supported Thatcher at the voting booth, but they never embraced all the ideological baggage she aggressively carried with her. After eleven years of Thatcher, a majority still desire a government that demonstrates social concern. In polls taken after Thatcher's third victory, six out of ten voters supported maintaining health care as an entirely public service, 55 percent favored collectivism instead of self-reliance in welfare policy, and 79 percent desired a society that valued social concern more than the creation of wealth (Young, 529). Labour responded to the public's desires by staking its political future on being able to deliver social services more efficiently (e.g., improvement of adult education and worker retraining programs and stronger management of the NHS) and to sustain fuller employment. Chastened by and sensitive to the historic political changes that took place at home and abroad during the previous decade, Labour also projected a more limited idea of what the central government can achieve. It envisioned a future state that "will be more decentralized, more regulator and facilitator than provider and director" (Leadbeater, 16). The vision is mundane, safe, and unromantic, more politically reactive to Thatcher's ethos, than a genuinely imaginative alternative, but probably the only politically sensible one at this historical juncture.

Thatcher's relationship with the opposition Labour party was by necessity an antagonistic one, but her relationship with intellectuals and artists was even more embattled. Thatcher never pretended to be an intellectual. She directed her mind toward solving concrete problems rather than speculating about abstract political ideas. But nobody could deny that she was extremely sharp and capable of complete mastery of political and economic detail and policy. She also utilized a number of well-known intellectual advisers and supporters, like philosopher Anthony Quinton, aging "Angry Young Man" Kingsley Amis, and historians A. L. Rouse, Robert Conquest, and Hugh Thomas, among others. The die, however, was cast when after first taking office, she cut deeply into university funding and eliminated three thousand university jobs. In 1985 a government green paper, *Higher Education into the 1990s*, called for the universities "to serve the national economy more effectively" (Young, 414). The disinterested and nonutilitarian quest for knowledge now found itself subject to Thatcherite cost-benefit analysis. The universities took their rage out on Thatcher in the only way they could, Oxford bestowing the unusual rebuff of refusing to grant her an honorary degree.

The arts establishment displayed a similar revulsion, attacking her as much for what they viewed as her persona—voice, clothes, personal tastes—as for her cutting state support to arts institutions and her overall political agenda. Though Thatcher never exhibited any particular interest in the arts beyond a poem by Kipling or a Freddy Forsyth thriller, she was no more of a philistine than Labour prime ministers like Wilson and Callaghan. Still, institutions like the Royal Shakespeare Company or the Royal Opera House "that depended on the public purse started at a disadvantage in the Thatcherite scale of priorities . . . (and) had to justify its existence against ever stiffer presumptions of guilt" (Young, 413). Consequently, Thatcher treated the arts, and the film business—notwithstanding her personal preferences (she disliked film)—no differently than any other business. For example, the Thatcher government passed a new Films Bill in 1984-85, one that applied market principles to the movie industry. The bill abolished the 1947 Eady Levy, a law that had distributed a percentage of box-office receipts to British-made films, and provided no replacement for these lost revenues. It also abolished a 25 percent tax break for investment in film production and privatized the NFFC (National Film Finance Corporation), thus eliminating the "only direct form of government involvement in the field of commercial film production in Britain" (Roddick, 14).

The Thatcher government's denial of aid for British film production merely compounded the long-term problems of a historically sick industry whose audience continued to decline: the average Briton attends the cinema on an average of once a year. In contrast with the generous subsidy policies of Western European countries like Sweden, even British governments committed to state intervention rarely gave much economic support to film production. The British film industry, of course, never freed itself of Hollywood domination. This colonization holds both for the preeminence of American films in British movie theaters and on television, and for Hollywood's success at weaning away many of England's top directors (e.g., Alan Parker, Ridley Scott, Stephen Frears) to work in a secure, well-financed industry and achieve more lucrative careers. Film in Britain also confronted the generally protheater, anticinematic bias of the arts establishment, and faced competition for an audience with some very striking and original television programming (e.g., Dennis Potter's *The Singing Detective*) and home video — Britain having one of the highest ownership and rental rates in the world. In contrast with the film industry, television remains a heavily subsidized business in which most film people, including directors like Ken Loach, Michael Apted, and Stephen Frears, among others, have done a great deal of creative work. Another difficulty that the industry faces is that two major chains, Rank and EMI, and two smaller ones, Cannon-Classic and the Star Group, dominate national film distribution. All of these chains primarily show Hollywood films, making it difficult for independent, intellectually difficult, and stylistically experimental British films to receive nationwide exposure.

Despite, however, the industry's economic precariousness and limited resources, the eighties saw an exciting renaissance of British film. The revival, brought on by renewed American interest in British film because of *Chariots of Fire*'s (1981) success, was fueled by America's expanded cable television market. More important for the development of a low-budget, intellectually (though rarely formally) adventurous cinema was Channel Four. This adventurous British television channel exhibited an interest in subsidizing film production and commissioned films from independent producers. During the eighties, a number of out-of-the-mainstream, commercially risky films like *The Draughtsman's Contract* (1982), *The Ploughman's Lunch* (1983), *Another Time, Another Place* (1983), and *My Beautiful Laundrette* (1985) received most of their funding from Channel Four, which allocated the greater part of its drama budget to producing feature films. These films were first released in movie theaters and subsequently shown on television. In addi-

tion, despite the Thatcher government's unwillingness to aid the film industry, it did establish a general mood that encouraged economic risk-taking and
experimentation with new and more innovative business practices (e.g.,
Channel Four).

Thatcher's prime contribution to British filmmaking was not the business
climate she created, but the subject matter her policies and the culture she
helped create provided British directors. The majority of English films of the
eighties never engaged in open critiques of Thatcherism, but the ethos she
created seemed to become the implicit or explicit subject of many of the period's best films. Of course, many films, like John Boorman's visually striking
Excalibur (1981), John Irvin's intimate *Turtle Diary* (1985), and Bruce Robinson's rite-of-passage *Withnail and I* (1986), seem untouched by Thatcherism. But from Ken Loach's spare, documentary-style film about drifting, unemployed youth in Sheffield, *Looks and Smiles* (1981), to Peter Greenaway's
stylized allegory of Thatcherite greed and vulgarity, *The Cook, the Thief, His
Wife, and Her Lover* (1990), a large number of British films responded to
Thatcherism.

The film that began the renaissance and helped grant British directors the
confidence to confront English subjects was Hugh Hudson's Oscar-winning
Chariots of Fire. A favorite of President Reagan, *Chariots* offered a conventional, inflated paean to a triumphant, 1924-Olympics-winning England, one
skillfully evoked by the use of a booming sound track, a great many slow motion shots of handsome young men running on the beach, rich period detail,
and romantic superimpositions. Shrewdly, this film uses the victory of anti-
establishment characters, at odds with the insidious bigotry and genteel
snobbery and hypocrisy of the English establishment, to exult in nationalistic
feeling and implicitly endorse the Thatcherite ethos. The film's driven central
figure, Harold Abrahams (Ben Cross), a Jewish immigrant financier's son
who rejects his Cambridge University masters' idea of gentlemanly values,
hires a professional coach to train him for the Olympics. Abrahams and his
Italian-Arab coach, Sam Massabini (Ian Holm), are seen by the Cambridge
masters as both ethnic outsiders and aggressive arrivistes—both their class
and nationality are held against them. However, Abrahams wins the Olympic
one-hundred-yard dash and becomes the "model Englishman" of the Gilbert
and Sullivan song, one fully assimilating into the Establishment he always
hungered to enter, ultimately being buried in an Anglican church service accompanied by a choir singing Blake's traditional hymn "Jerusalem."

Chariots of Fire remains overtly critical of an England built on rigid class
demarcations and aristocratic hauteur, but in its stead it implicitly endorses
the Thatcherite ethos of a nation based on a meritocracy of the ambitious,

Heroes of the 1924 Olympics, Eric Liddell (Ian Charleson) and Harold Abrahams (Ben Cross), in *Chariots of Fire* (1982), the movie that began the British film renaissance.

the diligent, and the gifted. In the film's vision, the Establishment's values begin to shift, becoming more tolerant of individual difference and comprehending that the future no longer rests solely within their control. But the film's idea of a more dynamic, diverse nation, one where a man like Abrahams has the chance to succeed, is depicted with as much uncritical sentimentality as the Cambridge masters treat their own hierarchical and racist vision of Britain. It's a fitting message for a Thatcher-ruled England where the traditional class lines give way to individual achievement, usually defined in terms of wealth and status.

Other, less exportable eighties films with British subjects deal with contemporary England rather than some luminous historical moment. For example, Lindsay Anderson's mordant and angry film, *Britannia Hospital* (1982), stands devoid of even one sympathetic character. Its bitter, heavy-handed satire caricatures all segments of British society — megalomaniacal scientists; resentful and indolent workers; morally unconscious, drug-stupified television people; absurd aristocrats; and ranting, violent leftist demonstrators. Anderson permeates his Britain with strikes, terrorist attacks, and riots. This grotesque version of Britain of the late seventies — the last years of the Callaghan administration — conflated with the first strike-filled years of Thatcher's reign, shows Anderson as totally cynical and despairing about the aspirations of the Left, expressing only contempt for a despised British establishment. In fact, his anguish about the chaotic state of the nation here extends to a totally pessimistic view of the human condition itself.

A much quieter film, Richard Eyre's *The Ploughman's Lunch* (1983), deals directly with Thatcherism. Subsidized by Channel Four, this sardonic, literate, and stylistically conventional movie perceptively satirizes London media life, as well as the political and social climate of Thatcher's England. The film centers around an ambitious, opportunistic BBC radio news editor of working-class origins, James Penfield (a subtle, muted performance by Jonathan Pryce), who avidly pursues class, status, and an unattainable upper-class woman, Susi (Charlie Dore). Penfield, an unpleasant and even repellent character, represents a fitting antiheroic figure for an ethos that eschews social concern and commitment in favor of the celebration of individual success. Penfield can pretend his working-class parents don't exist when it suits his purposes. He remains passively remote from his dying mother, the emotional desperation of a colleague, and the moral fervor of the Greenham Common women. He also displays a gift for adapting his political convictions to the person he's talking to — turning into a proponent of imperial England and the invasion of Suez when talking to his conservative publisher, and anti-Suez and sympathetic to socialism when talking to a left-leaning historian.

The Ploughman's Lunch does more than focus on one driven careerist's saga. Eyre totally entwines James's fortunes with a pointed critique of the moral emptiness of British public life. The BBC news staff meetings function as gatherings of wary, cynical professionals who lack any moral or intellectual response to the news. They aim to find the right balance, to provide a great deal of soft news and avoid controversial stories, like the Greenham Com-

Stranded in the countryside, British journalist James Penfield (Jonathan Pryce) is cornered by the Greenham Common protesters, to whom he promises press coverage, in *The Ploughman's Lunch* (1983).

mon women, that could upset the bland social order they wish to convey. In other spheres, book publishing turns into merely the packaging of commercial products, while advertising creates fabricated pasts like the supposed eighteenth-century "ploughman's lunch"—invented in the sixties in some London marketing office.

The "ploughman's lunch" is a metaphor for all the falsifications—private and public—that Penfield and other men on the make in Thatcher's England construct. Penfield diligently writes a book on Suez, revising its humiliating history so that it can be viewed as a predecessor worthy of the imperial Falklands victory. To top all these fabrications off, Eyre seamlessly fuses footage of the 1982 Tory party conference in Brighton with his fictional story. At that conference, Margaret Thatcher makes political capital by invoking the successful Falklands invasion as a sign of the renewal of the British spirit—one more powerful example of how hype and promotion substitute for reality. Like most of the eighties films critical of Thatcher, *The Ploughman's Lunch* offers no defined leftist or other specifically political alternative to her ethos. The only socialist in the film, Ann Barrington (Rosemary Harris), a middle-aged historian, lives a life of affluence and total comfort in a grand Norfolk house, while still indulging in empty, reflexively leftist critiques of the Labour party. The prototype of the academic socialist, her insulated, privileged ev-

Rosemary Harris plays Ann Barrington, an academic socialist whose life is at odds with her politics, in *The Ploughman's Lunch*.

eryday life is totally at odds with her political convictions. While the Greenham Common protesters' moral passion is treated sympathetically, they are still seen as ineffectual and a touch absurd (Quart, 48-49).

A richer, more emotionally complex and optimistic work than *The Ploughman's Lunch*, one that provides a direct and corrosive critique of Thatcherism, is Mike Leigh's *High Hopes* (1988). Leigh, a much more original, idiosyncratic director than Eyre, and a man rooted in experimental theater, uses little camera movement and builds the film around a minimal and loosely structured narrative. In *High Hopes* Leigh evokes the social mood and class tensions of Thatcher's London through the actions and interactions of his seven main characters—three couples and the aging, isolated mother of the film's main character, Cyril. In creating his slice of London, he moves from satire to farce to genuine pathos. The central, most sympathetic and nuanced characters in the film are Cyril (Philip Davis) and Shirley (Ruth Sheen). Shaggy-haired, left-wing, bohemian, and marginally linked to the working class, Cyril smokes pot, reads *Lenin for Beginners*, and works at a dead-end job as a motorcycle messenger. An alien in Thatcher's Britain, he is a man without interest in money and status, one who must angrily adjust to being treated as invisible by an impersonal, profit-obsessed society. The couple even own a cactus named Thatcher.

Cyril, choked with feelings of class resentment, still does obeisance to

Shirley (Ruth Sheen) and Cyril (Philip Davis), a left-wing, working-class couple in *High Hopes* (1988), directed by Mike Leigh.

Marx and his vision of society. Although committed to social change, he ruefully admits that he sits on his ass in despair because he just isn't sure what to do politically. Shirley may be bucktoothed and ungainly, but her radiance and warmth make her seem beautiful at times, and she is connected to the world in a more concrete and knowing and less ideological way than Cyril. Leigh displays little use for leftist slogans or sentimentality. A woman friend of Cyril and Shirley's who anxiously spouts leftist rhetoric about changing the world and going to help the peasants in Nicaragua looks like someone whose politics function more as a psychologicial lifeline than as a thought-out commitment. The film's animus, however, is not directed at the Left, but at the other two couples, who adapt, in different ways, to the Thatcherite ethos.

Leigh uses the snobbish Tory couple who live next door to Cyril's depressed, disconnected mother, Mrs. Bender (Edna Dore), as venomous comic caricatures to send up gentrification and Thatcherite social callousness. The wife, Laetitia (Leslie Manville), conveys the brittle, harsh inhumanity of a pint-sized Thatcher, as she briskly advises Mrs. Bender to buy her house so she can resell it for a nice profit. The couple use expressions like "tip-top" and "posthaste"—sounding like extras from "Brideshead Revisited"—though much of their manner derives from aspiration and mim-

Laetitia (Lesley Manville) and Rupert (David Bamber), representatives of Thatcherite values, in *High Hopes* (1988).

icry rather than inheritance. Mrs. Bender is obviously an embarrassing neighbor for this upwardly mobile couple to have—a melancholy, downscale, working-class widow, one whose presence only lowers their street's property value.

The third couple centers around Cyril's hysterical, nouveau-riche sister, Valerie (Heather Tobias), a shrill, overdressed vulgarian who puts her makeup on with a trowel. Valerie's husband is a lecherous lout of a used-car dealer, and they predictably live in an overstuffed, garish suburban house. But despite Valerie's success, at least along Thatcherite lines of making money and acquiring material goods, she remains unsure of her class position and painfully tries to imitate Laetitia's yuppie dress and manner. (The traditional class structure and style still carry a great deal of social weight in Britain.) Leigh's portrait of a leopard-skin-coat-wearing Valerie sometimes goes over the top, but the pathos of days spent exercising, consuming, and hungering for affection from her abusive husband gives the stereotype some redeeming poignance.

In contrast to his satiric treatment of the smug, odious Tory couple and the unhappy, selfish Valerie and her boor of a husband, Leigh depicts Cyril and Shirley in a more naturalistic fashion. They demonstrate more than a single dimension, and their intimate behavior—talking, fighting, having sex—feels utterly genuine. Leigh holds out a touch of hope for Cyril and Shirley in a society riven with avarice and lack of compassion. By the film's conclusion, Cyril clearly knows that this society won't suddenly be transformed in accordance with the high political hopes he still holds in his head: pursuing Marx's vision of a classless society is now merely, in his words, like "pissing in the wind." But he isn't defeated; in fact, without the film providing any explanation for the emotional change, he feels more serene, more willing to come to terms with life's injustice and have a child with Shirley— something he previously refused to do. *High Hopes* provides no political alternative to Thatcherism, but it suggests ways to live more humanly, even amid the social inequity and meanness of Thatcher's England. Those grander high hopes of radical political change no longer have much viability, but Cyril balances his political disillusionment with the more modest hope of building a humane and caring life with Shirley (Quart and Quart, 47, 56-57).

In addition to *High Hopes*, other British films deal directly with Thatcherism, like Chris Bernard's small fable *A Letter to Brezhnev* (1985) and David Drury's *Defence of the Realm* (1985). The former centers around two working-class women who feel permanently imprisoned in a depressed Liverpool suburb, until ironically a Russian sailor arrives to offer one of them hope. The latter film, a well-made, paranoid thriller, poses direct political questions about the functioning of Thatcher's police-state-like security services, and the conservative press's willing collaboration with their murderous activities.

More imaginative and intellectually resonant than most of the British films of the eighties were Stephen Frears's and Hanif Kureishi's literate and ironic *My Beautiful Laundrette* (1985) and *Sammy and Rosie Get Laid* (1987). Both films depict Thatcher's England as dominated by racism, greed, and social injustice, but they eschew an orthodox leftist perspective for a more ambiguous, unpredictable point of view. Frears and Kureishi avoid sentimentalizing victims of prejudice or economic deprivation and, though men with leftist sympathies, equally subvert both schematic leftist thinking and respectable authority. Their commitment is to an anarchic, impulsive, and sexual life, and consequently, they are sympathetic to characters with size and panache— even if they turn out to be capitalist rogues and authoritarian executioners. In fact, the only unqualified villain in the two films is an absurdly posh-accented, arrogant Margaret Thatcher.

Other directors, like Marek Kanievska and Michael Radford, use the past implicitly to criticize present-day Britain. Kanievska's decorative *Another Country* (1984), set in an archetypal public school in the thirties (though it could be England of the eighties), views the sadism and power games that dominate student life as morally bankrupt and ominous apprenticeships for future political power. Radford's *Another Time, Another Place* (1983) is a luminously composed exploration of the clash of cultures—expressive, emotionally open Italian POWs versus chill, repressed Scots—in rural northern Scotland in 1944. The film, less concerned with depicting the reality of Scottish life during World War II, strongly affirms a woman's sexuality and humanness as she struggles to break from the constraints of a dour and rigid community. Both *Another Time, Another Place* and Radford's imaginatively visualized version of Orwell's novel *Nineteen-Eighty-Four* (1984) place their emphasis on human feeling, love, and the inner life as antidotes to either a constricted communal life or the horrors of collectivism and state terrorism. Radford's films abhor repressive dogmatism, rejecting all political ideologies and systems for a belief in the freedom to express all the contradictory and flawed elements that being human entails. Stating that England in the eighties is too complex a phenomenon for any ideology to explain, Radford claims that we inhabit a world where "all the things we were taught to believe have crumbled away" (Park, 100). For Radford, the only belief system functioning in England in the eighties was Thatcherism, an ideology that utterly repelled him.

Directors and screenwriters like Leigh, Frears, and Kureishi may not exactly echo Radford's sentiments, but they too convey that both the Thatcher ethos and the traditional leftist political alternatives to her rule were no longer viable in the England of the eighties. Cultural and social structures that once reverberated morally and politically—like left-wing politics, the unions, the church, and even the class system—no longer played the same social role. In her desire to transform Britain into a more assertive, efficient, profit-oriented society, Margaret Thatcher created a world of rapidly changing, often socially and morally alienated values, a world that severed itself from many of the institutions and norms that once dominated British society. For eleven years she controlled and shaped the British political and social landscape, looming as a larger-than-life figure in the consciousness and vision of some of its best film directors. Most of their films expressed a revulsion with Thatcherism; still, their anger rarely turned to vaporous and schematic polemics, evolving instead into the complex formal texture and imagination of art. Thatcher never provided direct help to the film industry, but her powerful, often oppressive, presence moved British filmmakers to burn brightly for at least one decade.

Works Cited

Economist. 1990. "The Thatcher Record: To the Victor These Spoils." Nov. 24-30, 17-20.
Leadbeater, Charlie. 1990. "A Head without a Heart." *Marxism Today*, July, 16-17.

McFarlane, Brian. 1986. "A Literary Cinema? British Films and British Novels." In *All Our Yesterdays: 90 Years of British Cinema*, edited by Charles Barr. London: British Film Institute.

Park, James. 1984. *Learning to Dream: The New British Cinema*. London: Faber and Faber.

Quart, Leonard. 1985. "The Ploughman's Lunch." *Cineaste* 14 (3): 48-49.

Quart, Leonard, and Barbara Quart. 1989. "High Hopes." *Cineaste* 17 (2): 47, 56-57.

Roddick, Nick. 1985. "If the United States Spoke Spanish We Would Have a Film Industry. . . ." In *British Cinema Now*, edited by Martyn Auty and Nick Roddick. London: British Film Institute.

Young, Hugo. 1989. *The Iron Lady*. New York: Farrar Strauss Giroux.

Three

The Last New Wave: Modernism in the British Films of the Thatcher Era

Peter Wollen

Independent filmmakers of the eighties reacted strongly against the effects of Thatcherism. They responded to the imposition of market criteria in every sector of society, to political authoritarianism, to the "two nations" project of Thatcherism, and to the leading role of the City, in films as various as Peter Greenaway's *The Cook, the Thief, His Wife, and Her Lover* (1989), Derek Jarman's *The Last of England* (1987), Terry Gilliam's *Brazil* (1985), Stephen Frears's and Hanif Kureishi's *Sammy and Rosie Get Laid* (1988), Mike Leigh's *High Hopes* (1988), Laura Mulvey's and Peter Wollen's *Crystal Gazing* (1980), and Reece Auguste's *Twilight City* (1989). Paradoxically, these are all London films, precisely because of the success of Thatcher's polarization of the country between North and South—a polarization that, as shown in the films, is doubled within the metropolis itself. Their roots can be traced back to the sixties—to the art world, the satire boom, experimental theater, and the post-1968 avant-garde. It was in these areas that a modernist impulse had finally made itself felt in British culture and had eventually combined with an emphasis on the visual dimension of television, theater, and film. Together, these films provide a definitive picture of the Thatcherization of London.

Negatively, Thatcherism has aimed to destroy the postwar Keynesian settlement, dismantle the public services provided by the state, and eliminate obtrusive foci of political opposition. Positively, Thatcherism combines three elements: (1) an economic "unregulated market" neoliberalism, (2) a politically neoconservative authoritarianism, and (3) a social "two nations" project, dividing the country geographically, between North and South, and socially, in terms of the labor market, between a de-unionized "peripheral" sector and a "core" company union sector. The "two nations" project, of course, hits ethnic minorities especially hard and encourages a sharp division between "inner city" and suburb. Thatcherism is a modernizing movement in a very specific sense. It aims to modernize the finance, service, communications, and international sectors of the economy, but not domestic manufacturing industry or civil society. New "core" industries, largely dependent on international capital, are consolidated in the South, while the North of the country is left as a peripheral, decaying hinterland. The South, organized around the City of London, traditionally the hegemonic pole of the economy, is increasingly decoupled from domestic manufacturing industry. Thus Thatcherism, terrified that the City will lose even more of its world role, given the continuing relative decline of the British economy, has an Atlantic rather than a European outlook in its international policy and aims to provide the point of entry into Europe for American and Japanese capital. Money rather than goods are paramount. Socially and visually, the citadels of international capital are abruptly juxtaposed with the decay of London's old industries and docklands.[1]

The Thatcher years provoked a long-delayed efflorescence of British film, still largely unrecognized in Britain itself. It can be seen, I believe, as a "British New Wave," coming long after the idea of a New Wave had crumbled away in most other European countries. The first New Wave, of course, exploded on the world from France in the "Miraculous Year" of 1959, which launched Truffaut's *Les Quatre Cents Coups*, Resnais's *Hiroshima Mon Amour*, and Chabrol's *Les Cousins*. Godard's *A Bout de Souffle* followed in 1960, also the year of *L'Avventura*, the first film of Antonioni's trilogy. This, in turn, drew attention to the work of Pasolini and, soon, Bertolucci. A few years later, Fassbinder, Syberberg, and Wenders were grouped together as the core of a somewhat belated "German New Wave." Since then critics gathered at festivals around the world have sought out "New Waves" wherever they could, broadening their net to include the Third World and hailing the Brazilian, African, and Chinese "New Waves." No one thought of looking again at Britain, which, having missed the bus in the sixties, could hardly expect a second chance. Besides, the British were notoriously unvisual, unartistic, and uncinematic. What was it Truffaut had said? "Aren't the words 'Britain' and 'Cinema' incompatible?"[2]

It has been argued that the "Angry Young Men" films of 1959–63 were the "British New Wave," rather than the "Jeune Cinéma Anglais," as the French, who certainly ought to have known, dubbed it at the time.[3] Yet surely to call these films New Wave is both inappropriate and misleading. First, the idea of a New Wave was intimately linked to the project of directorial "authorship."

A good case can be made for Lindsay Anderson as a bilious but authentic "auteur" (something he himself might well deny in a fume of irascibility), but nobody has made a serious claim for the auteurist credentials of Reisz, Richardson, Schlesinger, and others. In fact, it would be much more plausible to argue for the producer-director duo of Relph and Dearden as auteurs, filmmakers whose "social problem" cycle, beginning with the *Blue Lamp* in 1950 and continuing through, via *Sapphire* (1959) and *Victim* (1961), to *A Place to Go* in 1963, preceded and paralleled the work of the Angry Young Men. Moreover, in "daring" to deal with race and homosexuality, for whatever headline-grabbing reasons, they showed greater courage, prescience, and, indeed, political sense than their more celebrated and supposedly more progressive and innovative younger colleagues.

Second, the idea of a New Wave involved putting film first and not subordinating it to literature or theater, as Truffaut argued in his notorious polemic against adaptation in *Arts* magazine. The Angry Young Men films, however, plainly put film second. Their success was directly derived from the success of the original plays and novels by Osborne, Amis, Braine, and Sillitoe. *Look Back in Anger, Room at the Top, The Entertainer, A Taste of Honey, Saturday Night and Sunday Morning*, and *The Loneliness of the Long Distance Runner* came out in their original forms between May 1956 and September 1959. The film versions, which came out after a three-year interval, between 1959 and 1962, clearly depended on the prepublicity and acclaim already generated by their literary sources for their initial impact. Moreover, Woodfall Films, beginning with *Look Back in Anger* (1959), set a pattern by having the original writers first collaborate on the film scripts with professional scriptwriters and then write them entirely. Osborne, Sillitoe, and Delaney all wrote their own scripts for the film adaptations of their work. The same procedure was followed with *This Sporting Life* (1963), written by the author of the novel, David Storey (and directed by Lindsay Anderson), and with John Schlesinger's *Billy Liar* (1963), written by Keith Waterhouse and Willis Hall, based on their own play of Waterhouse's novel! This film of an adaptation of an adaptation is about as far from Truffaut's ideal of auteurism as you can get.[4]

Third, both critics and the directors themselves explicitly justified the Angry Young Men films in terms of "realism." Their attitude reflected an old shibboleth and plaint of the British cinema establishment, both in production and reception, best summed up by Michael Balcon's programmatic preference for "realism" over "tinsel."[5] This system of value, though most strongly entrenched on the Left, ran all the way across the political spectrum. For the Right, as with the Left, the aesthetic preference for realism was bound up with nationalism. "Tinsel," of course, was identified with Hollywood escapism and, in contrast, realism evoked local pride and sense of community. It meant showing ourselves honestly to ourselves, rather than indulging in other people's alien and deceptive fantasies. British critics praised films they liked in terms of their realism and damned those they did not as escapist trash. The French New Wave, however, aimed to transcend this shallow antinomy. The third term that made this possible was, of course, "modernism." The films of Resnais and Godard, even when adaptations, placed themselves clearly in a modernist tradition, as did Truffaut's crucial *Jules et Jim* (1962). Resnais, to take the most obvious example, collaborated with writers like Robbe-Grillet and Duras. The *Cahiers* group followed the path blazed by the Nouveau Roman and recognized Jean Cocteau as their godfather. Yet in Britain filmmakers fetishized the second-rate novels of regionalists, realists, and reactionaries.

The history of modernism in Europe followed a definite geographical pattern, which reflected an underlying historical reality.[6] The more a country felt the ambition to catch up economically and culturally, the more an aggressively avant-garde section of its intelligentsia embraced and radicalized a version of modernism. After the collapse of the old absolutist regimes, avant-garde artists often rejected the search for new modes of personal expression in favor of a depersonalized rationalism or functionalism. They attempted to subordinate the arts to industrial and technological needs and imperatives, and to merge the artist with the masses. Thus in backward Russia, the avant-garde moved rapidly from symbolism to futurism and then, after the impact of the October Revolution, to constructivism. In Italy futurism developed its own technocratic ideology and, in Germany, expressionism gave way to the Bauhaus. In France, where the ancien régime had been toppled more than a century before, cubism was followed by the much weaker current of purism, around Le Corbusier, but also, more significantly, by surrealism. The surrealists, like the constructivists or the later Bauhaus artists, lined up on the left politically, and yet reacted with hostility to the norms of modern industrial development, unlike their counterparts in revolutionary Russia or Germany. In Britain, after the brief flurry of vorticism, modernism never took root in any lasting way.

Britain, of course, was both the homeland of the Industrial Revolution, the pioneer of manufacturing capitalism, and the European country with the most remote and attenuated experience of absolutism. Modernism, in its pure form, appealed to very few in Britain, especially not in England. England's most committed modernists were very often expatriates—Eliot, Pound, H.D., Wyndham Lewis. In the visual arts, vorticism rapidly dissolved

and modern currents were smoothly amalgamated into the English landscape tradition, as in the work of Ben Nicholson or Henry Moore. A mild and
heavily romanticized anglicization of surrealism surfaced briefly and then
sputtered to a halt. In the world of literature and in taste-setting journalism,
there was a bloodless transfer of power to the Bloomsbury group, within the
traditional intelligentsia itself, and an increasingly emollient modernism was
assimilated into the ongoing high culture with hardly a break. Indeed, the
most effective protagonists of modern literature — Eliot and Leavis — argued
for modernism in frankly traditionalist terms. Far from wanting a break with
the past, they saw modernism as the culmination of a long national literary
history. This history now needed only to be reassessed retrospectively,
rather than brusquely overthrown. Moreover, modernism was treated as
something that had already happened and been absorbed, rather than as an
ongoing project.[7]

Modernism first impinged on British film culture during the silent period
with the London Film Society and the journal *Close Up*. But the coming of
sound quickly wiped out these tender plants, as it did much stronger film
avant-gardes elsewhere. The *Close Up* circle, around the writers Bryher and
H.D., produced Kenneth MacPherson's *Borderline* (1930), financed by Bryher (then married to MacPherson), and starring H.D., alongside Paul and
Eslanda Robeson. It remains the one outstanding British avant-garde film of
the period. However, *Close Up* folded shortly thereafter, and its contributors
lost heart and dispersed.[8] Meanwhile, after the collapse of the London Film
Society, its moving spirit, the irrepressible Iris Barry, left for New York in
1930.[9] In New York she met Philip Johnson at a cocktail party and soon afterward, she was hired by Alfred Barr to run the new Museum of Modern
Art's film program. Thus the modernist impulse was transferred from London to America, where the Museum played a crucial role in the survival of
avant-garde film through the thirties, enabling it to resurface again in the forties. In Britain, of course, this did not happen.

The Film Society's most significant outcome was its impact on Alfred
Hitchcock, a habitual and doubtless punctual attender at screenings. There
Hitchcock not only mingled with the cultural elite but also absorbed modernist aesthetic ideas, which he later attempted to nurture within narrative film.
Hitchcock experimented with sound in his first talking picture, *Blackmail*
(1929), but soon retreated into conformity. Nonetheless, once he felt his career in the industry was secure, both in Britain and subsequently in the
United States, he cunningly contrived a place for experimental ideas within
commercial genre films — the Salvador Dali dream sequence in *Spellbound*
(1945), the ten-minute takes in *Rope* (1948, produced by another Film Soci-

ety alumnus, Sidney Bernstein), the "pure cinema" project of *Rear Window* (1954), the montage murder sequence in *Psycho* (1960), and so on. Hitchcock's collaborator, Ivor Montagu, whom he met through the Film Society, also worked with Eisenstein, and many echoes of Eisenstein appear in Hitchcock's own work. But, in general terms, Hitchcock seems to have drawn the conclusion that modernist experiments were best contrived as a kind of illicit contraband, which he could smuggle in and secretly enjoy, while lapping up the praise and the dollars for his success within the mainstream of the industry.

During the thirties, the surviving vestiges of twenties modernism were channeled into the state-sponsored British documentary movement. John Grierson, a Scot, remained more open to modernism than other British producers and hired coworkers (like Alberto Cavalcanti, a Brazilian, and Len Lye, a New Zealander) who had impeccable experimental film credentials: Cavalcanti's *Rien que les Heures* (1926) was a landmark of the French avant-garde and Lye had made his abstract film *Tusalava* for the London Film Society in 1928. Nonetheless, the main drift of Grierson's project was to subordinate modernism (in its Russian form) to realism and to national propaganda. Grierson was impressed by Eisenstein's vision of an epic, silent cinema based on the masses and achieving its dramatic effects through formal means rather than character identification, and he believed it could be transposed to fit British documentary and propaganda film. Grierson's documentaries aimed to represent the society at large rather than particular individuals. They were meant to inform rather than entertain. In this context, he could draw productively from Eisenstein and Pudovkin. Similarly, other modernists could have a role to play within his team. Thus, in this unlikely setting were to be found artists like Lye, W. H. Auden (who wrote the voice-over for *Night Mail*, 1935), and Humphrey Jennings (a chief organizer of the London surrealist exhibition of 1936).[10]

To critics at the time, Grierson's efforts seemed to combine the realism they desired with a prudent preservation of modernist elements in an acceptable, marginal role. Meanwhile, Alexander Korda became the standard-bearer for narrative film in Britain, launching a series of costume dramas celebrating the popular high spots of British history and a cycle of extravagant imperialist epics, mainly directed by his brother, Zoltan Korda.[11] Korda's initial success with *The Private Life of Henry VIII* (1933) sprang from a canny combination of grandiose costume spectacle with music-hall comedy, but he was never able to repeat it, and his backers, Prudential Insurance, abruptly withdrew their support in 1937. Korda, however, did succeed in inspiring the British cinema world with the idea that they could and should set their sights on Hollywood as a model to be emulated. He pointed the way toward Rank's brave attempt to take on Hollywood after the war and, more recently, the pathetic false dawn of David Puttnam. Meanwhile, British cinema continued to churn out a series of "quota quickies": George Formby vehicles and vernacular potboilers for the domestic audience. But when the deadly grip of heritage drama and pierhead comedy finally broke down during the 1939-45 war, it was romanticism, and not realism, that carried the day: whether the operatic Technicolor romanticism of the Archers and Gainsborough or the contorted black-and-white "man-on-the-run" romanticism of the "spiv" film and Carol Reed.[12]

The war years saw a revival of English romanticism in response to the need for an idealized reaffirmation of British history and shared values (as perceived within the dominant ideology) and, on the other hand, for release into fantasy and dream to relieve the stress, hardship, and agony of war.[13] During the war, film production was necessarily limited, but nonetheless the national mood is much better conveyed by the visual ambition and expansive romanticism of Olivier's *Henry V* (1944) than by the restrained grittiness of Coward and Lean's *In Which We Serve* (1942), however much the critics may have welcomed the realism they felt that it conveyed. After the war was won, still sheltered from American competition, British cinema blossomed. This period saw not only Powell's and Pressburger's trilogy of *Black Narcissus* (1947), *The Red Shoes* (1948), and *Gone to Earth* (1950), in which a series of intensely desirous women are thwarted and finally plunge over the edge to their death, but also Carol Reed's trilogy of *Odd Man Out* (1947), *The Fallen Idol* (1948), and *The Third Man* (1949), in which appealingly desperate heroes are caught in paranoid labyrinths of pursuit and betrayal.

It is important to stress the strength of this "new romanticism," as the parallel movement in painting and poetry is called, because it partly explains the success of the Angry Young Men films in the next decade. In 1945 the top box-office film was *The Seventh Veil*, a sublimely over-the-top drama of female desire, classical music, and psychoanalysis. The same year, Cavalcanti, having left Grierson's documentary unit, made a small masterpiece of the grotesque in *Dead of Night* and followed this up, in 1947, with *They Made Me a Fugitive*, the definitive expressionist "man-on-the-run" film. Thus even a hero of "documentary realism" showed himself the master of "docklands romanticism" (along with Robert Hamer and *It Always Rains on Sundays*, 1947). British films, none of them remotely "realist," dominated the domestic box office for four straight years, until American political and economic power became irresistible and the British finally capitulated to Washington arm-twisting and a Hollywood boycott in 1948.[14] Both *The Third Man* and

Gone To Earth were coproductions with Selznick and, apart from them, the most impressive films from 1949 onward were Hitchcock's transatlantic *Under Capricorn* (1949), Dassin's *Night and the City* (1950), and Huston's series of "runaway productions" beginning with *The African Queen* (1952). The stage was now set for the critics at last to welcome a truly "realist" counterblast to Hollywood, one that simultaneously reacted against the romanticism and aestheticism of earlier British film.

However, the Angry Young Men were not the only cultural countercurrent of the fifties. In 1956, the same year that *Look Back in Anger* was produced at the Royal Court Theatre (May 8), the exhibition *This Is Tomorrow* opened at the Whitechapel Gallery (August 8).[15] This was the culmination of the work of the Independent Group of artists, architects, and critics and the emblematic beginning of British pop art. Both the Angry Young Men and the Independent Group, founded in 1952, reacted strongly against the diluted modernism of the traditional intelligentsia, a decaying amalgam of Bloomsbury and Cold War pieties. However, while the Angry Young Men turned back toward a provincial Little Englandism, the Independent Group openly welcomed American consumer culture in their struggle against the English countryside and the villa in Tuscany, celebrating science fiction, Hollywood movies, tailfins, and advertising. The Angry Young Men were resentfully anti-American, although they did energize their English populism with a taste for traditional jazz, uncontaminated either by Tin Pan Alley or by postbebop modernism. "Trad" enlivened the sound tracks of Reisz's *Momma Don't Allow* (1955) and Richardson's *Look Back in Anger* (1959). Visitors to *This Is Tomorrow*, on the other hand, were greeted by a giant Robbie the Robot (from the sci-fi movie *Forbidden Planet*) and a wall montage celebrating CinemaScope. A leading proponent of the Independent Group's work, Lawrence Alloway, went on to become a kind of godfather to the auteurist film magazine, *Movie*, in the early sixties.

Pop art was a way to outflank the dominant elite culture by turning simultaneously to popular consumer culture and to the avant-garde tradition. Reyner Banham, for instance, carefully placed pop technophilia in the context of the modern movement, and Richard Hamilton, the pioneer pop artist, turned back to Marcel Duchamp as a revered ancestor. Pop broke through to a wider cultural audience with the 1961 appearance of a new phalanx of artists, the Young Contemporaries, encouraged by Alloway, and then Ken Russell's benchmark television show, *Pop Goes the Easel*, the following year. In retrospect, we see that the nonexistent British "New Wave" of the time would have been much more closely linked to pop than to the Angry Young Men. Pop prefigured the sixties transformation of British culture. When the transformation came, however, it was expatriates who showed the way, at least as far as the cinema was concerned: Richard Lester, especially with *The Knack* (1965); Joseph Losey, who made *Modesty Blaise* (1966); and Antonioni, whose *Blow-Up* (1967) became the archetypal film of the decade. These directors aligned themselves much more closely with their French counterparts. Their scripts derived from absurdism rather than realism—Harold Pinter or the Goon Show. Local directors appeared very late in the decade— Cammell's and Roeg's *Performance* was shot in 1968, but its distributors cravenly delayed its release until 1970. Alongside Roeg, John Boorman and Ken Russell both developed into "auteurs," but basically they were neoromantics (low-key and high-key, respectively), clearly anti-Kitchen Sink, but only incidentally modernist.[16]

We can better see the long-term importance of the sixties for British film in the subsequent work of Derek Jarman and Peter Greenaway. Both went to art school in this period, Jarman after getting a literature degree at London University, in deference to his family, and Greenaway in preference to going to university, in defiance of his family. Jarman and Greenaway both set out to make films within the visual arts tradition. The dominant painters in Jarman's world were gay—David Hockney and Patrick Procktor. He was also close to Ossie Clarke on the fashion scene, which interlocked with the art world during the sixties. Hockney's significance, of course, sprang not only from his success as a painter, but also from his public declaration of homosexuality and its increasingly crucial presence in his art. Jarman himself, however, was not a pop painter, but a landscapist who moved toward abstraction. His early paintings show monoliths on English "west country" hills—descendants of Paul Nash or Henry Moore. Jarman is deeply attached to the landscape around Swanage in Dorset (which appears many times in his films), where he spent many childhood holidays and whose unique features Paul Nash also celebrated in his surrealist paintings. Jarman's own landscape tour de force at Prospect Cottage on Dungeness, a garden of Elizabethan flowers, stones, and driftwood, over which looms a massive nuclear power station, recreates the surrealist world of Chirico, with the respect for the "genius loci" always felt by Nash. There is a lasting tension in his work between a delirious neoromantic Englishness and a pop modernism, always in touch with "street culture." His two influential teachers at university were Eric Mottram, who introduced him to William Burroughs's *Naked Lunch*, and Niklaus Pevsner, who directed him to Gothic cathedrals, Lincoln, Canterbury, or Ely. The eerie elegiac tone of his recent films has its roots in this metaphysical historicism and in his deeply ambivalent nostalgia for childhood, fed by an intransigent anger and a will-to-resist rooted in gay culture.[17]

In his films, rather than his paintings, Derek Jarman first articulated the gay world in which he lived, its tastes, routines, extravagances, and crises. Filmmaking began for him as a personal art of home movies, strongly contrasted with his professional work as a set designer for Ken Russell. The crucial turning point came when he turned down Russell's invitation to design *Tommy* (1975) and determined instead to make his own first feature, *Sebastiane* (1976). What strikes me now about *Sebastiane* is no longer its place as a pioneering transposition into film of age-old visual motifs aestheticizing beautiful, tormented boys in Mediterranean settings, but its "high camp" silver Latin dialogue track. To me, this makes the film like an opera, whose libretto is in a foreign language, foregrounding the role of performance and visual composition. Dialogue has always seemed an awkward necessity for Jarman, and he has increasingly been happiest with preexisting literary texts — *The Tempest* (1979) or *The Angelic Conversation* (1985) — or, as with *War Requiem* (1989), musical texts. (Here he carries out Michael Powell's old ambition of the "composed film," in which the music preceded the filming, as in episodes of *Black Narcissus* or, of course, *The Red Shoes*.)[18] Greenaway, on the other hand, is fascinated by words and overloads his sound track with dialogue, sometimes as though the characters were mouthpieces for an abstruse disputation taking place outside the film.[19]

Peter Greenaway was much more directly influenced by sixties pop artists, such as R. B. Kitaj (after whom a star is named in *Drowning by Numbers* [1988]) and Tom Phillips, the creator of *A Humument*, with whom he collaborated on his television film *Dante's Inferno* (1989), the pilot project for *Prospero's Books* (1991). In Greenaway's case, the fascination centers on artists who explore the relationship between words and images, between literature and painting. Greenaway discovered Kitaj's paintings at the same Marlborough Gallery show in 1963 that Derek Jarman also visited. Like Greenaway, Kitaj maintains an impenetrably enigmatic relation to his sources. Like Greenaway, too, he is drawn to the arcana of old engravings, incunabula, emblems, or maps. Kitaj has sought to people his paintings with imaginary characters, like those in novels, who appear in a series of works. In the same way, Greenaway too has his caste of imaginary characters, presided over by Tulse Luper, who crop up in film after film, sometimes in central roles, sometimes as fanciful marginalia. At heart, Greenaway, like Kitaj, is a collagist, juxtaposing images drawn from some fantastic archive, tracing erudite coincidental narratives within his material, bringing together Balthus and Borges in a bizarre collocation of bizarre eroticism and trompe l'oeil high modernism. Kitaj also, of course, is a cinephile, through whose painting,

Kenneth Anger and Michael Powell (1973), we can trace a strange connection between the myth-worlds of Greenaway and Jarman.[20]

At first sight, Derek Jarman and Peter Greenaway have little in common. Indeed, Jarman is notorious for his vitriolic attacks on Greenaway. Yet both were products of sixties art schools, both were trained as painters and still are painters, both developed a strong visual style and dedicated themselves to making personal films marginal to the populist mainstream of the industry, both pay court to narrative while shamelessly revealing that their true interests lie elsewhere. Both can be seen, in a certain sense, as modernists. Both, in another sense, can also be seen as neoromantics, steeped in a personal vision of the English landscape, endlessly revisiting and rejecting the temptations of Victorianism and antiquarianism, returning much more willingly to their memories of childhood, mediated through home movies and family snapshots for Jarman, and through pored-over children's book illustrations for Greenaway. Derek Jarman accuses Greenaway of succumbing to antiquarianism in *The Draughtsman's Contract* (1982), a vice he attributes first to Poussin and thereafter to the Victorians. In contrast, he cites his own *Caravaggio* (1986), with its contemporary references on image and sound track, its obvious debt to Pasolini, its inauthentic modernity. But Greenaway does not see *The Draughtsman's Contract* as authentic. On the contrary, he reacts angrily to a comparison with Kubrick's *Barry Lyndon* (1975): "My film is about excess: excess in the language, excess in the landscape, which is much too green—we used special green filters—there is no historical realism in the costumes, the women's hair-styles are exaggerated in their height, the costumes are extreme. I wanted to make a very artificial film."[21] In the same interview, he dismisses *Chariots of Fire* (1981, also Derek Jarman's most hated film) as reactionary and lacking any real aesthetic, even that of a *Saturday Night and Sunday Morning* (1960).

The difference between them, of course, lies in their divergent strategies for avoiding antiquarianism. Derek Jarman explicitly modernizes, introduces contemporary references and false touches, interprets Caravaggio's life and art through a filter of topical and personal preoccupations and tastes. Greenaway, on the contrary, exaggerates the archaism, pushing all the elements into an unreal and peculiarly inauthentic realm of caricature and pastiche, trying to turn a Restoration comedy into *Last Year at Marienbad* (1961). *Prospero's Books* (1991) follows in the same tradition by recreating the high Renaissance world of masque, pageant, and emblem in exaggerated splendor, while at the same time placing the play within Prospero's mind and experimenting with video effects and infography. The risks run by the rival strategies are clear. Jarman opens himself to the charge of anachronistic travesty,

Greenaway to that of lavish overindulgence. When I saw *The Draughtsman's Contract* at its premiere at the Edinburgh Film Festival, I was nauseated by the excess of Englishness, the hyperbolic heaping of English language on English acting on English landscape on English country-house murder on English preciousness and whimsy, the dilettantish celebration of eccentricity and games-playing. The modernist dimension of Greenaway's work, the side that takes us toward Hollis Frampton's *Zorn's Lemma* or toward the Oulipo writers in France,[22] toward an intricate conceptualism or a Nabokovian dandyism, can appear overingenious and willfully bizarre—another rerun of Lewis Carroll, yet with its shadow side made ever more apparent in erotic tableaux and Jacobean cruelty.

Derek Jarman is much more intimately linked to "New Romanticism." His most prominent disciples (John Maybury and Cerith Wyn Evans) were part of the "Blitz crowd" and his own work is related not only to this "club scene" new romanticism,[23] but to a much deeper, more long-lasting tradition: to the medieval poets, the Elizabethans (not only Marlowe and Shakespeare, but magicians, alchemists, and herbalists), Blake and Shelley, the late Victorians, the Apocalyptics, and, of course, Michael Powell and Emeric Pressburger. Modernism in Britain has prospered precisely in alliance with the underground currents of this broad national-romantic strain in the culture. Neoromanticism fitted intimately with the experience of the war, in poems by Edith Sitwell, Dylan Thomas, or T. S. Eliot, in drawings or paintings by Moore and Piper, in films by Humphrey Jennings and Powell and Pressburger. This wartime mood still runs through Jarman's films, especially in *The Last of England* (1987), with its recurrent imagery of a blitzed and burning London, recalling also the Great Fire of 1666, the burning of the Houses of Parliament painted by Turner, and the burning down of his own studio. "Fire turned nasty." It was no longer the comforting glow of childhood hearth and picnic bonfire. The palette of *The Last of England*, too, like that of Jarman's more recent paintings, is all tarry black and fiery red, made to look like cathedral stained glass.

Whereas the mainstream of romanticism has always expressed and consolidated national myths, Jarman's subverts them. Underlying the imagery of the blitz and the wasteland lies a critique of a destructive society and government—in a word, of Thatcherism. The desolate cityscape is contrasted with the imagery of the garden, as the state terrorism of *Jubilee* (1977) was contrasted with the closing masque of *The Tempest* (1979), the two films linked through the role of two Renaissance magicians, John Dee and Prospero. Jarman's political commitment draws on the sense of an alternative tradition, on the great homosexual texts—Plato's *Symposium*,

Shakespeare's sonnets, the paintings of Caravaggio. At the same time, it is inseparable from his day-by-day involvement in the gay world, in the struggle against Clause 28 and the solidarity of gay men in the face of AIDS as they confront an authoritarian and homophobic regime whose leader's insistent moral appeal was to "Victorian values" and against the "permissive society."[24] The key turning point, for Jarman, came with the Royal Jubilee of 1977 and its riotously sinister shadow, punk. Jarman's *Jubilee* is a protest against the whole horrendous notion of the "second Elizabethan age," the backdrop of national grandeur and creativity against which Britain's economic and cultural decline was played out for twenty-five years. After that, of course, Thatcherism came as a movement not of renewal, but of vengefulness against everything she disapproved of that had somehow still managed to survive.

Peter Greenaway emerged from a strangely contradictory background. On the one hand, he worked for the government Central Office of Information, making films meant to express the British way of life, and, on the other hand, he made idiosyncratic "structural films" in his own free time. His affinities are with "international" modernism—before making *The Draughtsman's Contract*, he screened films by Fellini, Bertolucci, Rohmer, Straub, and Resnais for the crew, so that they could understand his intentions. At the same time, he secretly remade his own earlier *Vertical Features Remake* (1979), in which a group of film scholars try to reconstruct a lost film from a series of surviving views. Greenaway is also close to movements in modern art and music that employ modular and serial structures. Like many conceptual artists, he is fascinated by lists, grids, catalogs, counting games, and random procedures, which appear in his work as "coincidences" or "accidents." He is also fascinated by mysteries and their concomitant troop of red herrings, deceptive riddles, and false trails, the stock-in-trade of the peculiarly English form of the cerebral detective story. His films are made under the twin signs of the taxonomy and the enigma. Such an aesthetic is perhaps strongest in an intrinsically nonrealist art like music, but even in literature and painting, it subordinates content to formal preoccupations, so that subject matter often seems no more than a pretext. The structure comes first and the content—say, a series of fictions—is then fitted into it, a lesson Greenaway learned from John Cage. This school of modernism, unlike neo-romanticism, was historically decoupled from politics, yet, under the pressure of Thatcherism, Greenaway too turned to political invective in *The Cook, the Thief, His Wife, and Her Lover*.

Greenaway's antipathy toward Thatcherism stems from an ethical and aesthetic dislike for the philistinism and vulgarity of her regime, her exaltation of the profit motive, her determination that art and scholarship should only be supported if they served an economic function, her authoritarianism, her social philosophy of frugality and order for the poor combined with greed and license for the rich. Thus an expensive restaurant was a logical setting for his film, a place where Spica's own authoritarianism, greed, and license can be publicly indulged. Moreover, one of Greenaway's recurrent preoccupations is with the food chain, the process of ingestion of the weak by the strong and the dead by the living, in curious configurations of cruelty and death with sex and dinner. At the same time, the restaurant is symbolically a cathedral, a cinema, and an art museum, the chef its officiating priest and artist. As in other Greenaway films, the woman is the controlling character, bent on revenge on the world of men, destroying the figure of the artist en route. The brutalization of an innocent child recalls that of Smut in *Drowning by Numbers* (1988), a grueling moment when a ludic commedia dell'arte is suddenly transformed into a macabre Jacobean drama. Indeed, as Greenaway puts it, "The Jacobeans were looking over their shoulder at the grand Elizabethan age; Britain still looks over its shoulder at the Great Empire. In Jacobean times, syphilis was the new sexual scourge; we now have AIDS. There's a certain comparison in that sexuality has become complicated, so there's a similar spirit of melancholy. The same sensation of fatalism exists vis-à-vis the sort of cruelty we see every day, especially cruelty in the home, the abuse of children, and so on."[25] From their very different angles, Greenaway and Jarman unexpectedly converge on a surprisingly similar standpoint.

Both Greenaway and Jarman made key films for the British Film Institute (BFI) Production Board, under Peter Sainsbury: *The Draughtsman's Contract* (1982), suggested by Sainsbury, who asked Greenaway whether he had ever thought of making a dialogue film, and later, Jarman's *Caravaggio* (1986). The board had become completely divorced from its experimental function until Sainsbury, former editor of the avant-garde journal *Aftermage*, was appointed in the mid-seventies. Sainsbury became something like a new, but decisively modernist and antirealist Grierson. Toward the end of the sixties, under the dual impact of New York "structural film" and the European experiments in narrative of Godard and others, a film avant-garde crystallized for the first time in Britain since *Close Up*. It was built around the BFI, The Other Cinema, the Workshop Movement, and the Independent Film-Makers' Association (IFA).[26] Neither Greenaway nor Jarman participated in the avant-garde debates and activities of the time, which they saw, perhaps, as too politically doctrinaire or too potentially time-consuming. In a way, their noninvolvement probably made it easier for them to break out of the earlier pattern of their filmmaking, unencumbered by a baggage of past positions and pronouncements. Also, they did not confront Thatcherism head on, as "political filmmakers," but from a less explicit artistic position within which their political anti-Thatcherism emerged.

Nonetheless, films like those of Greenaway and Jarman should be seen as part of a wider and disparate shift in British film, due in part to a decisive shift toward the visual arts as a source for cinema, and in part to the theoretical and practical consolidation of a film avant-garde in the IFA and at the BFI. The emergence of a post-Godardian "political modernism" at the BFI, although it never achieved even the limited popular success of Greenaway or Jarman, helped to create an alternative pole of attraction within British cinema and thus the space between mainstream and countercinema that they later occupied.[27] Greenaway and Jarman are much closer in background and outlook to other directors emerging from the BFI and the workshops than they are to the upscale TV drama and ad directors who constitute the rump of the "film industry" left behind in Britain after the more ambitious of them have been called to the Coast. The other important condition, of course, was the fabulous collapse of Puttnamism and the flight of its leader to Hollywood, where his pretensions were ignominiously liquidated. "The British are coming" indeed.[28]

Thatcherism, by breaking the mold of British politics and carrying through radical right-wing cultural policies, directed, in essence, against the legacy of the sixties, succeeded paradoxically in politicizing filmmakers who had been formed during the comparatively liberal years of Wilson, the decade of sexual liberation, the last hurrah of welfare Keynesianism, and the belated entry of modernism into the general culture. This "delayed modernism," however, proved resilient enough to survive into the eighties. It decisively influenced a generation then in a position to make oppositional films first for the BFI, later for Channel Four, and eventually for independent producers within the industry or in Europe. As a result, Britain saw an efflorescence of filmmaking paralleled only in the forties. Britain finally produced the "Last New Wave," a series of uncompromising films made by original, oppositional, visually oriented modernist auteurs. It was worth waiting.

Notes

1. This analysis of Thatcherism emerges from debates carried on by a number of authors. See especially the following: Andrew Gamble, *The Free Economy and the Strong State* (Basingstoke: Macmillan, 1988); Stuart Hall, *The Hard Road to Renewal* (London: Verso, 1988); Bob Jessop, Kevin Bonnett, Simon Bromley, and Tom Ling, *Thatcherism* (London: Polity Press, 1988); Scott Newton and Dilwyn Porter, *Modernisation Frustrated* (London: Unwin Hyman, 1988); and Henk Overbeek, *Global Capitalism and National Decline: The Thatcher Decade in Perspective* (London: Unwin Hyman, 1990). For the general anti-Thatcherite cultural efflores-

cence under Thatcherism, see Robert Hewison, *Future Tense* (London: Methuen, 1990). Films coming from outside London, it should be noted, like Bill Forsyth's Scottish films or the Liverpudlian *Letter to Brezhnev*, seem strangely less bitter than the London films, although a vein of cynicism underlies the mood of astringent comedy and wry fantasy. Northern Ireland has been marginalized in the cinema, as in the political arena, although Alan Clarke's extraordinary television work there represented the most startling and successful convergence of political with formal preoccupations in any of the media.

2. These words are quoted without citation by Roy Armes, in *A Critical History of the British Cinema* (London: Secker and Warburg, 1979). They are requoted parodically in Peter Greenaway's *The Draughtsman's Contract*, with painting substituted for cinema. For another version, see also Truffaut's remark that there is "something about England that's anti-cinematic," in François Truffaut, *Hitchcock* (London: Panther, 1969).

3. Jacques Belmains, *Jeune Cinéma Anglais* (Lyon: *Premier Plan*, no. 44, May 1967).

4. On the Angry Young Men and their impact on the cinema, see Harry Ritchie, *Success Stories: Literature and the Media in England 1950-1959* (London: Faber and Faber, 1988); and Robert Hewison, *In Anger* (London: Weidenfeld and Nicolson, 1981). John Hill, *Sex, Class and Realism: British Cinema, 1956-63* (London: British Film Institute, 1986) provides a comprehensive survey of the movement in film.

5. See Robert Murphy, *Realism and Tinsel* (London: Routledge, 1989), which takes its title from Michael Balcon's pamphlet *Realism and Tinsel*, based on a talk given to the Film Workers Association in Brighton in 1943. This is available in *Michael Balcon's 25 Years in Films*, ed. Monja Danischewsky (London: World Film Publications, 1947). In his talk, Balcon especially stressed the contribution Grierson's unit had made as "the men who kept realism going on the screen" and the potential for a new type of film bringing a realistic treatment to "story elements" within the industry.

6. See Peter Wollen, "Scenes from the Future: Komar and Melamid," in *Between Spring and Summer* (Tacoma, Wash.: Tacoma Art Museum, and Boston: Institute of Contemporary Art, 1990).

7. For the postwar history of modernism in Britain, see Alan Sinfield, *Literature, Politics and Culture in Postwar Britain* (Oxford: Basil Blackwell, 1989). He is also very illuminating on the sexual and class politics of the Angry Young Men.

8. For *Close Up* and *Borderline*, see Roland Cosandey, "Re-assessment of 'Lost' Film," *Afterimage* (London), no. 12 (Autumn 1985), which contains a full bibliography. See also Anne Friedberg, "The Film Journal *Close Up*," (Ph.D. diss., New York University, 1983).

9. For the Film Society, see Jen Samson, "The Film Society, 1925-1939," in *All Our Yesterdays*, ed. Charles Barr (London: British Film Institute, 1986).

10. For Humphrey Jennings, see Mary-Lou Jennings, *Humphrey Jennings* (London: British Film Institute, 1982).

11. Sir Alexander Korda can be seen as one of the roster of émigré knights described by Perry Anderson in "Components of the National Culture," *New Left Review*, no. 50 (July-August 1968), along with Sir Isaiah Berlin, Sir Ernst Gombrich, Sir Lewis Namier, and Sir Karl Popper. Yet Korda, it should be noted, worked with the revolutionary Bela Kun regime in Hungary and was a refugee from counterrevolutionary dictator Admiral Horthy. Later, however, he became an intimate and patron of Churchill and his circle.

12. For the music-hall, pierhead, and seaside tradition, best exemplified by George Formby, the ukelele-playing hero of the Beatles and Morrissey, see Murphy, *Realism and Tinsel*. Murphy's chapter "The Spiv Cycle" also provides the best introduction to this riveting British equivalent to film noir. A "spiv" was a petty racketeer involved in the postwar black economy. He wore flash ties, suits with wide lapels, and a sneer or grin.

13. For wartime and postwar romanticism, see especially David Mellor, *A Paradise Lost* (London: Lund Humphries, 1987); and Robert Hewison, *Under Siege* (London: Weidenfeld and Nicolson, 1977).

14. The best brief treatment of the British struggle against the economic power of Hollywood, led by Harold Wilson, is in Murphy, *Realism and Tinsel*.

15. See *This Is Tomorrow Today* (New York: P.S. 1, Institute for Art and Urban Resources, 1987); and, for the subsequent shift in British popular culture, Dick Hebdige, *Hiding in the Light* (London: Comedia, 1988).

16. For a general treatment of the 1960s, see Robert Hewison, *Too Much* (London: Methuen, 1986).

17. The indispensable sources for Derek Jarman are his two books of journals, Derek Jarman, *Dancing Ledge* (London: Quartet, 1984), and *Modern Nature* (London: Century, 1991). See also the special number of *Afterimage*, "Derek Jarman . . . of Angels and Apocalypse," *Afterimage* (London), no. 12 (Autumn 1985). I have also drawn from Derek Jarman, *Derek Jarman's Caravaggio* (London: Thames and Hudson, 1986), *The Last of England* (London: Constable, 1987), and *War Requiem* (London: Faber and Faber, 1989).

18. Michael Powell was inspired by Friedrich Feher's film *The Robber Symphony*, which is described by Graham Greene in his review in the *Spectator*, May 24, 1936, reprinted in Graham Greene, *The Pleasure-Dome* (Oxford: Oxford University Press, 1980).

19. For Greenaway, I have drawn mainly from Peter Greenaway, *Papers* (Paris: Dis Voir, 1990), which contains a selection of his artwork with his own commentary, and Greenaway, *Fear of Drowning by Numbers* (Paris: Dis Voir, 1988). A number of Greenaway's scripts are also published.

20. For Kitaj, see Marco Livingstone, *R. B. Kitaj* (Oxford: Phaidon Press, 1985). Kitaj did actually introduce Kenneth Anger and Michael Powell to each other: "I brought Anger and Powell together because they admired each other. They're both quite mysterious and since I introduced them, I painted them together in their disjunction."

21. See Peter Greenaway, "Meurtre dans un jardin anglais," *L'avant-scène cinema* (Paris), no. 333 (October 1984). The translation of Greenaway's remarks is my own.

22. For the Oulipo group of writers, see *Oulipo*, ed. Warren F. Motte, Jr. (Lincoln: University of Nebraska Press, 1986).

23. For new romanticism and Blitz culture, see Caroline Evans and Minna Thornton, *Women and Fashion: A New Look* (London: Quartet, 1989).

24. Derek Jarman is one of a number of gay filmmakers who made films in Britain during the Thatcher years, including Terence Davies, Isaac Julien, John Maybury, Ron Peck, and Cerith Wyn Evans.

25. See Gary Indiana's interview with Peter Greenaway, in *Interview* 20 (March 1990), 120-21, on the occasion of the New York release of *The Cook, the Thief, His Wife, and Her Lover*.

26. Reliable sources are few for this period in British cinema. For the black workshops, see especially *Blackframes*, ed. Mbye B. Cham and Claire Andrade-Watkins (London: Celebration of Black Cinema and MIT Press, 1988); and Coco Fusco, *Young, British and Black: The Work of Sankofa and Black Audio Film Collective* (Buffalo, N.Y.: Hallwalls/Contemporary Arts Center, 1988).

27. See D. N. Rodowick, *The Crisis of Political Modernism* (Urbana: University of Illinois Press, 1988).

28. "The British are coming!" was the media slogan propagated after *Chariots of Fire* won an Oscar. It is strange that the next British Oscar sweep, for *The Last Emperor*, had no discernible impact whatever in Britain, presumably because its director was an Italian. Conversely, a director like Ridley Scott, even though he has retained his personal and working ties with Britain, has been systematically neglected. Yet Scott's vision of the city in *Blade Runner* (1982) has much in common with its British counterparts.

Four

Images for Sale: The "New" British Cinema

Thomas Elsaesser

The Thatcher Years: Hard Times, Interesting Times

The British cinema during the 1980s—the Thatcher Years—enjoyed a Renaissance. Indeed, early on in the decade even Hollywood helped to celebrate its rebirth: Oscars for *Chariots of Fire* (Hugh Hudson, 1981); the appointment of its producer, David Puttnam, as director of production at Columbia Pictures; more Oscars for *Gandhi* (Richard Attenborough, 1982). The 1980s also saw notable hits on the art cinema circuit with *A Letter to Brezhnev* (Chris Bernard, 1985) and *My Beautiful Laundrette* (Stephen Frears, 1985), recognition for auteurs like Peter Greenaway, John Boorman, and Nicolas Roeg; plaudits in Berlin for heretic iconoclasts like Derek Jarman; and commercial successes for international directors like Stephen Frears, Ridley Scott, Adrian Lyne, and Alan Parker. In addition, a more hard-bitten, controlled professionalism among directors eclipsed the volcanic and fizzling talents of a Ken Russell and a Lindsay Anderson from the previous decades. This group, by and large, opposed the ideological rigidities of Thatcher, matching the Iron Lady's temperament with an equally steely determination not to whine or indulge in left-wing romanticism.

During the decade, more British films were made than at any time since the 1950s, or at least more British films attracted international awards or coverage. In Britain the cinemas were filling up again, albeit for American blockbusters, but whatever the attraction, a revival of audience interest might just, in the long run, be good for British movie business, as well. One could begin to talk of a "British film culture" without having to invoke François Truffaut's famous quip about "British" and "cinema" being a

Director Alan Parker (on the set of *Mississippi Burning*), one of the British directors to achieve international success during the 1980s.

contradiction in terms. Movies were also helped by the lively interest television took in the cinema, thanks to a popular preview program like Barry Norman's "Film" on BBC1, the retrospectives on BBC2's "Film Club" and "Moviedrome," the "South Bank Shows" devoted to filmmakers, "The Media Show" on Channel Four, and the coproduction/cofinancing or in-house filmmaking of television, especially BBC's "Screen Two" and Channel Four's "Film on Four" series, with a helpful hand from the British Film Institute (BFI) Production Board. Out in the streets, however, the scene became further depleted: fewer and fewer cinemas, even among the Rank/EMI-Cannon duopoly, and a dying out of independent neighborhood cinemas as well as art houses.

In the country at large, million of Britons during the Thatcher era were living through hard times. Others found them interesting times, because her government brought about polarizations in the body politic not seen since the late 1920s: the definitive breakup of a social consensus that had maintained a common discourse about what was important to the national interest across the political spectrum. With Thatcher, the very terms by which to voice dissent were challenged, a point of some importance when considering the different political styles that emerged: from Arthur Scargill's miners' strike to David Owen's Social Democrats, from the militant faction on the Liverpool City Council to Nicholas Ridley on Germany. In the cinema's case, the different filmmaking styles (too readily lumped together as "postmodern") broke with the consensus idiom par excellence: "realism." In short, the Thatcher years implicitly and explicitly asked what it meant to be British—or English, Scottish, Irish, or Welsh, or to be from the North, the Midlands or the South. The decade also questioned what it meant to be a British filmmaker. The polarizations along lines of class, of race, of region, of nationality and of language recalled similar breakups elsewhwere in Europe. They make the 1980s a period of momentous social shifts well beyond Thatcherism and support the view that violent social tensions are often the best soil for the flowering of resilient, contesting, and confrontational arts, obliging artists to rediscover themselves as social counterforces and moral consciences.

An obvious topic would be to investigate whether one can trace the breakup of the consensus in the cinema of the 1980s, as well. Yet equally relevant is whether the kind of self-questioning of national identity just hinted at can be distinguished from another response, no less prominent in the 1980s: self-promotion, also pursued in the name of national identity. Given the increasing dependence of the arts on money (a condition always true of the cinema) and the fact that those granting money increasingly demand that the arts demonstrate their usefulness, what might be the status of such a national identity, especially where it defines itself in economic terms: as competitive edge, conquest of markets, and brand-name awareness, while nonetheless relying on images and stories rather than goods and services for its meaning and substance?

Not Another British Cinema Renaissance . . .

Screenwriter Colin Welland's cry "The British are coming" at the Oscar ceremony for *Chariots of Fire* set the tone for the decade, releasing a flood of pent-up emotion and producing acres of print about the British film renaissance. But whenever the word "renaissance" crops up in the context of the British cinema (as it seems to do at least once every decade), one needs to be wary. Chances are the film industry is in deep trouble. This was the case around 1984–85 when, still flushed with the success of *Chariots of Fire*, a string of media events culminating in the British Film Year of 1985 persuaded the public to see not the small acorn but the mighty oak tree: to ignore the continuing decline of an indigenous film industry, the decreasing share of British-made films in British cinemas, and an exodus to Hollywood of directors, cinematographers, and specialists in many filmmaking crafts (especially sound, sets, and animation).

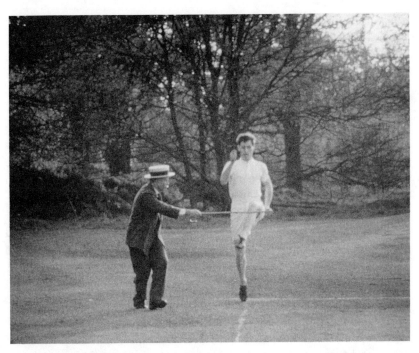

"The British are coming!": Sam Mussabini (Ian Holm) trains sprinter Harold Abrahams (Ben Cross) for the 1924 Olympics, in *Chariots of Fire* (1982).

Scanning the titles trumpeted as New British Cinema at the 1984 London Film Festival, one wonders if what took place was a large-scale relabeling of the goods, a quick fix for the deep-seated structural ills of mainstream filmmaking. Suddenly, half the drama output of British television found itself named "cinema." While some "Plays for Today" deserved to be called movies (*Rainy Day Women*, 1984, scripted by David Pirie, for instance), even more television films should never have been showcased in the cinema, although coproduction deals (sometimes with foreign companies) made this obligatory. Thus, Chris Peachment could write about *Loose Connections* (Richard Eyre, 1984), "What we have here is something that would not be diminished by showing on video. Which may be perfectly acceptable to its director . . . but is not what one would hope to say about something consciously made for the cinema" (Peachment, 152). More damning still, Jeremy Isaacs, then head of Channel Four, thought the efforts by the independent filmmaking sector fell between both stools: "too slight for the cinema, too slack for television" (Isaacs, 118), while for the critic John Brown a major vehicle of the film industry, *The Dresser* (Peter Yates, 1984), despite its "elaborately promoted status (The Royal Film, the Oscar nominations) as a big screen movie [could not disguise the fact that it] operates as a big screen extension of television traditions" (Brown, 190).

A renaissance implies a renewal. What was it that was stirring, moving, breaking through frozen ground? Talent? Commercial success? Big Themes? Big Names? The organic metaphors flowing from those panegyric pens homogenized divergent if not contradictory phenomena. In the case of the British cinema in the mid-1980s, these ranged from fiscal changes affecting investment depreciation (the end of tax shelters, in short), to judicious programming (film critic Derek Malcolm's term of office as director of the London Film Festival proved particularly rich in this respect), to taking in an anniversary (fifty years of the British Film Institute in 1983), to the trial-and-error period of a new television network (Channel Four's buying and commissioning policy), and to the low rental rates of home video recorders and prerecorded tapes (making Britain by the early 1980s "the largest home video market in Western Europe," according to *American Film*, May 1983).

Talk of a renaissance, however, rekindled the question of what a national cinema could be, what it has been, and who needed it. The British film industry always had problems asserting itself economically against overpowering Hollywood competition. Interestingly, in the periods when it held its own, or whenever a discernible strategy emerged (during the war years, or the 1950s), its success sprang as much from an ideological move as from an economic boost. This is what one learns from the classic studies. *A Mirror for England* was the programmatic title of Raymond Durgnat's influential book, and Charles Barr showed in what elaborate ways "projecting Britain and the British character" was Michael Balcon's motto at Ealing Studios. In other words, whether during the war or immediately after, propaganda, patriotism, and "projection" have functioned as integral parts of a successful national cinema.

Reporting on the 1981 Berlin Film Festival's retrospective of Balcon's work, David Robinson marveled at "just how rich the British cinema was in the 1930s and 1940s," and concluded that it had to do with "craftsmanship and a sure and determined sense of a national identity. . . . The films have a sort of confidence that they can sell themselves without recourse to vast budgets, or running after 'international' (that is American) appeal" (*Times*, February 27, 1981).

Robinson was not alone in thinking that an "emphasis on British themes gives . . . films the sinew of authenticity." The writer Alan Bennett put it equally succinctly:

Behind a lot of the questions that are raised lurks an unspoken one: how do

we make it big in America? Risking being hauled before Colin Welland in the
Barnes Magistrates Court, charged with insulting behavior, I'd like to ask
why do we want to? . . . [T]he European directors I admire . . . don't eat
their hearts out because they're not big in Arkansas. Why should we? Mrs.
Thatcher has the answer, but does she know anything about films?
(Bennett, 122)

To which one might reply that she may not have known about films, but her
speech writers knew a thing or two about self-promotion. She projected
"British themes" and the "sinews of authenticity" pummeled out of flabby
jingoist nostalgia, or more humbly put, she constructed national myths out of
the bric-a-brac of history, xenophobia, and paranoia.

Thatcher's Britain: An Invention of the Media

The dilemma when writing about cinema in the age of Thatcher is quite simply this: The Thatcher years were an invention of the media, or at the very
least, the result of a complex and often collusive love-hate relationship between the Thatcher government, the press, and television. Most commentators agree that the connection between politics and television—not just in
Britain—has become too close for comfort for democracy. But since the
connection between film and television has become even more inextricable,
it is almost impossible to construct for the cinema during this decade a
straight opposition between confrontational artists and compliant public opinion, nor indeed for those working in the audiovisual media, an opposition between the hard times for some and the interesting times for others.

What remains most vividly about the decade is the so-called Saatchi effect. In politics, it pinpointed the close ties between the Conservative Central Office and a well-known advertising agency: the massive deployment,
from within No. 10, of the prime minister's press secretary Bernard Ingham,
and the promotion and preferment of flamboyant industrial entrepreneurs or
"boardroom buccaneers" such as Lord Hanson (of the Hanson Trust), Lord
King (Chairman of British Airways), and Lord Weinstock (Chairman of
GEC). These men, a newspaper once pointed out, Margaret Thatcher rewarded as Queen Elizabeth I once rewarded Francis Drake. For the cinema,
the Saatchi effect blurred the lines between the different kinds of self-aware-
ness: that which probes and that which promotes. When Norman Stone,
writing for Rupert Murdoch's *Sunday Times*, made his much-publicized attack on filmmakers like Derek Jarman and Stephen Frears ("Sick Scenes
from English Life"), he quite simply hated what they showed. Clearly alien
to Stone was the idea that a filmmaker's shocking or disturbing images might

be essential to making a certain reality visible, not just to the eye but to one's moral and emotional senses. Stone could assume, without questioning it, that at issue was England's image in the world, since national cinema worked as advertising: the agency should look after the client.

On the other hand, as the high-risk business for self-made men and buccaneers par excellence, the film industry should have appealed to the Thatcher philosophy. Yet even Puttnam and Attenborough found it hard to catch the prime minister's ear when it came to mitigating, with the help of central funds, the effects of abolishing the Eady Levy, the tax write-offs and other economic measures detrimental to the film industry. In one sense, of course, the film industry in any European country always looks toward state support, as did the New German Cinema; the French government also directed massive aid to its film industry. In Britain, government perceived the film lobby as looking for "handouts," and thus as anathema to free-marketeers. But equally in the pursuit of new (and this means American) markets, British cinema should have enjoyed the government's benevolence on a par with Plessey, Westlands, or Rover Cars. After all, Britain under Thatcher became a nation of national brand names, company logos, icons, and slogans: identity under the reign of "The Image."

How then can one read the relations between the British cinema and Thatcherism? When neither official rhetoric nor central government supported the small but nonetheless real impact of British films internationally, the whole spectrum, from Alan Parker to David Puttnam, from Dennis Potter to Peter Greenaway, from Derek Jarman to Stephen Frears, turned scathingly anti-Thatcher. But did this necessarily mean that Britain in the 1980s had either a critical, self-questioning or a combative, society-questioning cinema?

What "We" Can Sell to "Them"

The answer must be, both and neither. Both, insofar as one can easily name dozens of films highly critical and satirical, somber and desperate about the state of Britain. Neither, insofar as the terms of the debate about the cinema shifted sufficiently to make "critical" and "combative" almost irrelevant notions. Superficially at least, the debate on both sides concerned markets, box office, image, and impact. As to "why we want to make it big in America," for instance, film journalists had no doubt. Perhaps the Thatcher ethos was well understood and accepted. More likely, the home truth had sunk in that no successful European film industry can make films for its own market alone. Investment calculated on a purely national revenue basis makes the homegrown product look too cheap to be attractive to domestic audiences, those who vote with their feet for pictures with production values. On the other hand, journalists like Margaret Hinxman thought that "precisely the qualities that have made *Chariots of Fire* such a hit across the Atlantic" were the ones apparently advanced by Rank, Lord Grade, and EMI for turning David Puttnam down when he approached them for financing: "It has no name stars in it, its subject was sport, above all, it was too British" (*Daily Mail*, January 31, 1982). Here, then, appears another dilemma: either too British or not British enough. Yet this presents too easy a juxtaposition. At issue is what kind of Britishness "we" could sell to "them," in turn balancing an appeal to "insider knowledge" about England and Britain with what the world knew, or thought it knew, about Britain.

Such a proposition raises a number of further points. First, we must differentiate between the projection of what one could call a "social imaginary" of Britain and the projection of a "national imaginary," one for "us" and one for "them." The distinction might even mark off television productions from film productions, with the latter necessarily destined for an international audience. Mamoun Hassan rightly points out that, as far as television goes, "international sales provide the jam" because the bread and butter is a national audience. The BBC has to justify its license fee, while the paymasters of commercial television are "the advertisers, [who] wish to sell their goods . . . in Birmingham, West Midlands, and not Birmingham, Alabama" (Hassan, 116). But he underestimates the quite tangible "commercial good will" that tourism, the publishing trade, luxury cars, or British quality knitwear and leather goods derive even from the relatively paltry sums changing hands between American PBS stations and ITV for "Upstairs Downstairs" or "Brideshead Revisited." From television to films, and from style magazines to record sleeves, the Thatcher years taught the British media a crucial lesson: the importance of an image culture, rather than a film culture.

Film Culture: A Foreign Import?

I once argued that Britain lacked a film culture from the grass roots up, as existed in France: meaning a large number of filmgoers who could recognize a traveling shot by Vincente Minnelli or a sequence edited by Sam Fuller. Equally important, I thought, was a generation of cine-literate as well as cinephile writers and directors. Hence the early enthusiasm for Chris Petit (a film critic turned director), whose reputation as a director always seemed slightly higher among the cinephiles than their judgment of his films, and the high praise for David Pirie (a film critic turned scriptwriter): "*Rainy Day*

Women is a film . . . highly conscious of its choice of vocabulary, operating within un-fashionable dialects in the face of a dubious art-house accent from draughtsman to ploughman, putting its energy into story-telling and discovering its themes in the process" (Brown, 190).

But I now wonder whether an emphasis on a film culture that, with the advent of television, risks becoming either scholastic or antiquarian, if it insists on filmmakers being cine-literate (knowing the "language of cinema") or cinephile (quoting from John Ford or Jean-Luc Godard), misconstrued the role of a tradition. During the years between 1968 and 1975, when a new generation of British film critics struggled to have the study of film accepted as a valid intellectual endeavor, the dialogue of the deaf between a certain journalistic establishment and the university film theorists narrowed the options of a film culture: on one side, the demand for a "materialist" practice and a countercinema, on the other the condemnation of semiology and psychoanalysis as the "Screenspeak" of "pod-people."

One could also think of another kind of divide — perhaps more appropriate for the age of media globalization: that between the insider's and the outsider's view of Britain, where the outsider could well be from Scotland, Ireland, or Liverpool, and the insider from Hollywood. Historically, the "outsider-as-insider" view of Britain has often proved most memorable, as in Joseph Losey's films, especially in his collaborations with Harold Pinter, which epitomize an image of Britain in the 1960s that still survives, even if it never achieved cult status. To the Losey-Pinter partnership one should add Roman Polanski's *Repulsion* (1965) and *Cul de Sac* (1966), as well as Jerzy Skolimowski's *Deep End* (1970): films where the pastiche element has, over the years, taken on a patina that gives them a truth missing from the films of Lindsay Anderson or John Schlesinger.

The precise relation of Britishness to a (cinema- or television-based) film culture is important, even if one argues that a strong national cinema must feed on its predecessors and thus stand in a vampiric relation to what has gone before. Identity and pleasure in the cinema remain connected to questions of narrative, the art of repetition, and recognition. One strategy of both television and the cinema as socially significant forms of self-representation might well be the energy either medium puts "into story-telling and discovering its themes in the process" (Brown, 190). But film culture partakes also of the pleasure of the quotation and the in-joke, the reworking of known styles, genres, idioms, and themes. Imitations, irony, remake, pastiche, parody are modes of sustaining a sense of cultural identity or a myth of the nation.

National Audiences, or . . .

What of the national audience for either British television or British cinema, insofar as the cinema still has such an audience? Does it care about national identity when it comes to entertainment? For viewers in the north of England, the lifestyles in "Dynasty" or "L.A. Law" are about as real as the lifestyles of the Yuppie stockbrokers living in London's Dockland or the Home Counties. Is the "national cinema" question, then, more than a figment of someone's (the critics') imagination, or a promotion ploy of doubtful use for products not marketed by way of genre or star? The unclassifiability of a production range drawn from television drama, film/TV coproductions, commercial feature films, and former film-school debuts is self-evident. But it is equally self-evident that the mid-1980s "renaissance" was tied up with the showcasing of large numbers of British films at jamborees like the London Film Festival.

Festivals are the Olympics of the show-business economy, even though not all are as market-oriented as the Cannes Festival. What competes at festivals are less individual films than film concepts, film ideas, sales angles, or what Stephen Heath called a film's "narrative image" (Heath, 44). Created by the press backup, by promotional activity that suggests several sources of appeal or cultural access in a film, these images can be generated by sheer numbers (if diversity is tied together with a label) or, more frivolously, by emphasizing a newsworthy item either in a film or surrounding it. What counts at festivals is novelty, discovery, the element of surprise. With the paying public afterward, it is more a matter of what they already know or recognize, the familiar that they discover in the different. A native public, therefore, may be flattered by the attention that others—other critics, other media, other audiences—give to the homegrown product or talent, as was the case with *A Fish Called Wanda* (Charles Crichton, 1988). The most celebrated heroes, therefore, often win their highest accolades abroad.

Critics thought the hype surrounding the British contingent at such festivals was rather over the top: "The current rash of hyperbole about the new British cinema will fade. Of course much of the TV drama 'showcased' at the London Film Festival was merely routine. The pendulum always swings too far at first" (Millar, 121).

Yet bulk remains crucial in launching a national cinema. The New German Cinema emerged internationally at the 1974 Cannes and 1975 New York festivals, mainly from the sheer number of films by three or four directors. These filmmakers' earlier work fed distribution demands, which in the case of Fassbinder amounted to some ten or twelve films. Producers or directors must have sufficient films, for demand once generated must be met quickly. Hence the close interdependence of film and television as delivery systems, neither of the same narrative material nor of a necessarily different experience, but of two distinct cultural discourses continually implying and pointing to each other. In the case of British films in the 1980s, the persistent danger was that if films never circulated outside television, then the associations evoked by the label British Cinema would fade; if the label exists successfully, but the industry cannot provide enough product to fit it, then television will offer its product under the label: both were the case, with diminishing returns for the idea of a national cinema. The objective conditions for the renaissance, therefore, were not so much the existence of Channel Four and its commissioning policy, but the coexistence of Channel Four, the BFI Production Board, the National Film Finance Corporation, and two or three risk-taking producers (David Puttnam, Simon Perry) and production companies (Virgin, Chrysalis, Palace) living "inside the whale" of all the available sources of film financing. Their films — by the very heterogeneity of cultural and economic values that entered into the filmmaking process — were open texts, changelings rather than bastards, traveler's checks rather than forgeries in the currency markets of film culture.

Therefore, as far as a "brand image" is concerned, Britain faced an interesting dilemma. In its efforts to promote a particular national cinema, it stood somewhere between Germany and France. Despite the nouvelle vague, French filmmakers over and over define themselves (positively or negatively) by reference to their own cinematic traditions, their cosmopolitan international film culture, and a heavily theorized cinephilia. Think of Eric Rohmer and Bertrand Tavernier at one end, and of *Jean de Florette* and *Cyrano de Bergerac* on the other. In West Germany, where an idea of a national cinema imposed itself only in the 1970s, diverse directorial talents accumulated enough films to appear before an international art-house audience as a group whose work reflected on the country from which they came. What could Britain offer in the way of either image or group identity to an art cinema audience? In Germany, it was invariably a director-star combination (Fassbinder and Hanna Schygulla; Herzog and Klaus Kinski; Wenders and Bruno Ganz) or "trilogies" that provided genre association; in Britain, films are one-offs, with occasionally an "engine" to pull a few others in its train. Could this add up to a national cinema? On the other hand, British media products, in terms of an industrial infrastructure, are poised not between competing European cinemas, but between commercial Hollywood and commercial television, with the independent sector in both film and television up until the mid-1980s (prior to the quota) much more marginalized than the

French or Italian art cinema. The British film industry rests on a strong technical base and unrivaled craftsmanship in certain specialized areas — heavily used by the Americans as long as sterling was weak against the dollar. Its television industry is highly competitive and sufficiently funded to buy what talent and services it needs from the theater, the film industry, or the literary establishment.

The real crisis for a new British cinema, therefore, came in the distribution and exhibition of material produced for television as well as for the cinemas. Without the tradition of an art cinema, British society only slowly incorporated the institutions (Regional Film Theatres, film magazines) necessary to create a coherent image for different kinds of film at their point of reception and consumption. The two major distribution/exhibition chains always preferred to handle American films, partly because they could acquire, in addition to the film, the advertising, promotion, and marketing directly with the product. Such films prove much easier to handle than something that needs not only a market but an image, as well. By contrast, the biggest French distributor, Gaumont, undertook a vast expansion and diversification program that made it both desirable and necessary for a distributor to invest in the production even of art-house films, something that Rank and EMI have been notoriously reluctant to do and for which the stakes in Britain may indeed be too high.

Gaumont expanded and diversified into new areas of filmmaking only to the degree that it could distribute these films adequately — be it by exporting to Italy, Germany, and the United States, or by splitting their Parisian and provincial theaters into ever more mini-units. It gave the company a higher turnover of films, but also allowed them to keep a "sleeper" in repertory without clogging up the schedules for their blockbusters. Gaumont's extraordinary monopolistic position and strong vertical integration meant that this policy benefited both production and exhibition. In Britain, it seems that the smaller, London-based distributors/exhibitors (Artificial Eye, the Screen group, and the Gate cinemas) tried something very similar: to acquire enough venues to enter the market as a biggish buyer, which in turn gave them the number of films that makes programming policy respond to variable and unpredictable demand.

. . . National Imaginaries

With this in mind, we might return to our topic: national cinema. If we exclude what I earlier called the "social imaginary" of television and concentrate on the "national imaginary," the cinema of the 1980s stands in a highly instructive relation to what precedes it, while it also helps us to identify how the cinema under Thatcher is distinctive. We can read a number of motifs, narratives, and images as a kind of identikit rather than an identity of Britain, and can construct from them mythologies, or mythemes. But does such an emphasis on the recycling and recombining of already existing images not risk collapsing filmmaking entirely with that obedient manipulation of images and references one now identifies as the curse and legacy of the Thatcher image culture? Perhaps. Yet what would it mean to oppose this image culture with a stern recall to realism and a search for that favorite catchword of the New German Cinema, "authentic images"? In Britain's case, this would be a call for images of misery and degradation, of unemployment and urban blight, of pollution and police harrassment, of violence and racism. But is this not a retreat to another kind of conservatism, no less nostalgic than Heritage England or Edwardiana, and no less demagogic than the Enterprise Culture?

British cinema celebrates its renaissances with such regularity because it always functions around another polarization — what one might call an "official" cinema and an "unofficial" cinema, a respectable cinema and a disreputable one. The renaissances always signal a turning of the tables, but only to change places, not the paradigms. Official: Basil Dearden, Noel Coward, David Lean; unofficial: Powell and Pressburger, Gainsborough melodrama. Official: Ealing comedies; unofficial: *Carry On* comedies. Official: *Room at the Top* (1958), *Saturday Night and Sunday Morning* (1960), *This Sporting Life* (1964); unofficial: Hammer horror, *For King and Country* (1964). Official: *Sunday Bloody Sunday* (1971); unofficial: *Secret Ceremony* (1968). One could go on . . . official: *The Ploughman's Lunch* (1983); unofficial: *Brazil* (1984); official: *Chariots of Fire* (1982); unofficial: *Hope and Glory* (1988). Sometimes it appears as if the same films get made every twenty years or so: *Local Hero* (1983) a remake of *Whisky Galore* (1949) and *The Maggie* (1954); *The Ploughman's Lunch* a remake of *Room at the Top* (or, as Charles Barr has pointed out, of *Darling*, 1965); and *Chariots of Fire* a remake of *In Which We Serve* (1942).

This Jekyll-and-Hyde, yin-yang quality of the British cinema, first analyzed by Raymond Durgnat, has in its "realism versus romanticism" version become one of the orthodoxies of academic film studies. Its deeper psychic economy, as it were, rests in the fact that for every mythic or cliché image of Britain, there is a countercliché. Rare are the films that let both myth and countermyth assert themselves, which is why *Brief Encounter* (1945) has such a special place in the canon. One of the main changes in the 1980s is

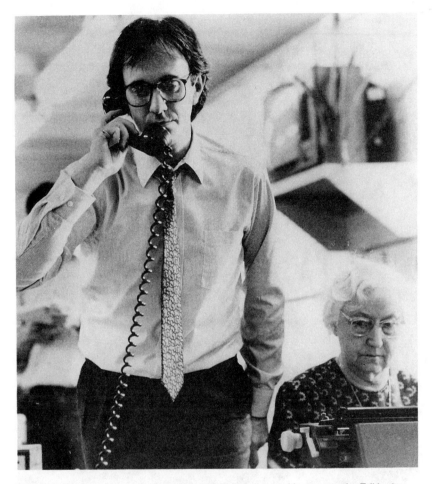

BBC Radio journalist James Penfield (Jonathan Pryce) dictates his story on the Falklands crisis in *The Ploughman's Lunch* (1983), an example of Britain's "official" cinema.

that more films meshed the traditions: under Thatcher, reality itself became fantastic, for some a fairy tale (*A Room with a View*, 1985), for most a nightmare (*Jubilee*, 1976; *The Last of England*, 1988; *Sammy and Rosie Get Laid*, 1988; *No Surrender*, 1986). Others saw the future as high-tech and shabby at the same time: *Brazil*, for instance, a very British film by an American director (Terry Gilliam), not dissimilar from *Blade Runner* (1982), a very American film by a British director (Ridley Scott).

For much of the 1980s, the mythemes remain in place. On one side: home counties, country house, public school, sports, white flannel, rules, and

Roy Baty (Rutger Hauer) saves Deckard (Harrison Ford) in *Blade Runner* (1982), a very American film by British director Ridley Scott.

games; Edwardian England, Decline of the Empire, Privilege, and Treason; male bonding, female hysteria. On the side of the countermyth: Scotland, Liverpool, London; dockland, clubland, disco, football, punk, race riots, National Front; working-class males, violent and articulate; working-class women, sexy and self-confident. No one would mistake this as realistic, yet the films that fit the scheme range from *Letter to Brezhnev* to *The Draughtsman's Contract*, *A Passage to India* to *The Last of England*, *My Beautiful Laundrette* to *Another Country*, *The Long Good Friday* to *Educating Rita*. Most of these images of Britain sell better in Birmingham, Alabama, than in Birmingham, West Midlands, because they encapsulate what "we" try to sell to "them." But on closer inspection, one sees that the films that did well in both places, whether coming from the "official" or the "unofficial" cinema, gave the myths a special edge, mixed the stereotypes in unexpected ways, or enacted the cliché to poignant perfection. Thus, they released a rich cultural sediment of meaning by which members of a national and historical community explain themselves to themselves and express themselves to others. In effect, the density or cross-hatching of references has assumed the place of "realism." Consider, for instance, how little relation to the historical facts the prevalence of stories about public school spies and traitors has. It is not only since the advent of satellites that spies have become irrelevant to information gathering or to national security. Yet because the complex of playing fields—Oxbridge, homosexuality—is able to articulate and negotiate such a number of important oppositions and contradictions (traitors to one's class/traitors to one's sex/traitors to one's country), its reality to Britain is of a different order than merely historical or sociological, and therefore we can expect some version of it even to survive the end of the Cold War.

Materializations of the Image

During the 1980s, British films and television have successfully marketed and packaged the national literary heritage, the war years, the countryside, the upper classes, and elite education. In a sense, they emulated the British record industry, rock musicians, and the rag trade, a lesson the Americans learned quickly after the Second World War, when commerce started following Hollywood rather than the flag. That the communication and media industries participate in the commodity exchange systems of capitalism should not surprise anyone who knows about ownership and control in these industries, and that images, clichés, narratives are now fully caught up in the same game simply takes the process to its logical conclusion. Like the natives in Third World countries who impersonate themselves for the sake of the tourists, Britain appears the victim of its own sophisticated media-making, the materialization of its own imaginary. Feeding from the myth and the countermyth in equal measure, the images give a semblance of verisimilitude to its public life by the sheer diversity of recognizable stereotypes.

Such a circulation of representations is useful politically (as the Thatcher government knew full well) insofar as it fixes a complex and shifting reality (e.g., nationhood and social cohesion at times of crisis and decline) into images commonly accepted as true and meaningful as soon as they crop up everywhere, forcing even the opponent to do battle on the same terrain. Britishness in the cinema may thus be a synthetic myth, but it remains no less powerful for that because it is held in place by binary oppositions and polarities that attract each other. Due to the violence of the social tensions that the uneven distribution of the wealth generated by North Sea oil brought to almost all regions and communities of the British Isles, Britain during the 1980s was probably the most colorful country in Europe. In this respect, the 1980s were a rerun of the Elizabethan or the Victorian age, if only by virtue of the immense contrasts between rich and poor, energy and waste, violence and ostentation. But when history returns, to paraphrase Marx, it usually does so as tragedy and farce. No wonder, perhaps, that Dickens was the author most often adapted on television during the period, or that when Margaret Thatcher finally resigned, the main evening news program was followed by a montage of the day's images to a text made up of quotations from Shakespeare's history plays.

One tends to imagine little effective political opposition to Thatcher, but in the years to come we may recognize the wealth of talent in writing and journalism that etched the decade's image in acid. Much of the talent found its way into television, less into the cinema. But film, after all, was not about documentation, information, investigation, or even satire (all the province of television), but rather about myth and the stereotype, both beyond realism and fantasy and closer to allegory and to games played according to the rules. Yet both the myths and countermyths of the British cinema strongly speak of Britain as a class society, maybe even a caste society. In this respect, at least, less has changed during the Thatcher years than might at first appear. While her social policies broke up one kind of consensus, another was formed, one using the same elements but striking from them a different coinage. Hence the impression that in the New British Cinema the sum of the parts, at least for now, is greater than the whole. The cinema under Thatcher contributed greatly to an unmistakably British image culture, but perhaps not so much to a film culture. Once more, talking about British cinema implies a look at British television, for the national imaginary hides, but also implies the social imaginary. But that is another story.

This essay includes portions of my "Images for England (and Scotland, Ireland, Wales . . .)," published in *Monthly Film Bulletin*, September 1984, in a three-part investigation of the present state of British cinema (the other essays in the series were by Raymond Durgnat and Charles Barr). I wish to thank the British Film Institute for permission to use the material.

Works Cited

Barr, Charles. 1977. *Ealing Studios*. London: Cameron and Tayleur.

Bennett, Alan. 1984. "My Scripts, Where Wheelchairs Make Up the Armoured Division, Are Not Ready-made Movie Material." *Sight and Sound* 53 (2): 121-22.

Brown, John. 1984. "Home Fires Burning." *Sight and Sound* 53 (3): 188-90.

Durgnat, Raymond. 1970. *A Mirror for England*. London: Faber and Faber.

Elsaesser, Thomas. 1972. "Between Style and Ideology." *Monogram* 3: 2-10.

Hassan, Mamoun. 1984. "Journalism and Literature Use Words. . . . " *Sight and Sound* 53 (2) 116.

Heath, Stephen. 1981. "Narrative Space." In *Questions of Cinema*, 19-75. London: Macmillan.

Hinxman, Margaret. 1982. *Daily Mail*, January 31.

Isaacs, Jeremy. 1984. "If We Can Sustain the Impetus. . . . *Sight and Sound* 53 (2): 118.

Millar, Gavin. 1984. "I for One Am Not Going to Wait Around. . . . " *Sight and Sound* 53 (2): 120-21.

Peachment, Chris. 1984. "London/Munich Loose Connections." *Sight and Sound* 53 (2): 151-52.

Robinson, David. 1981. "Berlin Festival Report." *Times*, Feb. 27.

Stone, Norman. 1988. "Sick Scenes from English Life." *Sunday Times*, Jan. 10.

Five

History with Holes: Channel Four Television Films of the 1980s

Paul Giles

This essay examines how Channel Four contributed to British filmmaking in the 1980s and how involvement with television affected the aesthetic shape of many British films during this era. The writer and director Mike Leigh, interviewed in *American Film* (1989), claimed that during the 1970s and 1980s in Britain "all serious filmmaking was done for television" (Fitch, 12). Leigh exaggerated here, of course; still, media critics in the United States usually fail to appreciate how extensively British cinema remains institutionally and artistically bound with the London stage and television companies. In America, the typical television movie appears as an inexpensive B-movie program negotiating some current social problem and containing the most conventional narrative forms of romance and melodrama.[1] British television broadcasts this kind of material, too, but during the 1980s the medium also offered space to many of the country's best writers and directors, whose films for the small screen surpassed most "British cinema" during this period.

Commentators too often frame the study of television with an apocalyptic, all-encompassing rhetoric, from Raymond Williams's notions of continuous "flow" in the early 1960s, through Marshall McLuhan's "global village" later that decade, to Jean Baudrillard's postmodernist reduction of television to a flattened medium "delivering its images indifferently, indifferent to its own messages" (Baudrillard, 50). But as John Caughie argues, these theories of television "universalize a local, national experience—the U.S. experience—as the essence of television" and ignore how this experience is constituted differently in other countries (Caughie 1990, 48). British television, for example, exists within a tradition of state-approved public service.

Since its establishment by Royal Charter in 1922, BBC Television, which has been on the air since 1936, has carried no advertising and remains financed by the government's annual license fee charged to all owners of television sets. The second BBC channel, BBC2, was set up in 1964 to complement the program schedules of its senior partner. Before the advent of Channel Four, the only other option available for British viewers was their local station of Independent Television, a network that began broadcasting in 1955, financed principally by advertising. Independent Television consists of fifteen regionally based companies presided over by the Independent Broadcasting Authority (IBA), recently renamed the Independent Television Commission (ITC). We must recognize, therefore, that market forces have never competed freely within British television. In 1984, the market-oriented Thatcher government passed its Cable and Broadcasting Act, which allowed a more general expansion of cable and satellite television, but progress during the 1980s was slow. By the spring of 1990, only about 93,000 homes subscribed to cable services. Satellite television started up later, in February 1989, though by spring 1990 it reached about one million homes.[2]

Two obvious difficulties characterize this British model of broadcasting: first, a relative lack of choice for the consumer; second, the perennial threat of government interference. The BBC jealously guards its editorial independence, though the 1980s demonstrated that such independence is a precarious business. The Conservative government vituperatively criticized the BBC for its insufficiently "patriotic" reporting of the Falklands war and the U.S. bombing of Libya; it openly exercised political influence in the appointment of BBC governors and administrators; it pressured all the television companies to censor a number of supposedly "obscene" broadcasts. Indeed, in 1988 the government established a "Broadcasting Standards Authority" to develop a stringent code on representing sex and violence. Yet, as Colin MacCabe shrewdly remarked, the scrutiny that any given medium receives from the censors is a sure index of its cultural importance at a particular moment in history. To say British television in the 1980s was subjected to political censorship also testifies to the psychological and aesthetic power of the medium, its ability to help shape the way people think. In this sense, the circumscribed nature of consumer choice offered potential advantages for ambitious writers who understood television as a public arena for fiercely contesting meaning and ideology.

Thus British television offered considerable inducements to filmmakers: substantial financial rewards, a highly visible medium, a captive audience. The viewing figures, as David Hare said, are "crazy." Anywhere from three million to twelve million people watch a single work on a single evening

(Hare, 49). A conservative figure of eight million roughly equates to filling an average-sized theater in London every night for six years. Americans accustomed to flicking past fifty television channels may find it difficult to appreciate the power each individual broadcasting station wields when only four of them exist, as in Britain during most of the 1980s. In this sense, the situation seems more like American television in the network-dominated 1950s than in the cable market of the 1980s. Accordingly, British television filmmakers felt, as Alan Bennett put it, that they were "addressing the nation" (Bennett et al., 121). Stephen Frears similarly remarked that he made *My Beautiful Laundrette* (1985) for Channel Four because he wanted a large number of people to see and talk about the film (Howkins, 239). The statistics reinforce this shift toward television as the focal point of social narratives and popular memory. For instance, 74 percent of the British population never visit a cinema (Lane, 36), but every British adult in 1988 watched on average over twenty-five hours of television each week (Harvey, 61). As a consequence of these structures of public broadcasting, British television has traditionally generated what John Caughie calls "a collectively shared experience" (Caughie 1986, 168), a discourse predicated upon the compulsive pleasures of familiarity and communal recognition. The most successful British television films internalize these communal aspects of television, allowing audience members to witness these easily identifiable aspects of popular memory; yet, such films also interrogate those comfortable assumptions, inducing the audience to reconceive its perspectives upon past and present in new and unsettling ways.

The whole question of what constitutes "successful" television, as Charlotte Brunsdon notes, became an unfashionable academic issue during Thatcher's reign (Brunsdon, 59), as television studies focused more upon the sociological conditions of transmission than upon the semiotics of the televisual text. Various studies of audience responses to standard light entertainment made up the most influential works in this area, with a few notable exceptions: John Caughie sought to define "the specific ways in which representations are produced on television and the ways in which they circulate" (Caughie 1985, 98), while Brunsdon recently expressed renewed interest in the development of "a televisual aesthetic" (Brunsdon, 69) and stressed the "importance of retaining the notion of text as an analytic category" (63). Promoting a critical discourse about television, however, should not involve simply erecting "taste" or "discrimination" or "quality" as fetishes in themselves. Much of what passes for "quality television," especially old-style BBC serializations of "classic" novels, exhibits mediocre aesthetic qualities. Such a critical discourse depends rather upon aesthetic quality, the recognition that certain texts bear a density and a complexity that actively challenge the viewer to reflect upon them. Television art, like all good art, ranges beyond mere fine "taste"; it possesses the power to startle, to challenge, to make its audience think. The best television fiction does just this. Yet, the medium's artistic achievements remain mostly invisible because we lack an appropriate critical language to describe them.

Gavin Millar articulates one useful strategy in response to this critical lacuna, totally eliding the television origins of such works: he simply claims these television films as "part of the British cinema" (Bennett et al., 120). Quite apart from the different modes of production, though, exhibition and distribution restrictions ensure that few of these works circulate widely among an international film audience. How many American reviews of British cinema in the 1980s include the BBC film *An Englishman Abroad* (1983), written by Alan Bennett and directed by John Schlesinger, or *Saigon: Year of the Cat* (1983), directed by Stephen Frears from David Hare's script? These remain two of the finest British films of the decade, made by two internationally renowned film directors. Extraordinarily, they ran against each other on different channels during the same evening, and their subsequent unavailability testifies to the chronic accessibility problems that beset the study of television fiction. After the critical success of *An Englishman Abroad*—a poignant reconstruction of the exile suffered by Guy Burgess (Alan Bates) after his exposure as a Soviet spy—screenwriter Alan Bennett ruminated on how some of his earlier works directed by Stephen Frears for London Weekend Television might have "fared almost as well" had they enjoyed exposure to "a better class of critic" at the London Film Festival before their fleeting television incarnation, as was the case with *An Englishman Abroad*. Now, complained Bennett, these old films "languish in the archives of LWT with no prospect of ever being seen again" (Bennett et al., 122).

Channel Four, which began broadcasting on November 2, 1984, institutionalized this close relationship between television and film production, both in the "Film on Four" series and, later on, through the channel's financial investment in feature films under the "Film Four International" umbrella. However, Channel Four's modes of production differed importantly from earlier television practices. Whereas the BBC and Independent Television previously produced their own dramatic material and purchased viewing rights to films after their theatrical release, Channel Four's charter required the broadcasting of programs made by independent suppliers. Hence Channel Four defined itself more as a "publishing house," a policy stemming from the Annan Committee's report in the late 1970s, which recommended some decentralization within broadcasting institutions. John Ellis argues that this policy of broadening the production base and increasing access to the screen for underrepresented minority interests was one of the last political by-products of the pre-Thatcher era. Although Channel Four opened three and a half years after Thatcher assumed power, says Ellis, its essential organizing principles were laid down earlier, so that the station remains "inflected by Tory ideology but not born of it" (Ellis 1986, 11). Thus the government established Channel Four as a nonprofit body, a subsidiary of the Independent Broadcasting Authority. Funded indirectly through advertising, the new channel was to arrange its program schedules to complement existing Independent Television services.

Had Channel Four started a couple of years later, its tone would probably have been very different. The Conservative government's parliamentary bill *Broadcasting in the '90s: Competition, Choice and Quality*, published in November 1988, proposed that by the early 1990s Channel Four's advertising air time should be sold on a competitive basis separately from the Independent Television authorities, a move that would inevitably force the station to attune itself more toward demands of the mass market in its quest for a larger overall share of the audience. Significantly, though, this government white paper described Channel Four's programming record as "a striking success" and recommended that by 1992 the BBC and Independent Television should follow the fourth channel's example by obtaining 25 percent of their original programs from independent producers. This report marked a distinct change from the early 1980s, when Conservative politicians accused the home secretary of "letting the loonies on the air." Then, Cabinet Minister Norman Tebbitt informed Jeremy Isaacs, first controller of Channel Four, that "the different interests you are supposed to cater for" were not those of "homosexuals and such," but rather "Golf and sailing and fishing" (Isaacs 1989, 65-67). In its early days, when it enjoyed a reputation for being both highbrow and liberal, Channel Four frequently became the target of the populist right-wing press and was often involved in the kind of censorship controversies that beset all of British television at this time. The arguments in the mid-1980s over screenings of Derek Jarman's films *Sebastiane* (1976), *Jubilee* (1978), and *Caravaggio* (1986) remain the most obvious examples of this inquisitorial climate that hovered over Channel Four.

Nevertheless, between 1981 and 1990 Channel Four partially funded the production of some 170 films by independent companies, and it quickly became a major player in the impecunious arena of the British film industry. By Hollywood standards, of course, the resources available to Channel Four were miserly: David Rose, the first commissioning editor for fiction, made twenty films in his first year for a total of $9.6 million, the average budget of one Hollywood feature (Park, 8). Usually production companies released these films first in the theaters, thereby gaining enough critical notice and reputation to make their subsequent appearance on television something of a special event. A few films arrived in theaters after their television appearance, usually with unhappy financial results. Toward the middle of the decade, after several failures on the commercial cinema circuit, Channel Four supported fewer films entirely from its own finances, instead collaborating on the funding with organizations such as the Goldcrest Company, the National Film Finance Corporation, and others. Still, the general prominence of Channel Four cannot be denied: ten out of the twenty-eight British features made in 1984 had Channel Four investment (Jack C. Ellis, 376), and the company gradually developed a strong presence at film festivals. At Cannes in 1987, for example, David Rose accepted the Rossellini Award for the contributions made by Channel Four to filmmaking, while in the same year the British journal *Sight and Sound* congratulated Channel Four for providing "film-makers with a continuity of financial support not seen since the heyday of Michael Balcon's Ealing Studios" back in the 1940s (Kent, 260). By the end of the 1980s, other British television companies started to emulate their example, with both Granada and the BBC coproducing more and more feature films.

As with the Ealing cinema, we can identify a particular kind of aesthetic style as characteristic of the Channel Four movie. John Ellis describes Ealing comedies as negotiating a series of "aspirations and utopian desires," wherein the petty bourgeoisie express their resentment against an increasingly bureaucratized postwar world (Ellis 1975, 115). Channel Four films work with something similar, insofar as they often juxtapose what is foreign, strange, or sinister with the safe haven of the drably domestic. Although "Film on Four" offerings addressed many potentially disturbing themes, they usually framed and contained them by structures of reassuring normalcy. For instance, in *Another Time, Another Place* (1983), director Michael Radford visually represents the Italian prisoners of war billeted upon an isolated farm in Scotland from the crofters' point of view, so that the Italians come to seem devils dressed in black, satanic figures who carry pitchforks over their heads as if wearing diabolic horns. The sexual knowingness of these Italians tantalizes Jane (Phyllis Logan), her marital misery reinforced by a sense of geographical isolation. Jane's laconic husband, Finlay (Tom Watson), responds less sympathetically to the glamour of foreignness: he will, he says, be "thankful to be rid of them lot" now that the war is ending. Phyllis, left to gaze longingly out of the window, tells herself, "There's other days, and other places." Yet, as the heavy weight of familiarity associated with the BBC radio programs that waft over this bleak Scottish landscape implies, for

The allure of the foreign: Jane (Phyllis Logan) dances with Luigi (Giovanni Mauriello) in *Another Time, Another Place* (1983).

Phyllis, other times and places will exist only in her fantasies. Recognition of these old BBC favorites binds the viewer into complicity with that sense of repressive familiarity that the film disseminates, and hence engenders an air of fatalism. Such styles of fatalism or inertia are characteristic of many different types of television production. As theorists of television situation comedy show how its narratives traditionally rotate upon an axis of transgression and restitution, with "order" reestablished after the mild allure of the forbidden, so Channel Four films in the 1980s often follow a similarly conservative pattern, albeit in a more sophisticated way.[3]

The form of this threat varies, of course: homosexuality in *Another Country* (1984), *Maurice* (1987), *Prick Up Your Ears* (1987); West Indians and the drug culture in *Playing Away* (1986); Jewishness in *Sacred Hearts* (1984); Americans in *Stormy Monday* (1987) and in *The Dressmaker* (1988); the Soviet Union in *A Letter to Brezhnev* (1985). The latter movie features a Liverpudlian girl (Alexandra Pigg) who defies her family and British consular advice by flying to Russia to pursue a Soviet sailor she met during a night on the town. Scripted by Frank Clarke and directed by Chris Bernard, this film features a creative team that also worked on the Channel Four soap opera "Brookside," again set in Liverpool. This authorial link with Brookside helps explain the film's sensitivity to Elaine's domestic plight, shut up in her parents' deadly suburban house where the continuous noise of the television only partially drowns out the perpetual family quarrels. To put it another way, *A Letter to Brezhnev* deals more convincingly with containment than with escape. As Martin Auty has written, the public mind associates television with "naturalism" and cinema with "the realm of fantasy" (Auty, 63), and, in the terms of this hypothesis, *A Letter to Brezhnev* fits more comfortably with its televisual than with its cinematic characteristics.

It would not, then, be difficult to argue that Channel Four films implicitly reinforce dominant conservative national ideologies, however much they explicitly seem to challenge such concepts. Jeremy Isaacs's contention that these films should reflect "our preoccupations here in Britain" rather than be geared for "a bland international market" (Bennett et al., 118) uneasily overlaps those "national concerns" articulated by William Whitelaw, patriarchal home secretary at the time of Channel Four's inception. Whitelaw, a loyal member of Thatcher's government for many years, wanted a channel that would provide space for "minority interests," a television station "somewhat different, but not too different" (Docherty and Morrison, 11). Clearly Whitelaw's views of "national concerns" were not synonymous with the "preoccupations" of Isaacs. The former, concerned frankly with repressive tolerance, remarked that "if they don't get some outlet for their activities, you are going to run yourself into more trouble" (Docherty and Morrison, 11). Isaacs, on the other hand, had no obvious vested interest in television as a means of social control. But for many radical filmmakers, these positions stood too close to each other for artistic comfort. Directors such as Chris Petit, Derek Jarman, Alan Parker, and Lindsay Anderson, all outspoken in denouncing the general timidity of British cinema, found such pusillanimity reinforced by the unwelcome restrictions imposed by television production codes. Jarman openly associated Channel Four's small-screen cinema with the Thatcherite "little England" of the 1980s, complaining that the "TV men" only wanted films to "complement the ads" (Jarman, 86) and accusing fellow directors such as Frears and Peter Greenaway of conformity to the demands of the television medium. Petit similarly scorned British cinema as being merely "television hardback" (Walters, 62), while Alan Parker described Channel Four as a cage within which the trapped filmmaker beats frantically against the bars (Houston, 153). More thoughtfully, Anderson addressed what he saw as the restrictions of the Channel Four medium in a 1989 interview: "I think the real difference is the kind of subject liable to be financed by Channel Four, which leads to some of the new British films being a bit lacking in the ambition one associates with a cinema film. There is a certain restriction of imagination or idea, rather than the feeling that if you make a film financed by television you have to restrict it in terms of technique or style" (Pratley, 95).

The theater of embarrassment: Shirley (Ruth Sheen), Cyril (Philip Davis), and Cyril's mother (Edna Dore) look over the rooftops of London in *High Hopes* (1988).

What I want to argue, however, is that the whole issue of television aesthetics should be seen as more complex than Anderson suggests here. Despite those confining parameters and the structural containment observed in many Channel Four movies, the best of these make skillful and sometimes experimental use of their small-screen medium, creatively exploring the whole idea of limits. Here aesthetic complexity becomes a crucial critical factor: while most television films simply reflect the dominant ideology, the most illuminating reflect back actively upon it. In Mike Leigh's *High Hopes*, to take one example, the thematic as well as formal emphasis rests on physical claustrophobia and psychological immobility. The central characters find themselves locked into a round of urban poverty and obligations to cantankerous relatives, the grotesque scenario peppered with frequent cups of tea and trips to the lavatory. This theater of embarrassment challenges its onlookers by bathetically subverting the expectations of cinematic narrative and engendering a sense of queasy familiarity, a recognition of the film's disconcerting proximity to the trials of daily living. This is not, said Leigh, a form of naturalism, but rather "heightened realism" (Fitch, 12): Leigh draws the viewer into uncomfortable empathy with his landscapes, exploiting the medium of television as a repository of the banal and the everyday to valorize that empathy. Despite its abjuring of the transparent window of naturalism, *High Hopes*, as Gilbert Adair says, produces "an *effet du réel*" (Adair, 65), an illusion of verisimilitude inextricably interwoven with the structures of television and predicated upon a mimetic relay of ordinary domestic life. Leigh made most of his films in the 1970s and 1980s exclusively for television, and, though *High Hopes* played in cinema theaters, it remains a film crucially informed by a televisual perspective.

From this point of view, we can recognize the automatic preference for cinema over television as little more than nostalgia for a more traditionalist aesthetic ideology. In 1984 Mamoun Hassan, then managing director of the National Film Finance Corporation, inveighed against what he took to be Channel Four's "hybrid" form of cinema by claiming television as more akin to "journalism," and cinema to "literature": "Television films and programmes have to be topical; cinema films have to be more universal than timely. . . . Television is at its best dealing with concepts, explaining and describing (it is no accident that the drama documentary is the preferred form of television drama); cinema is at its best when it concerns itself with the ineffable, with that which cannot be expressed" (Bennett et al., 116). One hears this kind of reactive idealism—"universal," "the ineffable"— repeatedly in critiques of Channel Four films; but, as Fredric Jameson remarks, such fetishizing of cinema over television is reminiscent of quests for that original "aura" of a unique work of art that Walter Benjamin famously claimed had been undone by the twentieth-century age of mechanical reproduction (Jameson, 217).

A similar blind assumption of "cinematic" principles led Mike Poole to criticize *High Hopes* on the grounds that "what is always absent . . . is any capacity for change—in Leigh's world people are denied any kind of development" (Poole, 29). The model Poole implicitly invokes is the "aura" of cinematic narrative style grounded upon enigma, resolution, fluidity, and change. The cinema, paradigmatically a medium of the gaze, forces an audience to identify intensely with the action and to be transported by it. Television, by contrast, establishes itself upon the casual glance, upon interaction with its viewers, upon recognition rather than identification.[4] As Herbert Zettl says, "We look *at* the movie screen, but *into* the event on television" (Zettl, 5). Such a distinction risks relapsing into overly essentialist divisions between the two media, when, of course, the thrust of this essay suggests points of intersection between them. The point remains, however, that the ideological lens of an earlier art form has too often misrepresented Channel Four's films during this period. Pauline Kael, for example, complained that *High Hopes* "isn't really conceived as a narrative of film. It's conceived as a group of skits that the director will extend and fuse" (Kael, 96-97). Yet such rejection of linear sequence characterizes a medium that prioritizes montage over hermeneutic resolution. Television, says Sandy Flitterman-Lewis, "provides a fragmentary and discrete series of microstagings" (Flitterman-Lewis, 193); by contrast, classical cinema foregrounds processes of sequential development, what Stephen Heath calls "narrativization" (Heath, 43).

We can see obvious examples of this different emphasis in the most widely watched television serials. The "plots" of "EastEnders" or "L.A. Law" exist as open-ended and amorphous; the narrative lines flow and converge, sometimes turning repetitively back upon themselves, but rarely reaching the cathartic climax we expect in a cinema production. The pattern in television serials reflects that in *High Hopes*, where any clear-cut resolution to the dramatic situation would seem artificial. Camille Paglia observes that television is "a genre of reruns, a formulaic return to what we already know" (Paglia, 51); I would suggest that the best television films harness this expectation of familiarity to comment upon the repetitive or compulsive aspects of national life. In many of these films, we find that the mise-en-scènes possess a statuesque quality reinforced by the relative immobility of the camera. Shots of action across the screen remain far less common than in the old-style movies, and this restrictive idiom represents the less fluid, more humdrum environment that television so well epitomizes. Television's reliance on dialogue rather than exotic or spectacular visual effects also contributes to this mood of confinement. In the case of *The Dressmaker*, a 1988 film set in wartime Liverpool, such confinement connotes a gothicized repression, a deathly refusal by Aunt Nellie (Joan Plowright) to face her niece's emerging sexuality or the changing social world outside. Of course, such formal processes do not, in themselves, ensure the excellence of television films. While the most challenging texts interrogate their audience's expectations of familiarity and force them to reconsider what such familiarity means, other films tend merely toward banality, a soap-opera-like reworking of the already too well known. Claiming that television films by definition surpass cinema films would be as falsely absurd as the opposite assertion. Yet we should understand that the aesthetic principles of television and film are not directly interchangeable, any more than those of painting and photography may be substituted.

The conjunction of two distinct modes of production fosters this illusion of realism in television films. On the one hand, television gives the spectator an impression that what he or she is watching happens "live": this, says Jane Feuer, binds the viewer into an imaginary presence, "a sense of immediacy and wholeness" (Feuer, 16). On the other hand, film engenders an impression of historicity: the idea that these events once took place in the material world. David Hare writes about his great preference for film over videotaped television productions precisely because video lacks that "visual finesse" and "stylistic density or texture" (Hare, 48) that enable film to imply a complex historical world, the very stuff of Hare's fiction. Margaret Morse theorizes this difference in terms of film's assimilation of the Renaissance rationalization of perspective, designed to represent the truth of an object in space, rather than a television studio's two-dimensional surfaces, which eliminate all such spatial depth (Morse, 6). Consequently, television drama shot in a studio on videotape has a more atemporal feel, as though everything takes place in a vacuum. Back in 1977, when he was producing *Licking Hitler* for television, Hare spurned the use of video and declared himself willing to wait a whole year until one of the film slots became available at BBC Birmingham. Hare was supported on this occasion by his producer, David Rose, then head of drama at BBC Birmingham, later to become commissioning editor for fiction at Channel Four; Hare remarked gratefully that Rose's "allegiance to the film system is absolute" (Hare, 47). Crucially, this televisual ontology of the live event, when crossed with the historicity of film, produces an illusion of the past unfolding as if in the present, as if happening "live." A great many of the Channel Four films made in the 1980s portray the past, not so much in a simple "nostalgia-deco" way (Jameson, 225) but rather in a manner that maintains a complex, bifurcated perspective shifting between past and present. These films foreground the difficulties of a contemporary representation and reclamation of the past, and highlight the elaborate apparatus locking Britain into its historical destiny. But their force also derives from how they translate history into a feigned simultaneity with the here and now, drawing upon television's fictive authorization of its discourse as a current event.

The frequent announcement after the opening title sequences of "another time, another place" can be seen as one of the clearest distinguishing characteristics of these Channel Four movies: "Spring 1954, London" in *Dance With a Stranger* (1984); "Michaelmas Term 1909, Cambridge" in *Maurice*; "The North of Scotland, Fall 1944" in *Another Time, Another Place*. Other films immediately seek to establish a specific historical time and place by easily identifiable signs: a bus headed for the Welsh town of Pwllheli together with Helen Shapiro singing "Walking Back to Happiness" in *Experience Preferred but Not Essential* (1982); newsreels of the 1948 England-Australia cricket internationals in *P'Tang Yang Kipperbang* (1982); icons from the Festival of Britain and Queen Elizabeth II's coronation in *Prick Up Your Ears*;

BBC shipping forecasts and the "Billy Cotton Band Show" on the radio in *Distant Voices, Still Lives* (1988). Such icons spark off communal memories to establish a bond of identity between the text and its viewers. Yet the best of these films engage in a complex dialectic of familiarity and defamiliarization, a dialectic probing and problematizing the hallucinatory images of the past evoked. Hare's 1985 film *Wetherby*, for instance, juxtaposes two different time periods, the 1950s and the 1980s, and elucidates seemingly inexplicable events of the present in terms of that deterministic historical continuity established by the film's images of the repressive 1950s, when ubiquitous family tea parties mask gaping sexual insecurity. The opening sequence of this film — mostly financed by Channel Four — features a discussion about Richard Nixon: "Do you remember?" "It wasn't so long ago." "Only ten years." "It's funny how people forget." This conversation anticipates the general tone of Hare's film, concerning the burdens of time, the vagaries of memory, and the perplexities of decoding and reordering the past. John Caughie suggests that the cinema elicits audience identification with its protagonists by the classic point-of-view shot, but that television fiction relies more upon the reaction shot, the audience witnessing knowledge dispersed to a wider group of characters (Caughie 1990, 54). This style of reaction shot permeates *Wetherby* and Hare's other television fiction, his emphasis falling upon groups of people responding to forces of history and events not of their own making.

Dramas set in the past have represented part of television's staple diet for many years, as countless BBC adaptations of Victorian novels readily testify. More specifically, D. L. LeMahieu writes about how the Edwardians seem like "imagined contemporaries" of late-twentieth-century Britains: LeMahieu argues that the popularity of films such as *A Room with a View* (1985) — which had Channel Four involvement — and television serials like *Upstairs, Downstairs* and *Testament of Youth* exemplify how British conservatism sought to annex this supposedly golden era as an arcadian valorization of its own traditionalist time. This wish fulfillment pure and simple, along with a similar kind of synthesized nostalgia, permeates several of the Channel Four films, particularly in the "First Love" series that David Puttnam's Enigma company produced for television: Philip Saville's *Those Glory, Glory Days* (1983), about a young girl's fanatical support for a London soccer team in the early 1960s, and Desmond Davis's version of Edna O'Brien's novel *The Country Girls* in the same year. These examples demonstrate excessively domesticated television films, the kind of production Lindsay Anderson and Derek Jarman railed against.

Magic realism: Joely Richardson as the young Jean Travers, with Robert Hines as Jim, her 1950s lover, in *Wetherby* (1985).

Yet in the Channel Four film *Wish You Were Here* (1987), written and directed by David Leland, different perspectives begin to emerge. Though this story concerns a rebellious girl growing up in East Anglia during the 1950s, the iconography of nostalgia remains rigorously framed by narrative structures weaving in and out of time. Leland shifts from the end of the war in 1945 to the picture palace movies of the 1950s to account for the claustrophobic climate of postwar Britain. The film self-consciously reconstitutes past time: the inhabitants of this seaside town loom out from the screen in statuesque fashion, as though caught in a series of still photographs; a plethora of shots heightens the style of projection and displacement that refracts objects through doorways and windows, as if to signify how this film is peering back on the 1950s from the distant vantage point of the 1980s. Moreover, Leland replicates the ways in which Lynda (Emily Lloyd) remains inextricably bound up with her dreary heritage by allowing the film's audience to empathize with the cultural icons represented here. The fish-and-chips stands, the Gracie Fields photographs, the sentimental war movies—all of these serve to lock the viewers, like Lynda herself, within the contours of collectively shared experience and popular memory. In this sense, Leland's film—whose very title implies nostalgia—crystallizes that urge toward identification and recognition that, as John Caughie suggests, the discourse of television customarily trades upon, promoting a sense of transference that allows the audience to witness these fictional scenes as if they were real. *Wish You Were Here* amalgamates its aesthetic self-consciousness with these more choric aspects of television, harnessing the medium's ability to involve its mass audience in a series of binding recognitions, yet also keeping the audience slightly off balance so that these recognitions are not transmitted merely in an unproblematic manner.

We can understand this dialectic of familiarity and defamiliarization in television fiction's reconstitution of the past as a mode not of realism but of magic realism. Refusing the glossy fetishes of simplified nostalgia, magic realism introduces "history with holes, perforated history" (Jameson, 130): it insists on the structural disjunction between past and present that exists simultaneously with any attempt to reconstitute the lost objects of other eras. Many of the most effective Channel Four films of the 1980s did not simply fictionalize history; they also implicitly commented on how history itself becomes fictionalized. Thus magic realism's disjunction between event and memory, between the object and its name, expanded into a broader investigation of how national mythologies are created, how history is reinvented and rewritten, sometimes unscrupulously. Richard Eyre's Channel Four film *The Ploughman's Lunch* (1983) remains the most obvious example of this, with its suggestion that the Suez crisis and the Falklands war were both repackaged for the history books like commodities in the advertising market. The film's theme of manufactured appearances is underscored by its scenes shot at the Conservative party conference in Brighton, an event notoriously staged with great care for the national television cameras. As if to reemphasize the interdependence of film and television in this production, Eyre's team received permission to shoot footage at this conference only through Channel Four's contacts with Independent Television News (Forbes, 235).

The distorting mirrors of the television medium again function self-reflexively in the Channel Four serial *A Very British Coup* (1988), which features a beleaguered Labour party prime minister (Ray McAnally) eventually going on television to complain about the media conspiracies undermining his administration. A more international reworking of this theme, the deflection of history into Machiavellian fictions, can be found in Tom Stoppard's treatment of the Polish Solidarity crisis, *Squaring the Circle* (directed by Mike Hodges), screened by the "Film on Four" series in May 1984. Described by Stoppard as "an imaginative history," this film was shot entirely in the studio with an assortment of gimmicky, alienating devices to reinforce the narrator's assertion: "Everything that follows is true, except the words and the pictures" (Woolley, 33). The film depicts Lech Walesa (Bernard Hill) playing elaborate mind games with the old Russian bureaucrats as he tries to establish freedom in Eastern Europe. As with *The Ploughman's Lunch*, Stoppard's work represents politics as a series of elaborate intrigues, a deadly playing field where the disjunction between the rhetoric of the image and the more intangible processes of history is always teasingly apparent.[5]

Such displacement of history into fiction takes on a kind of ontological status in television films of the 1980s. Television films train their glance back on television itself, exploring the contradictions inherent in this medium's own recycled vision of the world. In this way, the fictional dialectic of familiarity and defamiliarization exposes those fissures and ambiguities latent within the nation's domesticated understanding of history. *A Letter to Brezhnev* undermines the stereotypes of "evil" Russians regurgitated by the news media back in the pre-*glasnost* days; *Prick Up Your Ears* provides a more hard-edged, sexualized angle on the cutesy commodification of Brian Epstein and the Beatles in the 1960s; *Saigon: Year of the Cat* painfully undercuts official American rhetoric about the Vietnam War by portraying the evacuation from this lost city as undignified and frightening. A memorable moment occurs in *Saigon* when the American ambassador (E. G. Marshall), who sets himself up to launch into a grand speech about his country's contribution to the Vietnam cause, suddenly finds himself brusquely hustled away by his troops be-

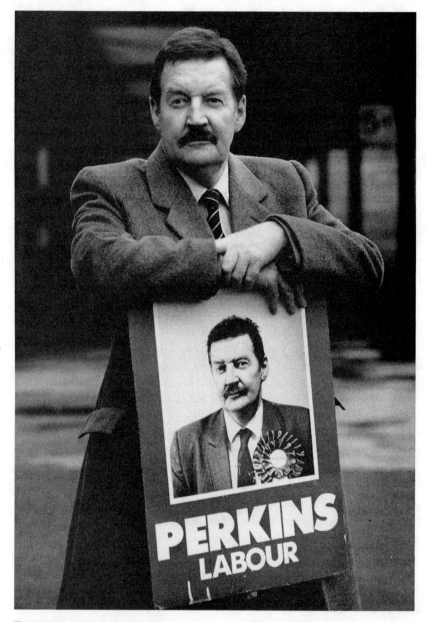

The distorting mirrors of the media: the prime minister (Ray McAnnally) with his
simulacrum in *A Very British Coup* (1988).

Imaginative history: Leonid Brezhnev (Frank Middlemass) conspiring with First Secretary Gierek (John Woodvine), in *Squaring the Circle* (1984).

cause there simply is not time. This bifurcated perspective, where rhetoric and image fail to confirm the validity of each other, also appears in several of the most effective BBC serials of the 1980s: in Alan Bleasdale's *The Monocled Mutineer* (1986), which plays off the military and political machine of the First World War against a startling sense of the ragged resistance to that organization among ordinary soldiers; in Troy Kennedy Martin's *Edge of Darkness* (1985), which concerns itself with the ruthless cover-ups perpetrated by British intelligence in order to protect the state's illegal experiments with nuclear energy.

All of these texts, especially the BBC serials, attracted predictable political controversies; yet, in this decade television broadcasts found themselves becoming increasingly politicized, whether they actively sought such a status or not. A widespread anxiety appeared about the Thatcher government aggressively restricting freedom of information, with television—the prime conduit of this information society—becoming a central target for censorship.[6] Richard Collins observes that the government at this time "made unprecedently explicit use of its powers . . . to prohibit transmission of particular messages" (Collins, 6), most notably in banning statements by speakers on behalf of Sinn Fein and the Ulster Defence Association, two lawful political organizations. The heavy-handed nature of this legislation contributed to a wide-ranging feeling of unease in liberal circles. As Harold Pinter, hardly an

extremist, put it: "When the Conservatives came to power, one of their platforms was that they wanted to save the country from state control. . . .
What has actually taken place is that no state power has ever been stronger
in this country" (Ford, 6).

For "stronger," we might perhaps substitute the phrase "more apparent."
Sally Hibbin, producer of *A Very British Coup*, points out that the whole idea
and apparatus of the state became more visible when the postwar political
consensus in Britain fell apart, leading to far sharper disagreements about
what should constitute national security interests. Consequently, the
Thatcher government provided a milieu where television films like *A Very
British Coup* and *Edge of Darkness* could no longer be dismissed as "just a
paranoid fantasy, left-wing conspiracy theory" (Petley, 96).[7] As Malcolm
Bradbury recognized, many British fictions of this time "are filled with
strange conspiracies that frequently became curiously true" (Bradbury, 8).
Hence television, necessarily implicated within the apparatus of this information society, lost any vestige of political innocence. The television screen
no longer was a mere window on the world, what John Ellis called "a safe
means of scanning the world outside" (Ellis 1982, 170); by the 1980s, this
screen appeared more sinisterly as a medium that was, in a metaphorical
sense, watching the viewer, helping to construct his or her psychological attitudes by its carefully regulated flow of information. This phenomenon was
not confined exclusively to Britain, of course, as the ingenious screen performances of Ronald Reagan demonstrate, but it was exacerbated in Britain
because of the nation's status as a small, centralized country with relatively
few channels of information. In this sense, the Channel Four work of Peter
Greenaway—discussed in detail elsewhere in this book—could be seen as a
metatext for British television films of the 1980s. Greenaway's emphasis in
The Draughtsman's Contract (1982) and elsewhere on both obfuscation and
decoding—the construction and unraveling of a pictorial puzzle—might be
understood as a metaphor for the Thatcherite televisual medium where all
the assumptions of "naturalism" needed to be problematized and all the su-
tures of conventional representation probed.[8]

In the 1980s, Thatcher's own public image was a larger-than-life figure.
She became almost a caricature of herself, like "a duchess in a farce or a
pantomime dame," as Angela Carter described her (Carter, 8). Consequently, analyzing her political power in similarly simplistic or iconic terms,
rather than seeking to address its larger cultural context, remains a danger.
This occurred in several Channel Four films that tried too hard to comment
upon Thatcherism: *Stormy Monday*, to take one example, used the conceit of
"America week" in Newcastle-upon-Tyne to sprinkle its mise-en-scène with

large rosettes of Thatcher and Reagan, along with a caricatured speech on the values of self-reliance by the city's Thatcherite mayor (Alison Steadman). This kind of satiric scenario, however, ignores the possibility that most people who voted for Thatcher did not, in abstract terms, support such a dogmatic stance on "self-reliance," nor even admire the prime minister personally; opinion polls tended to suggest that many supported her for a much more complicated variety of social and economic reasons. It is true that Thatcher liked to portray herself iconically, as the guiding philosophical spirit of Britain in the 1980s, but the actual historical situation was surely more complex than this. Ironically, then, films overtly hostile to Thatcher, such as *Stormy Monday*, colluded in the rhetorical force of this image she invented for herself, even in opposing it politically. This difference between manifest and latent political content is well illustrated in *Wetherby*, which David Hare claims as a deliberate attempt to evoke the tone of Thatcher's Britain (Hiley, 64). At one dinner-party scene during this film, Stanley Pilborough (Ian Holm) proffers a psychoanalytical explanation of the prime minister's behavior, claiming she is taking vengeance upon the country out of a series of private obsessions. More convincing than this, however, are the impersonal elements in Hare's film: its analysis of time, history, and memory, together with its projection of how the past flows inexorably into the present. Often the most perceptive critiques of Thatcher's England came when directors and writers kept the pantomime villain herself at a safe distance, or when— as in *Wetherby*—Thatcher represented a cumulative product of postwar British history rather than just a grotesque aberration.

The Channel Four films of the 1980s, then, increasingly mark an implicit acknowledgment of the specific terrain of their aesthetic medium and of the ways in which this medium worked with the discourses of social convention, popular history, and communal memory. A hard-edged negotiation with such discourses helped to produce that dialectic between familiarity and defamiliarization characteristic of the best television films of this decade. As David Hare observes, the idea of eight million invisible people simultaneously watching a television production is so disorienting, so hard to conceptualize, that authors and critics sometimes contain this bewilderment by imagining that viewers cannot distinguish between superior works of fiction and "dogfood commercials" (Hare, 49). But, suggests Hare, the truth of the matter is very different: in late twentieth-century Britain, the television film functions as a uniquely democratic art form, unique in bridging general accessibility with the power to reshape people's perceptions and so, potentially, to change their lives.

Notes

1. For a recent analysis of American television movies, see Schulze.
2. Figures on cable and satellite television are taken from Feist and Hutchison, 63, and *ITN Factbook*, 935.
3. On situation comedy, see, for instance, Eaton.
4. In making this distinction, I follow Ellis, *Visible Fictions*, 137-38.
5. *Squaring the Circle* is a classic example of a major work by a major writer that is, at the present time, almost invisible because of the lack of accessible television libraries.
6. Media censorship in Britain was particularly prevalent during the Falklands war. For an account of this, see Harris.
7. The quotation comes from Lynda Myles, producer of *Defence of the Realm* (1985), another film about government suppression of information. Myles said this film, directed by David Drury, "turned out to be extremely prophetic" in relation to Thatcher's Britain (Petley, 96).
8. Many films that addressed issues of representation were shown in Channel Four's "Eleventh Hour" series, a showcase for more obviously avant-garde works that were screened for smaller audiences late at night. In this essay, however, I have chosen to concentrate upon the more well known and widely seen Channel Four productions.

Works Cited

Adair, Gilbert. 1988-89. "Classtrophobia: *High Hopes*." *Sight and Sound* 58 (1) 64-65.
Auty, Martyn. 1985. "But Is It Cinema?" In *British Cinema Now*, edited by Martyn Auty and Nick Roddick, 57-70. London: British Film Institute.
Baudrillard, Jean. 1988. *America*. Translated by Chris Turner. London: Verso.
Bennett, Alan, Mamoun Hassan, Jeremy Isaacs, and Gavin Millar. 1984. "British Cinema: Life before Death on Television." *Sight and Sound* 53 (2): 115-22.
Bradbury, Malcolm. 1990. "Write Angles." *Listener*, Feb. 15, 8-9.
Brunsdon, Charlotte. 1990. "Television: Aesthetics and Audiences." In *Logics of Television*, edited by Mellencamp, 59-72.
Carter, Angela. 1983. "Masochism for the Masses." *New Statesman* 3 (June): 8-10.
Caughie, John. 1985. "On the Offensive: Television and Values." In *TV and Schooling*, edited by David Lusted and Phillip Drummond, 53-66. London: British Film Institute.
_____. 1986. "Popular Culture: Notes and Revisions." In *High Theory/Low Culture: Analysing Popular Television and Film*, edited by Colin MacCabe, 156-71. Manchester: Manchester University Press.
_____. 1990. "Playing at Being American: Games and Tactics." In *Logics of Television*, edited by Mellencamp, 44-58.
Collins, Richard. 1989. "White and Green and Not Much Read: The White Paper on Broadcasting Policy." *Screen* 30 (1-2): 6-23.
Docherty, David, and David Morrison. 1987-88. " . . . Somewhat Different, but Not Too Different." *Sight and Sound* 57 (1): 10-13.
Eaton, Mick. 1978-79. "Television Situation Comedy." *Screen* 19 (4): 61-89.
Ellis, Jack C. 1990. *A History of Film*. 3rd ed. Englewood Cliffs, N.J.: Prentice-Hall.
Ellis, John. 1975. "Made in Ealing." *Screen* 16 (1): 78-127.
_____. 1982. *Visible Fictions: Cinema, Television, Video*. London: Routledge and Kegan Paul.
_____. 1986. "Broadcasting and the State: Britain and the Experience of Channel 4." *Screen* 27 (3-4): 6-22.
Feist, Andrew, and Robert Hutchison. 1990. *Cultural Trends. Issue 6: August 1990*. London: Policy Studies Institute.

Feuer, Jane. 1983. "The Concept of Live Television: Ontology as Ideology." In *Regarding Tele-vision: Critical Approaches—An Anthology*, edited by E. Ann Kaplan, 12-22. Frederick, Md.: University Publications of America–American Film Institute.

Fitch, Janet. 1989. "High Hopes." *American Film*, March, 12.

Flitterman-Lewis, Sandy. 1987. "Psychoanalysis, Film, and Television." In *Channels of Dis-course: Television and Contemporary Criticism*, edited by Robert C. Allen, 172-210. Chapel Hill: University of North Carolina Press.

Forbes, Jill, and Tim Pulleine. 1983. "Crossover: McEwan and Eyre." *Sight and Sound* 52 (4): 232-37.

Ford, Anna. 1988. "Harold Pinter: Radical Departures." *Listener*, Oct. 27, 4-6.

Hare, David. 1982. "Ah! Mischief: The Role of Public Broadcasting." In *Ah! Mischief: The Writer and Television*, edited by Frank Pike, 41-50. London: Faber.

Harris, Robert. 1983. *Gotcha! The Media, the Government and the Falklands Crisis*. London: Faber.

Harvey, Sylvia. 1989. "Deregulation, Innovation and Channel 4." *Screen* 30 (1-2): 60-79.

Heath, Stephen. 1981. *Questions of Cinema*. New York: Macmillan.

Hiley, Jim. 1985. "The Wetherby Report." *Observer Magazine*, March 10, 64-65.

Houston, Penelope. 1986. "Parker, Attenborough, Anderson." *Sight and Sound* 55 (3): 152-54.

Howkins, John. 1985. "Edinburgh Television." *Sight and Sound* 54 (4): 238-39.

Isaacs, Jeremy. 1989. *Storm over 4: A Personal Account*. London: Weidenfeld and Nicolson.

ITN Factbook. 1990. London: Michael O'Mara.

Jameson, Fredric. 1990. *Signatures of the Visible*. New York: Routledge.

Jarman, Derek. 1987. *The Last of England*. Edited by David L. Hirst. London: Constable.

Kael, Pauline. 1989. "The Current Cinema." *New Yorker*, Feb. 20, 95-98.

Kent, Nicolas. 1987. "Commissioning Editor: David Rose Interviewed." *Sight and Sound* 56 (4): 260-63.

Lane, Stewart. 1986. "Out Dated." *Listener*, April 24, 36.

LeMahieu, D. L. 1990. "Imagined Contemporaries: Cinematic and Televised Dramas about the Edwardians in Great Britain and the United States, 1967-1985." *Historical Journal of Film, Radio and Television* 10: 243-56.

MacCabe, Colin. 1988. "The South Bank Show Lecture: Is Television About to Enter the Dark Ages?" *Listener*, Feb. 11, 10-12.

Mellencamp, Patricia, ed. 1990. *Logics of Television: Essays in Cultural Criticism*. Blooming-ton: Indiana University Press.

Morse, Margaret. 1985. "Talk, Talk, Talk—The Space of Discourse in Television." *Screen* 26 (2): 2-15.

Paglia, Camille, and Neil Postman. 1991. "She Wants Her TV! He Wants His Book!" *Harper's*, March, 44-55.

Park, James. 1982-83. "Four Films for 4." *Sight and Sound* 52 (1): 8-12.

Petley, Julian. 1988. "A Very British Coup." *Sight and Sound* 57 (2): 95-97.

Poole, Mike. 1982. "Improvising the Real." *Listener*, Sept. 2, 29.

Pratley, Gerald. 1989. "35 Days in Toronto." *Sight and Sound* 58 (2): 94-96.

Schulze, Laurie Jane. 1986. "*Getting Physical*: Text/Context/Reading and the Made-for-Televi-sion Movie." *Cinema Journal* 25 (2): 35-50.

Walters, Margaret. 1987. "Safe British Cinema." *Listener*, Dec. 17-24, 62.

Woolley, Benjamin. 1984. "Being Poles Apart." *Listener*, May 24, 33.

Zettl, Herbert. 1978. "The Rare Case of Television Aesthetics." *Journal of the University Film Association* 30 (2): 3-8.

Six

The Repression of Communities: Visual Representations of Northern Ireland during the Thatcher Years

Brian McIlroy

> I remember once, in the early days of the troubles, the local RUC
> received a call one wintry night from a Protestant farmer
> reporting intruders on his property. As the patrol car turned into
> his drive, they saw a colour television plonked smack in the
> middle of the road. One constable got out to remove it—and was
> blown to kingdom-come. In Ulster, the medium really is the
> message.
>
> —John Naughton

John Naughton's striking anecdote above inspired me to explore the ways in which film directors and screenwriters approached the subject of Northern Ireland's violence during the years 1979-90. The Thatcher years produced many works that still require contextualization. "The troubles" in Northern Ireland (which "started" in 1968-69) have certain inbuilt impediments as a film topic, primarily the sheer complexity of Ireland's history with, and governance by, Great Britain. Margaret Thatcher came to power with mainstream opinions on Northern Ireland's position in the United Kingdom; as long as the majority of the population of the northern six counties wished to stay under British rule, she would defend that desire. In effect, this policy (which the Labour party also endorsed) put the British government and the Irish Republican Army (IRA), who seek to reunite the country against the wishes of the majority Protestant population of Northern Ireland, on a collision course for over twenty years. Thousands have suffered injury and death from this guerrilla war.

The claims for separation from the United Kingdom were helped by the rampant constitutional anomalies. For example, in Northern Ireland, unlike England, Scotland, and Wales, the major political parties—Conservative, Labour, Liberal Democrats—never were allowed or encouraged to form local branches. Instead, political parties in Northern Ireland reflect specifically the Irish-British dimension: two Unionist parties supported mainly by the Protestant population argue for the continued connection to Great Britain;

the Social Democratic and Labour parties supported mainly by the Catholic population argue for a gradual move to a United Ireland. On both sides of these parties more extreme ones exist, including Provisional Sinn Fein, the political wing of the IRA, which has significant (but *not* majority) support in Catholic nationalist areas in Northern Ireland.

The IRA has made itself felt as a military force throughout the United Kingdom and has never been slow to capitalize on a media opportunity. A thorn in Margaret Thatcher's side, she will have to guard against it for the rest of her life, since the IRA murders of retired policemen represent a consistent pattern. In the midst of Thatcher's election campaign in 1979, her close friend and shadow secretary of state, Airey Neave, was murdered by the Irish National Liberation Army, a more left-leaning organization than the socially naive Provisional IRA. Thatcher, in her early period of office, instructed her ministers to seek a peaceful internal arrangement within Northern Ireland. Meanwhile, she inherited from the Labour government a slew of problems concerning special category status for terrorist prisoners. This special status officially ended in April 1980, quickly followed by the "blanket" protest (in which prisoners refused to wear prison clothing), which turned into a series of hunger strikes. The most famous hunger striker, Bobby Sands, was elected a Westminster M.P. in a by-election, while he was starving himself to death.

Thatcher refused to grant special status to terrorist prisoners, and after ten men died, the IRA leaders called the strike off.[1] Though this emotional battle was a propaganda victory for the IRA, it also showed the resolve of Thatcher, a woman not afraid of confrontation, as she proved again during the British miners' strike and the Falklands/Malvinas crisis. On the political front, plans for "rolling devolution" for Northern Ireland never garnered much interest, but in 1982 a local assembly convened after provincewide elections. The Catholic nationalist parties declined, however, to take their seats, leaving the Unionists to talk to themselves.

Instead of attending the assembly, the constitutional nationalists discussed matters with elected representatives from the south of Ireland. These talks resulted in the New Ireland Forum Report released in 1984, which called for three main options to be considered by the British and Irish governments. Thatcher's negative response, later coined the "Out, Out, Out" speech, was characteristically to the point: "I have made it quite clear—and so did Mr. Prior when he was Secretary of State for Northern Ireland—that a unified Ireland was one solution that is out. A second solution was confederation of two states. That is out. A third solution was joint authority. That is out. That is a derogation from sovereignty. We made that quite clear when the Report was published" (Kenny, 82).

Her strong criticism came only a month after a bomb attempt on her life at the Conservative Party Conference (October 1984) killed five people, so Thatcher was in no mood for fudging the issues. Nevertheless, a great deal of hard bargaining behind the scenes over the next year led to an ingeniously worded (it avoided defining the present status of Northern Ireland) Anglo-Irish Agreement, one signed in November 1985.

This agreement gave a formal voice, for the first time since the formation of the Northern Ireland state in 1921, to Southern Irish elected representatives in the running of the province. Although restricted to matters of security and the treatment of the Catholic nationalist community, it offended the Unionist parties who refused to recognize the legitimacy of the agreement and began to encourage acts of civil disobedience. The accord represented an attempt to isolate the IRA and its violence. For the remainder of her term, Thatcher's ministers sought to strengthen the accord in spite of Protestant resistance. This policy included banning all terrorist spokespeople from appearing directly on television.[2] Through all these complex political negotiations, "the troubles" ebbed and flowed.

Because the films dealing with Northern Ireland invariably grapple with IRA violence, as well as the violence that happens in response, they usually fall within the thriller genre, since it contains all the ingredients necessary for conspiracy, intrigue, murder, and star-crossed lovers. Belfast's rugged streets move characters from innocence to experience. In many ways, this tendency to use generic conventions and formulas betrays a conservative choice: it emphasizes the universal quality of a film's narrative and, in so doing, avoids a concerted attempt to demythologize the Northern Ireland "problem." But given cinema as a powerful cultural force in society, it remains important, first, to point out how films underwhelm or repress history and politics; second, to understand how they also undermine specific communities. So the haphazard group of films dealing with Northern Ireland follows a fatalistic aesthetic, much in the same way as Polanski's *Chinatown* convinces us that societal corruption so pervades our world that it swallows up the individual seeking to do good.

The history of films dealing with Ireland as a whole has been charted in a series of books published in the late eighties (Rockett; Slide; McIlroy; Curran). We see from these works that Ireland's struggle with England for independence has attracted many filmmakers: from Brian Desmond Hurst's *Ourselves Alone* (1936) through Michael Anderson's *Shake Hands with the Devil* (1959) to David Lean's *Ryan's Daughter* (1970). These films look at violence within Ireland, among Irish people, and conclude that compromise is possible for those who are not fanatics. Of the three directors above, only Hurst was an Irishman. English and American filmmakers tend to bring Ireland to the Irish. Like many other small countries sharing a common language with a larger country, Ireland's national images have been foisted upon it by outsiders. John Ford's *The Quiet Man* (1952), for instance, remains a favorite among Irish viewers of all ages: it presents a flattering, romanticized version of the country, an escapist revision of reality through rose-technicolor spectacles.

The film that influenced many screenwriters and directors considering Northern Ireland as a subject is Carol Reed's *Odd Man Out* (1947). The pursuit of an IRA gunman through the streets of Belfast provided Reed with a convenient metaphor to explore the metaphysical themes of the outsider — and of salvation. Reed's combining of the thriller genre with film noir allows him to suggest the universal aspect of the gunman's actions, and consequently viewers will be disappointed if they seek only a political statement from the film. This unwillingness to be historically or locally precise springs not only from a fear of being accused of partisanship but also from a fear of confusing the non-Irish audience, those not expected to understand the byways of Irish politics as containing vital information for narrative resolution. Assumptions about the spectator thus lead to a simplification of issues and feelings, an observation discussed at length by John Hill (Rockett).

Although one can say very little about the Northern Ireland situation without someone attacking the critic as misguided and/or prejudiced, it seems important to take a stand on delineating the problems of representation. The easiest and most conventional method of approaching the conflict opens filmmakers to charges of sectarianism because it too neatly divides the warring groups into three camps: (1) the Catholic community and its paramilitary offshoots (particularly the IRA and the Irish National Liberation Army); (2) the "security forces" (the British Army; the locally recruited Ulster Defence Regiment; the police, and the Royal Ulster Constabulary; and (3) the Protestant community and its paramilitary offshoots (particularly the Ulster Defence Association and the Ulster Volunteer Force). Such a framework allows a filmmaker, particularly in the field of documentary, to give the impression that the security forces either keep the warring factions apart or, indeed, the reverse, keep them fighting and thereby prevent a solution. Immediately, readers may object to the use of the words "Catholic" and "Protestant," preferring the less religious terms "Nationalist" and "Unionist." But it remains a fact that Catholics populate the vast majority of Nationalist organizations, and Protestants the Unionist groups. Most filmic representations accept this generalization of Northern Ireland's simmering political scene. To term someone a Protestant or a Catholic in this context conjures up a whole history of social, economic, and political attitudes not confined to religious affiliation.

Grave misconceptions and misunderstandings between the two communities in Northern Ireland have spread to the film representations of the people in Ulster, and to that extent, film and TV-film production has often added to the mystification. By dividing my subsequent discussion into the three sections mentioned above, I will take the sectarian positions "by the throat," as it were. The first, and most "appealing" to filmmakers, is the depiction of the Catholic community and the paramilitary organizations emanating from it.

The Catholic Community and the IRA

The majority of film and television productions dealing with the province focus on the minority population of Roman Catholics in Northern Ireland, a subject area prone to censorship. A TV drama reviewer in 1982 commented that "in television alone, upwards of 40 programmes have been suppressed in part or in whole during the past decade" (Poole, 33). Since then, the most famous case of censorship has been the BBC film *Real Lives* (1985), which profiled two Irish extremists, one Protestant and one Catholic. The furor over the initially banned film resulted from Martin McGuinness's (of Provisional Sinn Fein) voiced opinions in favor of an organization (the IRA) that in 1984 almost murdered the prime minister and most of her cabinet colleagues. A letter from the home secretary sent to the BBC Board of Governors indicated his concern over the film's possible transmission. The board voted against the screening. In reaction, journalists led a one-day strike at the BBC, protesting the blatant intervention of the Thatcher government. Matters worsened when Thatcher appeared on a news program and thanked the board for their "judicious" decision not to screen the documentary. On the surface, it appeared that the Board of Governors had bowed to government pressure, and the IRA received yet another propaganda victory. In the heat of the moment, commentators overlooked that until the last few years of Thatcher's term the British government had allowed the reporting of Sinn Fein. By contrast, the Irish Republic banned Provisional Sinn Fein access to broadcasting in 1975 because of its unequivocal support of the "armed struggle."

Most films blindly accept the assumption that the Catholic community is an oppressed minority. Since the IRA casts itself as the protector of this beleaguered community, filmmakers deal with the IRA. At the start of Margaret Thatcher's term of office, three films with references to the IRA caused considerable comment. Two of these, with American directors but diverse financial backing, were the most direct and explicit. Arthur MacCaig's *The Patriot Game—A Decade Long Battle for the North of Ireland* (1979) utilized television footage from a number of international TV stations to build its visual argument that the British troops present in Northern Ireland continue to play the role of imperial oppressors. The film vehemently supports the IRA armed struggle, ostensibly showing how history makes it inevitable. According to the *Variety* review in 1980, the Irish Northern Aid Committee, subsequently investigated by the American authorities over allegations that it transferred money directly to the IRA, used the film as a fundraiser. So controversial was the film that two special screenings were held in the Royal Court Theatre in London in June 1979, since most British distributors declined to handle the picture.

Dealing with the IRA also functions as the main subject of the two other films released in 1979: John Mackenzie's *The Long Good Friday* and Tony Luraschi's *The Outsider*. In a sense, they reveal the "tentativeness" of a British production versus the "boldness" of a foreign-financed production, a general thesis advanced by John Hill (Rockett).

John Mackenzie's film looks primarily at gangsterism in 1970s London. Bob Hoskins plays working-class mobster Harold Shand, who makes good by sheer graft and appropriate violence, a precursor to Spica in Greenaway's *The Cook, the Thief, His Wife, and Her Lover* (1989). Shand, the nouveau riche, eventually runs into an older, more efficient "family," that of the IRA. As the screenwriter conceived it, "The hero would be a Thatcher man gone mad—the ultimate self-made capitalist and utterly patriotic" (Keefe, vi). The problem with the film from an Irish nationalist perspective is that IRA violence simply functions as a form of gangsterism (which to British governments it has always been). In this way, the film reflects an English realpolitik. The history of the film's postproduction reveals that financial backers were uneasy with the depiction of the IRA as this unstoppable, incorruptible force. Mackenzie never helps the audience move beyond gangsterism because he never investigates the IRA. It is, in effect, the evil deus ex machina. What is fascinating is that the IRA infiltrates the underworld in Britain and is treated as an inexplicable, though amazingly efficient, force. This attitude of respect tinged with incomprehension remains the essential British view today.

Tony Luraschi's *The Outsider* focuses on young Irish-American Michael (Craig Wasson), who, filled with songs and stories from his Irish-born grand-

Danny (Stephen Rea), in pursuit of revenge, clutches the weapon that has replaced his saxophone-playing career, in Neil Jordan's *Angel* (1982).

father, comes to Northern Ireland to join the IRA. Michael accompanies the IRA on special missions, including the murder of a magistrate. The naive American soon learns that the IRA and the British army stay caught in a struggle without regard for the kind of romanticized idealism Michael exhibits. Luraschi presents the IRA as a duplicitous group of men who use the young man for their own purposes. Ironically, Michael's grandfather turns out to have been the sinner of all Irish sinners: an IRA informer. Brutal, violent, and direct, *The Outsider* nonetheless bravely questions the presence of the British army, the shadowy role of the Ulster Defence Regiment, the interrogation techniques of the Royal Ulster Constabulary (RUC), as well as the kangaroo courts of the IRA. This film, too, ran into distribution problems because of its topicality, especially scenes where police torture a blind IRA sympathizer.

The first truly remarkable Irish-directed "Northern Ireland feature" was released in 1982. Neil Jordan's *Angel* has received a great deal of attention from commentators who validate its aesthetics by remarking that both sides in the Northern Ireland "troubles" are condemned. Danny (Stephen Rea), the sax player, becomes a gunman for reasons of revenge after a Protestant gang murders a deaf-mute he has befriended. Some critics argue that the specifics of religion/allegiance are unclear; but, a knowledgeable viewer knows that because the policeman is the ring leader of the gang this is almost certainly a Protestant paramilitary group.

Interestingly, the clue of a clubfoot sets off Danny's search for revenge. A nonspecific Irish saying to determine religion is to ask whether someone kicks with the "other" or "left" foot. In this instance, the culprit kicks with a malformed foot! The film's underlying premise is that police corruption and murder (represented by the Protestant community) destroy Danny's humanity and lead him to violent acts. Danny is, then, the IRA, "the people" radicalized into action. Literally, he is a son without parents, one who finds his voice—first by sax playing and then by gunplay. He eliminates the "cancer" of Protestantism and contently leaves a Jewish head of police—significantly called Bloom (a cute Joycean echo)—to sort out the mess at the end.

Pat O'Connor's *Cal* (1984), taken from Bernard MacLaverty's novella of the same name, follows the literary source very closely and traces a young Catholic boy's story. He and his father are the only Catholics left on a Protestant street and suffer accordingly. The film also looks at how a young Catholic man becomes involved in the operations of the IRA. Not unlike many reluctant activists, Cal (John Lynch) is seduced into working for the IRA—half through threats and half through promises that if he complies with "small jobs" he will be left alone to live his own life later. The IRA leader, Skeffington (John Kavanagh), presents his involvement through his crippled father, a parallel to the crippled father of the murdered RUC man for whose death Cal is partly responsible; Skeffington's father once was heavily committed to the cause of national liberation. Through his choice of characterization and shooting style, O'Connor indicates how the IRA leaders see themselves as fighting some kind of holy war. Skeffington, for example, is strangely puritanical and disapproves of bad language. At one point, Cal meets the IRA leader in a pigeon- and bat-infested stone-wall enclosure and, because much of their discussion is shot from above at an angle, it implies that the world of the IRA is unnatural. The brutal representation of the gunman Crilly, who actually murders the RUC man while Cal assists, conveys the sense that the IRA leadership easily manipulates young and violent men who are little more than gangsters.

Both *Angel* and *Cal* were critical and commercial successes, but three films in the 1980s dealing with the Catholic community and the IRA particularly impress because they originate from Irish women: Pat(ricia) Murphy's *Maeve* (1981), Stuart Burge and Anne Devlin's *Naming the Names* (1986), and Anne Crilly's *Mother Ireland* (1988). These three films explore the role of (Catholic) women in the Republican movement. Murphy's film charts the return of Maeve (Brid Brennan) from "open-minded" England to her Republican "ghetto," where she finds herself constantly warring with chauvinist ideas from within and without her specific environment. The male soldiers who taunt her on the streets display misogynist attitudes little different from the male Republican leaders and advocates in her own community. By deliberately eschewing a conventional narrative—one feels distanced from much of the supposed linear visual presentation by occasional direct address to the camera and a complicated mise-en-scène—Murphy calls into question the patriarchal structures that support the presence of the British army in Northern Ireland, as well as those that support the Republican movement in Catholic Nationalist areas.

In *Naming the Names* (a TV film for the BBC), a young Catholic woman, Finn (Sylvestra Le Touzel), is arrested for luring a Protestant judge's son to a park where the IRA apprehends and murders him. The critical event in Finn's life, the Protestant firebombing of her home in 1969, almost kills her guardian grandmother, while Finn is making love with an English journalist. When her grandmother does die a few years later, an orphaned Finn depends on her English boyfriend to keep her from the IRA, though he remains unaware of her predicament. Their breakup seals her fate with the IRA. Circumscribed by the streets of her West Belfast ghetto, Finn repeats only the names of these streets when quizzed by the police for her IRA contacts. The Catholic community, shown to be frightened and impotent in the 1969-70 period, becomes totally radicalized by the mid-1980s, as evidenced by the argument in Belfast City Library between Catholic Finn and Protestant Henry:

> HENRY: Take Parnell, for example—Charles Stewart Parnell, a Protestant, a leader of the Home Rule, was destroyed by the Roman Catholic clergy over his divorce case.
>
> FINN: He was destroyed by Gladstone, and the English nonconformists. . . . And when has any Protestant movement had a Catholic leader?
>
> HENRY: Come on, they're not exactly queuing up at the door, are they?
>
> FINN: How could they be? What of the wars of the constitution?
>
> HENRY: That's not relevant.
>
> FINN: A Protestant parliament for a Protestant people. And it's not relevant?! You think that's all right? It's economic, rational . . . ?
>
> HENRY: You get angry very quickly. Who's done that to you, Finn? [She gets up and leaves]

They both run out into the street and face the large sign on the City Hall: "Belfast Says No," a reference to the Unionist resistance to the Anglo-Irish Agreement:

HENRY: Confirmed what they've [the Unionists] always believed. The British government are the real Republicans!

FINN: Welcome to Belfast.

The third film, *Mother Ireland*, a documentary video that features many Irish women's attitudes concerning their social and political position in Ireland, achieved a certain notoreity for its interview with Mairead Farrell, one of the three IRA suspects shot dead in Gibraltar by a British SAS unit. She complains that the Republican movement often fails to be fully aware of women's issues. To what extent audiences should feel pleased that Farrell can be just as involved in terrorist activities as any man remains problematic. Nonetheless, her direct engagement with social and political realities reflects the radicalization of many women in Northern Ireland.

Other Catholic women who dominate the video include Rita O'Hare of the magazine *Republican News*; journalist Nell McCafferty; filmmaker Pat Murphy; feminist Republican activist Bernadette Devlin; and women who supported the Nationalist movement during the War of Independence and the Civil War. Director Crilly forcefully brings out the discrepancy between the Mother Ireland image of compassion and suffering and the reality of modern Irish women who, at least in the Republican movement, demand and receive recognition that violence and feminism can (and do) go hand in hand.

The Security Forces

To put it mildly, the screen versions of the security forces in Northern Ireland have not been particularly sympathetic. Yet even here discrepancies exist. So, for example, one group, the Ulster Defence Regiment, has hardly been tackled at all, even though it carries out much of the army-style operations—roadblocks, patrols, and the like—in Ulster. Like the RUC, this force is predominantly Protestant in makeup. Their colleagues in the RUC, however, have been more severely treated. For instance, in Ken Loach's *Hidden Agenda* (1990), the police callously murder Irish Catholic and American civilians, violently carry out house searches, and bitterly resent "foreign" interference. This fact is exemplified by the chief constable of the RUC in the film, Brodie (Jim Norton), who resists the investigation of Kerrigan (Brian Cox) and Ingrid (Frances McDormand). Loach offers no explanation as to why Brodie believes in his cause. Yet to understand the nuances of this particular situation, some background is necessary to discuss it further.

On December 12, 1982, an undercover unit of the Royal Ulster Constabulary murdered Seamus Grew and Roddy Carroll. Grew and Carroll were

Police inspector Kerrigan (Brian Cox) and human rights activist Ingrid (Frances McDormand) arrive in a nationalist ghetto to interview an SAS deserter with information incriminating highly placed Conservative politicians, in Ken Loach's *Hidden Agenda* (1990).

members of the Irish National Liberation Army, an extremist offshoot from the Official IRA. Both men were traveling home to Armagh City when a speeding car overtook them and forced them off the road. At close range, Grew and Carroll were shot to death, though neither man was armed or wanted for any specific crime. Murders like these by the undercover RUC unit led to a police inquiry into what became known as the "shoot-to-kill" policy in Northern Ireland. Deputy Chief Constable John Stalker of the Greater Manchester constabulary headed an internal investigation authorized to present a report, one recommending what charges, if any, should be laid against police officers in Northern Ireland. Before Stalker could present his findings, he was "disgraced" back in Manchester by allegations that he kept company with criminals. Though proved false, these allegations removed Stalker from the Northern Ireland investigation.[3]

Commentators and authors put forth many theories to explain this bizarre twist of events, one of the most popular claiming that Stalker found connections between clandestine operations and their authorization from within the higher levels of the British government. Also in the conspiracy vein, it later emerged that the former Labour prime minister Harold Wilson had been the target of a CIA-inspired plan to discredit him. Hearing this, some quickly assumed that right-wing forces actively made conditions conducive for the rise of Margaret Thatcher and her conservative agenda. Loach attempts to combine these two theories in his film *Hidden Agenda*.

In the movie, an American Civil Liberties Union lawyer, Paul Sullivan (Brad Dourif), is killed while uncovering the story behind an ex-SAS soldier, Harris (Maurice Roeves), involved in a conspiracy against Wilson's Labour government in the 1970s. Loach ties the Conservative party supporters' shenanigans against the Labour party government of the 1970s (shades of the TV series "A Very British Coup") with the alleged "shoot-to kill" policy in Northern Ireland many years later. He fails, however, to make this connection stick. Two separate issues are (half) addressed here, one well (Conservative party conspiracy) and one confusingly (the British policy within Northern Ireland). The director stacks the decks from the very beginning. We see policemen make a house arrest, former detainees allege ill-treatment inside police stations, a police/SAS/MI6 unit kill Frank Malloy and the American lawyer with "efficiency," and British undercover agents kidnap (and kill off-screen) Harris on Dublin's streets—thereby suggesting that England continues to "invade" the Irish Republic.

Loach opens with two quotations: one from Margaret Thatcher states that Northern Ireland is as much part of the United Kingdom as her own constituency, and one from James Lalor, a nineteenth-century Irish Republican, indicates the imperative of Irish independence. To imply that Thatcherism and Conservative party "dirty-tricks" supporters in the 1970s remain part and parcel of an alleged "shoot-to-kill" policy in Northern Ireland without investigating IRA violence and murder makes one question the ethics of Loach's intertwining of fictional filmmaking and politics. His film seems more an exercise in political correctness, a response to recently published material (Doherty) than a true engagement with the real issues (many of which can be usefully scanned in Ryder).

Loach's negative depiction of the RUC stands with good filmic company. The corrupt police in *Angel* are involved in murder, and, in *Cal*, the police rather earnestly beat up the Catholic protagonist for his part in the murder of one of their own. The graphic murder of the RUC man in *Cal*, replayed often in flashback to underscore the protagonist's guilt and desire for redemption, never contextualizes or explains the province's problems.

In *Naming the Names*, a policeman interrogates Finn while others watch through closed-circuit-television surveillance, as a policewoman stands silently beside her and looks on disapprovingly. Policewomen are noticeably missing in most contemporary films dealing with the RUC. Perhaps filmmakers and writers feel their presence weakens the frame they hang around the picture of Northern Ireland: male, Protestant security forces exploiting and repressing female, Catholic civilians, including feminist Republican activists, as seen in such films as Murphy's *Maeve* and *Anne Devlin* (1984), and Crilly's *Mother Ireland*. To be sure, the presence or numbers of policewomen do nothing to subvert patriarchal structures, but they do complicate the rather simplistic accusations of misogyny at the root of Protestant policing. *Maeve*, through its distancing devices, does point out that the Republican movement finds it extremely difficult to integrate women.

The British army in action appears as background "filler" in nearly every film dealing with Northern Ireland. Some television documentary programs isolate their experience, but only a few narrative fictional films have similar goals. A. F. N. Clarke's *Contact* (BBC Screen 2, 1985), based on his own recorded experiences in Belfast and South Armagh while he was in the British Parachute Regiment, captures precisely the tension and boredom of patrol and rest periods. The soldiers are young, violent, frightened, and curious all at the same time. One striking scene serves to sum up this weird atmosphere: after a comrade dies in action, the soldiers move toward the dead man, as if finding it psychically necessary to see the injuries inflicted. Every sound on patrol represents possible danger, and Clarke makes the audience feel almost continuously on edge.

Karl Francis's *Boy Soldier* (1986), one of the less conventional male treatments of the British army, looks critically at the ridiculous go-between status of the army. Unique here is the Welsh emphasis. Without Channel Four, funding for this project would not have been secured, and it comes across as one of the more sophisticated treatments of the British army in recent years. Wil (Richard Lynch), a young Welsh soldier serving in Northern Ireland, sees his best friend killed on the streets. In a state of panic, he shoots a young man brandishing a knife. The public unrest at this "civilian murder" demands Wil's sacrifice. Clinging to his principles of honesty, Wil refuses to lie for expediency and subsequently suffers maltreatment from his English army superiors who see little difference between the Irish and the Welsh. The process of brutalization, carefully traced by Francis, suggests that ultimately the army is an inappropriately blunt instrument to use in the delicate Northern Ireland situation. But Francis also suggests that the real value the army offers for working-class British males resides in its sense of a close community.

The Protestant Community and Its Paramilitary Offshoots

One must look hard for a likeable or sympathetic Protestant character in films dealing with Northern Ireland; in fact, one rarely discovers a well-

Cal (John Lynch) and Marcella (Helen Mirren) ponder the social and psychological ramifications of their relationship, in Pat O'Connor's *Cal* (1984).

rounded protagonist or antagonist. Quite simply, filmmakers display little interest in developing approaches to the Protestant community, preferring to rely on comfortable stereotypes. For example, the Protestant voice is painfully missing in Loach's *Hidden Agenda*: the one million Protestants of the North of Ireland remain invisible in his constellation. Images of Protestantism are conveyed merely by a long shot from a high window during the 12th July celebrations (when the Protestants commemorate the victory over Catholic James II by Protestant William of Orange in 1690), and by the chief police officer Brodie who "resists" Kerrigan's investigation. What other Protestants we see are involved in violence or implied bigotry.

In O'Connor's *Cal*, the Protestant family members with whom the Catholic boy interacts are severe, distrusting, and terribly cozy with the trigger-happy security forces. Protestant youths assault Cal in another example of Protestant intimidation. In Peter Smith's and Alan Bleasdale's otherwise comic *No Surrender* (1985), a Protestant terrorist threatens a former comrade with exposure of his daughter's mixed marriage with a Catholic. Finally, we see the more "liberal" Protestant murder his more "extreme" former colleague, a hardly sympathetic portrayal despite the screenwriter's intent to achieve it. Violence, and malicious violence at that, seems integral to most filmmakers' conceptions of the Protestant male community.

This contention opens up a new area: how have filmmakers considered Protestant women and violence? As Richard Kearney (1988) observes, Edward Bennett's *Ascendancy* (1981) and Kieran Hickey's *Attracta* (1983) show male violence paralyzing and repressing women to an extent that they assume mythic proportions—essentially the all-suffering Mother figure. Of course, given the blatant pro-Republican bias of Anne Crilly's *Mother Ireland*, Protestant women simply are excluded from the video documentary. But this view of Irish Protestant women fails to account for the violence that radicalized certain women to join the security forces.

Only *Naming the Names* offers an interesting portrayal of an Irish Protestant, even though reviewers misread the character as English (Pascal). Henry Kirk (Michael Maloney), the son of a local judge, is studying Irish history at Oxford. While at home, he travels to the Catholic Falls Road Bookshop to look at their Irish collection in search of materials for his Ph.D. thesis. The bookshop assistant, Finn, is steeped in Irish history but, given the de facto separate education systems in Northern Ireland for Catholics and Protestants, from a purely Republican perspective. Finn and Henry form a romantic attachment, both claiming that they have English partners. In this way, writer Anne Devlin emphasizes the love-hate relationship both Irish Catholics and Protestants have with the English mainland.

Finn delivers the two volumes of R. M. Sibbert's *Orangeism in Ireland and Throughout the Empire* (1914-15) to Henry, and this history of Orangeism written by an Orangeman sparks a lively debate. In the midst of their discussion, Henry utters the Protestant position rarely articulated verbally or visually on television and film:

FINN: You think that's all not irrelevant now? Gladstone and Home Rule?

HENRY: No, no, Gladstone tended to dismiss the Protestants as a bigoted minority. Successive British governments are making the same mistake.

FINN: What is your thesis, briefly, in a line?

HENRY: The Protestant opposition to home rule was rational. Because at the time Ulster Protestant industries, linen, shipbuilding, were dependent on the British market. Home rule would have ruined Ulster financially.

FINN: But it wasn't just about money, was it?

HENRY: No, no. The Protestants were also worried about being discriminated against in a largely Catholic state.

FINN: They were worried?

HENRY: Yes, I think those fears were justified.[4]

The fact that I must quote a dialogue interchange to establish a Protestant portrayal is significant. No filmmaker in Britain and Ireland has thoroughly investigated a visual representation of the Protestant community, one that reaches beyond the easiest of stereotypes.[5] If anything, filmmakers fetishize what they conceive as minority opinions. This reductiveness creates terribly imbalanced fictional renditions, despite the painstaking efforts of local television stations to provide fair treatment of each community in current affairs and news programs (Cathcart). Consequently, violence and the issues surrounding it in Northern Ireland received an extremely skewed representation between the years 1979 and 1990, a time during which a minority oppositional cinema has dominated our perceptions.

Over the Thatcher years, mainstream filmmakers became more assertive and aggressive in their representations of the Northern Ireland "problem." Films and videos toward the end of Thatcher's "reign," such as Ken Loach's *Hidden Agenda* and Anne Crilly's *Mother Ireland*, confidently and directly criticize the British government's role in Northern Ireland. These films, in particular, struggle with a complicated politics; yet, they often fail to provide a stimulating visual treatment. At the other end of the spectrum, films concerned primarily with character continued to do well at the box office, including Neil Jordan's *Angel* and Pat O'Connor's *Cal*. These films repress history and politics for fear of distancing the non-Irish audience. In general, filmmakers and videographers have served well the ideological position of the Catholic nationalist community in Northern Ireland. The position of the security forces has been sketchily treated. The Protestant unionist community has largely been ignored. Although narrative films can play a crucial role in the cultural reconcilement of Northern Ireland's communities, we find neither comfort nor proof in the productions made during the Thatcher years. We do, however, see bolder attempts than hitherto in articulating anti-British politics.

Notes

1. A useful blow-by-blow account of the hunger strikes may be found in Liam Clarke's *Broadening the Battlefield: The H-Blocks and the Rise of Sinn Fein* (Dublin: Gill and Macmillan, 1987).

2. In the post-Thatcher era, "talks about talks" appeared to promise a new agreement involving all mainstream political parties, but in mid-1991 these meetings broke down, leaving Thatcher's legacy in place.

3. In addition to Doherty (1986), useful books on various aspects of the Stalker case include the following: Peter Taylor, *Stalker: The Search for Truth* (London: Faber and Faber, 1987); The Committee on the Administration of Justice, *The Stalker Affair: More Questions Than Answers*, 2nd ed. (Belfast: CAJ, 1988); John Stalker, *Stalker* (London: Harrap, 1988); Kevin Taylor with

Keith Mumby, *The Poisoned Tree* (London: Sidgwick and Jackson, 1990); and David Murphy, *The Stalker Affair and the Press* (London: Unwin Hyman, 1991).

4. Socially speaking, southern Ireland remains one of the most conservative countries in Europe. In 1983 and 1986, respectively, access to abortion and divorce were rejected in referendums. The latter issue, in particular, confirmed Protestant fears of a united Ireland.

5. The appearance in 1990 of Thaddeus O'Sullivan's *December Bride*, which focuses on the rural Protestant community of the Strangford Lough area, is a remarkable exception.

Works Cited

Cathcart, Rex. 1984. *The Most Contrary Region: The BBC in Northern Ireland, 1924-1984*. Belfast: Blackstaff Press.

Curran, Joseph. 1989. *Hibernian Green on the Silver Screen: The Irish and American Movies*. New York: Greenwood Press.

Doherty, Frank. 1986. *The Stalker Affair*. Dublin: Mercier Press.

Hitch. 1980. "The Patriot Game—A Decade Long Battle for the North of Ireland." *Variety*, June 18, 24.

Kearney, Richard. 1988. "Nationalism and Irish Cinema." In *Transitions: Narratives in Modern Irish Culture*. Manchester: Manchester University Press, 173-92.

Keefe, Barrie. 1984. *The Long Good Friday*. London: Methuen.

Kenny, Anthony. 1986. *The Road to Hillsborough: The Shaping of the Anglo-Irish Agreement*. Oxford: Pergamon Press..

McIlroy, Brian. 1989. *World Cinema 4: Ireland*. Trowbridge, Wiltshire: Flicks Books.

Naughton, John. 1985. "The good spies come back." *Listener*, Jan. 10, 33-34.

Pascal, Julia. 1987. "Personal Troubles." *Listener*, Feb. 5, 31.

Poole, Michael. 1982. "The Long March," *Listener*, Nov. 4, 33.

Rockett, Kevin, Luke Gibbons, and John Hill. 1987. *Cinema and Ireland*. London: Croom Helm.

Ryder, Chris. 1989. *The RUC: A Force under Fire*. London: Methuen.

Slide, Anthony. 1988. *The Cinema and Ireland*. Jefferson, N.C.: McFarland.

Seven

Re-presenting the National Past: Nostalgia and Pastiche in the Heritage Film

Andrew Higson

The critical celebration of the revival of British production in the mid-1980s was in part an acknowledgment that British films were once more forces to be reckoned with in the international marketplace. While the obligation to succeed internationally requires to some degree an effacing of the specifically national, certain films have used the national itself—or at least, one version of the national past—as their prime selling point. Images of Britain and Britishness (usually, in fact, Englishness) became commodities for consumption in the international image market. The films I have in mind are the cycle of quality costume dramas, or what I will refer to here as the heritage film, and they include *Chariots of Fire* (1981), *Another Country* (1984), *A Passage to India* (1985), *A Room with a View* (1986), *A Handful of Dust* (1987), *Maurice* (1987), and *Little Dorrit* (1987) (and more recently *The Fool* [1990] and *Where Angels Fear to Tread* [1991]). My interest in these films is in the way they represent the national past, and in how this representation works for contemporary spectators. I will argue that the past is displayed as visually spectacular pastiche, inviting a nostalgic gaze that resists the ironies and social critiques so often suggested narratively by these films (see also Wollen).

The heritage cycle and its particular representation of the national past is in many ways symptomatic of cultural developments in Thatcherite Britain. The Thatcher years, of course, coincided with an international capitalist recession that accelerated Britain's decline as a world economic power, but that also saw the growth of multinational enterprises, including the European Community. Inevitably, these processes disturbed traditional notions of national identity, which were further upset by the recognition that British society was increasingly multiracial and multicultural. At the same time, the government adopted political and economic measures, often sharply contested, that tended to encourage high unemployment, marked inequalities of income and standards of living, and a more general social malaise among the dispossessed that drifted periodically into social unrest.

The heritage cycle is only one strand in the British cinema of these years, and it can usefully be contrasted to other British films like *My Beautiful Laundrette* (1985), *A Letter to Brezhnev* (1985), and *Passion of Remembrance* (1986). These films are set firmly in the present, away from the centers of power, in an unstable and socially divided postimperialist and/or working-class Britain, where identities are shifting, fluid, and heterogeneous. The heritage films, on the other hand, provide a very different response to developments in Thatcherite Britain. By turning their backs on the industrialized, chaotic present, they nostalgically reconstruct an imperialist and upper-class Britain (or its other side, the picturesque poverty of *Little Dorrit*). The films thus offer apparently more settled and visually splendid manifestations of an essentially pastoral national identity and authentic culture: "Englishness" as an ancient and natural inheritance, *Great* Britain, the *United* Kingdom. It would be wrong, however, to suggest that these films resonate unequivocally with Thatcherite politics. They are too ambivalent to sit easily in such an equation and in various ways propose more liberal-humanist visions of social relations, at least at the level of dialogue and narrative theme. It is this tension between visual splendor and narrative meaning in the films that makes them so fascinating.

Heritage films operate at very much the culturally respectable, quality end of the market, and are key players in the new British art cinema, which straddles the traditional art-house circuit and the mainstream commercial cinemas in Britain. These are the sort of films that are invited to festivals and that win prizes. They are discussed in terms of an authorship that, at least in the case of the literary adaptations, is doubly coded—in terms of both film director and author of the source novel. Their audience is primarily middle-class and significantly older than the mainstream film audience, and they appeal to a film culture closely allied to English literary culture and to the canons of good taste. The hand-to-mouth production base of these films, along with the terms of their reception and circulation, indicate that they function within a *cultural* mode of production, as distinct from Hollywood's *industrial* mode of production (Elsaesser, 3): their significance is accounted for culturally rather than financially, even though several of them (including *Chariots of Fire*, *A Passage to India*, and *A Room with a View*) were considerable box-office successes.

Reproducing Englishness: cricket practice, in *Another Country* (1984).

We must also recognize that this cycle of films, as with so many recent British films, depends on television in a variety of ways. Several were partially funded by television companies: *A Room with a View* and *Maurice* by Channel Four; *A Handful of Dust* by London Weekend Television). Hugh Hudson and Charles Sturridge, the directors, respectively, of *Chariots of Fire* and *A Handful of Dust*, came from the television industry. All of the films arguably owe as much to the tradition of the BBC classic serial and the quality literary adaptation on television as they do to the filmed costume drama or to art-house cinema (on the classic serial, see Kerr). Thus, in addition to the films already mentioned, the cycle of heritage adaptations should also perhaps include two prestige television serials of the early 1980s, "Jewel in the Crown" (1983) and "Brideshead Revisited" (1981), the latter directed by Sturridge. Indeed, Channel Four's policy—and its influence on the policies of other television companies—of cofunding filmed dramas for a theatrical as well as a televisual release, rather than funding serialized drama on video, temporarily replaced the television classic serial in the mid-1980s, while employing many of its aesthetic conventions for the films that emerged. (More recently, Channel Four has favored drama shot on video, and/or serialized drama, with no plans for theatrical release.)

John Corner and Sylvia Harvey argue that the radical economic and social reconstructions of Britain in the 1980s required the Thatcher government to find novel ways of managing the conflict between old and new, tradition and modernity. They identify the key concepts in this process as "heritage," with its connotations of continuity with the past and the preservation of values and traditions, and "enterprise," with its connotations of change and innovation. The terms are vitally interconnected: "What has come to be called 'the heritage industry' is itself a major component of economic redevelopment, an 'enterprise,' both in terms of large-scale civic programmes and the proliferation of private commercial activity around 'the past' in one commodified form or another" (Corner and Harvey, 1991c, 46). One of the more obvious manifestations of official concern with the values and properties of the past can be found in the National Heritage Acts of 1980 and 1983. As Patrick Wright shows, these acts reworked concepts of public access and use in terms of commodification, exhibition, and display, encouraging the forthright marketing of the past within a thoroughly market-orientated heritage industry (Wright, 42ff; see also Hewison). The heritage industry has thus developed as a vital part of contemporary tourism and related service industries such as the leisure industry, which of course embraces cinema.

The heritage film and its reconstruction of the past thus represents just one aspect of the heritage industry as a whole. Of course, the heritage impulse, "one of the most powerful imaginative constructs of our time" (Samuel, preface xii), is not confined to Thatcherite Britain, but is a characteristic feature of postmodern culture. The heritage industry may transform the past into a series of commodities for the leisure and entertainment market, but in most cases the commodity on offer is an image, a spectacle, something to be gazed at. History, the past, becomes, in Fredric Jameson's phrase, "a vast collection of images" designed to delight the modern-day tourist-historian (Jameson, 66; see also Urry, chaps. 5 and 6). In this version of history, a critical perspective is displaced by decoration and display, a fascination with surfaces, "an obsessive accumulation of comfortably archival detail" (Wright, 252) in which a fascination with style displaces the material dimensions of historical context. The past is reproduced as flat, depthless pastiche, where the reference point is not the past itself, but other images, other texts. The past as referent is effaced, and all that remains is a self-referential intertextuality (Jameson, 60ff). Yet, at the same time, the sense of pastness and historicity are important, for as Andreas Huyssen suggests, the search for tradition is a vital feature of the contemporary response to the felt failure of modernism.

The heritage films, too, work as pastiches, each period of the national past reduced through a process of reiteration to an effortlessly reproducible, and attractively consumable, connotative style. The films turn away from modernity toward a traditional conservative pastoral Englishness; they turn away, too, from the high-tech aesthetics of mainstream popular cinema, however nostalgic and pastiche-like it may also be. Where Hollywood in recent years has specialized in the production of futuristic epics, the heritage film prefers the intimacy of the period piece, although their visual splendor lends them an extravagant, epic scale. The postmodernism of these films is actually an antimodernism that clothes itself in all the trappings of classical art — but the more culturally respectable classicisms of literature, painting, music, and so on, not the classicism of Hollywood (indeed, the image of Americanness against which Britishness/Englishness is contrasted in *Chariots of Fire* is explicitly technological and machinelike).

The image of the past in the heritage films has become so naturalized that, paradoxically, it stands removed from history: the evocation of pastness is accomplished by a look, a style, the loving recreation of period details — not by any critical historical perspective. The self-conscious visual perfectionism of these films and their fetishization of period details create a fascinating but self-enclosed world. They render history as spectacle, as *separate* from the viewer in the present, as something over and done with, complete, achieved. Hence the sense of timelessness rather than historicity in relation to a national past which is "purged of political tension" and so available for appreciation as visual display (Wright, 69). As Cairns Craig suggests, this is "film as conspicuous consumption" (10) — or rather, because it is only images being consumed, it is a *fantasy* of conspicuous consumption, a fantasy of Englishness, a fantasy of the national past.

Yet at the same time, the version of the national past offered is above all a modern past, an imaginary object invented from the point of view of a present that is too distasteful to be confronted head-on. Thus Raphael Samuel shows how Christine Edzard's *Little Dorrit* produces a Dickens for the 1980s, despite, or perhaps precisely because of, the care taken to reproduce period details (Samuels 1989c). Samuel contrasts the 1980s Dickens, which seeks to conserve the heritage of Victorian values, with the grotesque realism, the "dark Dickens" of the 1940s, when the Victorian period was being re-viewed as problematic and repressive. Thus Edzard's film cleans up the city's slums and workshops, its inhabitants and their authentically period costumes: "The artefacts so lovingly assembled turn the London of [Edzard's] film from a prison-house — Dickens' guiding metaphor — into a showcase of period delights" (Samuel 1989c, 51). The film effaces the gothic aspects of the novel in favor of a conservationist urban pastoral in which "London is . . . a playground, and poverty — provided it is safely period — picturesque" (Samuel, 1989b, 284).

A Dickens for the 1980s: the picturesque poverty of *Little Dorrit* (1987).

In a move typical of the heritage industry (Wright), these key films in the *national* cinema of the 1980s are fascinated by the private property, the culture and values of a *particular* class. By reproducing these trappings outside of a materialist historical context, they transform the heritage of the upper classes into the national heritage: private interest becomes naturalized as public interest. Except, of course, these are still films for a relatively privileged audience, and the heritage is still refined and exclusive, rather than properly public in the sense of massively popular. The national past and national identity emerge in these films not only as aristocratic, but also as male-centered, while the nation itself is reduced to the soft pastoral landscape of southern England untainted by the modernity of urbanization or industrialization (or, in the case of *Little Dorrit*, to a tasteful urban pastoral). In each instance, the *quality* of the films lends the representation of the past a certain cultural validity and respectability.

These films share a particularly strong group style, not least because of the degree to which they work as pastiches. The central intertextual focus of the cycle, and of the broader historical genre that informs these films (see Higson, chap. 4), is undoubtedly the adaptation of literary and theatrical properties already recognized as classics within the accepted canon of plays and novels: for example, Dickens's *Little Dorrit*, E. M. Forster's *A Passage to India*, *A Room with a View*, and *Maurice*, and Evelyn Waugh's *A Handful of Dust*; but also *Another Country*, adapted from the play by Julian Mitchell, and Kenneth Branagh's adaptation of Shakespeare's *Henry V*. In each case, the "original" text is as much on display as the past it seeks to reproduce. The literary source material, of course, functions as an important selling point, playing on the familiarity and prestige of the particular novel or play, but also invoking the pleasures of other such quality literary adaptations and the status of a national intellectual tradition. The genre can also invent new texts for the canon by treating otherwise marginal texts or properties to the same modes of representation and marketing.

The genre involves much more than simply the adaptation of literary or dramatic texts and plunders the national heritage in other ways, too. Almost all of these films contain a recurrent image of an imposing country house seen in extreme long shot and set in a picturesque, verdant landscape. This image encapsulates much that is typical of the films as a whole, and indicates that the notion of heritage property also needs to be extended to cover the types of ancient architectural and landscape properties conserved by the National Trust and English Heritage, and the costumes, furnishings, objets d'art, and aristocratic character-types that traditionally fill those properties. These properties (the term, with its theatrical connotations, seems more than appropriate) constitute the iconography of the genre. In what is both a bid for historical realism (and visual pleasure) and a function of the nostalgic mode (seeking an imaginary historical plenitude), the past is delivered as a museum of sounds and images, an iconographic display. This iconography brings with it a particular moral formation and set of values, which the films effortlessly dramatize at "significant" historical moments.

The intertextuality of the heritage cycle is also particularly noticeable in the casting of the films. The same actors play similar roles and class types in several different films, bringing a powerful sense of all the other heritage films, costume dramas, and literary adaptations to each new film. In fact, these films draw on two groups of actors: on the one hand, established actors who specialize in character parts (Denholm Elliot [*A Room with a View, Maurice*], Judi Dench [*A Room with a View, A Handful of Dust*], Maggie Smith [*A Room with a View*], Simon Callow [*A Room with a View, Maurice*]) and who bring with them all the qualities and connotations of the British theater tradition; on the other hand, various younger actors virtually groomed for their parts in the heritage films (Helena Bonham Carter [*A Room with a View, Maurice, Where Angels Fear to Tread*], Nigel Havers [*Chariots of Fire, A Passage to India*], Rupert Graves [*A Room with a View, Maurice, A Handful of Dust, Where Angels Fear to Tread*], James Wilby [*Maurice, A Handful of Dust*], Hugh Grant [*Maurice*]).

The iconography of heritage Englishness: white flannels, summer hats, Edwardian fashion (watching cricket in *Maurice* [1987]).

Set against the intertextual, generic qualities of these films are the discourses of authorship and authenticity, which stress originality and uniqueness rather than similarity and repetition. These discourses work in various ways: the literary adaptations strive to reproduce the tone that distinguishes the book, to respect the "original" text and the "original" authorship. The period films, which, of course, include the literary adaptations, seek to reproduce the surface qualities that define the pastness of the particular period. Yet, at the same time, there is a foregrounding of filmic authorship, too, the attempt to make a unique and original film. Each strategy is a means of stressing authorship, originality, authenticity—but the authenticities are not all of the same category, each potentially pulling in a different direction, while the generic qualities *deny* the sense of originality altogether. Paradoxically, the preoccupation with authorship, the display of good taste and a self-consciously aesthetic sensibility, are themselves generic qualities that bind the films together. Literary authorship, the process of writing itself, is foregrounded in the recurrent narrative episode of a character writing or reading a letter or a book, either aloud or in voice-over, thus celebrating the purity of the word. Literary adaptations also, of course, foreground the authenticity of the "original" by their effort to reproduce dialogue from the novel for characters in the film, or to transpose the narrative voice of the novel to the

speech of those characters. There is also a studied reference to and reproduction of other art objects and art forms — classical paintings, statues, architecture, and music all add weight to the tasteful production values of these
films.

Narratively, the films move slowly and episodically rather than in a tightly
causal manner; they demonstrate a greater concern for character, place, atmosphere, and milieu than for dramatic, goal-directed action. There is also a
preference for long takes and deep focus, and for long and medium shots,
rather than for close-ups and rapid cutting. The camera is characteristically
fluid, but camera movement is dictated less by a desire to follow the movement of characters than by a desire to offer the spectator a more aesthetic
angle on the period setting and the objects that fill it. Self-conscious crane
shots and high-angle shots divorced from character point of view, for instance, are used to display ostentatiously the seductive mise-en-scène of the
films. This is particularly clear in the two Merchant-Ivory films. In *A Room
with a View*, there is a typical interior shot of Lucy playing the piano at the
Pensione Bertolini: Lucy, the ostensible focus of *narrative* interest, sits in
the background, while artifacts and furnishings fill and frame the foreground;
the camera gracefully, but without narrative motivation, tracks slowly around
one splendid item of furniture to reveal it in all its glory. In the same film, the
shots of Florence are always offered direct to the spectator, unmediated by
any shots of characters within the diegesis looking at the view. Such shots, in
fact, *follow* the views, rather than preceding and thus motivating them. Insert shots of Cambridge function similarly in *Maurice*, having only a minimal
function as establishing shots. In this way, the heritage culture becomes the
object of a public gaze, while the private gaze of the dramatis personae is
reserved for romance: they almost never admire the quality of their surroundings. Heritage culture appears petrified, frozen in moments that virtually fall out of the narrative, existing only as adornments for the staging of a
love story. Thus, historical narrative is transformed into spectacle; heritage
becomes excess, not functional, not something to be used, but something to
be admired.

All in all, the camera style is pictorialist, with all the connotations the
term brings of art photography, aesthetic refinement, and set-piece images
(Higson, 93ff). Though narrative meaning and narrational clarity are rarely
sacrificed, these shots, angles, and camera movements frequently exceed
narrative motivation. The effect is the creation of heritage space, rather than
narrative space: that is, a space for the display of heritage properties rather
than for the enactment of dramas. In many respects, therefore, this is not a
narrative cinema, a cinema of story-telling, but something more akin to that

mode of early filmmaking that Tom Gunning calls the cinema of attractions. In this case, the heritage films display their self-conscious artistry, their landscapes, their properties, their actors and their performance qualities, their clothes, and their often archaic dialogue. The gaze, therefore, is organized around props and settings—the look of the observer at the tableau image—as much as it is around character point of view.

The use of flamboyantly designed intertitles in *A Room with a View*, while emphasizing the episodic nature of the narrative, suggests another affinity with very early cinema. It redundantly indicates narrative action before it takes place, and in so doing, interrupts the actual telling of the tale and highlights the artifice of the diegesis. Indeed, such films often seem more concerned to *show* the "original," whether a novel or a period, a building or a landscape, than to tell an internally coherent tale. As Samuel notes of *Little Dorrit*, "the film resembles nothing so much as a series of cameos in which the chapters of the book are replayed as scenes" (Samuel 1989b, 281).

The emphasis on spectacle rather than narrative draws attention to the surface of things, producing a typically postmodern loss of emotional affect: emotional engagement in a drama is sacrificed for loving recreations of the past, or rather, beautifully conserved and respectfully observed spectacles of pastness. This is particularly odd in dramas that are in almost every case organized around a romance, an imagined romance, or a romantic triangle, and that include a fair share of narrative coincidence, fateful intervention, and obstacles thrown in the path of love. But, if this is the stuff of melodrama, in this case emotions are underplayed, while sensationalism and contrivance are tastefully obscured. The excitements of the love story lie submerged by the trappings of the period piece.

A more generous reading of these films might suggest that, in the displaced form of the costume drama, the heritage film creates an important space for playing out contemporary anxieties and fantasies of national identity, sexuality, class, and power. Temporal displacement and cultural respectability license the exploration of taboo subjects such as the homoerotic passions of *Another Country* and *Maurice*. Such films may then produce a pointed critique of the limits of the present social and moral formation. After all, the nostalgic perspective always involves a dialogue between the imagined past and a vision of the present; it never simply talks about the past. Like Forster's novels, several of the films dramatize a vision of liberal-humanist values in a materialistic world, and Alison Light argues that "the return to Edwardian England in the '80s [is] as much a rejection of Thatcherism and its ethics as a crude reflection of it." She suggests that "what the films have picked up on is the romantic longing within liberalism for making unions despite differences of nationality, sexuality, social class" (Light, 63). Thus, if the films seem at first to attempt to escape from the cultural heterogeneity of contemporary Britain by celebrating a class apparently secure in its self-knowledge and self-sufficiency, it is clear that they also dramatize the effort of different social identities to connect with one another across cultural and social boundaries, so reinvoking the liberal consensus. Thus, we have the gay love affairs of *Maurice* and *Another Country*, the trans-class relationships of *Maurice* and *A Room with a View*, and the interethnic friendships of *Chariots of Fire* and *A Passage to India*.

Peter Widdowson argues that Forster sought to affirm his liberal vision through art, and one might suggest that the tasteful artistry of the heritage films enables them to affirm such a vision. But there are problems with applying this argument to the films. In their concern for authenticity and fidelity in the reproduction of pastness and the "original" text, they fetishize artistry, as well as the past itself—or at least its filmic image. The strength of the pastiche in effect imprisons the qualities of the past, holding them in place as something to be gazed at from a reverential distance, and refusing the possibility of a dialogue or confrontation with the present. Even those films that develop an ironic *narrative* of the past end up celebrating and legitimating the *spectacle* of one class and one cultural tradition and identity at the expense of others through the discourse of authenticity, and the obsession with the visual splendors of period detail. Mise-en-scène and drama thus work against each other in their construction of the national past: images of permanence, tradition, grandeur, and continuity counteract the narratives of impermanence and cultural fluidity, and the ironies of the Forsterian voice. Undoubtedly, Forster's novels are also overly concerned with Englishness, but rarely is that identity framed as permanent and unchanging. On the contrary, Forster argues for a liberal-humanist refashioning of Englishness, rather than a simple assumption of an already formed national identity. Indeed, he savagely derides as sham the suburban middle-class Englishness of the Halls in *Maurice*, yet their household in the film is rendered desirable in its accumulation of the antique collector's signs of Edwardian period style: "the society which Forster is criticising becomes almost involuntarily an object of veneration" (Hollinghurst, 1225).

Almost all of the novels and other stories that provide the sources for the heritage films of the 1980s have some edge to them of satire or ironic social critique, and the films in various ways try to reproduce this sensibility. But it seems clear that it is the pictorial qualities of the exotic period settings that have attracted the filmmakers as much as the moral critique. As a consequence, that which is in the source narratives abhorrent or problematic be-

comes prettified, elegant, and seductive. For instance, while the owners of
Hetton Hall in *A Handful of Dust* constantly worry about the unfashionable
qualities of their vast gothic pile, and the money it takes to maintain it, in the
film the hall is positively alluring and resplendent. As one reviewer comments, "The Duke of Norfolk's country seat, Carlton Towers [which stood in
for Hetton Hall] . . . is the star of stars" (Walker, 32). The pleasures of pic-
torialism thus block the radical intentions of the narrative.

The conservationist desire for period authenticity rarely equates with the
desire for faithful adaptations of the source text in the literary adaptations.
Indeed, in the adaptations of the Forster and Waugh novels, contemporary
social satires and comedies of manners are transformed into period pieces.
Similarly, Samuel argues that, in the case of *Little Dorrit*, "the film's preoccupation with period effects is singularly at variance with Dickens himself,
who was notoriously cavalier in his treatment of history and contemptuous of
notions of heritage" (Samuel 1989b, 283). Samuel goes on to claim that
Dickens was not a period novelist, but drew ideas, images, and characterizations from different historical periods, self-consciously fabricating the fiction and creating "a fantasy of Victorian England" (283). While Forster is indeed a writer "who manifests and is attentive to the social and historical
context out of which he derives" (Bradbury, 3), he is not a novelist of place,
but rather of ideas and manners. Place, setting, and mise-en-scène in Forster are dealt with in very general terms, rather than observed with the obsessively detailed eye of the art directors of the films adapted from his novels. The novels explore what lies beneath the surface of things, satirizing the
pretentious and the superficial, and especially those who are overly concerned with keeping up appearances rather than acting according to the passions of the heart. The films, however, construct such a delightfully glossy
visual surface that the ironic perspective and the narrative of social criticism
diminish in their appeal for the spectator.

A Room with a View, for instance, can be read as a satire on the repres-
sions of the middle classes and a reaffirmation of generative, life-giving
forces. As a critique of Victorian values, it may well be nostalgic for the emotional simplicity and libidinal spontaneity of the fairy-tale romance. But in the
film, Maggie Smith plays the repressive life-denying figure of Catherine Bartlett so powerfully, so charismatically, that it becomes once more attractive.
The film delights in her performance of Victorian primness, as it delights in
the equally excessive performances of Simon Callow and Daniel Day Lewis.
Similarly in *Maurice*, Clive Durham (Hugh Grant) becomes a far more attractive and fascinating character than Maurice (James Wilby) himself, partly
because of Grant's boyish good looks and sublimely camp performance full of

The attractions of performance, the delights of high camp: Daniel Day Lewis as Cecil Vyse in *A Room with a View* (1986).

exaggerated gestures and mannerisms. Yet it is Maurice's sensibility that the narrative requires us to share; indeed, the film purports to criticize all that Clive eventually represents. Clive is, in the final analysis, horrified by Maurice's sexuality; he cannot confront it, preferring instead, like Catherine Bartlett, to save face, to keep up a respectable appearance, to look the part.

Forster's satirical impulse is also undercut in *A Room with a View*. On one level, it is there in George's (Julian Sands) description of Cecil (Daniel Day Lewis) to Lucy (Helena Bonham Carter): "[Cecil] wants you for a possession, something to look at, like a painting or an ivory box, something to own and display. He doesn't want you to be real and to think and live." But in the end, the film adopts Cecil's pretensions, displaying its possessions and making every effort to fashion each image "like a painting." The film attempts to criticize people who have a fear of being seen doing the wrong thing, encapsulated in Cecil's anxious, furtive looks about him before he kisses Lucy, his fiancée, for the first time; the other side of this fear is a love of being seen and admired by the right kind of people, as when Cecil looks around the gathered society at his mother's house for the nods of appreciation at *his* good taste as Lucy plays the piano. Yet the film itself circulates in society in the same way, desperately wanting to be viewed by the right kinds of audiences, ceaselessly displaying its good taste in just as knowing a way as Cecil.

But if satire or moral critique requires an ironic distance from the characters and their settings, surely this is achieved in the refusal of psychological depth and emotional engagement? Surely such shallow characterizations as the emotionally empty and materialistic protagonists of *A Handful of Dust*, and their desire to keep up appearances, can be read as representations of ironically superficial characters? Indeed they can, except that all these figures, and the space they inhabit, are so lovingly, beautifully, and seductively laid out that a desire for the other, for the lost perfection of the spectacle, narrows any ironic distance that may have been intended. Period authenticity and heritage conservationism represent precisely the desire for perfection, for the past as unimpaired paradigm, for a packaging of the past that is designed to please, not disturb. Satire, however, requires the contrary, the tainting of the paradigm and the disturbance of perfection.

Forster's novels were themselves, of course, nostalgic narratives, but the desire for period authenticity tends to refashion the nature of the nostalgia. Forster yearned for a mid-Victorian golden age rather than for the Edwardian present. His novels respond to a felt crisis in liberal-humanist values and play out a pastoral concern for a passing rural England, one encroached on by industrialization, suburbia, and London society. They demonstrate "a profound, almost mystical, response to the English countryside and its living embodiment of the past [but] perceive it to be in the process of radical and destructive change" (Widdowson, 58). At the end of *Maurice*, as he and Alec go off into the greenwood, Maurice realizes that "they must live outside class. . . . But England belonged to them. That, besides companionship, was their reward. Her air and sky were theirs, not the timorous millions who own stuffy little boxes, but never their own souls" (Forster, 208-9). England, in other words, is a pastoral scene without the trappings of class celebrated in the films, but the scene is already impaired by the spread of suburbia. The Forster films, on the other hand, look back nostalgically to an *Edwardian* golden age. The greenwood of Merchant-Ivory's *Maurice* and the ruralism of their *Room with a View*, the pastoral community of Summer Street, and the sincerity, companionship, and moral support of the bourgeois family are offered as part and parcel of the period they depict; they have not yet become the lost objects of nostalgic desire. The pastoral of the films therefore invents a new golden age, one that the novels depict as already tainted and unstable.

The narratives of *Chariots of Fire* and *Another Country* try to avoid this problem through their flashback structures, suggesting that the nostalgia of the representation is actually that of the ostensible narrator: Aubrey Montagu (Nicholas Farrell) in *Chariots* and Guy Bennett (Rupert Everett) in *Another Country*. The latter, closeted in a dingy Moscow flat surrounded by the trappings of Englishness (the Harrods mug, the cricket ball, the old school photographs), looks back on his last years at a highly privileged English public school during the 1930s. Here, as in *Maurice*, the nostalgic image of a perfect national past is deliberately set up, only to be destroyed ("flawlessly staged then condemned" [Finch and Kwietniowski, 77]) by uncovering its shortcomings, especially its systematic exploitation and abuse of gay men. But at the same time, there is a lingering desire to celebrate that past in the loving recreation of the period piece. The film tries to contain this residual nostalgia by projecting the tale as Bennett's memory. But the vision of the past rapidly becomes the film's central diegesis, the range and scope of camera shots used suggesting that it is our vision rather than the partial vision of a character. Even before the possibility of a flashback is established, the title sequence creates a nostalgic perspective by cutting between a delightful English pastoral scene and the gray concrete of Bennett's Moscow apartment block. The tastefully melancholic music and the image of passing through a dark tunnel before being able to appreciate the full glory of the pastoral scene further underlines the sense of recalling a cherished but lost memory.

Other heritage films also create the nostalgic experience. Thus the imperialist fantasies of national identity found in the cycle of films and TV programs about the Raj, such as *A Passage to India* and "Jewel in the Crown," and the more recent films looking at the last days of the British Empire in Africa, such as *White Mischief* (1987), can be seen as conservative responses to a collective, postimperialist anxiety. Retreating from the social, political, and economic crises of the present, they strive to recapture an image of national identity as pure, untainted, complete, and in place. Yet like so many nostalgic narratives, they return to a moment of stability and tranquility in the social order as they themselves chart the process of decay, the fall from this utopian national ideal: in most cases, they chronicle the corrupt and decadent last days of imperialist power, a period when that power was already coming under attack, the pure identity becoming tainted, and the culture in decline. As a whole, the heritage films deal with the last of England: not just the end of Empire, but the betrayal of the nation in *Another Country*; the corrupt decadence and moral decay of the upper classes in *Another Country* and *A Handful of Dust*; the death of liberal England; the efforts of the aristocracy to make way for new blood in *Chariots of Fire* (see Johnston). The idea of heritage implies a sense of inheritance, but it is precisely that which is on the wane in these films: there can be no issue from the sexless and/or homosexual relationships of *Maurice* and *Another Country*; the son is killed in *A Handful of Dust*; Brideshead is destroyed; and in almost every case, there is a marked absence of strong father figures. Nostalgia is then both a narrative of loss, charting an imaginary historical trajectory from stability to instability, and at the same time a narrative of recovery, projecting the subject back into a comfortably closed past.

The nostalgic narrative of *Another Country* illustrates just this complexity. At the end of the film, the journalist interviewing Bennett asks if he misses anything. Bennett hesitates; choral music fades in, and he replies, "I miss the cricket!" End of film. The choral music here conjures up memories of the first scene of the flashback to the 1930s, a memorial service in the school quadrangle and the site of Bennett's first overdetermined gaze at his loved one, Harcourt (Cary Elwes), another boy at the school. Cricket also conjures up a specific memory, again of a particularly passionate exchange of looks between Bennett and Harcourt on the cricket field. If only those perfect scenes could have lasted forever, the system in place, homosexual desire able to live a secure, passionate, if closeted life! If only the past in all its perfection could have remained in place, unimpaired. But the film goes on to show that this image of perfection is indeed already impaired, the product of a militarily authoritarian system that is openly corrupt and exploitative.

In these films, however, the sense of impending narrative-historical loss is always offset by the experience of spectacular visual pleasure. Their reconstructions of the national past feast on the spectacle of authentic objects, clothing, and other signs of an apparently secure heritage, contrasted with the often fearful exoticism of other cultures. Thus even a film like *A Passage to India*, which purports to criticize British imperialism, shows the cinematic spectacle of the British in power. The theatricality of the Raj, and the epic sweep of the camera over an equally epic landscape and social class is utterly seductive, destroying all sense of critical distance and restoring the pomp of Englishness felt to be lacking in the present. Similarly, *Another Country*'s critique of the details of class power, and the whole system of privilege, inheritance, and tradition, is lost in the welter of period detail. As Craig puts it, "The death of inheritance . . . is counteracted by the seeming permanence of the architecture, landscape, and possessions that fill the screen" (Craig, 11). In *Maurice*, Forster describes Clive Durham's country house as on the verge of decay, rather than magnificent ("it struck [Maurice] once more how derelict it was, how unfit to set standards or control the future" [Forster, 209]). In the film, the outhouses are decrepit, ladders are everywhere because the house is being repaired, and the sitting-room ceiling is leaking ("Why is my house falling down?", asks Clive), but the crumbling inheritance

The mise-en-scène of power, the perfection of posture: schoolboy style in *Another Country*.

is never foregrounded as much as the remaining magnificence of the house: the splendor of the society in place always undercuts images of the last of England. Visual effect, the complete spectacle of the past, becomes an autonomous attraction in itself, once more displacing any narrational qualities the mise-en-scène may have.

"The national past," Patrick Wright argues, "is capable of finding splendour in old styles of political domination and of making an alluring romance out of atrocious colonial exploitation" (254). The comment seems particularly appropriate for the heritage genre, one that obsessively constructs (often upper-class) romances around authentic period details. Class, gender, and race relations, and the values of the ruling elites, are in effect re-presented as just so much mise-en-scène, elegantly displayed in splendid costumes, language, gestures, and all the props (the properties) of the everyday life of one or another class. The history of exploitation is effaced by spectacular presentation. The past becomes once more unproblematic, a haven from the difficulties of the present.

The mise-en-scène of power, the theatricality of the Raj, the spectacle of privilege: these films construct a fantasy of extravagance, decadence, promiscuity, and passion (frequently, of course, a homoerotic passion: there is a continual insistence on the pleasures of the male body). If such a fantasy is in some ways a critique of the more mundane and repressive present, that cri-

The knowing theatrical gaze: Guy Bennett (Rupert Everett) eyes his loved one in *Another Country*.

tique is always contained by being accessible only through a facade of class privilege firmly set in the past. But that facade, constructed in the self-conscious artistry of these films, is itself extravagant. The discourse of authenticity is treated so seriously, and taken to such lengths, that it becomes almost self-parodic: the meticulous period piece as knowing artifice and extravagant frivolity. From this point of view, the films scale the heights of camp, which Susan Sontag defines as "the theatricalisation of experience" (114). In a passage that seems designed to comment on the heritage cycle, she suggests that "camp art is often decorative art, emphasising texture, sensuous surface, and style at the expense of content" (107). Such art requires a peculiarly intense but superficial gaze from its admirers. In *Another Country*, for instance, Bennett's gaze at his loved one is so intense and self-conscious that it becomes almost a parody of desire. The look is always knowing; there is never any doubt that both the subject and the object are aware of the look, as too are the spectators of the film. What is remarkable is the theatricalization of the gaze, its exaggerated, camp quality. It is this same knowing theatrical gaze for which the heritage films of the 1980s display their wares.

One of the key features of the Thatcher years was the denationalization of the economy, a process that was justified in terms of the concepts of enter- *Social* prise and competition. Inevitably, there was a certain cultural denationaliza- *national* tion, as well. The privatizing ethics of popular capitalism shifted the empha- *id.* sis from community values and notions of consensus and collective identity to the values of individual enterprise and the marketplace. The production of new market-led identities thus challenged long-standing class-bound and deferential notions of national identity. As Corner and Harvey suggest, the self-made individuals of the enterprise culture "refuse the certainties of the old patrician aristocratic order, they overturn the stately world in which everyone knows their place and they challenge, in the process, the rules of *noblesse oblige*" (Corner and Harvey, 1991b, 8).

These challenges to the traditional settlement of national identity are to some extent compensated for in the fantasy worlds of the heritage films. They thus provide a platform from which either a liberal or a more traditionally conservative critique of the Thatcherite project could be mounted. This raises the important question of how well these films accord with the official management of heritage in the 1980s. Margaret Thatcher herself both called for a return to "Victorian values," and, during the Falklands/Malvinas conflagration, invoked the spirit of Churchill and the Second World War. It is notable, however, that very few of the heritage films of the 1980s have actually been located in the Victorian period (*Little Dorrit* is the obvious exception), and most are set before the outbreak of the Second World War. Significantly, none of these films tell stories of nineteenth-century entrepreneurs on the make, accumulating vast private fortunes at the expense of public welfare — even though it is surely Victorian capitalism and the dramatic industrial transformations of that period that provide the ideal role model for Thatcherism. Similarly, while these films tentatively narrate the stories of enterprising and innovatory individuals who reject convention — after all, these are virtually requisites of a classical narrative structure — narrative development is in the end downplayed. Nor is enterprise generally couched in overtly competitive and materialistic terms, except perhaps in the case of *Chariots of Fire*, with its aggressive plea for meritocratic justice; but even here, the expected climax of individual competition is set to one side in favor of a jingoistic national struggle at the Olympic Games. Other films, especially the Forster adaptations, are in various ways critical of the sort of materialistic society that Thatcherism promoted — yet, at the same time, these films visually celebrate the possessions of the upper classes.

Corner and Harvey suggest that Thatcherism "has at once challenged, popularised and commodified the values of a more ancient, patrician and rural conservatism" (Corner and Harvey 1991b, 14); this is a more than apt

128   ANDREW HIGSON

description of the function of the heritage films of the 1980s. They do criticize the values of this upper-class Englishness in various ways, as we have seen; but they do also popularize this social formation as one whose possessions are worth acquiring, or at least admiring. They also popularize this social formation as one in which the contemporary spectator might find refuge from the radical and often problematic transformations of the 1980s. Yet the liberal-humanist visions of social union in so many of these films implicitly criticize rather than celebrate the values of the marketplace, suggesting a flight from Thatcherism rather than concord with its Victorian antecedents or its contemporary effects. The ambivalence of these films to both the past and to the Thatcherite present is, as we have seen, the ambivalence of nostalgia. On the one hand, there is the reassurance of apparent continuity with the past; on the other hand, the societies depicted are often already in decline, even if visually the suggestion is otherwise.

In closing, it is worth noting another group of contemporary British costume dramas dealing with the more recent past, including such films as *Dance with a Stranger* (1985), *Wish You Were Here* (1987), *Hope and Glory* (1988), *Distant Voices, Still Lives* (1988), and *Scandal* (1989). These films concentrate on the everyday lives and memories of "ordinary people," and in many cases push female characters to the fore, to some extent democratizing the genre and offering a rather different range of narrative pleasures and identifications. The converse of this, however, is that their representation of the past remains in a conservationist mode such that even the mise-en-scène of ordinariness delights the eye, and invites the collector's curiosity.

This chapter could not have been written without the many discussions I have had about these films over the last few years with Matthew Brown and other undergraduate and postgraduate students and colleagues at the University of East Anglia. I would also like to acknowledge my particular indebtedness to Patrick Wright's *On Living in an Old Country*.

Works Cited

Bradbury, Malcolm. 1966. "Introduction." In *Forster: A Collection of Essays*, edited by Malcolm Bradbury, 1-14. Englewood Cliffs, N.J.: Prentice-Hall.
Corner, John, and Sylvia Harvey, eds. 1991a. *Enterprise and Heritage: Crosscurrents of National Culture*. London: Routledge.
_____. 1991b. "Introduction: Great Britain Limited." In *Enterprise and Heritage*, edited by Corner and Harvey, 1-20.
_____. 1991c. "Mediating Tradition and Modernity: The Heritage/Enterprise Couplet." In *Enterprise and Heritage*, edited by Corner and Harvey, 45-75.
Craig, Cairns. 1991. "Rooms without a View." *Sight and Sound*, June, 10-13.

Elsaesser, Thomas. 1989. *New German Cinema: A History*. London: British Film Institute/ Macmillan.

Finch, Mark, and Richard Kwietniowski. 1988. "Melodrama and *Maurice*: Homo Is Where the Het Is." *Screen* 29 (3): 72-80.

Forster, E. M. [1908] 1972. *Maurice*. London: Penguin.

Gunning, Tom. 1990. "The Cinema of Attractions: Early Film, Its Spectator and the Avant-garde." In *Early Cinema: Space, Frame, Narrative*, edited by Thomas Elsaesser with Adam Barker, 56-62. London: British Film Institute.

Hewison, Robert. 1987. *The Heritage Industry*. London: Methuen.

Higson, Andrew. 1990. "Constructing a National Cinema in Britain." Ph.D. diss., University of Kent at Canterbury.

Hollinghurst, Alan. 1987. "Suppressive Nostalgia." *Times Literary Supplement*, Nov. 6, 1225.

Huyssen, Andreas. 1981. "The Search for Tradition: Avant-garde and Post-modernism in the 1970s." *New German Critique* 22: 23-40.

Jameson, Fredric. 1984. "Post-modernism, or the Cultural Logic of Late Capitalism." *New Left Review* 146: 53-92.

Johnston, Sheila. 1985. "Charioteers and Ploughmen." In *British Cinema Now*, edited by Martyn Auty and Nick Roddick, 99-110. London: British Film Institute.

Kerr, Paul. 1982. "Classic Serials — To Be Continued." *Screen* 23 (1): 6-19.

Light, Alison. 1991. "Englishness." *Sight and Sound*, July, 63.

Samuel, Raphael. 1989. "Preface." In *Patriotism: The Making and Un-Making of British National Identity*. Vol. 1, *History and Politics*, edited by Raphael Samuel, x-xvii. London: Routledge.

———. 1989b. "Docklands Dickens." In *Patriotism: The Making and Un-Making of British National Identity*. Vol. 3, *National Fictions*, edited by Raphael Samuel, 275-85. London: Routledge.

———. 1989c. "Dickens on Stage and Screen." *History Today*, Dec., 44-51.

Sontag, Susan. [1964] 1983. "On Camp." In *A Susan Sontag Reader*, 105-19. London: Penguin.

Urry, John. 1990. *The Tourist Gaze*. London: Sage.

Walker, Alexander. 1988. "*A Handful of Dust*." *Evening Standard*, June 9, 32.

Widdowson, Peter. 1977. *E. M.Forster's "Howard's End": Fiction as History*. London: Sussex University Press/Chatto and Windus.

Wollen, Tana. 1991. "Nostalgic Screen Fictions." In *Enterprise and Heritage*, edited by Corner and Harvey, 178-93.

Wright, Patrick. 1985. *On Living in an Old Country: The National Past in Contemporary Britain*. London: Verso.

Free from the Apron Strings: Representations of Mothers in the Maternal British State

Mary Desjardins

Hope and Glory (1987) and *The Krays* (1990) are two internationally successful British films made in the latter part of Margaret Thatcher's political
rule that offer images of mothers compatible with a number of the possible
representations of the "maternal" constructed in psychoanalytic discourse
and its appropriation by feminist discourses. *Hope and Glory*, for instance,
features the oedipal mother, as its young male protagonist struggles to find
adult role models in an increasingly feminized British home front during
World War II. The mother in *The Krays* suggests one version of the phallic
woman psychoanalysis has described as the pre-oedipal mother holding life
and death powers over the defenseless infant. Along with her own mother
and sisters, Violet Kray usurps the place of the patriarch, infantilizes her
sons, and willfully ignores their brutalization of other men. Because she de-
spises how men have oppressed women, she seeks to banish all rivals to her
son's power and to the power *she* holds over her sons.

This essay explores these representations of the maternal, but one
should not apply psychoanalytic concepts to these films in an ahistorical context. In fact, what interests me about these two films is how their positioning
of mothers as central forces in the narratives seems significant in the historical context of 1980s Great Britain, a period in which both prime minister and
monarch are women and mothers. Although I will ultimately offer some suggestions in regards to that significance, the questions here have more to do
with how the *discursive field* of Thatcherite Britain has negotiated an understanding of the maternal in relation to the state. Two questions seem central
to this understanding: (1) What does it mean to represent the maternal in
films in a nation whose political agenda is to free the people from what

Thatcher identified as "the apron-strings of the governess state" (quoted in O'Shea, 22), in other words, to free them from a state rhetorically figured as an infantilizing maternal? (2) How does a government in the process of constructing a contemporary popular memory that will reassert an older, glorious national identity mobilize representations of the maternal to that end?

Both questions concern political and representational strategies and/or values with which the Thatcherite government became notoriously associated. The right-wing conservative government under Thatcher's rule as prime minister from 1979 to 1990 was characterized by a dismantling of many of the institutions and symbolic supports of the previous coalition and Labour governments. This entailed a rejection of "big government" — pejoratively termed by many as the welfare state and by Thatcher as the governess or nanny state — through an increased privatization of state-owned companies and housing, a weakening of trade unions, a lifting of controls on foreign exchanges, and a levying of a poll tax that lessened taxes for the wealthy and increased the tax burden for the working and middle classes. In a provocative essay on Thatcher politics and the film *The Ploughman's Lunch*, Tony Williams argues that the implications of such a rejection was a movement of "national consciousness toward social Darwinist 'Victorian values' " (Williams, 11).

In privileging government policies that on the social level resembled Darwin's "scientific" precept of evolution as "survival of the fittest," Thatcher's regime eliminated another set of Victorian values: "the cult of True Womanhood," which heroicized traditional maternal capacities because they were supposedly morally superior to those which enabled men to compete in an exploitative marketplace. In other words, in the Thatcher years, competition among free enterprisers replaced a maternal state seen as infantilizing and therefore incapacitating its citizens. The government's contribution in constructing a contemporary popular memory that reinstates an earlier, powerful national identity based on "pluck" (self-initiative) and imperial values is crucial to the successful "maturation" of British citizens. Restoration of an earlier national identity similar to that held by Britain during and right after World War II, for example, means a national identity forged *before* the women's movement, when women were most manipulated as producers and reproducers by a series of nationalistic pronatalism propaganda.

This essay focuses on *Hope and Glory* and *The Krays*, not only because the films pay most attention to the historical specificity of the maternal, but also because they suggest World War II as a crucial moment or reference point for real, social women as well as a contemporary popular memory for Britain. Of course, for many feminist historians and scholars of film noir and the woman's film, World War II also represents a privileged historical moment. At that time, twentieth-century women entered a public consciousness constructed in part by powerful mass media institutions in the form of radio and the cinema. As the films under discussion suggest, women were also able to most figure in the private unconscious during this period. In both *Hope and Glory* and *The Krays*, mothers on the home front substitute for absent or weak patriarchs, increasing the psychic hold between mother and child. The films' perspectives on the value of such a substitution differ, as do the ways they participate in the construction of a contemporary popular memory of World War II. *Hope and Glory*'s production of memory of the war presents a unified ground for past and present, whereas *The Krays*'s memory of that period consists of a contradiction between the dominant contemporary meanings of the war and the particular disruptive memories that cannot find their place in the public field.

My conceptualization of "popular memory" is derived from a series of written exchanges in the 1970s on the British Telefilm *Days of Hope* (McArthur, 1975/76; MacCabe 1975, 1977; Tribe) from work done by the Popular Memory Group associated with the Center for Contemporary Studies in Great Britain, and from the British Film Institute's 1983 Summer School on "National Fictions: Struggles over the Meaning of World War II." Work of the latter two groups was given impetus by the Falklands war of 1982, when, as Colin McArthur argues, "the left and liberal opinion generally experienced what could only be described as a deep sense of shock at the massive resurgence of a regressive definition of British national identity" (McArthur 1984, 54). McArthur and other participants in the BFI Summer School further argue that "the central historical experience in this refurbished national identity was the Second World War and the over-arching rhetoric of its enunciation by the Thatcherite government was Churchillian" (ibid.). In other words, the Thatcherite government at once constructed and drew upon a popular memory of Great Britain and World War II to support its contemporary claims about war and the nation. Popular memory functions here as "a version of the past which connects it up to the present so as to produce popular conceptions" of who a particular people or nation are, where they have come from, and why their society is as it is (Dawson and West, 9).

The popular memory of World War II constructed within the Thatcherite years positions the war period as part of an unfolding destiny of the British people. Memory is a work of discovery, confirming a unified subject. One concern of the various scholars analyzing this construction is to replace the aforementioned notion of memory and history with one that sees history as "something perpetually constructed in a specific juncture" (Tribe, 321). This understanding of popular memory can help to place the mythology of World War II in the terms and conjunctures constructed in the war years themselves, as well as in the Thatcherite period in which the films under discussion were produced and received. This understanding remains attentive to "disruptive" memories of the war as well as to those belonging to the dominant public field, to the displacements affected by and the pressures resulting from the need to rearticulate the past in the present, with both the past and present national history the process and result of popular struggle.

Both *The Krays* and *Hope and Glory* begin with self-conscious evocations of the process of memory and history. *Hope and Glory*, the autobiographical film of director John Boorman's childhood experiences in wartime London, when his mother took over as head of the family in his father's absence, begins with a newsreel of Chamberlain's admittance that appeasement has failed. *The Krays*, the biographical film of the notorious Kray brothers, gangsters who loved their mother "too much" and terrorized London in the 1960s, begins with the voice-over narration of the Krays' mother, as she recounts a dream in which she is a bird keeping her egg warm and safe. The beginning of *Hope and Glory*'s narrative, with newsreel footage of events securely ensconced in public memory, holds the promise of exposing how the filmic institution mediates history and memory, while *The Krays*'s beginning clearly positions its conception in the personal, and since this specific memory is of a dream, as a manifestation of the unconscious. That *Hope and Glory*'s construction of popular memory of World War II begins with a self-reflexive gesture and with an event recognizable to the collective does not ensure that public struggle will be represented or serve as some kind of model of representation in its status as a set of contradictions. *Hope and Glory*'s beginning with the failure of appeasement is, however, quite significant. Chamberlain's shameful policy provides the "lack" motoring the war in popular mythology during World War II, and in Thatcherism's construction of memory of World War II in the postwar period. In the words of Graham Dawson and Bob West:

> Thatcherism has reworked the meanings of that moment when
> appeasement collapsed, so as to re-establish continuity with that previous
> glorious history: a continuity now broken, not by the disasters of 1940, but
> by the period of the post-war consensus, 1945-79. Britain has fallen from
> "her" previous supremacy, but can be great again. The Thatcher
> government is the self-appointed heir of the glorious past. (Dawson and
> West, 9)

Hope and Glory marks its difference from the Thatcherite rhetoric of

Mothers on the home front substitute for absent or weak patriarchs, increasing the psychic hold between mother and child, in John Boorman's *Hope and Glory* (1987).

greatness by constructing a memory of the war from the point of view of the child, a subject whose experiences are usually excluded in representations of war and popular memory. Boorman stated in interviews that he made the film as a tribute to the wartime contributions of his mother and aunts. As typically ignored or underrated experiences, the activities and feelings of women and children work to fragment "consciousness into a contradiction between one's preferred general meanings and the displaced, but persistent, particular memories, which if brought to life, can be most disruptive" (Dawson and West, 11). So in the film, the young Boorman and his sisters actually wish for war and bombings as a kind of liberation from the strictures of their ordered bourgeois life, his older sister becomes sexually active, and his mother expresses desire to be with men outside of monogamous marriage. These "persistent, particular memories" could disrupt a popular memory in the process of smoothing over contradiction or inadequately representing the experiences "which impede identification and the fusion of the personal and the general" (ibid.). They could expose the partiality or contradictions within the consensus politics of the war.

But ultimately the film fuses the personal lack with the social or national lack, with both resolved in fullness and unity. The shame of appeasement is resolved by a war in which class differences supposedly eroded, in which the people supposedly kept "a stiff upper lip," and in which, in Churchill's rhetoric, "the native soil" was protected from invasion. The "lack" of the young Boorman in *Hope and Glory* is an inadequate oedipalization due to the absence of fathers on the home front. So one of the film's memories potentially disruptive to a national popular memory—the experiences of mothers, sisters, and aunts—also functions as the source of the boy's insecurity and embarrassments. Boorman makes it clear throughout the film that mothers and other women have become a problem. The young boy squirms and chafes at signs of the feminized home front: watching the love story film he must sit through, witnessing his older sister having sex in a public place, overhearing his mother confess her love for his father's best friend. These traumas, and thus the boy's lack, are resolved when the mother's desire for infidelity is met with the literal destruction of the home—just after she confesses her love to her husband's friend on a train, the family's home is bombed out. The bombing forces her and the family to the home of her father, a misogynist who fills the gap left by the absent father, and constantly gives the boy lessons in how to undermine what he sees as an increasingly feminized culture.

The grandfather's house on the Thames River serves as both the pastoral paradise of Churchill fantasy and the place where the young Boorman has his first experience with the British film industry. The pastoral paradise of England, securely in the hands of the patriarch, serves as the site where Boorman will find his vocation in film—destiny of Britain and destiny of the oedipally resolved male individual converging at the film's conclusion. Past and present, individual and collective popular memory of the war come together as Boorman finds the man in the boy. Mother will be under the eye of her father, and the older sister, now pregnant, will marry her soldier boyfriend

Young Boorman and the grandfather, a misogynist who fills the gap left by the absent father, in *Hope and Glory*.

on the country estate. Women, who during the war were producers, wives, mothers, lovers, nurses, and soldiers, now will be confined to the institution of motherhood, contained within marriage or the care of secure patriarchs.

The Krays, directed by Peter Medak, puts a different value on the substitution of mothers for absent patriarchs on the home front, and because it cannot fully contain the disruptive memories of these mothers on the home front, exposes the gender and class problematics of the coalition politics of the war and even exposes the core of resentment that the Thatcherite government tapped in the later postwar period. While the opening memory of *The Krays* positions the maternal in a mythical space—in a dream of and by the all-nurturing mother—and thus works to further mystify it, the film also contains evidence of the inextricable connection between gender and class, and of their specificity in history. If the opening memory, which will be repeated at the end of the film in voice-over during mother Violet's funeral, succeeds in making the maternal an eternal, then at other points it counters that construction with memories of specific historical moments when women have been most oppressed and repressed by patriarchy. For example, in one scene, the young Kray boys huddle with their mother and aunts in a World War II air-raid shelter, while their maternal grandfather entertains the crowd with stories of Jack the Ripper. This kind of construction of memory, though

Frances (Kate Hardie) and Reggie (Martin Kemp) before Reggie "mothers" Frances to the
point of suicide, in *The Krays* (1990).

conveyed by a male, contains a memory of male violence against women (and
women of a certain class) that fuels feelings of resentment against men. Not
only is it just as potent a myth as the one of the simultaneously frightening
and loving phallic mother, but it is also a historical reality. The film constantly
reminds us of the difference between psychic fantasies and historical realities
and when the two might converge. Violet Kray often self-mockingly compares herself to the wicked mothers of fairy tales, but the violence of the
Kray boys and their male cronies and rivals results in actual murder and intrigue. Reggie even becomes the embodiment of an evil maternal when he
"mothers" his young wife to the point that she commits suicide. Violet even
sees this coming. As much as she loves her son, she says, Frances (Reggie's
wife) must learn to kick back at men, like she has.

The film also abounds with memories of World War II that disrupt the unified image of that war in popular memory. Violet and her mother constantly
remind men that they are children only thinking that they are in control, for
it was actually women who fought the war and continue to do so in the home
every day. In one scene, Violet's husband responds to these assertions by
claiming that she knows nothing of war, since she was confined to the home
during those years. When she claims that the home is full of death and heart-
ache that he would know nothing about, he moves to strike her. Violet threatens to slit his throat if he touches her, and the twins jump to her defense.

These memories, shown in the process of construction around the quotidian, provide a charge to what might be considered utterly banal motherly and
housewifely activities. In this way, the film mimics and then perversely
transvalues the British government's discursive strategies during the war
and postwar periods that made the home front a site of battle winnable by
mothers.

One memory of the war years, evoked by Violet's sister Rose, who is the
Kray twins' most beloved aunt, serves as an excessive disruption not only in
terms of its content (disrupting the popular memory of the war), but also as
a narrative disruption, coming after the happy moment of Reggie's wedding
and precipitating Rose's death. Back at Violet's house after Reggie's wedding, Rose tells of recently hearing a man on the bus boasting of his war
experiences. As the camera slowly tracks in on her face, Rose has a tortured
recollection:

> It was the women who had the war, the real war. The women were left at
> home, sitting in the shit, not in some sparkling plane or gleaming tank.
> They should have been with me when old Pauline Wooley went into labor.
> . . . Seven hours of screaming . . . and then I had to cut the baby's head
> off to save the mother's life. She died anyway. . . . So much blood. And the
> abortions! Poor girls. One day they'll drain Victoria Park Lake. And you
> know what they'll find? What glorious remnants of the Second World War?
> Babies. . . . Bullets and dead babies. Men! Mum's right—they stay kids all
> their fucking lives and they end up heros or monsters. Either way, they
> win. Women have to grow up. If they stay children, they become victims.

Ironically, it is this Aunt Rose and Violet who help keep their men in a state
of prolonged adolescence. But if the film suggests that strong mothers are
responsible for male violence—another way of containing the maternal by
claiming its subversion of the social order—it also intimates that if mothers
and aunts train their male children to kill other men, it is due as much to class
resentment as to gender vengeance.

This suggestion also disrupts the popular memory of World War II—from
its inception during the war through the present—as won because of a coalition government on the national level and a putting down of class boundaries
on the local level. But, in reality, society constantly struggled against disso-
lution, and the lower classes felt resentment because they were making
greater sacrifices than the upper-class "partners." These failures are never
adequately addressed in either the popular memory of World War II constructed during the war or in the Thatcher years.

In the latter period, the Conservative government located failure in the
postwar consensus period, with its concessions to unions and creation of a
welfare state. Thatcher's government wanted to liberate Great Britain from

"the apron strings" of the maternal state through privatization and promotion of free enterprise. In *The Krays*, Violet, her sisters, and their mother locate failure in the coalition government of World War II as they identify over and over again the oppression of women during the war. They also attack the postwar consensus years, as they reward the Kray twins for gaining social status not through identification with working-class unionization, but through a vicious pursuit of individual success and power in the marketplace, even if the marketplace must be taken by force. The film perversely suggests that Violet Kray had the idea for "mothering" free enterprise rather than having the welfare state "mothering" the lower classes before Margaret Thatcher did, all while doing the everyday duties of mothering and keeping the family together. "For what is the real driving force in our society?" asked Mrs. Thatcher in 1979. "It is the desire for the individual to do the best for himself and his family" (quoted in Ogden, 337).

Violet Kray hates her slacker husband because he is a man and because he deserted during the war, but most of all because his cheating has gotten him nowhere in terms of social mobility. If men of a certain class can't succeed lawfully, Violet can't understand why they don't do so outside the law. She knows that men have the power no matter what side of the law they are on, and that women have no power except as mothers. She agrees with Rose that if women stay like children they become victims of the patriarchy, as does Reggie's wife Frances.

What does a film like *The Krays* suggest in a national and historical context in which a female prime minister tried to free the "people" from a supposedly infantilizing maternal state? Violet Kray uses the maternal to promote free enterprise. In many ways, Violet allies herself with the Thatcher philosophy that repects and gives Spartan nurturing to those who succeed through individual initiative. But neither the film nor Violet is so naive as to suggest that success through individual initiative is ever achieved without power that oppresses certain groups — whether that power be an infantilizing maternal that Violet can exercise over her sons, or patriarchal power that could jeopardize Violet and her matriarchal clan. She chooses to bind her sons to her so that patriarchal power will be exercised over other men.

At its conclusion, the film bring these gender and class issues together in a crosscut sequence that confuses which one has primacy. As the twins commit their most brutal crimes, those that will consolidate their power and send them to prison, where they remain today as working-class heroes — Violet sits at home watching a documentary of World War II on television. The murders are intercut with images of Violet watching and sobbing as a popular memory of World War II is constructed through the media and she

Violet's (Billie Whitelaw) closeness to her sons (Martin Kemp and Gary Kemp) is terrifying on both private and social levels, in *The Krays*.

finds her experience, once again, left out. As the television documentary ends, the boys come home, Violet turns to them and recounts the dream of her birdlike protection of her boys, which was the film's opening. Personal

The "homosocial economy" of the gangster group as doppelgänger of Thatcherite Britain, in *The Krays*.

memory—for Violet, a mythology of a powerful maternal—resists the public, media-made memory that marginalizes disruptive recollections. It is through such strategies—the constant contextualization and recontextualization of the personal memory and historical moment—that *The Krays*, more successfully than *Hope and Glory*, suggests the process of popular memory in all its contradictions.

I am not suggesting, however, that the depiction of the maternal in *The Krays* is radical or even necessarily progressive. The film's image of the mother can be appropriated by the spectator for a misogynistic or homophobic response. The film shows Violet Kray's closeness to her sons as having terrifying implications for both the private and the social.[1] Because the film suggests that Ronnie Kray, the homosexual twin, is the more violent of the two, classic homophobic and misogynist depictions of homosexuality and the maternal are potentially revived. It could be argued, however, that the depiction of homosexuality in this film is less concerned with the influence of the maternal (despite the mother's centrality) on sexual "deviance" and more concerned with exposing a "homosocial economy" of the male gangster society as a "doppelgänger" of the ordered society of Thatcher England, which *rejects* the maternal. Moreover, the film's focus on the victimization of women and mothers by men, which is seen as a historically specific victimization, makes the film a valuable text for an understanding of how the mother can be the subject and object of a historical representation, rather than dismissed or vilified as the "eternal unclean" of the abject.

The strategies in *Hope and Glory* and *The Krays* that centralize, but also evaluate, maternal and female concerns evidence many of the ambivalences Western societies feel about women in power since World War II, growing especially intense in ambivalence since the women's movement. Janice Winship has traced the debates about women's power in postwar Britain, arguing that the dominant discourse tried to reconcile a notion of "we the nation" with "we women" through constructing peace as a battle only women (especially mothers) could help to win (Winship, 197). This included figuring a popular image of Queen Elizabeth (crowned in 1953) as both ruler and devoted wife and mother (Winship, 208-10). While this imaging has continued to the present (with the queen's ruler image predominating during various IRA crises, her mother image predominating in a tabloid press concerned with the social foibles of her various sons or daughters-in-law), the introduction of a woman prime minister in the configuration of British ruler-mothers with Thatcher's election in 1979 brought many of the culture's resistances to feminism to the foreground. This was not because Thatcher represented feminism, but because, despite (perhaps because of) her own rise to power, by serving as one of its greatest detractors, she expressed the feelings of many. Her remark in 1978 that "the feminists have become far too strident and have done damage to the cause of women by making us out to be something we're not" (quoted in Ogden, 341) is representative of the position on women's rights and sexual difference that Thatcher took in her eleven years in office.

It is also representative of a culture that increasingly believes that we live in a postfeminist age, when feminism and the movements of other marginalized groups are no longer needed as positions of political resistance to the dominant culture. That feminism is no longer, or perhaps was never, needed is supposedly proved by the fact of Thatcher's election. Likewise, that feminism (and socialism) has gone "too far" and now given benefits to the undeserving is proved by an underclass that demands rights rather than working for them. When Thatcher remarked before her election, "You get on because you have the right talents" (quoted in Ogden, 341), she encapsulated the philosophy of free enterprise that would be invoked in her own country and in the United States whenever programs helping marginalized groups were weakened or dismantled. Whenever this attitude about winning through individual initiative was clothed in nationalistic terms reminiscent of the Churchillian rhetoric of World War II, Thatcher and her constituents participated in the state's construction of public memories.

The self-conscious positioning of mothers within narratives constructed around the bittersweetness (as in *Hope and Glory*) or the disruptiveness (as in *The Krays*) of memory must be seen in this context of a culture coming to terms with the place of feminism in a resurrected free enterprise world where even women can be leaders. *Hope and Glory* suggests its place for feminism when it recalls the mystery of women from the safety of nostalgia and a fully oedipalized male adulthood. *The Krays*, looking back at the war, postwar, and "swinging London" period of English history, exposes the connection between free enterprise and criminality that is surely as relevant to Thatcher England as Coppola's *Godfather* saga (1972 and 1976) was to Watergate and post-Watergate America. Although it pictures the terrifying power of the maternal familiar to misogynistic representations of mothers, the film also provides an outlet for the anger and for the memories of mothers who fought a war every day in the home. *The Krays* suggests, with a kind of irony and cynicism that seems particularly relevant to a historical context in which a woman can claim with *no* irony that "you get on because you have the right talents," that women can only save themselves from victimization if they control men to act in the name of capitalism on women's behalf.

Note

1. In an essay on Thatcher and Ruth Ellis (the last woman to be executed in Great Britain), Jacqueline Rose argues that the collective fantasy of state violence that characterizes Thatcherite Britain is connected to a collective misogynist fantasy that puts women on the very edges of the social. Ruth Ellis, who admitted calculating the murder of her lover, threatened to expose the constructedness of women as hysterics (as not responsible for their actions) and the connection between rationality and violence. Thatcher's defense of capital punishment is representative of a collective attempt to mask aggressivity from within by making violence appear from the outside, in the form of the Law. But Thatcher's supremely rationalized discursive strategies for defending capital punishment also threaten to deconstruct the oppositions between reasoned law and violence.

Works Cited

Dawson, Graham, and Bob West. 1984. "Our Finest Hour? The Popular Memory of World War II and the Struggle over National Identity." In *National Fictions: World War Two in British Films and Television*, edited by Geoff Hurd, 8-13. London: British Film Institute.
McArthur, Colin. 1975/76. *"Days of Hope." Screen* 16 (4). Reprinted in *Popular Television and Film*, edited by Tony Bennett et al., 305-9. London: British Film Institute.
_____. 1984. "National Identities." In *National Fictions: World War Two in British Films and Television*, edited by Geoff Hurd, 54-56. London: British Film Institute.
MacCabe, Colin. 1975. "Days of Hope—A Response to Colin McArthur." *Screen* 17 (1). Reprinted in *Popular Television and Film*, edited by Tony Bennett et al, 310-13. London: British Film Institute, 1981.

_____. 1977. "Memory, Phantasy, Identity: *Days of Hope* and the Politics of the Past." *Edinburgh '77 Magazine*. Reprinted in *Popular Television and Film*, edited by Tony Bennett et al., 314-18. London: British Film Institute, 1981.

Ogden, Chris. 1990. *Maggie: An Intimate Portrait of a Woman in Power*. New York: Simon and Schuster.

O'Shea, Alan. 1984. "Trusting the People: How Does Thatcherism Work?" In *Formations of Nation and People*, edited by *Formations* Editorial Collective, 19-41. London: Routledge and Kegan Paul.

Rose, Jacqueline. 1988. "Margaret Thatcher and Ruth Ellis." *New Formations* 6 (Winter): 3-29.

Tribe, Keith. 1977/78. "History and the Production of Memory." *Screen* 18 (4). Reprinted in *Popular Television and Film*, edited by Tony Bennett et al., 319-26. London: British Film Institute, 1981.

Williams, Tony. 1991. *"The Ploughman's Lunch*: Remembering or Forgetting History." *Jump Cut* 36: 11-18.

Winship, Janice. 1984. "Nation before Family: Woman, the National Home Weekly, 1945-1953. In *Formations of Nation and People*, edited by *Formations* Editorial Collective, 188-211. London: Routledge and Kegan Paul.

Part II

Filmmakers during the Thatcher Era

Nine

Power and Territory: The Emergence of Black British Film Collectives

Manthia Diawara

> Margaret Thatcher conducted the whole affair with absolute
> control. She pretends to be charming, and seductive, and on
> observation, I could see that she uses her gender in terms of
> being feminine, listening to men, in the ways she'd ask questions,
> and then she'll be like a mother and tell the men off.
>
> —Isaac Julien, "Downing Street Seminar," in
> *Diary of a Young Soul Rebel*

> I think it means that people are really rather afraid that this
> country might be swamped by people of a different culture. The
> British character has done so much for democracy, for law, and
> done so much throughout the world that if there is any fear that it
> might be swamped, then people are going to be rather hostile to
> those coming in. We are a British nation with British
> characteristics. Every country can take some minorities, and in
> many ways they add to the richness and variety of this country.
> But the moment the minority threatens to become a big one,
> people get frightened.
>
> —Margaret Thatcher, quoted in *Handsworth Songs*

The period 1985 to 1991 constitutes a black film movement in Britain that is
as significant politically and aesthetically as the Brazilian Cinema Novo, the
French New Wave, and the Argentinian Third Cinema. This essay will delineate some of the constitutive elements of the new black British renaissance
cinema in order to categorize it as a movement. For the sake of diasporic
specifity, I will concentrate on the films of three film collectives: Ceddo,
Sankofa, and Black Audio. The black British renaissance cinema, like surrealism in the 1920s and Cinema Novo in the 1960s, presents itself with
themes of discontinuity, boundaries, political agendas, and aesthetic manifestos that set it apart from British experimental cinema, the earlier black
British films, and the films of the black diaspora.

Many commentators already characterize the black British renaissance
cinema of the 1980s as a movement; one of these is Jim Pines—the first

journalist and cultural practitioner to seriously explore collectives such as Sankofa, Ceddo, and Black Audio. The notion of movement is also explicit in Kobena Mercer's articles on black British cinema. In "Recoding Narrative of Race and Nation," for example, Mercer states that "the prolific activity of the black independent film movement stands out as an area of development in contemporary film culture that is unique to Britain in the 1980s" (Mercer 1988b, 4). In his introduction to *Questions of Third Cinema* (1989), Paul Willemen describes black British cinema as constituting "the most intellectually and cinematically innovative edge of British cultural politics" (Pines and Willemen, 28). Alison Butler, for her part, sees in films such as *Handsworth Songs* "the hope that we are witnessing the arrival of new artistic forms and cultural movements" (Butler, 19). Finally, one must acknowledge the centrality of the theoretical writings by Stuart Hall, Homi Bhabha, and Paul Gilroy, around which pivot notions of identity, ambivalence, Englishness, and diasporic aesthetics crucial to an understanding of black British cinema.

The Historical and Political Context of the Movement

The history of the black British renaissance film of the 1980s has to be traced back to the emergence of the so-called minority arts in Britain since the mid-1970s. The riots associated with the 1976 and 1981 Nottinghill carnivals were followed by strategies of containment. Such policies resulted both in a militarization of the police against black youth in British cities and in the setting aside of funds for minority artists by the National Art Council, the Greater London Council, the British Film Institute, Channel Four, and arts councils of local governments. Naseem Khan's 1976 report, entitled "The Arts Britain Ignores," recommended the establishment of the Minority Arts Advisory Service (MAAS), which could encourage multiculturalism in Britain by recognizing "immigrant arts" and by providing creative spaces in schools and art centers for "minority artists." To put it in Kwesi Owusu's words, "MAAS would construct and maintain an up-to-date register of groups and publicize immigrant arts, and act as a pressure group to see through the implementation of the report's recommendations" (Owusu, 49). Naseem Khan, instrumental in setting up the agency, also acted as its de facto head, aided by a committee of black and immigrant artists.

While many artists benefited from funds generated by the Naseem Khan report, the idea of "minority art" angered black artists afraid of being ghettoized as a problem to be nurtured and protected in British society. Thus some artists challenged the new multiculturalisms, claiming that "they col-

lapse different cultural and artistic forms into a melting pot without necessarily acknowledging their individual modes of expression, and without challenging institutional and attitudinal racism, which deprecates their quality by
racial stereotyping" (Owusu, 43).

In 1982, barely a year after the 1981 Nottinghill riot, the Greater London
Council (GLC) sponsored a conference to reevaluate black artists' access to
media production. Black artists remained critical of how the GLC and the
newly created Channel Four television underfunded their creative projects,
or put white artists and producers in charge of representing black issues to
the public. Imruh Caesar, a black independent filmmaker at the GLC conference, brought out the need for "Black people to become the subjects, rather
than merely objects, of the camera" (Owusu, 86). The conference participants also criticized the timidity of Channel Four for not yet committing itself
to the training of black youth in directing, camera work, and production.
Channels Four's documentaries and television series, such as "Eastern
Eye," "Ebony," and "Black on Black," also received criticism for not going
far enough to address black spectatorship in British television. As Jim Pines
pointed out, some black spectators of Channel Four magazines on the black
experience argued that "programmes like *Black on Black* and *Eastern Eye*
should be more propagandist in their orientation. In other words, given the
dynamics of race politics in Britain at the moment, you should be concerned
with putting across black political and cultural views which are explicitly in
opposition to the white mainstream" (Pines 1983, 7). By propagandist,
Pines meant creating counterimages to BBC shows like "Love Thy Neigh-
bour," "Mind Your Language," and "Mixed Blessings," which portray racist
stereotypes of blacks in Britain. Channel Four's policy of nonracist situation
comedies such as "No Problem" aimed to undermine images of blacks as
muggers, as lazy and shiftless, instead positing images of blacks that emphasized their good citizenship, their hard work, and their ordinariness. In other
words, black spectators defined their relation to Channel Four by demanding
positive images; such images were supposed to be necessary to combat
mainstream television's construction of blacks. They wanted Channel Four's
cameras to shift the blame away from black youth by revealing and denouncing the metropolitan police's construction of the youths' image as muggers
and drug pushers in order to survey and punish it.

Both the GLC and Channel Four responded to the black artists' criticism
by setting aside funds for training black youth in their desired mediums and
helping them set up collective film and video workshops. Such workshops,
after all, helped to keep the youth off the streets and reduced the chances of
further uprising by a people affected by racism and unemployment. As Isaac

Julien puts it, "It also has to be noted why we are here, the struggles of black communities which have taken to the street to express their frustration, are continued and mirrored in other spaces, i.e. cinema" (Julien, in Auguste et al. 1988, 36). In the early eighties, black film and video workshops also had to overcome the obstacle of virtually closed unions. For blacks and women, as Jim Pines puts it, the Association of Cinematograph, Television and Allied Technicians (ACTT) "traditionally has been a highly protective union — indeed, it is a closed shop and reputedly one of the most difficult unions to get into. For those on the outside, the problem is that without a union card it is practically impossible to get employment in the industry" (Pines 1983, 20).

The Manifestos of the Movement

The early phases of the black workshops were marked by a search for a film language capable of expressing the many experiences of black people in Britain. At first the young filmmakers used conference sites to distinguish their positions on representation and aesthetics from, on the one hand, those of previous black filmmakers in Britain and the diaspora, and the white independent cinema of Britain and Western Europe, on the other. They also used the newly created workshops to screen films by Sembene Ousmane, Haile Gerima, Charles Burnett, and Julie Dash, which they discussed with audiences and compared to the practices of Third Cinema as amplified and applied to African, Asian, and black American films by Teshome Gabriel's new book, *Third Cinema in the Third World: The Aesthetics of Liberation* (1982). Sankofa and Black Audio Film/Video Collective were particularly interested in film theory and the applicability of Laura Mulvey's *Narrative Cinema and Visual Pleasure*, Homi Bhabha's notions of ambivalence and hybridity, and other uses of Lacan and Althusser in *Screen* and *Framework* in the late seventies and early eighties. The diaspora influence was linked to the works of black Americans such as June Jordan, whose *Civil Wars* helped the young black British to theorize policing in their own context; Manning Marable; Cedric Robinson; James Baldwin; and black women writers. The Caribbeans included C. L. R. James, George Lamming, Wilson Harris, Frantz Fanon, Aimé Cesaire, Edward K. Braithwaite, and Derek Walcott; the African influences included Ngugi Wa Thiongo and Sembene Ousmane. Crucially, however, the works of Stuart Hall and Paul Gilroy (*The Empire Strikes Back* and *There Ain't No Black in the Union Jack*) and the publications in the journal *Race and Class* were the most immediate influences on the new black British cinema.

By 1986, when the collectives were internationally famous for films such as *Territories*, *Passion of Remembrance* (Sankofa), and *Handsworth Songs* (Black Audio), a new film language had been forged that marked a significant departure from race relation films that constructed black presence in Britain as a problem, from white independent cinema that rendered race invisible, and from diaspora and Third Cinema films that lacked cinematic pleasure and took ambivalent subject positions.

Position papers and artistic and political manifestos by John Akomfrah, Martina Attille, Karen Alexander, and Reece Auguste outline the programs of the new black British cinema; they insist on its specificity within the larger context of independent filmmaking in Britain. In 1983, John Akomfrah's article in *Artrage* announced the birth of Black Audio Film/Video Collective. For Akomfrah, Black Audio Film/Video Collective was created to address three main areas in film activities. First, they questioned the mainstream media's representation of black people: "to look critically at how racist ideas and images of black people are structured and presented as self-evident truths in cinema. What we are interested in here is how these 'self-evident truths' become the conventional pattern through which the black presence in cinema is secured" (Akomfrah, 29).

In the second place, Akomfrah posits Black Audio's need to inventory the "available techniques within the independent tradition and to assess their pertinence for black cinema. In this respect our interest did not only lie in devising how best to make 'political' films, but also in taking the politics of representation seriously" (29). By adding the dimension of the "politics of representation" to their agenda, Black Audio problematized the whole notion of black people's "relation to images." They demonstrated that the issue of representation was not resolved by simply shifting from negative images to positive images. Positive images, they believed, were as embedded in stereotypes as negative images, and only a politics of representation could account for the filmmaker's relation to the images that he or she arranged on the screen. As Stuart Hall put it:

How things are represented and the "machineries" and regimes of representation in a culture do play a constitutive, and not merely a reflexive, after-the-event, role. This gives questions of culture and ideology, and the scenarios of representation—subjectivity, identity, politics—a formative, not merely an expressive, place in the constitution of social and political life. (Hall 1988, 28)

Finally, Akomfrah described the need for a collective practice in Black Audio's approach to film, as opposed to privileging the director as the sole creative force in a film. The collective approach emphasized the division of labor among the producer, the director, the persons in charge of distribution and publicity, the audience for the film, and so on. To put it in Akomfrah's own words:

> The strategy was to encourage and emphasize collective practice as a means of extending the boundaries of black film culture. This would mean attempting to de-mystify in our film practice the process of film production; it would also involve collapsing the distinction between "audience" and "producer." In this ethereal world film-maker equals active agent and audience usually equals passive consumers of a predetermined product. We have decided to reject such a view in our practice. (Akomfrah, 29)

The three points Akomfrah put on the table for Black Audio Film/Video Collective helped them address the issue of stereotypical representation of blacks by the police and the media in Thatcherite Britain, as well as to posit the possibility for the emergence of a film style specific to black Britons. For Akomfrah, a theory of difference was necessary both for deconstructing structured presence/absence of blacks in the media and for the grounding of a politics of representation that was not fixed: "The search is not for 'the authentic image' but for an understanding of the diverse codes and strategies of representation" (Akomfrah, 30).

For her part, Martina Attille of Sankofa Film Collective explained that her group was first concerned with the experience of black people and policing in Britain. To better understand this phenomenon, they investigated the strategies of containment, the varieties of black communities, and the systems of power and control. According to Attille, "Despite the diversity of black life in Britain, images of black people are defined in very narrow terms and contained as problematic, policing being a predictable arena" (Attille, 53). Sankofa's goal was, therefore, to bring the multiple identities and values of black subjects out of the shadows in order to expose the stereotypical images mobilized by the police to maintain black youth as the problem in Britain. Sankofa Film Collective used the notion of pleasure and multiple subject positions as elements of their film language, giving voices back to black people and revealing the diversity of their lives in Britain. For Attille, a pleasurable cinema is necessary to draw people into the film:

> We wanted the film to appeal to young people, the politically aware and those who could become politically aware, a film for Europe about being young and black in Britain at a time of uncertainty. We also wanted the film to retain its original integrity—e.g., the realities of policing in its broadest sense—and to assert the politics of being a black woman, always active. (Attille, 53)

Sankofa Film Collective also emphasized gender and sexual politics as constitutive elements to shape their film language. For Attille, putting gender and sexuality in the foreground was one of the ways Sankofa distinguished itself from the first generation of black filmmakers: "Sankofa's particular character in terms of race, gender and sexuality meant that the unfinished business of the 1960s/70s (black, gay and feminist movements) was something that we felt needed prioritizing in the present, particularly in relation to those three areas of experience" (Attille, 54).

Finally, the new black film collectives' search for a specific identitary experience in Britishness expressed itself in a specific film language that made them question the prevailing styles in diaspora and Third Cinema films, as well as in the British independent and West European cinema. No doubt the theories of Third Cinema, particularly Teshome Gabriel's application of the concept to the films of Sembene Ousmane and Haile Gerima, opened up the possibilities for an alternative film practice in Britain. As Reece Auguste put it at the Commonwealth Institute conference on Cultural Identities in 1986, the historical antecedents of the black film renaissance were "the early period of British black independent film production from Lionel Ngakane's allegorical *Jemima and Johnny* (1974), to the 1980s, with the films of Henry Martin, Horace Ove, Imruh Bakari Caesar and Menelik Shabazz, and the political and aesthetic intervention of Third Cinema, as a countermovement in film, which is critical of its own position, as it is of European cinema" (Auguste 1988, 33).

However, for Auguste, neither Third Cinema, with its emphasis on oppositional film style, nor the old British black independent films, which focused on race as a problem in Britain, adequately encompassed the hybrid and creolized space that was the subject of the new black cinema. As Auguste put it:

> Debates around Third Cinema have not in my view sufficiently addressed developments in the cinema by diasporic subjects living and working in the metropolitan centres of London, Paris, New York, etc. Thus it becomes immensely problematic when films from Britain are incorporated into this all-embracing conceptual framework called Third Cinema practice. Such a process does not allow adequate space for a critical evaluation of the distinctiveness of films emerging from Britain and other Western metropolitan centres. That level of analysis and critical reflection is most needed. (Auguste 1989, 215)

Similarly, Cassie McFarlene explained the difference between an earlier black British film like *Burning an Illusion* and the films of the black British renaissance like *Passion of Remembrance* and *Handsworth Songs* by arguing that the former is embedded in the discourse of ethnic absolutism, while the latter emphasize multiple-subject positions. As McFarlene put it, *"Burning an Illusion* was made at a period during which there emerged a new ideology of ethnic absolutism which focused on the black cultural formation in Britain as homogeneous. The question of the racial/cultural identity of black people in the Diaspora was at this period given priority over other factors arising out of the history of settlement" (McFarlene, 29). For McFarlene, a shift occurred with films by Sankofa and Black Audio, which were more in conversation with the independent white leftist experimental filmmaking, the recent developments in theory, as well as the latest issues raised by black women writers in the United States. McFarlene saw the emergence of a unique consciousness among the new wave of black filmmakers with regard to blackness and Britishness, gender and sexuality, desire and pleasure— issues that before were marginal in black films.

The black film renaissance distanced itself from independent British and Western European films, too, by emphasizing black subjecthood and notions of pleasure that were banned in the films of such directors as Peter Gidal (*Close Up*, 1983), Lezli-Ann Barrett, Laura Mulvey, Peter Wollen, and others. While the white experimental cinema did away with the subject and notions of identity, the black British deployed diasporic memories in their films. As Isaac Julien put it:

> On the left of avant-gardism is pleasure, which the avant-garde self denies, clinging to the purism of its constructed ethics, measuring itself against a refusal to indulge in narrative or emotions and indeed, in some cases, refusing representation itself, because all these systems of signs are fixed, entrenched in the "sin or evil" of representation. The high moral tone of this discourse is based on a kind of masochistic self-censorship which relies on the indulgence of a colonial history and a post-colonial history of cinema of white representations based on our black absence. The problematic that surfaces when black film-makers experiment with the idea of black film text and the subjective camera, is that subjectivity implies contradiction. But this is not, in itself, fixed. (Julien, in Auguste et al., 36]

The British Cinema Is Dead, Long Live Black British Cinema

To turn now to the themes that unify black British renaissance cinema as a movement I shall emphasize policing and diasporic aesthetics in the films. These themes are differently represented to question Englishness and blackness in the films, as well as to address the problematics of sexuality, class relations, and belonging in Britain. The representation of policing in the films draws from the treatment of the same subject by Stuart Hall and others (*Policing the Crisis: Mugging, the State, and Law and Order*) and Paul Gilroy (*There Ain't No Black in the Union Jack*), as well as from the uprisings against the police in Handsworth, Brixton, and Tottenham. The filmmakers intend to depict not only the manner in which the police and the mainstream press construct stereotypical images of black people in Britain and force the population to accept these images, but also the ways in which bodies are sexually constructed and maintained in certain positions. *Territories*, a film by Sankofa Film Collective, for example, depicts an image of two gay men dancing on the British flag under the watchful eyes of a policeman. Britishness as English puritanism is contested in this scene through the defiance of police surveillance and an appropriation of the Union Jack by blacks and gays.

The figuration of policing in the films takes on two levels defined by Paul Gilroy (1987) as the archaeology of representations of law-breaking. The first level shows the efforts by the police and the mainstream press to construct and maintain a monolithic and fixed image of blacks in Britain, while the second level deconstructs the first one and posits the possibility of multiple black subject positions. The first one links blackness to crime and argues that black law-breaking is un-English and therefore constitutes the main evidence that blacks are unworthy of belonging to the nation. The second level reveals the police's bias against black people by focusing on "the supportive relationship between the police and the local white residents harassed by the noise" (Gilroy, 97). It constructs an image of the law that suppresses black culture in its attempt to preserve a monolithic Britishness. The extent to which black people are seen as a threat to Britishness is shown in a television address by Margaret Thatcher that is quoted in *Handsworth Songs* and that serves as the second epigraph of my text.

Following Paul Gilroy's work, films like *Handsworth Songs* (Black Audio), *Territories* (Sankofa), *Passion of Remembrance* (Sankofa), and *The People's Account* (Ceddo) show both the Thatcherites and the Labour party colluding to maintain that black law-breaking distances them from authentic Englishness. *Handsworth Songs*, for example, represents the riots of Handsworth by placing its cameras with the mob, instead of placing them behind the police. Thus we see the police and the mainstream press as they approach their "victim." In one scene, the cameras track down a group of helmeted policemen as they chase and trap a black man with long dreadlocks. Parts of the scene are shown in slow motion as the police finally catch the Rasta man who vainly tries to escape them. The filming of the scene puts emphasis on the police outnumbering the man in dreadlocks, and on the brutality of the police against the helplessness of the man.

Also, in *Territories*, the police's representation of the streets as dangerous for elderly white women is turned against itself. In one scene, an old white woman clinging to her purse and looking frightened crosses a street full of young black males. The camera stays on her until she reaches the other end of the street, then the scene is reversed, sending her back to the beginning. Interpreted from the perspective of black youth's contestation of their construction by the police, this scene embodies several meanings. To begin with, it appropriates the discourse of the police and addresses the fears of the white woman, for whom the image of young black male connotes rape and mugging. In this sense, the presence of black youth turns the streets into hell, and crossing from one end to the other becomes a painful and long journey for the law-abiding white woman. But, by running the same image in reverse, the film literally deconstructs the stereotypic police construction of black youth. The image in reverse, because it is comical—or a bad joke at the expense of the old woman—unseats the authenticity of the image of the black youth the police have created in the woman's mind. As Paul Gilroy argues, "The struggle over signs and images [between the police and the black artists], particularly those which involve blacks, has become more important for the maintenance of order than the actual law-breaking that they denote" (109). *Territories* uses the theme of policing to "recompose" the signs of blackness and Britishness in Britain and to lift blackness from the pathological space created by police files.

Such films denote the theme of policing and black youth's resistance to it through recourse to images of burning buildings in Brixton, Handsworth, and Tottenham. Just as these buildings in smoke have come to symbolize black resistance in films like *Who Killed Colin Roach* (Isaac Julien), *Handsworth Songs, Passion of Remembrance, Territories*, and *The People's Account*, the names of black people, such as Colin Roach, Blakelock, Cherry Groce, and Mrs. Jarret, whose deaths are associated with the riots, have also come to symbolize black martyrdom in Britain.

Without doubt, the strongest indictment of policing comes from *The People's Account*, a film about the community's view of the 1985 riot in Broadwater Farm (Tottenham). Using interviews with people from Broadwater Farm and Burmingham, the documentary looks into the historical and contemporary relationship between black people and the police; their social and economic conditions; and the role the media, in collusion with the police, have played to "distort and undermine the fundamental reasons for the uprisings" (Ceddo press release, 1986). *The People's Account,* now famous for being censored by the Independent Broadcasting Authority (which must give its stamp of approval before films can be shown on British television), focuses mainly on policing, which distinguishes it from other films of the movement dealing with several themes at the same time. It compares the police's treatment of black people in Britain to the treatment of blacks in the apartheid system of South Africa. It accuses the police of "terrorist raids against

Black communities," describes black people as victims of police racism, and calls the events of Broadwater Farm a "classical example of self-defence by the [black] community." *The People's Account* is also known for its use of *uprisings* in the place of *riots* to underscore black people's revolt against discrimination, exploitation, and policing. Ceddo Film/Video Workshop considers film to be a guerrilla weapon in the general perspective of uprisings, just as Bob Marley's music was considered to be a weapon of liberation. It is in this sense that Ceddo film crews have been present among the crowd to film the police at the uprisings in Handsworth, Brixton, and Tottenham. Original footage from Ceddo archives can be seen in films like *Handsworth Songs* and Sankofa films.

The theme of the black diaspora figures importantly in many of the films. The filmmakers represent the diaspora as a way of resisting the pathological construction of blackness by mainstream media and of positioning blackness as a third and hybrid space that can be opposed to the ethnic absolutism of Englishness and other ethnicities in Britain. As Paul Gilroy put it, "Black Britain defines itself crucially as part of a diaspora. Its unique cultures draw inspiration from those developed by black populations elsewhere. In particular, the culture and politics of black America and the Caribbean have become raw materials for creative processes which redefine what it means to be black, adapting it to distinctly British experiences and meanings" (Gilroy, 154). For Stuart Hall, diasporic narratives often construct cultural identity either as "hidden histories, true essences of Caribbeanness or Africanness inside the many other more superficial or artificially imposed 'selves', which people with a shared history and ancestry hold in common" (Hall 1989, 69); or as difference and rupture, "points of deep and significant difference which constitute 'what we really are': or rather—since history has intervened— 'what we have become' " (Hall 1989, 70). While the first narrative empowers itself through archivism, excavation, and continuity, the other valorizes fragmentation, hybridity, and rupture. In either case, the filmmaker articulates his or her identity with different types of presences: African, American, Asian, and European.

Films like *The Passion of Remembrance, Handsworth Songs, Territories, Twilight City* (1989), *I'm British But* (1989), and *My Beautiful Laundrette* (1985) construct diasporic space as a third space. By third space I mean the familiar notion of hybrid spaces that combine the colors and flavors of different localities, and yet declare their specifity from each of those localities. In *My Beautiful Laundrette*, the Asian presence and the English presence are combined to produce a third space, which is occupied not only by the youth of Asian descent, but also by the white youth of the punk generation.

The construction of a third space is the subject of narrative deployment in *The Passion of Remembrance*. On one level, the youth construct their black Britishness through recourse to the black American funk style of the 1970s and the sexual politics legitimized by British feminism and poststructuralism, and by making a movement away from the 1970s reggae and the 1960s-derived black British nationalism and white British ethnic absolutism. On another level, *The Passion of Remembrance* constitutes a third space as the space for women and homosexuals whose struggles were not sufficiently highlighted during the civil rights movement. It is in this sense that heterosexuals seem lost in the open spaces of the film, while women lead the way.

Diasporic narratives are also used in the films for didactic and celebratory purposes. In films such as *Omega Rising: Woman of Rastafari* (1988) and *Time and Judgement* (1989), the African and Caribbean presences are emphasized in order to bring hidden histories out of the shadows. In *Time and Judgement*, director Menelik Shabazz combines images of Marcus Garvey, Haile Selassie, Nelson Mandela, and the Queen of Sheba with Afrocentric poems and images to denote how, after four hundred years of oppression, the African people "rose up with the rod of Moses and passed judgement" against "Babylon." In *Omega Rising*, Ceddo Film/Video traveled through Britain and Jamaica to reveal the role of women in the Rastafari movement that many consider patriarchal and sexist.

In films such as *Testament* (1989), *Looking For Langston* (1989), and *Handsworth Songs*, the African and American presences are questioned in order to envision their usefulness to the material conditions of black British identity formation. The narrative of *Looking for Langston*, for example, empowers itself by conjuring up Hughes and other figures of the Harlem renaissance. The film is looking back at that discourse of the turn of the century in order to empower its own discourse of the present, namely, black Britishness. In *Handsworth Songs*, Black Audio inserts enigmatic footage of Malcolm X in Birmingham to point to the similarities of white racism and black struggle in the United States and Britain. In *Testament*, too, the protagonist questions the "presence Africaine" in the makeup of black British identity by traveling to Ghana and articulating her British identity with the pan-Africanism of Nkrumah.

Other important thematizations of the diaspora in the films involve religion (*Dreaming Rivers* [1988], *Omega Rising*, and *Time and Judgement*), languages, music, and costumes of African, American, and European presences. All these diasporic narratives are used to situate blacks inside and outside Britishness, to delineate points of identification with blackness, and to mark the fluidity of identitarian positions.

In closing I'd like to return to the beginning of this essay, which places the black British film movement between 1985 and 1991, significantly one year before the reunification of Western Europe. Is it possible that identity politics no longer maintain their efficacy and that broader political coalitions are becoming more urgent? Perhaps the critique of essentialism, too, has influenced new narratives that privilege what Gianni Vattimo calls "weak thought." It is also possible that the recent decision by Channel Four not to support the workshops has precipitated the demise of the movement. One might also point to the return to authorship, implicit in the fame associated with names such as Julien, Akomfrah, and Shabazz, as an indicator of the end of an era. At any rate, the end of *Young Soul Rebels* (1991) marks a new era in black British filmmaking. As the four main characters get out of their couches and begin to dance, it becomes clear that they are tired of identity, separate communities, and Thatcherite Britain, and that they are leaving all that behind.

Works Cited

Akomfrah, John. 1983. "Black Independent Film-making: A Statement by the Black Audio/Film Collective." *Artrage: Inter-Cultural Arts Magazine* 3/4 (Summer): 29-30.

Attille, Martina. 1988. "The Passion of Remembrance: Background." In *Black Film, British Cinema*, ICA Documents no. 7, 53-54, London: Institute of Contemporary Art.

Auguste, Reece. 1989. "Black Independents and Third Cinema: The British Context." In *Questions of Third Cinema*, edited by Jim Pines and Paul Willemen, 212-17. London: British Film Institute.

Auguste, Reece, Isaac Julien, and Martina Attille. 1988. "Aesthetics and Politics: Working on Two Fronts." *Undercut: The Magazine for the London Filmmakers' Coop* 17: 32-39.

Black Phoenix: Third World Perspective on Contemporary Art and Culture. 1978. No. 2 (Summer).

Butler, Alison. 1988. "Handsworth Songs." *International Documentary*, Winter/Spring, 19-22.

Ceddo Press Release, 1986.

Gabriel, Teshome. 1982. *Third Cinema in the Third World*. Ann Arbor: University of Michigan Press.

Gilroy, Paul. 1987. *There Ain't No Black in the Union Jack*. London: Hutchinson.

Hall, Stuart. 1988. "New Ethnicities." In *Black Film, British Cinema*, ICA Documents no. 7, 53-54, London: Institute of Contemporary Art.

Hall, Stuart. 1989. "Cultural Identity and Cinematic Representation." *Framework* 36: 68-81.

Hall, Stuart, Charles Critcher, Tony Jefferson, John Clarke, and Brian Roberts. 1987. *Policing the Crisis: Mugging, the State, and Law and Order*. London: Macmillan.

Julien, Isaac, and Colin MacCabe. 1991. *Diary of a Young Soul Rebel*. London: British Film Institute.

Khan, Naseem. 1986. "The Arts Britain Ignores." In *The Struggle for Black Arts in Britain*, edited by Kwesi Owusu. London: Comedia.

McFarlene, Cassie. 1987. "Toward A Critical Evaluation of Black British Film Culture." Unpublished text, B. A. Film Photography and Television, London College of Printing.

Mercer, Kobena. 1988a. "Diaspora Culture and the Dialogic Imagination: The Aesthetics of Black Independent Film in Britain." In *Blackframes: Critical Perspectives on Black Indepen-*

dent Cinema, edited by Mbye Cham and Claire Andrade-Watkins, 50-61. Massachusetts: MIT Press.

———. 1988b. "Recoding Narratives of Race and Nation." In *Black Film, British Cinema*, ICA Documents no. 7, 4-14, London: Institute of Contemporary Art.

Owusu, Kwesi. 1986. *The Struggle for Black Arts in Britain*. London: Comedia.

Pines, Jim. 1983. "Channel 4: A Pandora's Box for Blacks?" *Artrage* 3/4: 2-5.

———. 1988. "The Cultural Context of Black British Cinema." In *Blackframes: Critical Perspectives on Black Independent Cinema*, edited by Mbye Cham and Claire Andrade-Watkins. Massachusetts: MIT Press.

Pines, Jim, and Paul Willemen. 1989. *Questions of Third Cinema*. London: British Film Institute.

Ten

Women's Independent Cinema: The Case of Leeds Animation Workshop

Antonia Lant

From the vantage point of the United States the contours of independent British film production in the 1980s appeared narrower than was the case. Economic, technological, and cultural factors all contributed to restricted distribution and exhibition patterns in the States, and while American festivals often screened British films, rental agreements rarely followed. Americans, for example, can book Sally Potter's *Thriller* (1979), *The Gold Diggers* (1983), *The London Story* (1987), and films by some of the London-based black workshops (Sankofa and Black Audio Film Collective); but no North American distributors exist for Pat Murphy's *Maeve* (1981) and *Anne Devlin* (1984), feature-length films partially funded by the British Film Institute (BFI) and made in the Republic of Ireland, or for the work of animator Vera Neubauer, or for regional workshops such as Amber Films in Newcastle, or Leeds Animation Workshop (LAW).[1]

Narrow U.S. distribution obscured the breadth of this cinema, but its invisibility also bore the imprint of underlying strata of constraint originating within Britain. Independent cinema distribution is in trouble there, too; at the time of writing the status of Circles and Cinema of Women, the two main British feminist distributors, was changing, and they now may have merged to form Cinenova. Difficulties of national distribution are amplified internationally on other grounds; the lengths, genres, styles, quality, and regional character of much filmmaking separates it from an American public. While features remain the standard product for cinema circuits, female feature directors number but few—Lezli-Ann Barrett, Laura Mulvey, Jan Worth, Beeban Kidron, Sally Potter. No British equivalents of Susan Seidelman, Kathryn Bigelow, or Penny Marshall exist. No women directed within the admittedly modest commercial sector in the eighties.[2] When the price of shorts (which women have more frequently made) is also substantial, the reasons for the scarcity of women's films, made or seen, at home and abroad begin to emerge with a vengeance (Merz, 67).

Besides the "inconvenient" (that is, varied) lengths of women's films, their content may be illegible or uninteresting overseas. The inspirational dictum of the seventies — "the personal is political" — has had a powerful corollary: the personal is also local, tied to specific audiences with specific knowledges. Murphy's *Anne Devlin* draws on the folk memory of an Irish heroine and the racism and other strains of Anglo-Irish relations (Gibbons); Creel Films' *It's A' Oor Ain* (1985) concerns Musselburgh miners and women's support groups during the 1984-85 miners' strike, while their *It's Handed Doon* (1986) is a drama/documentary about Fisherow fishwives whose creels (handwoven baskets) carry fish from market to customers; LAW's *Council Matters* presents the arcane structures of a local authority via cutout and cel-animated conversations between an inquiring girl and a latter-day cleaner-cum-witch.

Such films speak to audiences' encounters with the politics of strikes, unemployment, and local law and lore, in familiar dialects and landscapes. The regionalism of these works is one of their strengths — the cinema requires an informed audience, in which both film and viewer reverberate with local questions and experience, building audience loyalty and a regional culture of sorts.[3] But this cinema can never translate into a wider purview — the film arena of the United States — and still remain the same.[4] There it risks not being read at all.

The British television market has also shaped distribution patterns for independent cinema; televisual transmission and video rental became its dominant outlet in 1980s Britain.[5] In 1982, with the arrival of Channel Four, a quota of independent film broadcasting was mandated, and became programmed into the regular schedule, most notably in the "Eleventh Hour" slot, that eponymous, off-peak nighttime niche. The early eighties also saw a meteoric rise in the number of home video-cassette recorders in the United Kingdom, swelling from 2.5 percent of households in December 1980 to 51 percent in December 1986, and accompanied by further declines in the number of cinema-goers (Lewis, 57). While television, and particularly Channel Four, has been crucial to the survival of British cinema in the 1980s, it has inadvertently often had a countereffect on the international distribution of independent film, because of TV station attitudes that once a film has been aired, its chief, visible life is over. Preparing work for television also affects aesthetic decisions, making a work potentially unsuccessful on 16 mm, let alone on 35mm.[6] Last, the video modes in the United Kingdom and the United States—PAL and NTSC—are incompatible, prohibiting the export (and, incidentally, the pirating) of tapes without some effort and cost.

The somewhat impoverished picture of independent filmmaking visible across the Atlantic—resulting from the reasons outlined above—belies a unique and distinctive period of production in Britain, especially in the workshop sector. Women have participated in this "brave cultural experiment," which has now ended (Lovell, 102). Its demise signals one consequence of Thatcherist economic policies, with their emphasis on privatization, individual consumerism, and "enterprise culture" in which the arts and museums have to run on a profit basis or be subsidized by private monies rather than by citizens' taxes, and in which local authority funds for the arts have been massively cut.[7] Paradoxically the Workshop Movement, emergent in the early 1970s, thrived in the 1980s, on the Association of Cinematograph, Television and Allied Technicians (ACTT) Workshop Declaration (a pact directly funding independent cinema), on monies from metropolitan county councils (including the Greater London Council, which was "pioneering a new relationship between power and the people" [Hall 1988, 126]), and on the enthusiasm and needs of community activism, rallying around political causes such as the Greenham Peace Camp and the miners' strike. These social actions politicized new groups of women and mobilized cinema and video: *The Miners' Campaign Tapes*, for example, were made through workshop cooperation to spread information and raise funds.

This social network atrophied with the decade. Fewer unofficial community groups came to meet, a result of the privatization of people as much as property under Thatcher (Leadbeater, 143). LAW's film *Home and Dry?* states the undermining impact of government policy in bald terms: "The Government wants us to buy our own houses—once we have a mortgage, we aren't as free to strike." The landslide Conservative victory of 1983, the defeat of the miners' strike in 1985, the abolition of the metropolitan councils in 1986, and the effective dismantling of the Workshop Declaration in 1991, besides transforming audiences into separate persons, gradually sapped the independent filmmaking sector, even if, in Sean Cubitt's words, "the taste of a genuinely popular media culture is still in our mouths, and the need to produce it—open, accessible, accountable—has never been stronger" (Cubitt 1986, 13).

This essay will examine the context and conditions of 1980s independent filmmaking by focusing on Leeds Animation Workshop, a women's film collective based in Yorkshire, active since 1978 and still operating; it predates and survives Thatcher. Its work represents an aspect of British eighties film culture that usually escapes both academic discussion and international distribution, despite the fact that it is a highly successful cinema in its own right; of all the British film workshops, LAW recuperated the highest proportion of its production costs through distribution in the 1980s, most of it in self-distribution.[8] The outfit could be seen as a brand of enterprise culture, but one functioning by collective endeavor rather than an "atomized" Tory individualism (Leadbeater, 148). LAW's ten films to date confront major issues of the decade: privatization (*Council Matters*, 1984, 10 min.); nuclear proliferation (*Pretend You'll Survive*, 1981, 9 min.); environmental damage (*Alice in Wasteland*, 1991, 12 min.); domestic violence and sexism (*Give Us a Smile*, 1983, 12 min., and *Out to Lunch*, 1989, 12 min.); Third World debt and famine (*A Matter of Interest*, 1990, 13 min., and *Crops and Robbers*, 1986, 15 min.); child-care provision (*Who Needs Nurseries? We Do!*, 1978, 8 min.); the housing crisis (*Home and Dry?*, 1987, 8 min.); and worker safety (*Risky Business*, 1980, 15 min.).[9] The collective views these issues through the various lenses of feminist, gay, antiracist, and socialist politics, encapsulating complex arguments within broad historicogeographical frames in the space of a few minutes—and a few thousand drawings.[10] Dubbed "Woman's-Eye Propaganda," their animated shorts provide contexts for debate, education, and organization, raising questions as much as answering them in their "get-it-all-in-ism" style.[11]

Because of the range of topics addressed, and because of LAW's consistent output across the decade, a study of their work provides one way of charting the course of recent feminist filmmaking as it engages with the changing political pressures of the eighties. Of course, examination of a women's animation collective (incidentally the only one in Britain, if not the world) raises questions that differ from those raised by looking at the work of individual filmmakers; matters of funding, audiences, theoretical positions, aesthetic choices, and even quantities of footage apply differently. Other feminist film collectives have operated in Britain in the eighties, 20th Century Vixen, Red Flannel, and Sheffield Film Co-op among them. This brief study could not cover them all.[12] However, it can draw attention to the uneasy coexistence of regional, group filmmaking, sponsored by an unusual union-supported declaration, alongside a rigorous government program promoting private consumption and the "centralization of cultural power" (Cubitt 1991, 124).

My study will analyze LAW's works in chronological order, and will link them to surrounding sociopolitical movements and sister texts—films by women tackling similar issues in divergent ways. Potter and Mulvey have

used cinema to elaborate theoretical issues, particularly questions of realism, filmic pleasure, and the impossibility of "truly" representing women
through film despite its analogical force. LAW skirts the stylistic techniques
of the avant-garde and the challenge of "doing theory" through film, largely
because of the risk of alienating users. However, their choice of animation
can also be seen as a response to those aesthetic and theoretical dilemmas
facing filmmakers such as Mulvey and Potter, and expounded most fiercely in
Screen magazine during the seventies. Animation's antiliteral quality provided
an answer, albeit a different one, to debates about realism, and afforded LAW
the opportunity to make a populist feminist counter-propaganda from the
Left (Whitaker, 86).

British independent cinema has had a fairly long if shaky lineage, surviving
from the Workers' Film Association of the thirties, through the Free Cinema
movement of the fifties, and into the 1970s. Boosted by the events of May
1968 and the impact of the American avant-garde, the London Film-makers'
Co-op and Cinema Action were making and screening their own (and others')
films by 1970, as was The Other Cinema, an alternative distribution outlet
and exhibition site.[13] Several in this first wave of workshops were active in
the women's liberation movement: the Berwick Street Film Collective
(formed in London in 1972), the London Women's Film Group (begun in
1971; makers of *The Amazing Equal Pay Show*, 1974), and Four Corners
Films (started in London in 1973) (Whitaker, 85). Their films sought to challenge the politics of gender through documenting sexual inequality and
through questioning repertoires of visual culture and their impact in shaping
sociosexual norms. The Berwick Street Film Collective's *Nightcleaners*
(1972) aimed to support women's efforts to unionize as poorly paid contract
cleaners, but functioned more as a Brechtian interrogation of documentary
filmmaking codes (Johnston and Willemen).

   A member of the collective, Mary Kelly, subsequently embarked on a
massive art project that criticized the institution of motherhood in its social,
psychoanalytic, cultural, aesthetic, and even historical dimensions. This
work, her *Post-Partum Document* (hereafter *PPD*, 1973-79), incorporated
scribble drawings by her child, prints, Lacanian diagrams, typing, and quotidian objects (some infamous nappies, and pinned beetles presented to
Kelly by her son), while it eschewed representational images of the particular mother and child around whom the whole work turned. The project
brought the subject of motherhood into the art gallery, explicitly probing the
conjunction mother/artist, as well as the cultural prohibition on carrying out
both kinds of production (Pollock, chap. 7).

Laura Mulvey, a member of the London Women's Liberation Workshop (Family Study Group), under which the London Women's Film Group formed, and co-organizer of the 1972 Edinburgh Film Festival's women's event, made *Penthesilea* (1974) and *Riddles of the Sphinx* (1976) with Peter Wollen during the same period, in addition to publishing her influential article, "Visual Pleasure and Narrative Cinema." The latter ninety-minute film also scrutinized motherhood, women's work, the need for nursery provision, and representational conventions of all these. (Mary Kelly appears in the film, working on her *PPD* and interacting with her child.) In *Riddles*, Mulvey and Wollen disrupt the transparency of the cinematographic medium through off-centered framing (cropping the image of the mother, Louise, to show only her midriff region, thereby denying imagery of her face), 360-degree pans, fragmentation of the mother's "story" into thirteen parts, and the framing of her story with processed imagery of Egyptian travel footage, footage of solarized female acrobats, and a retelling of the Oedipus myth.

The imperatives for the formation of Leeds Animation Workshop and its first film, *Who Needs Nurseries? We Do!*, derive from this same historico-political context: for LAW, too, "motherhood, and how to live it, lay at the roots of the dilemma," to quote Mulvey in *Riddles*. *Riddles of the Sphinx*, *Post-Partum Document*, and *Who Needs Nurseries?* are different responses to the same dilemmas of representation, politics, and women's daily life. However, while the Mulvey/Wollen film has become a canonical text within the international feminist avant-garde — one of "The New Talkies" — and while Kelly's work was championed and eventually "released" as a book, no critical ink illuminated LAW's film, which steadily showed to local and regional action groups, at trade union meetings, at women's meetings, and at other community organizations.[14] Indeed, no critical ink has been spilled over LAW's films at all.

They have never entered the critical canon for a number of instructive reasons. First, the various working-class, female, young, old, and other audiences to which the films are addressed immediately understand them, even if they balk at them. This clarity of meaning derives from using certain elements of narrative, including cartoon characters, sequences of related events, and strong closing images, even if these might not "resolve" the questions raised by the film. It also stems from the use of accessible, melodic, rhythmic music scored for brass band (in *Council Matters*), electric piano (in *Risky Business* and *Pretend You'll Survive*), and bamboo instruments (in *Alice in Wasteland*), and imagistic sequences that also invite audience engagement through their rootedness in the everyday — the launderette, street, café, factory, supermarket. Closeness to their audience also

results from the consultation process integral to the workshop's methods of
research and scripting: before making a film they talk to activists, teachers,
and other potential users to assess their needs, often bringing a draft script
and storyboard to meetings. This may be a local process, but also regional,
national, and even international. For *Council Matters*, town halls in London
as well as garbage depots in Yorkshire were visited; for *Crops and Robbers*,
the collective met with liberation fighters from Namibia, South America, and
the South Pacific, as well as supermarket workers in Leeds.

While the films do not consistently deconstruct or dislocate content and
representation—do not engage in the distancing strategies of the filmmaking
avant-garde of the seventies and eighties and their critics—they do share a
feminist content with works such as Kelly's and Mulvey's, and similarly exist
outside the mainstream in terms of production, distribution, and exhibition.
LAW's films are borrowable at libraries and are screened at political meetings, in schools, colleges, and education and training sessions—generally at
a grass-roots level rather than in cinemas or on television—and for this reason the workshop refers to "users" of their films, conceiving them as tools to
facilitate debate and action.[15] However, the films have been shown in festivals all over the world—in Japan, India, Australia, Africa, and Canada, as well
as the United States and Europe—and have been requested by resource
centers in Colombia, Malaysia, Peru, India, and Korea, among other countries. They have been acquired for television in Germany, France, Holland,
and Cuba, and during the 1991 Clarence Thomas hearings in the United
States sections of *Out To Lunch* and *Give Us a Smile* were screened by CBS
News, as well as by BBC and ITV, to provide background coverage on the
issue of sexual harassment.

What gets lost in documenting the large, individual works of particular
artists (the traditional habit of film and art history) is an awareness of the
diversity among art practices, and here specifically feminist art practice.
Works do not necessarily appear in "official cultural sites"—commercial cinemas or academic magazines. In the words of Griselda Pollock and Rozsika
Parker, "there is a necessary relation and interchange between practical
strategies and strategic practices" (Parker and Pollock, 75). In LAW's films,
both sides of the equation are at work. Through animation LAW filmmakers
refuse the option of seamless, continuity editing and photographic realism;
and when using live action or photographic collage elements they throw
them into relief as representational, coded systems, rather than as naturally
occurring phenomena, by juxtaposing them with animation. These are strategic practices. On the other hand, the humor and transformative power of
animation and its cultural associations of accessibility and buoyancy enable

the workshop to reach and speak to its users, precluding the necessity for explanatory intellectual amplification (hence the absence of their work in cinema studies scholarship). This is a practical strategy.

Leeds Animation Workshop formed in 1977 when four women with backgrounds in experimental theater, sociology, and education joined forces in Leeds as the Nursery Film Group to campaign for the provision of more state nurseries for children.[16] Their first film, *Who Needs Nurseries? We Do!*, is worth examining in some detail, since its devices have become staples in the group's later filmic transformations of commercial habits of animation into political effectiveness.

LAW films typically present subject matter through an unconventional or traditionally unrepresented point of view.[17] In *Pretend You'll Survive* a housewife confronts her nuclear nightmares; in *Risky Business* worker Carol sustains a minor industrial accident and investigates its causes, visiting Mr. Potter, the safety officer who waters his plants as a diversion from employee needs; in *Council Matters* Freda, a char who uses her vacuum cleaner as a flying broomstick, explains how a local authority functions; in *Alice in Wasteland* Carroll's "Wonderland" is transformed as the expanding and shrinking Alice pursues the disposal of rubbish and inspects images made from torn color magazine and newspaper, symbols both of damage and reuse; and in *Who Needs Nurseries?* we hear and examine children's gripes.

That film's opening image initiates another LAW strategy—of evoking regional specificity in setting, characters, and audience. In the first drawing we see a cel-animated journalist spewing the rhetoric of "balanced" reporting plumily into his microphone; he professes to be interested in whether more nurseries are needed. Behind his head, however, looms a large, hand-scrawled poster for scrag end, local vernacular for cheap cut of meat. The geographical and class clash of interests, the North/South divide, are laid out in the juxtaposition of his posh accent with a hinterland meat market economy.[18] In the film's central section, children convene a large meeting presided over by three "chairbabies" who hear divergent opinions from children of all classes and races on whether they would like to attend a nursery. One pulls down a screen of statistics and the shrinkage of nurseries since World War II is made plain. A reproduced wartime poster ironically suggests how easily daycare was forthcoming in the past when national security was threatened.[19] In the film's last image, cel-animated children march rhythmically across the screen, carrying banners and mowing down the roving southern reporter with whom the film had begun. The children's drowning out of the southerner, who is concluding, against the evidence, that it is not

Freda's Hoovercopter in the Yorkshire landscape, in *Council Matters* (1984).

Alice surveys holes in the ozone layer, in *Alice in Wasteland* (1991).

known whether more nurseries are needed, speaks for the desire of a working class, and of mothers and children, to be heard.

While specific places are never overtly mentioned in LAW's films, local accents, vocabulary, and architecture feature prominently, enhancing an address to those close to home; the back-to-backs under Freda's Hoovercopter, the streets outside the factory in *Risky Business*, and the crier for the *Evening Post* in *Give Us a Smile* all sustain the identity of a Yorkshire setting.[20] Further, LAW employs only locally based people where possible, and completes the entire process of its filmmaking in Leeds.[21] It emphasizes local screenings: *Pretend You'll Survive* had its first public showing in the Leeds Trades Club; in the recent National Environment Week *Alice* showed on a video bus touring around Leeds. By inhabiting non-cinema venues, LAW has tried to expand and find a different audience, hoping "to get to people who don't go to cinemas, as well as those who do."[22] These attitudes toward audiences and exhibition are part and parcel of the politics of the women's movement: the determination to pull attention, monies, and identities out from under centralized capital authority (Parker and Pollock, 23). The back-to-backs in Leeds are geographically remote from Soho, London, the main location for animated cinema in Britain, but the ideological force of the distance and of its imperial/colonial overtones was made clear again in the "Looks North" section of a *Daily Telegraph* article on LAW during the making of *Home and Dry?* There Ivor Smullen "*discovers* a defiant six woman group working from a slightly down-at-heels Leeds suburb" (July 31, 1987, my emphasis).

Risky Business and *Pretend You'll Survive* followed *Who Needs Nurseries?*, continuing the use of searing wit and female viewpoints to urge audiences to consciousness, debate, and action. In the last frames of *Pretend You'll Survive*, a pun on the derided government pamphlet *Protect and Survive*, a woman rips up images of militarism, transforming them into a banner proclaiming "Don't Pretend—Protest!" *Risky Business* presents factory accidents resulting from a company's drive for profits at the expense of worker safety. Reggie the Robot, assistant to Carol, spouts excerpts from the Health and Safety at Work Act as Carol challenges management. In a Chaplinesque scene a machine swallows a worker, while in another Carol tussles with a massive dust monster, mindful of the apparently benign uses of cartoons in advertising of the Ajax "White Tornado" type. Elsewhere Carol finds the workers in contact with VBF, cryptic for "Very-Ide Bad-For-You-Ene," she discovers.

Both *Pretend You'll Survive* and *Council Matters*, made three years later, highlight the opposing aims of local and central government in Britain under

Thatcher. *Council Matters* proposes that city hall, while not perfect, is a re-source (unlike private enterprise) that people can use to improve their situation. It is a plea for local democracy, for citizens to get involved. In its image of central government using tax money to foster arms growth, *Pretend You'll Survive* is consistent with this message. This film was made expressly for disarmament campaign groups whose political momentum was growing in protest over the siting of U.S. cruise missiles at Greenham Common during the period of the making of the film; said the collective, "We set off originally to make a five-minute film about nuclear power but events overtook us in 1979-80."[23] Only four months after forty women marched from Cardiff to Greenham and spontaneously decided, on December 4, 1981, to set up camp and stay, the film began showing in Leeds.[24]

The experience of making *Pretend You'll Survive*, combined with the newly radicalized Leeds atmosphere of feminist art practice and politics, propelled LAW into becoming a women-only group, which they have been ever since.[25] The national spotlight had been turned on Leeds (and Bradford) through Peter Sutcliffe's rapes and murders of women committed over several years; dubbed "the Yorkshire Ripper," he was finally arrested and tried in early 1981. After Yorkshire police had warned women not to go out alone at night for fear of attack, local women's groups, lead by Women Against Violence Against Women, retaliated with demands for a curfew on men as more logical and just. In an obliquely related series of incidents, also in early 1981, Leeds was described hyperbolically as "the center of feminist ferment" in the local press after women, signing themselves "Angry Women," torched three Leeds stores — "Sex-shop," "Fantasy," and "Cupid" — to protest that "porn is violence against women."[26] Thousands of women signed petitions to dissuade Leeds Council from licensing more shops.

The audience and motivation for LAW's fourth and most controversial film, *Give Us a Smile*, grew out of these conditions.[27] It was released in 1983, the same year as Sally Potter's feature-length production, *The Gold Diggers*, and was scored by the same composer, Lindsay Cooper.[28] Just as it is instructive to recognize the shared political motivations of *Riddles, The Post-Partum Document*, and *Who Needs Nurseries?*, it is again useful to compare these two apparently different works — one known in the States, the other not — for they both explicitly question traditions of female representation in photographic pornography, fine art, household magazines, and film, by asking what kind of structures link market economy, female imagery, and women's struggles.

In Potter's film, shot in Iceland and London, two women, Ruby and Celeste (played by Julie Christie and Colette Lafont), trace their "origins" in "the connections between gold, money, and women" (Potter in Rosenbaum, 128). The connections prove to lie in exploitation and capital; as Ruby puts it, gradually claiming her identity, "I've been framed." The film draws on audience knowledge of Christie's career as a star, and on iconography of the white female film heroine, especially that of Griffith's melodramas and film noir. Francophone, black Celeste is a city bank employee who looks behind the figures she pounds into the computer to uncover male stereotypes of bureaucrats, servants, "anonymous pursuers and street terrorizers" (Potter in Rosenbaum, 129). In one of the more startling moments of the film, Celeste rides on a white charger into a ballroom (the outpatient's hall of the disused Royal Free Hospital) and whisks Ruby away from the tedium of formal dancing with uniformly suited men.

Give Us a Smile, LAW's first film to combine live action with animation, opens with imagery of an anonymous pursuer. His feet follow a woman's down a dark street; shot with live action, the scene is reminiscent of the opening moves of Michael Powell's *Peeping Tom*, with its stealthy piano chords, high-heeled shoes, and menacing shadows. The tension continues as now a cel-animated woman also walks a street and passes shops plastered with images of women she cannot understand but uncannily recognizes, like Christie's Ruby of *The Gold Diggers*. The collective's angry lyrics accompanying Cooper's score convey the problem: "Why do the things they say have to dominate my day? . . . Every window that I see tries to tell me how to be. . . . On every shelf I see my face—and there isn't any space to be alone." These words are interlaid with questions to rape victims taken from police reports: "You are in the habit of going into public houses, are you not?" "Are you on the pill?" "What did you expect if you shared a taxi with him?" "Did you say no when you meant yes?" These are also combined with phrases of street harassment: "Cor, look at the knockers on that!" "When did you last have it, luv?" "Cheer up, it might never happen," and, of course, "Heh, give us a smile."

LAW and Potter have both written of their hope of conveying a sense of discovery and pleasure for women through film, of presenting the opportunity for recognition, identification, and rethinking. In LAW's words, "We didn't want women to go away from the film feeling completely depressed. . . . We wanted it to be a positive piece."[29] Likewise Potter writes that "ultimately my own desire was and is to give pleasure; to heal the 'pleasure time blues' of the opening song" whose lines demand: "Please give me back my good night out,/Please give me back my leisure time" (Potter in Rosenbaum, 129). Potter's image of Celeste bursting in to rescue Ruby is reminis-

Breaking out of bondage, in *Give Us a Smile* (1983).

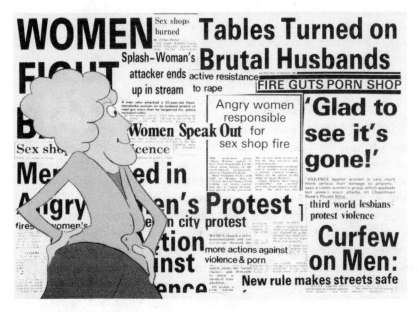

Alternative headlines, in *Give Us a Smile*.

cent in both spirit and iconography of that in *Give Us a Smile* when the tables turn and animated women begin to make their own images. A drawn woman recomposes a television show (for which all the credits are given to "a man" except wardrobe and makeup) with spray paint, brush, and matches. A black-and-white still cartoon of a woman, signed "a man" again, leaps off the page, out of her bondage, escaping from victim status to the sound of tinkling glass, while literalizing the distinction between animated and still cartoons. Another woman transforms typical tabloid headlines of attacks on women into ones of "Women Fight Back" and "Fire Guts Porn Shop," borrowed from recent Leeds women's actions. Elsewhere graffiti is added to stocking and cigarette advertisements, making them reveal their sexist suppositions.[30] And a porn shop disappears into crackling animated flames in the film's last shot.

Whether directing political energy against pornography is tactically sound has been the subject of intensive debate among feminists.[31] What the Leeds film provides through the imagery of animated arson, however, is a "fantasy of reversal," a release of the feeling of the possibility of change (Williamson 1984, 322). It is a desire parallel to that expressed by Potter for her own film, in her lyrics for its "theme tune" and in her work's final image of a Rosie the Riveter wielding her welding gun in a shower of sparks. While the two films diverge dramatically in length, and while Potter's might be more historically engaged and designated "an experimental or avant-garde film," and LAW's "a political film, in the agitational or militant sense," they both insist on the importance of drawing in an audience through the pleasure of music and image, and both use the motif of escape—be it from TV, a page, or a ballroom—to express the potential of a different future (Wollen, 31).

Give Us a Smile was the first of LAW's films to be made under the Workshop Declaration of 1982. This was an agreement between the British Film Institute, Channel Four, the Regional Arts Associations, the Independent Film and Video Association, and the Association of Cinematograph, Television and Associated Technicians (ACTT) facilitating funding, security, and continuity of employment in the "cultural and grant-aided sector" of film. LAW was among the first workshops to become franchised and was one of four to be sponsored by the British Film Institute rather than by Channel Four.[32] The declaration boosted LAW's ability to operate an "integrated practice" of distribution, exhibition, education, and training, as well as production. They carried this out perhaps more than any other workshop; as well as producing and distributing their own films they have participated in local, regional, national, and international cultural initiatives. They have organized, attended, and addressed screenings of their films and those of others; talked to audiences within and outside Britain; held regular training weekends and other courses; and acted as a film resource center, receiving visitors from several countries, as well as from local districts.

The declaration made all this possible because it offered long-term support and better working conditions (including union maternity leaves and allowances) and allowed collective members to participate in all aspects of production, rotating tasks rather than being forced to respect the usual union-marked divisions of labor.[33] It also allowed filmmakers to pay regular wages, and stated the collective's right to pay equal wages to all its workers. In terms of its provision of a more hospitable climate for film production, the declaration was the single most important event of the 1980s for the workshops. But its positive benefits were eroded by changes that minimized other sources of funding. *Home and Dry?*, the workshop's seventh film, was made just as the defeats of the second half of the eighties were beginning: the abolition of the Eady Levy in 1985, of capital allowances for British films in 1986, and of the Metropolitan County Councils in the same year.[34] Funding for the film came in under the wire from CHAR, the Campaign for the Homeless and Rootless, themselves sponsored by the Board and Lodging Information Programme of the Greater London Council.

Under Thatcher's housing policy, while some council tenants had become home owners, homelessness had reached the highest level on record, and council house building had slumped dramatically. The physical and emotional loss of homes was papered over in prime ministerial rhetoric: "The family is the building block of society. . . . It is the preparation for the rest of our life. And women run it" (quoted in Brunt 1988, 19). LAW's film confronts these contradictions—between ample metaphorical and minimal physical homes—via four female animated characters who tend their washing at the local launderette. A lesbian woman, an older single woman, and women from the Carribean and Pakistan whose home is Britain all present their dilemmas—staying in bad relationships for lack of alternative housing, living with the impermanency of bed-and-breakfast policy, not being consulted about their needs, and so on. Their collective anxiety is expressed through a Victorian sampler whose platitude "No Place Like Home" dissolves into "Nowhere to Go." As in *Who Needs Nurseries?* and *Pretend You'll Survive*, the film ends with images of banners, this time in Bengali and English, urging viewers to discuss, act, and protest.

In using female characters and voice-overs to express ideas and means of action, LAW insists that crises in housing, Third World debt, and environmental destruction, while on the surface unrelated to gender, have a particular and important impact on women. LAW's films highlight what Meehan has called the "feminization" of poverty under Thatcher, with its freezing of children's allowances, complication of access to maternity pay and reemployment, and privatization of health services, which "encourages the idea women should be at home to care for the sick and elderly" (Meehan 1990, 197-98).[35] In 1987 *Spare Rib* reported the following impact of 1980s Conservative policy on women: "Women's unemployment since 1979 has tripled from 327,000 to 934,000. Women are 44% of the workforce, 80% of the low paid workforce, and 2 out of 3 of those in poverty" (Whitlock, 15).

In the face of this evidence Thatcher persistently styled herself a "Housewife Prime Minister," particularly when addressing a female constituency. In an alliterative 1982 speech she compared running the national economy to running the domestic one: "Some say I preach merely the homilies of housekeeping or the parables of the parlour. But I do not repent. Those parables would have saved many a financier from failure and many a country from crisis" (quoted in McFadyean and Renn, 111). To the Conservative Women's Conference six years later she argued, "I cannot help reflecting that it has taken a Government headed by a housewife, with the experience of running a family, to balance the books for the first time in twenty years—with a little left over for a rainy day" (quoted in Brunt 1988, 19). Bea Campbell points out that in Thatcher's constant reference to the housewife in herself—and its value in sorting out the national economy—she has "made the domestic visible" (236). However, in bringing women "into the political conversation . . . as housewives" she renders "invisible the housewife who is also in waged work and . . . blurs the contradictions experienced by the wageless housewife" (Campbell, 236-37). LAW's films are peopled by the latter categories.

There is a necessary if paradoxical shared ground between LAW's focus on the domestic, everyday experience of their viewers and this housewifely aspect of Thatcher's rhetoric; one uncovers the tracks of the other.[36] And the two politics meet above all in the supermarket, in the motif of shopping, which recurs in Thatcherism's promotions of the promise of individual choice just as it does in LAW's images of connection between women's tasks and international politics. In the collective's words, the shopping mall is "no longer a morally neutral place."

As a woman scrutinizes products for sale in her Leeds supermarket in *Crops and Robbers*—tea, bananas, sugar—we and she are made aware, through drawing and intercutting, of the origins of these goods outside England, and the human, political, and economic price of their journeys to the shelf. In the film Mexico is represented as an outpost of the United States

The cultivated strawberry, in *Crops and Robbers* (1986).

where a cel-animated strawberry (reminiscent of the California raisins), re-
plete with underarm pesticide, is being fattened for export by plane up north
while local farmers go hungry. Crayoned cutouts of vegetables march in
ranks from Africa and South America to Europe, having decimated the local
flora. Through these and other compressed references to plantations, slav-
ery, food aid, and colonies we learn "Imperialism for Beginners," a lesson
that animation is superbly equipped to deliver (Petley, 355).

   Initially the film's voice-over belongs to First World politicians of the last
five hundred years, expressing imperialist international sentiments: "Food is
a weapon — it is now one of the principle weapons in our negotiating kit,"
and, "Let us remember that the main purpose of American aid is not to help
others but to help ourselves." Pieces are moved around a pseudo-Monopoly
board to convey the checks and balances of international trade and capital.
This long history and complex network of debts and surpluses weighs more
and more heavily on the old woman shopping in Leeds, whose poverty in-
hibits her consumption, and on the young woman price-tagging food along-

side her. Eventually the empire's voice is taken over by subaltern tongues, who call for First World people to recognize the connection between their own deprivations and decisions (in the supermarket) and the exploitation of the Third World. An end to multinational capitalism is demanded, and the entire board is upturned to symbolize this revolution. The final shots show ranks of women, of all ages and colors, marching down the shopping aisles.

In this film a double movement is at work: against the centralization that makes London/Parliament the holder of the purse strings and the focus of national culture (as in earlier films), but also toward making visible the concerns of working people globally—in Petley's words, "Poverty is not simply a third world matter" (Petley, 355). *Pretend You'll Survive, Crops and Robbers, A Matter of Interest,* and *Alice in Wasteland* link the domestic to the international, locating both subject matter and audience within a world picture—all four films abound with images of maps and globes. This geographical and social web is explained as a consequence of both past and present events, of the economic and social history of colonialism as it abuts contemporary struggles, particularly in the later films. In this way LAW is engaging the "politics of location," alongside Sheffield Film Co-op's *Bringing it All Back Home* (1987), Ngozi Omwurah's *Coffee Coloured Children* (1988), Black Audio Film Collective's *Handsworth Songs* (1986), Sankofa's *Passion of Remembrance* (1986), and so much other independent film of late 1980s Britain, which sees domestic poverty and labor as tied to that of postcolonial countries, and conceives personal histories as part and parcel of international, imperialist ones.[37]

An expanded visual vocabulary expresses the increased complexity of LAW's later analyses: in *Alice,* recycled envelopes, newspaper, and rubbish coalesce to form images of sprouting beans and continental drift; other drawings are made directly onto the celluloid, as usual, but thinner paint is used, mixed with glues, to produce watery stains evocative of pollution. *Crops and Robbers* employs pixillation in the movement of elements on the board game (a sort of 3-D animation), live action, cel and cutout animation, and slow-motion footage of a die falling through the air and landing on the board. The intermixing of techniques conveys the labyrinthine paths of imported goods as well as the interlacing of the ideas expressed. This general strategy is brought vividly home in a moment of apparent match-on-action; a crayon-drawn, engraved calabash overflowing with mixed tropical fruits cuts to a live action supermarket scene in which the price tagger apparently receives the goods, from off-screen, but now they are a uniformly packaged melon monoculture, photographically reproduced. The artisanal quality of colored drawing borders the processed character of live action photography in a mimesis of the international politics of food.

Out to Lunch, the last film I want to discuss, is the one that most directly examines the extended life of gender representation.[38] Here pencil-colored, hinged, cutout figures and collages of muscle-building and dietary magazine imagery deftly visualize conceptual and physical pressures on women to occupy "little space," either actually or verbally. Virginia Woolf's premise that "women have served all these centuries as looking glasses, possessing the magic and delicious power of reflecting the figure of a man at twice his natural size" is printed in white on a black screen in the opening moments of the film. The collective then literalizes Woolf's metaphorical image in a café setting. Sitting at a table, a woman listens to a man blathering unintelligible words; his reflection expands in her spectacles as she interjects, "That's fascinating," "How amazing," "Wonderful," "You're so clever." The café's animated chalkboard menu resonates with new linguistic significance, punctuating familiar, prandial encounters: on offer are "mussels" or "slimmer's special," "ego soufflé," "honey bun," "humble pie," "just desserts," and finally "piece of cake," as the waitress puts up her feet, having scooped her trying customers into the draining rack and having brushed letters spelling "manpower" into the bin. At two points the sexual politics of space are expressed through a changed vantage point for the audience, who now see an aerial view of the table. The new vision this unexpected angle creates evokes the spectator's raised consciousness of the gendered significance of daily habits, literally presented by the male "space invaders" who compress women to the end of the table.

According to LAW, this film campaigns for women to become "linguistically visible" and aims to "deepen and accelerate" this process, by sensitizing viewers to the woman-reflecting-man syndrome and by dismantling apron-wearing, waitress-style clichés. Margaret Thatcher has been no friend to feminism—her scorn for its efforts and her stated belief that man or woman, "you get on because you have the right talents" are well documented (quoted in McFadyean and Renn, 111). Yet she does offer a model of a new womanhood: "She has brought qualities of ruggedness and ruthlessness to femininity which perhaps only men hadn't noticed before in women" (Campbell, 246). She has not reflected men at twice their size but challenged them to housewifely knowledge in order to distinguish her work and express her power. However, while Thatcher's image counters the magnifying woman of LAW's café, hers has not been a prowoman politics. A single female Conservative prime minister is not equatable with collective female empowerment, production, and action.

Aerial view of space invasion, in *Out to Lunch* (1989).

Animation has been an aesthetic choice for other feminist filmmakers besides LAW—Ayoka Chenzira in the States, Vera Neubauer in Britain, and Nina Sabnani in India, for example. The reasons for their choice are multifaceted, linked to practical, economic criteria as well as to questions of representation, gender, and politics. Animation is user-friendly: in 1976, when future members of LAW were first considering filmmaking, only a handful of rentable 16-mm cameras existed in Yorkshire—live action filmmaking was not practicable outside London. Animation is woman-friendly: its technology is advantageous to women in whom is so commonly inculcated a fear or revulsion of machinery, a training to run away from it.[39] Animation can be done in low-tech, quiet corners (on the kitchen table, according to British animator Sheila Graber), away from glaring studio lights; it can be a way into cinema. Animation has also been collective-friendly: group decisions are more feasible when few or no actors absorb finances.[40] In Creyke's words, "Leeds film star Alice is paper thin, remains silent about her professional life and lives in a cardboard box." Without actors and studio rentals, less pressure exists for on-the-spot decisions. Although animation is very labor intensive, its simpler technology can reduce costs, another allure for independent filmmakers:

Defrocking racism, in *Out to Lunch*.

LAW reckons to spend about £5,000 per minute, while commercial animation costs may be up to £5,000 per second for hi-tech, computerized work.[41]

Beyond these practical attractions, animation holds a particular ideological niche in the wider culture that LAW both draws on, and redraws. Animation evokes American studios, fantasy, expensively produced worlds of immortality and immunity; in LAW's films characters and animals exposed to toxic fumes, intensive farming, and radiation simply perish, rather than rebounding like Tom or Jerry. Commercial animation has a repertoire of motifs for signaling femininity—ribbons, curls, frocks, eyelashes—exaggerated to the hilt in *Who Framed Roger Rabbit*'s Jessica Rabbit; one of the challenges for LAW is to find new means of representing women, still recognizable by audiences, without reproducing this constricting menu. The problem is encapsulated in an image from *Out to Lunch* in which an Asian woman is turned down for a waitressing job because the "uniform" will not fit her. The uniform is a cutout, aproned drawing of a white, blond woman, with tabs for attachment. It is the uniform Thatcher temporarily dons in her housewifely mode.

Animation has also been a tool for propaganda—for telescoping messages or transforming familiar images. It has been used to sell goods in advertising and to sell ideologies in wartime. LAW inherits this performance of politics through images—and admires Norman McLaren's *Hell Unlimited* (1938), for example. Animation provides LAW with an alternative to talking heads for conveying information succinctly and humorously, in a combination of visual and linguistic forms. Animation is to live action as poetry is to prose, says the workshop—representation of a distilled, precise kind. Only through animation may Alice encounter landfill, waste dumps, deforestation, genetic engineering (Cloney Island), ozone depletion, and acid rain, all in the space of twelve minutes. It is work in synch with an electorate that thinks "politically not in terms of policies but images." Work such as LAW's functions by "capturing people's political imaginations" in constructing issues "into an image" (Hall, 260).

One consequence of this compression (certainly the result of attendant economic factors, as well) is the creation of films short enough to be used in the classroom, allowing time for other events to follow screenings— discussion or a tandem film. They can take the traditional position of the Disney cartoon before the feature, wittily conveying in a few seconds the chief lessons of Dale Spender or Woolf, disseminating them, and inflecting understanding of adjacent texts.[42] *Crops and Robbers* was shown in a double bill with *A Question of Silence* in Leeds—two feminist perspectives on shopping mall politics. LAW films may not be avant-garde in the modernist sense of performing a distancing aesthetic critique of representation, but they can function alongside that avant-garde, emerging from the same politics but into a different ambit. They too find a route away from conventions of realism, but through the hybrid medium of art and photography that is animation.

Postscript

Over the winter of 1990 first Channel Four and then the BFI withdrew their support from the Workshop Declaration, making it essentially inoperable. Both Channel Four and the British Film Institute now wish to commission individual films and programs from workshops (as well as any other independent group or individual) rather than having a stake in the long-term running of an outfit, and wish to have explicit editorial input throughout production (Vale). However, the special rates and flexible union agreements worked out through the declaration only make sense alongside a commitment (whether it be from Channel Four, the British Film Institute, or other bodies) to continuity of funding for daily running costs and salaries; the declaration was "formulated to acknowledge the specific and exceptional conditions prevailing in the cultural and grant-aided sector and [was] designed to encourage the development and growth of stability and permanent employment in this sector" (ACTT, 10). That permanence is now threatened: Sheffield Film Co-op went on the dole in June 1991; LAW reduced their number of members from six to five, and are searching for alternative sources of funding with an increased urgency. During the week of my June 1991 visit, *Crops and Robbers* and *Out to Lunch* were being screened in the Leeds Art Gallery as part of the Leeds European Festival week on food! The next day two of the group were meeting their Euro-MP to discuss European funding for animation, a meeting that later bore fruit in the form of support for a film about occupational stress. The group is researching three other new projects: a lesbian subject titled *On the Line; Off Your Trolley*, about supermarket decisions; and a television "history" with animated inserts on a twelfth-century abbess, Hildegard of Bingen.

I thank Leeds Animation Workshop for our correspondence and discussions, and for the access they gave me to their films and archive in June 1991. I also thank Women Make Movies and First Run/Icarus for making films available for viewing, and Anne-Marie Smith for comments and especially her bibliographic suggestions. All illustrations are reproduced courtesy of Leeds Animation Workshop, 45 Bayswater Road, Leeds, West Yorkshire LS8 5LF (tel: 0532 484997).

Notes

1. LAW is currently negotiating U.S. distribution rights through Icarus/First Run in New York and Frameline in San Francisco. Their films are widely distributed in Canada and Australia.

2. To suggest the limited scope of that sector, twenty-seven British features were released in 1982, and thirty-four in 1983. Beeban Kidron's film *Antonia and Jane*, made for television, was theatrically released in the United States in 1991-92.

3. Cubitt (1991) discusses the challenge that video represents to centralized culture in its potential to build a democratic media network. There are also parallels between the Workshop Movement, in which the ability to record has been in the hands of local, often untrained, people, and the activities and motivations of Mass Observation in the 1930s.

4. See also Ed Buscombe's discussion of the pressures on British television to become more international after 1992 with the removal of trade barriers within Europe. He argues that a federal structure—currently in the form of the decentralized BBC—paradoxically allows for the production of regional fictional television, such as Alan Bleasdale's "Boys from the Blackstuff" and "GBH" (about Liverpool politics), as well as the popular soap opera "EastEnders." Such regional television will not find a large enough European market after 1992, he argues, and will perish (Ed Buscombe, "Nationhood, Media, Culture: Britain," paper for the Society of Cinema Studies Annual Conference, Los Angeles, May 24, 1991).

5. LAW began upgrading its videotapes in 1985, transferring them onto one-inch masters rather than low-band U-matic masters; most people were by then seeing their films only on video.

6. This important though sensitive topic is discussed by Whitaker, Lovell, and Williamson (1987), among others.

7. The term "enterprise culture" is thoroughly analyzed, in all its oxymoronic glory, in Caughie and Frith.

8. By the provisions of the Workshop Declaration, under which LAW's films have been made since 1982, any financial surpluses generated through production must be reinvested in the "activities and infrastructure of the Workshop" (ACTT, 3).

9. Besides these ten films, LAW has made a variety of short animated pieces, including a brief sequence for a Labour party political broadcast (1980-81); an extended title and end sequence for *Print It Yourself*, a four-part Channel Four series on community printing initiatives (1984); and an animated logo produced for Scan, a collective of Asian women making videos in London (1986).

10. LAW filmmakers work only in 16 mm. Their films usually require between 12 and 24 drawings per second, but over 50 may be used in more complicated, composite frames.

11. Coined by the Halifax *Evening Courier*.

12. Still less the scores of other, mostly unfranchised workshops producing films in Britain in the eighties. See Cubitt's (1986) discussion of the quantity and types of workshops, distinguishing between those emphasizing process and those emphasizing product in their filmmaking. About twenty workshops were eventually granted franchises under the declaration in all.

13. Sheila Whitaker excellently surveys this lineage and its recent evolutions. My account is indebted to her essay. See also MacPherson.

14. The expression "The New Talkies" was coined by the editors of *October* 17 (Summer 1981) to characterize those films informed by discourses of film theory, psychoanalysis, and semiotics, and proceeding from "the radical critique of representation" (p. 3).

15. LAW has written substantial accompanying notes for all the films, intended to aid discussion. *Who Needs Nurseries?*, *Risky Business*, *Pretend You'll Survive* and *Out to Lunch* have aired on Channel Four.

16. Only one of the group, Gillian Lacey, had professional experience in commercial animation—she had worked on *The Yellow Submarine* in a junior capacity, but had abandoned the field and had been teaching in London for seven years before moving to Leeds and becoming active in nursery campaigning. Another important founding member, Jenni Carter, had been a theater designer working at the Royal Court, London, among other venues, before moving up to Leeds, having a child, and entering the campaign. Currently, in 1991, the group has five members: Terry Wragg, Stephanie Munro, Janis Goodman, Jane Bradshaw, and Milena Dragic. Terry Wragg is the only member of the original Nursery Film Group still to be part of the collective.

17. Of course, to even talk of point of view implies the presence of characters or coherent personalities within the films, a convention of commercial cinema that a film such as *Riddles* sought to challenge.

18. The North/South divide is a symbolic one, conveying the division between privilege and nonprivilege. As Hall points out, in another context, the North is not uniform, "there are plenty of 'Southerners' living in the 'North' " (Hall 1988, 264).

19. Thatcher's Education Act of 1980 was to reduce the number of nurseries further through local authority spending cuts.

20. Islington Borough Council, London, funded a cockney soundtrack for *Council Matters*, amending the script and replacing the original Yorkshire brogue. The need for a new track, recorded by LAW in Leeds using speakers "imported" from London's East End, suggests how important accent has been in efforts to reach specific sectors of the British audience. As part of LAW's agreement in receiving grants from the local authority, films and videos purchased by residents of the City of Leeds are available at a reduced rate.

21. Until 1983, the collective had to transport all their drawings and props down to London to animate them, since there was no access to a rostrum camera in Leeds.

22. *Leeds Other Paper*, Nov. 27, 1981.

23. *Leeds Other Paper*, Nov. 27, 1981.

24. The women's peace movement, focused through Greenham, became the largest mass feminist campaign of the early 1980s, as Beeban Kidron and Amanda Richardson's film *Carry Greenham Home* (1983) documents. The camp grew to thousands: on December 12, 1982, 30,000 women holding hands circled the nine-mile perimeter fence of the future nuclear weapons base; a year later the missiles arrived as 50,000 women encircled the base.

25. The Leeds Women's Art Programme—for coordinating local women's art-making and study—began in 1981. It was modeled on the Feminist Art Program in California of 1970-71, and was the first such organization in Britain. The Leeds Women's Photography Project opened in the Pavilion for processing and exhibiting photography in May 1983. Although LAW was not directly involved with these groups, they strengthened the culture of women's artistic practice in the region, as did the exhibition of several sections of Mary Kelley's *Post-Partum Document* in Leeds in 1979, one of their earliest exhibition venues in Britain. See also Parker and Pollock, 1987, 33-35.

26. Halifax *Evening Courier* and *Leeds Women's Liberation Newsletter*, April 1981, reprinted in Kanter et al. 1984, 49, where the group is referred to by the name Sex-Shop Arsonists. Leeds still has a reputation for feminist activism, especially of the pro-censorship variety.

27. A furor blew up when the *Yorkshire Evening Post* printed a misleading front-page headline—"Leeds 'fun' cartoon prompted by the Ripper"—to announce the BFI's grant to the workshop for making the film, all the time capitalizing on the word "Ripper" to sell newspapers and obscuring the specific politics informing the project. The paper even interviewed the mother of one of Sutcliffe's victims for the story (*Yorkshire Evening Post*, May 29, 1981).

28. In an interview LAW recalled the energy given to women's filmmaking generally in Britain when Potter's all-women crew was making *The Gold Diggers* in 1982-83.

29. *Leeds Other Paper*, Oct. 21, 1983.

30. Here the film is indebted to Jill Posener and the graffitists whose work she documents. It also draws on Judith Williamson's *Decoding Advertisements* and Griselda Pollock's analyses of fine art's traditions of representing women. Pollock was consulted in the making of the film.

31. See especially the divergence of opinion among Williams, Koch, MacKinnon, and Stern (a contemporary example).

32. Channel Four purchased LAW's three earlier films, although *Give Us a Smile* was never broadcast because the particularities of buy-back agreements for animation took until 1991 to resolve. Again the film's length was a problem, since the channel usually paid so much per minute per program and this film was shorter than most, though more labor intensive. *Out to Lunch* was a commission from the channel's animation department, which later bought the TV rights to *Alice in Wasteland*. As all this suggests, it is their practice of animation that makes LAW anomalous within the workshop sector; they have been alone in that sector in receiving almost no benefits from the Independent Film Department of Channel Four save a small equipment grant toward the purchase of a secondhand Steenbeck. The other ten workshops to be franchised in 1983 were Amber Films (Newcastle), Birmingham Film and Video Workshop, Cinema Action (London), Four Corners (London), Front Room Productions (London), Newsreel Collective (London), North East Film Workshop (Rosedale, North Yorkshire), Open Eye Film and Video (Liverpool), Sheffield Film Co-op, and Trade Films (Tyne and Wear). By 1985 eighteen were funded, and the black workshops Ceddo, Sankofa, and Black Audio Film Collective formed part of this second wave—Ceddo formed in 1981-82, for instance, and became a franchised workshop in 1985.

33. Malcolm Le Grice points out that in eroding the traditional union concept of a division of labor, ACTT was bowing to the inevitable; changes in technology had made "that division less and less tenable" (Panel Discussion, 7). One can also recognize here the seeds of a weakening of the media unions under the Workshop Declaration, even though it was devised by union members, among others.

34. Parliament and County Hall had become increasingly polarized. Thatcher closed down the GLC and other metropolitan bodies broadly because they were clearly antinuclear, left-wing, benign authorities offering power to citizens as best they could (see Hall 1988).

35. Women, employed or not, have not voted in large numbers for Thatcher in any of her three elections (Hall 1988, 266; Segal, 214).

36. For discussions of Thatcherism and feminism see also Brunt (1988, 1990), Gardiner, Franklin, Lurie, and Stacey (1991); and Segal.

37. "The Politics of Location" was the title of a symposium held in Birmingham in October 1988 at the Midland Arts Center. The proceedings are largely reproduced in *Framework* 36 (1989).

38. *Out to Lunch* has been adapted as a book of cartoons for Penguin by Jane Bradshaw, due for publication in 1992. The film was originally titled *Just Desserts*, and briefly *Out of Bounds*.

39. See Cockburn for a discussion of women's exclusion and discouragement from technical education and employment, from high school onward.

40. LAW uses actors, at Equity rates, for voice-overs and occasionally on camera.

41. Through the Workshop Declaration the ACTT also agreed to union members working at especially negotiated lower rates because of the special circumstances applying to animation, and in recognition of the general tightness of funding for independent film.

42. Ideas in Dale Spender's *Man Made Language* were taken up in *Out to Lunch*.

Works Cited

ACTT Workshop Declaration. London: ACTT, 1984.

Brunt, Rosalind. 1988. "Conference Darling." *Spare Rib* 192 (June): 19.

_____. 1990. "The Politics of Identity." In *New Times: The Changing Face of Politics in the 1990s*, edited by Stuart Hall and Martin Jacques. New York: Verso.

Campbell, Beatrix. 1987. *The Iron Ladies: Why Do Women Vote Tory?* London: Virago.

Caughie, John, and Simon Frith. 1990. "The British Film Institute: Re-tooling the Culture Industry." *Screen* 31 (2): 214-22.

Cockburn, Cynthia. 1985. *Machinery of Dominance: Women, Men, and Technical Know-How*. London: Pluto.

Creyke, Anne. 1991. "Alice in Wasteland." *Yorkshire Evening Post*, Feb. 11.

Cubitt, Sean. 1986. "From Workhouse to Workshop." *Arts Express*, August/September, 13-14.

_____. 1991. *Timeshift: On Video Culture*. New York: Routledge.

Film Policy, as Presented to Parliament. 1984. London: HMSO.

Franklin, Sarah, Celia Lury, and Jackie Stacey, eds. 1991. *Off-Centre: Feminism and Cultural Studies*. London: Birmingham Cultural Studies, Harper Collins.

Gardiner, Jean. 1983. "Women, Recession and the Tories." In *The Politics of Thatcherism*, edited by Stuart Hall and Martin Jacques. London: Lawrence and Wishart.

Gibbons, Luke. 1986. "The Politics of Silence: *Anne Devlin*, Women and Irish Cinema." *Framework* 30/31: 2-14.

Hall, Stuart. 1988. *The Hard Road to Renewal*. London: Verso.

Hall, Stuart, and Martin Jacques, eds. 1983. *The Politics of Thatcherism*. London: Lawrence and Wishart.

_____, eds. 1990. *New Times: The Changing Face of Politics in the 1990s*. New York: Verso.

Johnston, Claire, and Paul Willemen. 1975/76. "Brecht in Britain: The Independent Political Film (on *The Nightcleaners*)." *Screen* 16 (4).

Kanter, Hannah, Sarah Lefanu, Shaila Shah, and Carole Spedding, eds. 1984. *Sweeping Statements: Writings from the Women's Liberation Movement, 1981-83*. London: Women's Press.

Kelly, Mary. 1983. *Post-Partum Document*. London: Routledge and Kegan Paul.

Koch, Gertrude. 1989. "The Body's Shadow Realm." *October* 50 (Fall): 3-29.

Leadbeater, Charlie. 1990. "Power to the Person." In *New Times: The Changing Face of Politics in the 1990s*, edited by Stuart Hall and Martin Jacques, 137-49. New York: Verso.

Lewis, Justin. 1990. *Art, Culture, and Enterprise: The Politics of Art and the Cultural Industries*. London and New York: Routledge.

Lovell, Alan. 1990. "That Was the Workshop That Was." *Screen* 31 (1): 102-8.

McFadyean, Melanie, and Margaret Renn. *Thatcher's Reign: A Bad Case of the Blues*. London: Chatto and Windus, 1984.

MacKinnon, Catharine. *Feminism Unmodified: Discourses on Life and Law*. Cambridge: Harvard University Press, 1987.

MacPherson, Don, ed. 1980. *Traditions of Independence: British Cinema in the Thirties*. London: British Film Institute.

Meehan, Elizabeth. 1990. "British Feminism from the Sixties to the Eighties." In *British Feminism in the Twentieth Century*, edited by Harold L. Smith. Amherst: University of Massachusetts.

Merz, Caroline. 1987. "Distribution Matters: Circles." *Screen* 28 (4): 66-69.

Panel Discussion. 1984. " 'Training' the Independents." *Screen* 25 (6): 5-16.

Parker, Roszika, and Griselda Pollock, eds. 1987. *Framing Feminism: Art and the Women's Movement 1970-1985*. London and New York: Pandora Press.

Petley, Julian. 1986. "Crops and Robbers." *Monthly Film Bulletin* 53 (634): 354-55.

Pollock, Griselda. 1989. *Vision and Difference: Femininity, Feminism, and the Histories of Art*. New York: Routledge.

Posener, Jill. 1982. *Spray it Loud*. London: Routledge and Kegan Paul.

Rosenbaum, Jonathan. 1984. "*The Gold Diggers*: A Preview." *Camera Obscura* 12 (Summer): 126-29.

Segal, Lynne. 1983. "The Heat in the Kitchen." In *The Politics of Thatcherism*, edited by Hall and Jacques. London: Lawrence and Wishart.

Spender, Dale. 1980. *Man Made Language*. Boston: Routledge and Kegan Paul.

Stern, Leslie. 1982. "The Body as Evidence." *Screen* 23 (5): 39-60.

Vale, Jo. 1989. "Screens First: On the Threat to Radical TV." *Guardian*, May 22.

Whitaker, Sheila. 1985. "Declarations of Independence." In *British Cinema Now*, edited by Martyn Auty and Nick Roddick, 83-98. London: British Film Institute.

Whitlock, M. J. 1987. "Five More Years of Desolation?" *Spare Rib* 180 (July): 15.

Williams, Linda. 1989. *Hard Core: Power, Pleasure and Machines of the Visible*. Berkeley: University of California Press.

Williamson, Judith. 1984. "Give Us a Smile." *Monthly Film Bulletin* 51 (609): 322.

_____. 1987. "Causes without a Rebel." *New Statesman*, August 21, 19-20.

Wollen, Peter. 1982. *Readings and Writings*. London: Verso.

Wollen, Peter, and Laura Mulvey. 1976. "Written Discussion." *Afterimage* 6 (Summer): 30-39.

Eleven

The Body Politic: Ken Russell in the 1980s

Barry Keith Grant

Ken Russell is commonly known—and most often summarily dismissed—as a director who indulges in visual excess. Unlike many other art-house auteurs, most notably Federico Fellini and Luchino Visconti, with whom he is often compared (or more accurately, contrasted), commentators commonly see Russell as vulgar, tasteless, excessive, puerile, misogynist, and even misanthropic. Critics established this view of Russell early in his career, at least since his last film for BBC television, *Dance of the Seven Veils* (1970), a biography of Richard Strauss that created a storm of controversy, including a parliamentary motion criticizing the film's "viciousness, savagery and brutality" (Baxter, 30). This reputation has remained entrenched ever since. Whatever prestige Russell gained with his third feature film, *Women in Love* (1969), a generally sensitive adaptation of the D. H. Lawrence novel, was largely negated by the two pictures that followed. *The Music Lovers* (1970) and *The Devils* (1971), much more flamboyant than *Women in Love*, displayed Russell's more notorious qualities: bold, startling images of eroticism, physical revulsion, and violence, and a rapid "kino-fist" editing style frequently incorporating unsubtle shock effects, combining in what Michael Dempsey vividly described as "hyperthyroid camp circuses" (Dempsey 1977/78, 24).

Unlike the films of his contemporary, Richard Lester, which share a certain visual energy, Russell's work concentrates less on exuberant *jouissance* than on the darker aspects of the sexual self. Thus, while critics touted the American-born Lester as the cinematic embodiment of "swinging London" in the sixties, they perceived Russell as the outrageous enfant terrible of British film in the seventies, a director whose "bad taste" and lack of "restraint" violated the decorum of serious British cinema, an aesthetically as well as morally conservative cinema (Armes, 33; Ellis, 27; Manvell, 50) seen as representative of British art and culture generally.

Russell, while aware that the critical rejection of his work is to some extent the result of the British context (Jaehne, 54), has played the part of "our own abominable showman" (Buckley, 13) with glee. His calculated description of *The Music Lovers* as "the story of a love affair between a homosexual and a nymphomaniac," for example, exploited the film's commercial potential, but also aroused the ire of cultured Britons. Not insensitive to good promotional hype, Russell embraced the role of enfant terrible, even going so far as to "assault" one of his most vociferous critics, Alexander Walker, on television and dismissing most others as narrow-minded and irrelevant. In his recent made-for-television autobiography, *A British Picture* (1991), subtitled "Portrait of an Enfant Terrible," the Russell figure sports a rainbow-colored shock of hair and, although he momentarily considers it, he steadfastly refuses to change his image.

While his persona has earned him a degree of notoriety, Russell has also been consistently marginalized in historical discussions of British cinema, despite the fact that his films provide a kind of dialectical response to the sublimated sexuality of the Angry Young Men films, the Hammer horror, and the *Carry On* movies that preceded him.[1] The book-length studies of British film mention him only briefly, or not at all. Conservative critics find him vulgar and disrespectful, while those of the Left view his obsession with romantic individualists politically counterproductive. Only a few—most notably John Baxter (1973), Joe Gomez (1976), and Michael Dempsey (1972)—bother to treat Russell's work with sustained attention. His recent films, moreover, received virtually no critical commentary, perhaps because they appear more diffuse and thus less indicative of Russell's auteurist reputation. Of the six that he made in the 1980s, only *Gothic* (1987) and *Salomé's Last Dance* (1988) obviously fit into his distinctive approach to biographies about artists; he made both *Altered States* (1980) and *Crimes of Passion* (1984) in the United States, far from the beloved Lake District, the distinctive English landscape that appears in so many of Russell's films.

But, in fact, Russell's work is hardly the distant voice or still life that critics have deemed it. Given the greater adventurousness in British cinema now than when he first came to prominence, particularly in the films of Nicolas Roeg, Derek Jarman (who began his film career as set designer of *The Devils*), and Peter Greenaway, Russell's more recent work has lost some of its ability to shock audiences, but it nevertheless remains distinctly British. Indeed, the features that Russell directed in the eighties grow from his earlier work, but are riven with tensions that suggest significant relations to the historical forces at work in recent British culture collectively known as Thatcherism.

In what follows, I propose an alternative reading of Ken Russell's work, one that situates his films squarely *within* the British cultural climate of the eighties rather than marginalizing them as an anomalous aberration. The films' thematic tensions, particularly their conflicts between masculine and feminine desire, and the director's own shifting sympathies express an ambivalence between the need to maintain traditional power structures and the necessity for change that constitute a uniquely rich, unresolved series of cinematic responses to the ideological project of Thatcherism. Russell's excessive style and his frequently campy or mock heroic tone not only exist at odds with the lofty seriousness of his subjects, but also suggest a view of contemporary British life that both embraces the neoconservativism of Thatcherism and resists it.

Typically conceived in terms of a dialectic between realism and fantasy, British cinema's strictest categories collapse in Russell's work. Accordingly, critics discuss him both as a realist (Armes, 300-307) and as a fantasist (Durgnat). The documentary, which has historically been so important in the evolution of British cinema, was largely absorbed into and compromised by the institution of feature filmmaking (Barr, 13; Walker, 155). But virtually alone (with the important exception of Peter Watkins), Russell reversed this influence, redefining British documentary "restraint" by combining realism with fictional devices to create the biographical "docudrama."

Given Russell's distinctive style, which led Stephen Farber (39) to evoke Dr. Johnson's description of the metaphysical poets ("the most heterogeneous ideas are yoked by violence together"), it is not surprising that his films relate uneasily to popular genres. Initially, after two unsuccessful apprentice movies with clear generic affinities, the Tati-like *French Dressing* (1963) and the spy thriller *Billion Dollar Brain* (1965), Russell's earlier films exist in opposition to generic conventions, frequently subverting them. Most obviously, his films about artists deflate the naive reverence of the typical Hollywood biography, which he views as dully conventional (Gow, 9). These movies, employing what Gomez identifies as a "tripartite perspective which incorporates the protagonist's own romantic self-image, a more objective view revealed by the perspective of time, and finally Russell's personal vision" (Gomez, 35), obviously work against the conventional linear narrative of the Hollywood biopic. Many of Russell's films, like the work of Dennis Potter, can also be considered musicals in which he foregrounds the relations between music, dance, and sexuality rather than, as in the classic musical, sublimating it. *The Boy Friend* (1972), Russell's homage to the Busby Berkeley musicals of the thirties, employs camp as a double-edged sword that simultaneously mocks and celebrates the classic Hollywood musical, although ultimately the film attacks the genre that inspired it by contextualizing the mounting of the show as a battle among individual egos rather than as a harmonious group effort.

By contrast, the recent films position themselves more comfortably *within* the genre system. Most obviously, *Gothic* (1968) mobilizes a particular form of the horror genre, as signaled by its generic title. In a sense, of course, most of Russell's movies are "horrifying," although *Gothic* and *Lair of the White Worm* (1988) remain his only sustained forays into the horror genre. Less glibly, one might argue that *The Devils* is an antihorror film, for by demythifying the supernatural it shows the source of horror to be psychological, the result of sexual repression. Although in *Gothic* Russell undercuts the genteel depiction of the discussions between Mary Wollstonecraft Shelley, Percy Shelley, and Byron at the Swiss Villa Diodati that led to the writing of *Frankenstein* (1818), as depicted in *Bride of Frankenstein* (1935), his film nevertheless remains faithful to the genre itself. Thus *Gothic*, appropriately, is filled with the iconography and appurtenances of the Gothic story: the heroine running through hallways in flowing white robes, mirrors that reveal ghostly images, specters in suits of armor, hidden rooms, raging storms, and so on. In the end, typically, the supernatural is explained away as a night of rampant imagination—indeed, one of Mary's visions is modeled on Henry Fuseli's famous painting *The Nightmare* (1781)—and in the film's coda, the following morning is sunny and civil, the group calmly posed for a *déjeuner sur l'herbe*.

Similarly, *Lair of the White Worm*, its tone more campy than ironic, features many of the stock characters of the horror genre, as well as its conventional thematic oppositions. And if it suggests a victory in the end for the horrific Other, it only provides the "antigenre" reversal that has itself become so conventional in recent years. *Crimes of Passion* also mobilizes the horror film, most obviously in the casting of Anthony Perkins, an icon of the genre primarily because of his role as Norman Bates in *Psycho* (1960), as a similarly insanely repressed character.[2] *Crimes* also demonstrates affinities with film noir, both visually, in its depiction of downtown urban nightlife, and in its narrative, the story of a sexual woman who lures a man away from his wife and responsible domestic existence—the basic noir plot (Damico, 54). *Altered States* constructs its psychic researcher protagonist, Eddie Jessup, as the conventional mad scientist figure of science fiction who transgresses "natural" boundaries. In the great cliché of the genre, he experiments in areas mortals were not meant to know (Bell-Metereau, 171-72).

China Blue (Kathleen Turner) walks the streets in *Crimes of Passion* (1985), a film displaying the visual style of classic film noir.

Genre movies function, on one level, to relieve cultural anxieties (Grant, Neale, Schatz). One of the primary mythological strategies (Barthes) for doing so makes culture into nature (Neale, Schatz)—an ideological operation made explicit in the metaphorical premise of *Altered States*. The move from generic opposition to accommodation is the result, at least in part, of the fact that American companies financed all of Russell's recent films, but this shift also suggests an attempt by the director to become more acceptable to the mainstream, indicative of Thatcherism's push toward greater prominence in the international marketplace during the eighties. Yet while some contemporary British films, like *Stormy Monday* (1988), critique this policy, economic issues remain virtually absent from Russell's recent films (although concern is expressed in *Altered States* about maintaining research grants). Rather, they are sublimated as generic conventions that attempt to resolve the cultural anxieties of which Thatcherism itself is in part a symptom.

In this regard, Russell's making of *The Rainbow* (1989), an adaptation of Lawrence's 1915 novel, is significant. Focusing on a bucolic Britain in the days of Empire, *The Rainbow* becomes a "heritage drama," which Charles Barr suggests is a virtual genre of British cinema (Barr, 12). In its reliance on nostalgia, heritage drama is a particularly conducive genre for the conservatism of Thatcherist ideology, the "mission" of which, according to Stuart Hall, has been "to reconstruct social life as a whole around a return to the old values—the philosophies of tradition, Englishness, respectability, patriarchalism, family, and nation" (Hall 1988, 39). A "prequel" to *Women in Love*, the film returns Russell to the material which first established his reputation and which, apart from *Tommy* (1975), represents Russell's only unqualified critical and commercial success. Russell emphasizes the connection by including cast members Glenda Jackson and Christopher Gable and using cinematographer Billy Williams and production designer Luciana Arrighi—all of whom contributed to *Women in Love*.[3] The casting of Jackson strikes a particularly resonant chord, for her role in the earlier film made her an international star; in *The Rainbow*, she plays, in effect, her own mother. The film thus exists in an aura of personal nostalgia. It suggests that Russell, even as he notes about his own artist characters (Baxter, 134), avoids the present by returning to the past.

At the same time as it invokes an era of past glory for its maker, *The Rainbow* also appeals to cultural nostalgia. Consumed with personal dilemmas of love and desire, Russell's Lawrentian characters recall Roy Armes's description of the good Englishman who, secure in Britain's industrial affluence and international power, "could pass through life and hardly notice the existence of the state, beyond the post office and the policeman" (Armes, 17). The discussions of Britain's presence in India and of democracy and class in *The Rainbow* appear less as explorations of political philosophy, whether about events then or now, than as weapons in battles of egos. Tellingly, the discussion about democracy and class takes place during a badminton match, a visual metaphor of their petty personal debates. Russell has voiced his discontent with recent British cinema: "Most British films these days," he avers, "are about people hitting each other over the head with bottles in Brixton"—political nihilism that he thinks is emphasized at the expense of the physical and spiritual beauty of the sceptered isle (Fuller, 2, 4; Jaehne, 54). Russell claims to prefer more nostalgic films, like *Yanks* (1979) and *Hope and Glory* (1987), a movie upon which he lavished rare praise (Jaehne, 54).

The Rainbow is Russell's contribution to the nostalgia cycle, the culmination of the deemphasis of political themes in his work. Only in *Savage Messiah* (1972) does Russell uncharacteristically set out to depict the artist as "worker" (Buckley, 14), although *The Devils*, with its examination of the political motives informing the persecution of Urbain Grandier, may be Russell's most political film. But even here, the narrative is removed to a distant past. For Russell, the patina of an idyllic past and the story of Ursula Brangwen, "an aristocrat of the spirit," serve to restore spirituality to the crass materialism of contemporary Thatcherite England (Fuller, 4). Certainly Russell's middle-period films *Tommy* (1975), *Lisztomania* (1975), and *Valentino* (1977) reveal his dislike of contemporary mass culture (Farber, 44), an antipathy not far removed from Thatcherism's view of cultural decline. Like Thatcherist ideology, these films, especially the last of the three, view mass culture and the decline of values as largely the result of Americanization. And, as if in response, his recent films express an "aristocratic" fear of cultural leveling, a reaction to the new England shown in films like *My Beautiful Laundrette* (1985) and *Sammy and Rosie Get Laid* (1987). For Russell, as for Ursula, the masses are cultural rubes, like the philistine tourists at the beginning and end of *Gothic*, reminiscent of Salomé's description of the Romans in *Salomé's Last Dance* as "brutal and coarse, with their uncouth jargon."

However, Russell does not embrace an appropriate corresponding style, an uplifting aesthetic in the Great Tradition of Leavis. He is satisfied merely for his movies to shock audiences out of complacency (Baxter, 201; Gow, 8). Thus, even as his recent narratives work within the constraints of genre, his style remains visually flamboyant, featuring a mise-en-scène clearly excessive to the requirements of conventional narrative structures. This characteristic excess appears, for example, in the Eisensteinian montages of Jessup's drug-induced hallucinations in *Altered States*; in the plethora of psychoanalytic signifiers that fill *Lair of the White Worm*; in the rapid-fire, aphoristic dialogue of *Gothic* and *Crimes of Passion*; and in the latter's overdetermined noir visuals, particularly in the depiction of the prostitute China Blue and the downtown streets she works.

In fact, Russell's excessive style is strikingly similar to that of classic Hollywood melodrama, a connection that, despite its importance for understanding this filmmaker's work, seems strangely unexplored. In the Hollywood melodrama, as in *The Rainbow* and Russell's cinema generally, social and political issues become translated into personal terms (Elsaesser, 282). The kinetic energy, rich mise-en-scène, and florid music of Hollywood melodrama—those moments of extreme stylization that break conventional codes of realism—have been explained psychoanalytically by several critics as an excess that reveals a "hysteria bubbling all the time just below the surface" (Elsaesser, 289), instances of what Freud termed "conversion hysteria" (Nowell-Smith, 117). In this approach, the film text becomes, in a sense, analogous to the physical body, the text's excessive style its symptomatology. This description of melodrama also applies to Russell's films, which in fact exhibit an obsessive preoccupation with the body. Indeed, the frequent

Jessup's (William Hurt) experiments in the isolation tank literalize the Russell protagonist's fear of the body in *Altered States* (1980).

description of Russell's style as "hysterical" is more apt than those who use the word negatively to dismiss the director realize.

Robin Wood expresses a common view that Russell's films display a pronounced hatred of the body (Wood, 909). Certainly the protagonists of both *Altered States* and *Crimes of Passion* feel trapped by their bodies, although of the recent films *Lair of the White Worm* most obviously endorses this view, as it may be read as a horror fable about AIDS: the vampirism of the reptilian femme fatale, Lady Sylvia, is an infectious "disease" passed through the bloodstream. But, in fact, Russell's films are complex texts that reveal a more ambivalent view of the body, often oscillating between revulsion, desire, and guilt. This ambivalence, most frequently articulated alternately as phallic celebration and anxiety about masculine identity, has its most famous instance in *Lizstomania* when Liszt envisions his phallus as a maypole worshipped by women, abruptly followed by the castration of his "howitzer-sized penis" (Dempsey 1977/78, 22) by spider-woman Princess Caroline in a guillotine.

Like their predecessors, the recent films are filled with imagery of ineluctable mortality ("not damp—decay!," as Shelley shrieks in *Gothic*), of all the natural shocks to which flesh is heir. As well, in *Salomé's Last Dance* Russell makes the age difference between Herod and Salomé a major element of Wilde's play by casting as Salomé the diminutive and alabaster Imogen Millais-Scott, whose Lolita-like charm strongly contrasts with the flabby, aged skin of Stratford Johns as the Tetrarch. As in the work of Peter Greenaway, Russell's films are obsessed with physical decay and death; but whereas Greenaway's films manage this anxiety through rigorously controlled, almost mathematical aesthetic structures, Russell's films refuse such containment.

If the result, typically, is the perception of aesthetic failure on the director's part—the typical responses that Russell mixes tones unsuccessfully or lacks "taste" and is "vulgar"—his "ill-wrought urns" are significant in that they also reflect contemporary cultural values and tensions no less than did Hollywood melodrama during the Eisenhower period. Regardless of Russell's claim to be himself unaware of his work dealing especially with a "politics of the body" (Gentry, 9-10), the body is clearly a privileged site of anxiety and struggle in Russell's films. It represents the body politic, especially the fear of cultural pollution and compromise by the inevitable social changes engendered by the post-Empire era and expressed as the political retrenchment and defensive nationalism that has characterized Thatcherist ideology. Russell's "shocking" images of physical decomposition and violence in his recent films are, perhaps, the visual equivalent of Britain's excessive show of strength in the Falkland Islands. The frequent artist figures in Russell's work who seek to remain aesthetically "pure" in the face of cultural "contamination" express Thatcherism's dismay with Labour's welfare state, which preceded its rise to power.

The site of conflict in the melodrama, usually located within the nuclear family (Kleinhans; Nowell-Smith), reveals a pattern of crisis precipitated by desire and repression. Again, this is also true of Russell's recent films. The woman's appeal as an indiscreet object of desire in *Salomé's Last Dance* casts a wedge between husband and wife ("It is strange that the husband of my mother looks at me like that," Salomé coyly observes). Her dance, like Dorothy Malone's in *Written on the Wind* (1956), is presented as a clear challenge to patriarchal authority. In *Gothic*, the genesis of *Frankenstein* is "explained" as Mary's response to the loss of her child, while she perceives Byron's philosophy of "free love" as a threat to her heterosexual coupling with Shelley. In *Crimes of Passion*, the marriage and family life of protagonist Bobby Grady is destroyed because of his desire for another woman. After admitting this attraction to his wife, Bobby talks to his young son, the two separated by a chain-link fence, an image of familial separation that is the inevitable result of such a "fatal attraction." And toward the end of *Lair of the White Worm*, one of the Trent sisters discovers her missing mother, but significantly, the fate of the father is never made clear—amid all the sexual anarchy depicted in the film, the patriarch simply vanishes.

Yet if these films display a masculine panic about sexual difference and empowerment, at times they also firmly reinstate patriarchy, as in the end of Oscar Wilde's play *Salomé* (1891), contained within *Salomé's Last Dance*, where a phallic spear by order of Herod summarily kills the threatening woman. In Russell's interpretation of the play, Salomé is a nymphet, a sexual woman who thereby is, in Claire Johnston's words, "a traumatic presence which must be negated" (Johnston, 213). Further, Russell uses Wilde himself as a figure that threatens heterosexual monogamy, and like his own Salomé, Wilde is eliminated as a threat to dominant ideology by being arrested at film's end. The paradigm of this hysterical reinstatement of the phallus in these films is the scene in *Crimes of Passion* where Bobby, whose placement as a narrative frame serves to contain the feminine rage of Joanna, mimes "the human penis" ("direct from the wild untamed jungles of Borneo," according to his friend's introduction) growing erect. Russell punctuates his performance at the backyard barbecue—even the hot dogs are wielded like phalluses—non-diegetically with the opening movement of Strauss's *Also Sprach Zarathustra*, thus giving Bobby's view of the phallus all the monumentality Kubrick earlier associated with this piece of music in *2001: A Space Odyssey* (1968).

In *The Rainbow*, Ursula's desire to desire ("the source of all truth and good," her teacher and lesbian lover, Winifred, tells her) threatens patriarchal tradition in that she wishes to transcend the conventional roles assigned to women. But in her employment as a teacher, Ursula quickly succumbs to phallic control, the part of the film Russell seems most to relish, since it receives particular stylistic emphasis. In short order Ursula changes her approach to teaching from the ideal of appealing to reason in the unruly (male) children to accepting the necessity of thrashing with a cane, which she does to one troublesome lad with such force that it breaks. As the unctuous head-master bluntly puts it, "Only my cane rules this school" — and, indeed, in one shot, the cane looms large in the foreground, the composition expressing the inevitability of male power. So even though Russell omits the novel's patri-arch Will Brangwen from his adaptation, his power is nonetheless present in Russell's Dickensian treatment of Ursula's teaching experience.

Thatcherism's reification of the family and patriarchy is responsible for the unsatisfyingly abrupt shift that marks the end of *Altered States*. Throughout the film Jessup is characterized, and his experiments contextualized, in terms of his sexual dread. For example, after imbibing the hallucinogenic mixture offered him by the Mexican Indians, Jessup envisions (recalling the fantasia of fleeting fame accompanying *The 1812 Overture* in *The Music Lov-ers*) himself and his wife, Emily, as nudes who turn to stone and are then eroded away by a sudden, fierce wind. Even in an impersonal dalliance with a student, he hallucinates a chasm in the floor between them, a space at once the pit of hell and a nightmare of vaginal horror (Bell-Metereau, 174). Inti-macy for him is consistently horrifying; his mocking description of family life as "clutter, clatter, and ritual" is nicely conveyed by Russell in, for example, the exceedingly narrow corridors of the Jessups' apartment. So, in terms of the film's sci-fi premise, his initial transformations to primitive man function as an objective correlative of Jessup's unacknowledged "animal lusts," while his last changes into sheer energy fulfill his fantasy of discorporation, a re-treat from the body and the inescapable fact of sexual difference (Sobchack, 21-24).

But then, in the climax, the film suddenly seeks to erase the hysteria it has expressed in having adopted Jessup's subjective point of view by requir-ing an abrupt and wide leap of faith. Emily reaches into the swirling mass of primal energy that Jessup has become and somehow retrieves him, restoring him to human form. From this experience he learns that "the ultimate truth of all is that there is no truth." As if in response to this newly perceived metaphysical absurdity, Jessup suddenly professes love for his estranged wife and family. Later that night he is now able, in turn, to rescue her from primal formlessness. In a final, reposeful moment they embrace. As several commentators have noted (e.g., Fox; Sobchack, 23-24), this ending forces an improbable volte-face upon the character of Jessup, who suddenly affirms the values of family and platitudes about romantic love. It also redefines Emily as wife and mother rather than as professional scientist, a reflection of Thatcherism's regressive view of women (Hall 1990, 21). Thus the film, like

The conflict in *Lair of the White Worm* (1988) is represented with the icons of the cross and the snake.

many recent American movies, privileges family and reinstates the power of the Father, an ideological project that may be characteristic not only of Reaganite entertainment but also that of his staunchest ally, Thatcher.

Lair of the White Worm is also about the struggle of patriarchy and British tradition to retain power. An updating of Bram Stoker's 1911 novel about a prehistoric serpent ("wurm") dwelling undetected for centuries in the English Midlands, the film focuses on a battle between patriarchal authority in the figure of Lord D'Ampton and the release of repressed (female) sexual energy in the form of the reptilian Lady Sylvia, high priestess of the worm cult. Russell represents this conflict with the images of the cross and the snake, respectively. When the virginal Eve touches a crucifix covered with venom expectorated by Lady Sylvia, she has horrifying visions (clearly evoking the more notorious scenes in *The Devils*) of nuns from the nearby ancient convent ("captive virgins praying to an impotent god") being ravaged by Roman soldiers, the Bosch-like scene presided over by the serpent-god. Lady Sylvia's "monstrous" sexuality threatens the moral fiber of the nation itself. She seduces a young fellow—a boy scout, no less!—and then abruptly reveals her fangs, her head quickly darting below the frame to emasculate him, a horrifying vision of the *vagina dentata*. Her sexuality is a direct challenge to the family, as the Trent sisters' missing mother is discovered under her influence to have become a vampire watching erotic videos; and even the local constable, icon of British law and order, becomes a vampire. Indeed, the nation has become so corrupt that there are few virgins left in Britain to sacrifice, and Lady Sylvia must check Eve on this score before proceeding further.

But ultimately the film is ambivalent about her. Even though she is frightening, she is also witty, lively, and refreshingly engaging, certainly a welcome opposite to the stuffiness of the two wooden patriarchal "heroes." Russell once noted that "there's a liberating force in music which . . . people can't help responding to, being primitive creatures at heart" (Baxter, 189) — a liberating lifting of the lid off the id perfectly visualized in the high angle shot of Lady Sylvia emerging from a woven basket and snaking across the floor in a tight lamé dress to the strains of "exotic" flute music, a direct contrast to the silly traditionalism of Angus's tartans and bagpipes.

Lair of the White Worm resembles *The Rainbow* in the sense that it too harkens back to the days of traditional British patriarchal hegemony. Significantly, in his adaptation Russell entirely omits the novel's important black character, Oolanga (whom Stoker frequently describes with intense racial hatred), instead simply giving us a white England apparently untroubled by racial difference. Yet the horror figured as sexual difference in the form of Lady Sylvia nevertheless suggests the mythic defense of traditional British culture through the sexual stereotyping typical of colonialism. As Ella Shoat has shown, colonialist discourse intertwines with patriarchal discourse; the colonized land is frequently represented as female, with the result that colonization is implicitly endorsed by the "masculinist power of possession, . . . penetration and knowledge" (Shoat, 57). (Interestingly, Shoat specifically identifies the figure of Salomé as a particularly clear instance of the colonized Other as a feminized projection of the white European male's colonial/sexual Imaginary [Shoat, 72].) Thus, Lady Sylvia in *Lair* is controlled by a recording of "Turkish charmer" music from D'Ampton's father's "North African collection" — that is, from a region that Britain no longer "collects," or, in other words, where it can no longer wield significant colonialist power.

The consistent threat to masculinity in these films suggests "the profound crisis of national identity" (Hall 1990, 21) to which Thatcherism is a response, the historical erosion of Britain's political power that Thatcherism seeks so strenuously to deny. Russell's films, then, are symptomatic of a nation scaling down from the heady days of Empire and its last moment of

Lady Sylvia (Amanda Donohoe) lifts the lid off the id in *Lair of the White Worm*.

greatness as a world power in the "swinging sixties" to more sobering contemporary political and economic realities. They mark the shift from a restrained national cinema, one dominated by a tasteful "tradition of quality" (Ellis), to the kind of stylistic indulgence indicative of a nation that, no longer exerting world power, can only turn inward.

Russell's films, filled with stylistic, generic, and thematic tensions, express both the values of British tradition and a disdain for them that mirrors the tensions inherent in Thatcherism, itself a bundle of "contradictory values" (Hall 1988, 53). Russell continues to prefer romantic individuals, usually artists, as his protagonists (Ursula Brangwen, Byron, and the Shelleys, obviously, while Jessup is a kind of "hunger artist" and China Blue a performance artist), most of whom abandon their idealism toward the end, their very struggle a reflection of Thatcherism's double emphasis on a "free market and strong state" (Hall 1988, 39). Russell's own appearance in the recent spy thriller *The Russia House* (1990) as a singular radically dressed agent amid a sea of nondescript, dark suits who is nonetheless rabidly conservative, not unlike Ed Begley's bellicose fascist General Midwinter in *Billion Dollar Brain*, cleverly employs the director's own persona and his work's characteristic dualities in its casting.

Russell's 1980s films remain consistent in their concerns and therefore distinctive in a national cinema that has been characterized by a marked absence of auteurs (Armes, 262). Certainly they reveal that tension between the filmmaker's material and his personality that generates the "interior meaning" said to be the hallmark of the classic auteur (Sarris, 513). Yet this is not to argue for the "greatness" of Russell as an individual director; for his films, despite their richness of personal vision, are at the same time revealing cultural expressions. Russell's work, like that of Fellini, Ingmar Bergman, and Woody Allen, may suffer from "boorish megalomania" (Walker, 392) and his films function as "pretexts for the effluence of his own fantasies" (Wood, 909), but they are not *simply* solipsistic exercises. Given that Russell works more by intuition than by intellect, it is not surprising that his work should have such cultural resonance. His imagination, which his BBC producer and "industrial paterfamilias" Huw Wheldon described as "like a bird being driven along on a huge gale" (Baxter, 118, 123), surely rides the winds of social and cultural change. In this sense, then, Russell's cinema, although usually dismissed as marginal within British film, is in fact central. If the "conventional binary opposition of realist and non-realist" practice in British film needs "reworking" (Barr, 15), such a reexamination would necessarily move Russell from the margin to the center.

Notes

1. *Carry On Dick* might well serve as an epigram for Russell's cinema.
2. Russell emphasizes the connection through close-ups of Perkins engaging in sexual voyeurism, as had Hitchcock in the earlier film.
3. In general, Russell's development of a stock company of both actors and crew, the creation of an extended "family," is at least partially motivated by a desire for comfort and security.

Works Cited

Armes, Roy. 1978. *A Critical History of the British Cinema*. New York: Oxford University Press.

Barr, Charles, ed. 1986. *All Our Yesterdays: 90 Years of British Cinema*. London: British Film Institute.

Barthes, Roland. 1972. *Mythologies*. Edited and translated by Annette Lavers. New York: Hill and Wang.

Baxter, John. 1973. *An Appalling Talent: Ken Russell*. London: Michael Joseph.

Bell-Metereau, Rebecca. 1982. "*Altered States* and the Popular Myth of Self-Discovery." *Journal of Popular Film and Television* 9 (4): 171-79.

Buckley, Peter. 1972. "Savage Saviour." *Films and Filming* 19 (1): 14-16.

Damico, James. 1978. "Film Noir: A Modest Proposal." *Film Reader*, no. 3: 48-57.

Dempsey, Michael. 1972. "The World of Ken Russell." *Film Quarterly* 25 (3): 13-25.

———. 1977/78. "Ken Russell, Again." *Film Quarterly* 31 (2): 19-24.

Durgnat, Raymond. 1977. "The Great British Phantasmagoria." *Film Comment* 13 (3): 48-53.

Ellis, John. 1978. "Art, Culture and Quality: Terms for a Cinema in the Forties and Seventies." *Screen* 19 (3): 9-49.

Elsaesser, Thomas. 1986. "Tales of Sound and Fury: Observations on the Family Melodrama." In *Film Genre Reader*, edited by Grant, 278-308.

Farber, Stephen. 1975. "Russellmania." *Film Comment* 11 (6): 39-46.

Fox, Jordan R. 1981. "*Altered States*." *Cinefantastique* 11 (1): 46.

Fuller, Graham. 1989. "Next of Ken." *Film Comment* 25 (3): 2-4.

Gentry, Ric. 1983. "Ken Russell: An Interview." *Post Script* 2 (3): 2-23.

Gomez, Joseph. 1976. *Ken Russell: The Adaptor as Creator*. London: Frederick Muller.

Gow, Gordon. 1970. "Shock Treatment." *Films and Filming* 16 (10): 8-12.

Grant, Barry Keith, ed. 1986. *Film Genre Reader*. Austin: University of Texas Press.

Hall, Stuart. 1988. "The Toad in the Garden: Thatcherism among the Theorists." In *Marxism and the Interpretation of Culture*, edited by Gary Nelson and Lawrence Grossberg, 35-57. Urbana and Chicago: University of Illinois Press.

———. 1990. "The Emergence of Cultural Studies and the Crisis of the Humanities." *October*, no. 53 (Summer): 11-23.

Jaehne, Karen. 1988. "Wormomania." *Film Comment* 24 (6): 52-54.

Johnston, Claire. 1976. "Women's Cinema as Counter Cinema." In *Movies and Methods*, edited by Bill Nichols, 208-17. Berkeley: University of California Press.

Kleinhans, Chuck. 1978. "Notes on Melodrama and the Family under Capitalism." *Film Reader* 3: 40-47.

Manvell, Roger. 1969. *New Cinema in Britain*. New York: Dutton.

Neale, Stephen. 1980. *Genre*. London: British Film Institute.

Nowell-Smith, Geoffrey. 1977. "Minnelli and Melodrama." *Screen* 18 (2): 113-18.

Sarris, Andrew. 1974. "Notes on the Auteur Theory in 1962." In *Film Theory and Criticism*, edited by Gerald Mast and Marshall Cohen, 500-515. New York: Oxford University Press.

Schatz, Thomas. 1981. *Hollywood Genres*. New York: Random House.

Shoat, Ella. 1991. "Gender and Culture of Empire: Toward a Feminist Ethnography of the Cinema." *Quarterly Review of Film and Video* 13 (1-3): 45-84.

Sobchack, Vivian. 1986. "Child/Alien/Father: Patriarchal Crisis and Generic Exchange." *Camera Obscura* 15: 7-34.

Walker, Alexander. 1986. *Hollywood, England: The British Film Industry in the Sixties*. London: Harrap.

Wood, Robin. 1980. "Ken Russell." In *A Critical Dictionary*, edited by Richard Roud, 2 vols., vol. 2, 909-10. New York: Viking Press.

Twelve

"Everyone's an American Now": Thatcherist Ideology in the Films of Nicolas Roeg

Jim Leach

In Nicolas Roeg's *Eureka*, an American gangster involved in a takeover bid for a Caribbean island is confident that the owner will eventually come to terms because he is "an American" and thus knows that "we're all on the same side." It is the middle of World War II, a time when national boundaries would seem to have been very clearly defined and when (according to cultural myths skillfully exploited by Margaret Thatcher) Britons discovered a sense of national purpose long since eroded. Yet the gangster declares that "everyone's an American now" and characterizes the war as a conflict between "Americans who all speak different languages." He looks forward to a time when even the Japanese will be "Americans" but does not find it necessary even to mention the British.

This homogenizing effect of American cultural power is illustrated by its spokesman: the gangster is named Mayakovsky (after the Russian poet), is of Jewish origin, but works for the Mafia. One of the agencies through which this power has been disseminated is, of course, the cinema. The narrative codes developed in Hollywood prevail in commercial cinema throughout the world, and American companies dominate film production and exhibition in many countries. In this essay I discuss the extent to which Roeg's cinema participates in or resists this process of "Americanization" and place Roeg's British perspective on "American" culture within the context of the ideological project of Thatcherism. Finally, the essay offers an analysis of the cultural and ideological implications in Roeg's films of the 1980s and a brief attempt to define their contribution to recent developments in British cinema.[1]

After starting out as a clapper boy in 1950, Nicolas Roeg became one of Britain's most respected cinematographers before establishing himself as a film director in the 1970s, a time when the "alternative" cultural movements of the previous decade began to lose their momentum. The new conservatism, signaled in Britain by Margaret Thatcher's rise to power, coincided with the virtual collapse of the British film industry after the brief economic boom in the late 1960s when the Hollywood studios invested heavily in the "swinging Britain" image. Two aspects of Roeg's films stand out in relation to this social and cinematic context: (1) ignoring the trend toward "safe" subjects, they continue the formal and sexual "daring" of 1960s cinema; (2) they are rarely set in Britain.

In fact, Roeg produces most of his films with American money, the major exception being *The Man Who Fell to Earth* (1976)—the first British-financed film shot entirely in the United States. Roeg's career thus seems to confirm Alan Parker's claim that American financing is now required if a British filmmaker wants to make films with more than a modest budget (Park, 104). Yet, unlike Parker and many earlier and more recent British filmmakers, Roeg never became a Hollywood filmmaker. His cinema exists in a kind of no-man's-land within which he activates and explores the tensions and contradictions in the new order and in the Thatcherist response to it.

During this period, television emerged as an important alternative source of funding for British filmmakers willing to accept budgetary constraints. Roeg never pursued this option, believing that his vision demands a large screen (Park, 85). Yet the contemporary experience of television plays a significant role in his films, where the spectator's attention often becomes divided among different elements within the image and on the sound track. Roeg likens this strategy to the way "people watch television and read a magazine at the same time looking from one to the other" (Waller, 27). Often this kind of viewing involves television screens within the film screen, as with the bank of monitors assembled by Newton in *The Man Who Fell to Earth* or the images and sounds from television sets on (or just off) screen that intrude on the action and dialogue in the opening sequences of *Castaway* and *Track 29*.

In Britain, commentators often cite the "distracted" kind of viewing television invites as evidence of the impact of American popular culture. One highly influential attempt to theorize this effect was the concept of "flow" developed by Raymond Williams after his exposure to commercial television in the United States. Williams claimed that viewers experience little sense of boundaries between programs and between the different kinds of reality that they represent (Williams, 118). Roeg's cinema suggests a parallel between this experience of "flow" and the erosion of national boundaries by American cultural power.

Televisual flow is built into the structure and imagery of Roeg's films, but the complex patterns it generates require concentrated attention from the spectator in order to grasp their full implications. Roeg uses the habits of television viewing to unsettle the intensity of cinematic viewing and thus to question the dominant assumptions about meanings and pleasure on which the so-called "information" and "consumer" society is based. He argues that "American" culture trains people to demand quick opinions that conceal the disturbing fact that "we go through life knowing absolutely nothing" (Combs 1985, 237). The need to generate clear meanings within the flow of television programming leads to a reliance on formulas and stereotypes that create an illusion of "mastery," a facade that discourages further inquiry into the "significance" of experience. Roeg's anticategorical cinema works against this attitude by insisting that, as the professor puts it in *Insignificance,* "you cannot understand by making definitions, only by turning over the possibilities."

In some ways, however, Roeg's resistance to traditional hierarchies and boundaries aligns his work with the "American" forces in contemporary culture. Like many other British directors, Roeg makes television commercials to support himself between film projects, and he argues that commercials often make use of techniques borrowed from films that (like his own) were "difficult" for their original audiences (Lanza, 35). By incorporating elements of the televisual flow of imagery into his films, while avoiding the illusion of "easy" consumption that television promotes, he acknowledges that social and cultural contexts must influence the making and viewing of films. All films, therefore, are to some extent complicit with the dominant ideology, but Roeg's films examine this complicity and encourage the spectator to reflect on the extent to which that ideology shapes his or her own responses.

Robert Kolker aptly describes viewing a film by Roeg as an experience that transforms us into "aliens in a strange land, trying to make sense of our perceptions, and failing" (Kolker, 84). Because this experience of perceptual failure has proved disturbing for audiences, critics, and producers, Roeg's films have been increasingly marginalized, receiving only limited distribution and critical attention. During the 1970s, many critics regarded the disruptive narrative structures of Roeg's films as part of an innovative project to create a cinema responsive to the new thinking about sexuality and identity in the "permissive" society. As Thatcherism tried to turn the tide against these new developments, seeing them as responsible for Britain's political and moral decline, Roeg's later films often seemed willfully obscure and indifferent to the changing ideological climate.

In *Performance* (1970), Roeg's first film (codirected with Donald Cammell), another gangster, this time a British one, exposes one of the central tensions within Thatcherism, even before Thatcher's rise to power. Harry Flowers admires the efficiency of the "Yanks" and uses brutal methods to force his competitors to "merge" with him, but he also claims a strong attachment to the traditional values of family life. Thatcherist ideology offered a similarly ambivalent response to the Americanization of the postwar world, although *Performance* makes clear that the established British ways of doing things were more sophisticated but hardly less ruthless than the "American" methods.

On the one hand, Thatcherism presented itself as a return to the values of an earlier period in which Britain possessed the political and cultural power that now belonged to the United States. Thatcher thus exploited and reinforced myths about Britain's decline to the status of a second-class nation and about the negative effects of American popular culture. On the other hand, Thatcher pointed to the United States (especially after the election of Ronald Reagan in 1980) as exemplifying the success of the "free enterprise" system over the "consensus" politics that, she felt, weakened postwar Britain by establishing a noncompetitive "welfare state." To Thatcher, "consensus" was "the process of abandoning all beliefs, principles, values and policies," and she advocated a return to the clear-cut definitions and boundaries that supposedly made life easier in the past—and in old Hollywood genre films (Derbyshire, 173).

Through its appeal to the past, notably in the comparisons between Thatcher and Churchill during the Falklands war, Thatcherist rhetoric sought to neutralize the myth of national decline. Thatcher presented herself as a strong leader capable of dealing with Britain's economic woes and with such contemporary problems as terrorism, pornography, and racial violence. A confusing bombardment of media images, often seen as the effect of an Americanized cultural environment, tended to magnify the impact of these problems. Thatcher thus blamed the media for spreading the demoralization she claimed to be fighting, conveniently ignoring the fact that it was the capitalist enterprise of the American media that had largely created the image of "swinging Britain" in the first place.

In his analysis of Thatcherism, Stuart Hall suggests that it offers a vision based on clearly defined boundaries and moral categories: "The language of law and order is sustained by a populist moralism. It is where the great syn-

tax of 'good' versus 'evil', of civilized and uncivilized standards, of the choice
between anarchy and order, constantly divides the world up and classifies it
into its appointed stations" (Hall, 37-38). Thatcherism thus generates "quick
meanings" that bring about an "elision between crime and disorder," so that
any challenge to the established order can be immediately dismissed as a
matter for the police (Kettle, 227). Although Thatcher did not invent this
"language," she synthesized it with the demands of corporate and consumer
capitalism. This mythical synthesis was, however, inherently unstable because of the tension between encouraging "the survival of the fittest" and
preaching "respect for moral absolutes" (Martin, 332).

The "moral absolutes" in Thatcherism opposed the social explanations for
human problems offered by the liberal ideology that shaped the postwar consensus and the welfare state. Thatcher argued that the reliance on social
"safety nets" weakens the individual but also that such social measures are,
in any case, too weak to control the disruptive forces at work in a hostile
world and in the dark recesses of human nature. Thus, the Thatcherist ideal:
a "self-sufficient" adult whose aggressive individualism can operate successfully in public life but who also needs the security provided by a family structure that offers protection from "a mean and nasty world" (Segal, 209). The
Thatcherist "adult" is normally a "father" or perhaps a woman able to demonstrate the "hardness" and aggression associated with "masculine"
behavior.

Thatcher exploited widespread frustration with a system in which the
state seemed to watch over the lives of individuals "from the cradle to the
grave" but whose rules and regulations only added to the muddle and confusion of modern life. She swept away the claims of liberal ideology by insisting that "there is no such thing as society," her way of saying that "people
had to accept responsibility for their own behaviour because anything else
would infantilize us all" (Willetts, 268).

Lindsay Anderson's recent claim that Roeg's films lack "a social element"
implies that they share the Thatcherist resistance to social explanations
(Hacker and Price, 54). These films certainly ignore the tradition of social
realism and explicit social criticism in British cinema, and, in fact, Britain itself is conspicuous by its absence. Yet though Roeg himself argues that films
should not deal in what he calls "partisan politics," he nevertheless describes his own work as an attempt to preserve, in "reactionary times," the
advances made in the 1960s and 1970s (Lanza, 34-35).

In confronting a powerful ideology forged from the welding together of
traditional moral categories and modern corporate imperatives, Roeg's films
do not operate completely outside the domain of this ideology but expose its

contradictions by showing its appeal *and* its limitations. Each film unsettles the spectator by suggesting that meaning is neither absent, as the complexity of contemporary experience often implies, nor absolute, as Thatcherism claims in response to this perceived absence of meaning; Roeg suggests rather that meaning is relative, a position that recognizes the need for meaning but refuses to allow this need to harden into an acceptance of fixed categories.[2]

Although Roeg's films of the 1980s are clearly not political allegories, they do disturb the secure categories on which Thatcherism depends. While the films (with the partial exception of *Castaway*) make no direct reference to British society and culture, they function as fables that subvert the underlying value system, the way of seeing inherent in Thatcherism. In particular, my analysis concentrates on the way in which the films' treatment of sexuality both appeals to and unsettles the ideological premises that underpin the Thatcherist discourse on the family, as well as on law and order.

The most controversial aspect of *Bad Timing* (1980) is its depiction of the "crime" whose investigation provides the motivation for the film's complex flashback structure. Alex (Art Garfunkel), an American psychologist working in Vienna, rapes Milena (Theresa Russell), a woman with whom he has been having an affair, while she lies unconscious and apparently dying. Some feminists expressed anger at the way in which the "camerawork, associative editing and narrative structure" compel "us in the audience to identify with this assault on the female victim" (Barber, 46). However, Teresa de Lauretis calls into question this perception of the film's strategies and argues that it works against the "visual pleasure" basic to mainstream cinema, which, according to Laura Mulvey's influential theory of spectatorship, privileges the male spectator. De Lauretis suggests that *Bad Timing* creates "unpleasure" by "undercutting spectator identification in terms of both vision . . . and narrative" (de Lauretis, 24).

While Milena's unconscious state does prevent us from identifying with her, it also works against the erotic investment apparently offered through identification with Alex as he cuts the clothes from her body and violates it. The film explicitly raises the issues of voyeurism and spying: Alex shows his students images of "political voyeurs" and tells them that "we are all spies"; he does "top secret" work for NATO. It goes further, however, by inviting the spectator to reflect on his or her complicity with such activities. The rape, in fact, culminates the process by which Alex, fascinated by Milena's "otherness," nevertheless tries to impose his own sense of order on her "untidiness"; this process is duplicated in the efforts of the Austrian police-

Milena (Theresa Russell) and Alex (Art Garfunkel) confront each other during the early stages of their affair, in *Bad Timing* (1980).

man, Inspector Netusil (Harvey Keitel), to prove that a crime has been committed.

Alex's objections to Milena's "untidiness" are ostensibly directed at the way she leaves things lying around, but he remains frustrated by her frequent disappearances and by her refusal to commit herself to a permanent relationship. When they take a vacation in Morocco, Alex proposes marriage by offering her a one-way airline ticket to New York. She pleads with him to enjoy "where we are now." By learning about her past and by building a future with her in his own "home" environment, he wants to possess her, and he sees her desire to live only for the present moment as a kind of moral "untidiness." But his encounter with this woman who refuses the terms of his (psycho)analysis leads to the emergence of the "untidiness" within himself.

When Alex arrives at Milena's apartment to find that she has cleaned and tidied it in order to please him, he responds by demanding that they make love. Her request that they should just talk to each other prompts him to make an excuse to leave. She rushes out after him, offers herself to him like a prostitute, and he takes her brutally on the stairs. Although some (male) critics stress Alex's humiliation, this sequence suggests that he *needs* her "untidiness" to justify his own sense of himself as the one who provides order, just as the inspector needs a "crime" to define himself as a man of law

(Gow, 29; Pym, 112). Later, after Milena makes her first suicide threat, Alex rushes to her apartment and finds her drunk, garishly made up, and wearing her bra over her blouse, the grotesque mirror reflection of his own repressed desires. When Inspector Netusil searches Milena's apartment for clues, he declares that he shares Alex's contempt for people "who live in disorder" and thus interfere with "our will to master reality." The law, however, fails to impose its shape on "untidy" experience, since Netusil is unable to extract a confession from Alex before they hear that Milena will survive (which means, apparently, that no "crime" has been committed).

The sudden cuts from Milena's body as she and Alex make love to that same body being violently worked on in the hospital provide the most obvious instances of how *Bad Timing* both permits erotic viewing and undercuts it. The film never establishes a stable relationship with its spectator. Its flashback structure is sometimes clearly motivated by the consciousness of a character but at other times such motivation is ambiguous or even absent. Roeg presents some flashbacks as Alex's memories during his wait in the hospital corridor, but at least two early flashbacks seem to originate with the unconscious Milena, and it remains possible that Netusil fantasizes the entire rape scene. The film constantly threatens to fly apart, suggesting that the spectator's experience incorporates the tension between Alex's sense of time and Milena's, the drive to narrative closure competing with a desire to experience the present moment to the full.

A similar tension operates in *Eureka* (1983), but here the forces of disorder dominate the film's imagery and structure. As Harlan Kennedy observes, "Roeg hurls heady visual juxtapositions at us — in a bid to storm the syntactical frontiers between shot and shot, scene and scene, metaphor and reality, parable and paranormal" (Kennedy, 21). These disruptive strategies reflect a tension built into the conception of the film as a treatment of the figure of the self-sufficient individual. Paul Mayersberg, who wrote the screenplay, suggests that the search for gold functions as a metaphor for the human "desire for self-realisation" (Milne, 282) but, even as Jack (Gene Hackman) insists on the integrity of his own individual will, the film's "fairy-tale" imagery connects his discovery to cosmic forces whose existence shows, as Roeg puts it, that "our actions are connected to everything and everyone around us" (Kennedy, 21). While the film seems to endorse Jack's Thatcherist desire to take responsibility for his own actions, it simultaneously insists that these actions form part of a complex web of cultural meanings created by past events and representations.

In his discussion of *Bad Timing*, Ian Penman suggests that, for Roeg, "bliss" can never be expressed "as an isolated perfection" but only "as an effect within the interplay of a whole range of problematic discourses" (Penman, 109). *Eureka*'s title focuses attention on the "bliss" of the single moment of discovery, which the film attempts to convey through a battery of visual and musical effects. One of these is a musical quotation from Wagner's *Das Rheingold*, and its effect illustrates the "problematic" functioning of the discourses in this film. The familiarity of the music denies the uniqueness of the moment, while the allusion to Wagner associates Jack's quest with a cultural tradition taken up by Nazism and thus foreshadows his later isolation from the struggle against fascism during World War II. The operatic grandeur is, in any case, undercut when Jack's histrionic celebrations only evoke memories of many similar demonstrations by prospectors in other films (including Chaplin's *The Gold Rush*, a poster for which we will see later in the film).

After leaving the vast, frozen spaces of the Yukon, Jack tries to isolate himself from the political turmoil of the outside world in the confined space of his tropical island mansion. Though he found the gold only after he rejected the "home" offered by Frieda (Helena Kallionites), a brothel owner in the Yukon, he uses his wealth to establish a family within which the tensions take on the archetypal dimensions of Greek tragedy and Freudian psychodrama. His attempts to control his island and his family through the power of his will prove futile in the face of the "American" invasion, suggesting a Thatcherist view of Britain's plight. However, when Jack is brutally murdered, the film never resolves the uncertainty about whether the killing is a reprisal for his "un-American" rejection of the takeover bid or whether his son-in-law (Rutger Hauer) has taken revenge for the humiliations suffered in their struggle for control over Jack's daughter (Theresa Russell).

The killing, simultaneously a product of the threat from outside and of the tensions within the family, is carried out in a way that resembles the voodoo rituals practiced on the island. Jack even acquiesces in his own death, recognizing that his life after the ecstatic moment of individual triumph has been an anticlimax. Though the film suggests that the forces that destroy Jack are ultimately unknowable, the blown-up photograph of the body exhibited at his son-in-law's trial looks like the well-known images of Hiroshima victims (the end of the war is announced during the trial). His desire to isolate himself from a "mean and nasty world" (from history, politics, and society) generates the same outcome produced by the historical forces he tries to escape. The death of the self-sufficient man reveals the complex interconnectedness of things and people that Jack denies in his attempt to "master" his family and his environment.

Eureka calls into question Jack's claims to self-sufficiency by linking his experiences to images stored in the spectator's cultural memory. This strategy becomes the main source of the unsettling effect in *Insignificance* (1985). The spectator is confronted with actors impersonating four "stars" of American culture. Known only as the Professor (Michael Emil), the Senator (Tony Curtis), the Actress (Theresa Russell), and the Ballplayer (Gary Busey), they are unmistakably modeled on Albert Einstein, Joseph McCarthy, Marilyn Monroe, and Joe DiMaggio. The film thus sets up a gap between the performances in the "present" and the established star images. By showing these characters grappling with the relationship between their public personae and their private selves, Roeg undermines the supposedly "fixed" quality of these star images. This representational instability parallels the disturbance caused by the Professor's theory of relativity, which challenges traditional belief in the fixed state of the universe and, in turn, the moral absolutism grounded in this belief.

The mythical encounter between these characters takes place in a New York hotel room during the Cold War period, when the "American" culture celebrated by Mayakovsky in *Eureka* consolidated its dominant position. The Professor, who escaped to America from fascism in Europe, remains haunted by an awareness that his ideas helped create the atomic bomb. Despite its practical uses, the theory of relativity generates hostility from those threatened by its scientific complexity. The Senator can respond only by branding the Professor a "communist," while the Ballplayer suspects any intellectual activity that might raise questions about the American dream. The Actress, however, comes closest to the film's own strategy when she uses toys and other props to act out a playful (and necessarily simplified) version of the Professor's theory.

The Actress's childlike use of "play" to demonstrate the Professor's theory both reinforces and cuts through the stereotype of the "dumb blonde," suggesting that the new way of seeing is a threat only to a particular "adult" view of the world. That this view belongs to the modern "American" ideology is confirmed by the Professor's encounter with the hotel's Indian elevator operator. The Indian greets the Professor as a Cherokee, presumably because the theory of relativity supports the belief of "a true Cherokee" that "wherever he is, he is at the center of the universe." Although the Indian finds it hard to sustain this belief in an elevator and feels that he is no longer a Cherokee because he watches television, he later uses the power of imag-

The Actress (Theresa Russell) uses toys to demonstrate the theory of relativity to the Professor (Michael Emil), in *Insignificance* (1985).

ination to escape from his "American" environment when he performs a traditional chant on the hotel roof while wolves howl all around him.

The Cherokee belief, suppressed in the course of American history, accords with the Actress's demonstration of relativity, which she sums up as showing that "all measurements of time and space are necessarily made relative to a single observer." The Ballplayer inadvertently demonstrates her point when he summarizes the American view of history by commenting that "if it wasn't for Columbus, we'd all be Indians." Traditional belief and modern scientific theory both imply that people should "take responsibility for their world"; but, according to the Professor, Americans refuse this responsibility and instead establish a "star" system that invests human beings with absolute values. These fixed points of reference provide the basis for "quick opinions," thus eliminating the need for people to think through difficult issues for themselves.

The Professor's theory becomes part of a myth of science in which $E = MC^2$ functions simply as a sign of the power of science that is then manipulated by the Senator for his political purposes. Sexuality, too, is subjected to a similar process, as the construction of a glamour image turns the Actress into a projection of male fantasies. This image acts as a screen for repressed sexual feelings liable to emerge in grotesque forms, as Milena demonstrated to Alex in *Bad Timing*. The Actress, first seen on location in the city streets during the filming of a shot in which her skirt is "blown up around her ears" by a blast of air from the subway (an allusion to the now iconic image of Monroe in *The Seven Year Itch*), later tells the Professor she is glad that he was not there. While the crowd in the street saw "a star doing glamorous things," she says, he would have seen "a girl showing her legs to a bunch of jerks."

The crudity underlying the glamour image also appears in the film's depiction of the Senator. He is seen having sex with a woman who seems to be the Actress but who then pulls off her wig to reveal that she is a prostitute impersonating the star. When he finds the real Actress in the Professor's bed, he mistakes her for a prostitute who looks like the Actress and comments that the Actress "only got where she is by doing what you're doing." He rejects her offer of sex in exchange for the safety of the Professor's papers by punching her, causing a miscarriage. His brutality underlines the hypocrisy of an ideology that takes what it cannot master (relativity, sexual desire) and uses it to create a commodity (atomic bomb, glamour image) that then destroys what the ideology claims to protect (peace, family life).

If the central issue in *Insignificance* is the relationship of the "real" to the cultural imaginary, *Castaway* (1986) involves a return to the real through its representation of the cultural reality of contemporary London and the natural reality of the island on which Gerald (Oliver Reed) and Lucy (Amanda Donohoe) are cast away. Yet, as Richard Combs points out, the realism of *Castaway* is deceptive since the film suggests that the real may remain "inaccessible, even when living naked on a beach" (Combs 1986/87, 70). By reducing mastery to a question of survival (as with the children in the Australian outback in Roeg's *Walkabout* [1971]), the situation of the castaways tests the cultural categories within which the real is experienced. Gerald and Lucy find themselves in a transitional world where nature turns much of their cultural backgrounds into nonsense, but where their behavior remains culturally conditioned; similarly, the film places us in an unstable relationship to the characters, in which we both share and remain outside their experience and become aware that the cultural codes from which they are escaping affect the processes of our own spectatorship.

Gerald's desire to escape to a desert island parallels Jack McCann's attempt at self-realization through the purchase and protection of his island. But, as in *Eureka*, the dream of freedom from cultural constraints gets quickly undermined. The drawings used in the opening credits relate Gerald's desire to memories of *Robinson Crusoe*, while his advertisement for a "girl Friday" suggests the combination of cultural and sexual fantasy that underlies his project. When Gerald first sights the island, he calls it their

The struggle to survive on their desert island takes its toll on Gerald (Oliver Reed) and Lucy (Amanda Donohoe), in *Castaway* (1986).

"home" for the next year. A series of quick cuts confronts us with images of fish in the sea, animals on the island, and the boat seen from the uninhabited island. These shots, which recall the treatment of the animal life of the outback in *Walkabout*, expose the human presumption in Gerald's claim and suggest that the intruders' relationship to each other and to the island will inevitably be shaped by the cultural patterns that they think they have left behind.

In the opening sequences, as the film intercuts between Gerald and Lucy acting out their unrewarding personal lives in London, we see, hear, or read media reports on such events as a sex-murder trial, a sex-change operation, and the shooting of the pope. Scandal and sensation have driven out any interest in politics, and the basic image is of the cultural and moral decline diagnosed by Thatcherism. The prurience of the British media gives way to the freedom of the desert island on which Lucy proves more ready than Gerald to shed the constraints of clothing. While this leaves the film open to charges of being a "rather pretentious" treatment of "what is basically exploitation material" (Cook, 43), it does set up a tension between "debased" cultural codes within which nudity inevitably becomes "exploitation" and the "natural" values that life as a "noble savage" is supposed to activate.

Although the couple separate at the end of the film, their island experience leads to a tentative sense of renewal that calls into question the culture/

nature dichotomy that inspired their adventure. Ironically, Roeg suggests the possibility of renewal through images of "grotesque" sexuality and "untidiness" that echo those in *Bad Timing*. After Gerald disappears for days to a neighboring island, where he works as a mechanic for the native community, Lucy desperately tries to seduce him by painting black stockings on her bare legs. Like Milena, she uses a "masquerade" to make visible the perverse quality of the sexual demands made on her, but in *Castaway* the result is a passionate episode of lovemaking during a storm that wrecks their "home." As a result of Gerald's activities as a mechanic, their pristine desert island has come to resemble a junkyard, but this "untidiness" also signals a renewal when he decides to stay with the islanders because his mechanical skills give him a valued place in their community.

While *Castaway* calls into question a way of seeing that depends on an absolute opposition between culture and nature, *Track 29* (1987) presents a vision of American culture from which nature has almost entirely disappeared. As in *The Man Who Fell to Earth*, this culture is tested by the arrival of a character who is both alien and British. According to the science-fiction narrative of the earlier film, Newton comes from another planet, but David Bowie's British origins are evident beneath his alien persona. Martin (Gary Oldman), the equivalent figure in *Track 29*, is ridiculed by the people of the small American town in which the film is set, because of his English accent and vocabulary. His status as a character is highly suspect, however, because he first appears as a two-dimensional cutout and later can only be seen by Linda (Theresa Russell), who thinks he is the child taken from her when she was fifteen and brought up in Britain by foster parents.

Although Martin's arrival can be at least partially explained as a manifestation of Linda's sexual frustration, since she is married to a doctor (Christopher Lloyd) who treats her as a child and refuses to allow her to have a child of her own, Martin's Britishness owes more to the film's British authors than to the fantasies of their character.[3] He also reminds us of the cultural movements of the 1960s, as he traces his birth back to the time of "flower power" when people believed in "peace and all that shit."

Martin is dropped off in town by a truck driver who may be his father, since, like the bumper-car attendant with whom Linda had sex on her fifteenth birthday, he has the word "MOTHER" tattooed across his chest. His powerful and gleaming rig is first seen at the end of a panning shot that begins on Martin and moves across a large American flag. Linda's husband, Dr. Henry Henry, is also associated with the American flag, which appears behind him as he delivers the keynote address at "Trainorama," a convention of model railroad enthusiasts who see their hobby as the basis for a political and moral revival in the United States. Henry describes their models as "a record of what built this great nation" and thus as a link with a past in which "we knew who we were, what we were, and where we were going."

According to Roeg, *Track 29* is about "how we become the person others want us to be although we stay the child that we originally were" (Hacker and Price, 355). A political platform based on a return to the past becomes highly suspect in a film in which all the characters act out fantasies of regression to childhood. Martin declares that he is "sick to death at being grown-up" and insists on enjoying the "American childhood" of which he has been deprived. As a doctor, Henry cares for geriatric patients in their second childhoods, but his own adult world centers on a model railroad. Linda's relationship with Henry is expressed through baby talk, while her childlike state is attributed to the traumatic effect of being deprived of her child when she was "a very scared little girl with an overbearing father and a dimwit mother."

The film's representation of the adult world remains highly ambiguous. It is a world in which speculations about "the shape of the universe" (like those in which the Professor was engaged) have become material for television cartoons. At the end of the film, a bloodstain on the ceiling suggests that Linda has killed Henry but, when she asserts her new independence by leaving the house, she adopts a glamour image like that of the Actress in *Insignificance*.[4] The film also offers the idea of play as an alternative to the fixed images and moral absolutes that govern adult life. If Henry's railroad reveals his desire to construct an alternative world that he can control, the film acknowledges its own (partial) complicity with this project when its own set is confused with Henry's models. Thus, when Henry leads the delegates at Trainorama in a rendition of "Chattanooga Choo Choo," Roeg intercuts the celebrations with an orgy of destruction in which Martin smashes Henry's model railroad and the truck demolishes Linda's bedroom. The film destroys its own fantasy world as we watch a figure from Linda's imagination destroy the model associated with her husband's fantasy of a return to the American past.

Like all Roeg's films, *Track 29* offers less a reflection of the world as it is than a model that maps out the shape of modern American culture and plays with its own (and our) integration into that culture. These films suggest that the demand for law and order rests on fear and that rigid moral categories generate the very disorder they are intended to control. Law, psychology, science, and technology, in Roeg's films, all offer systems of meaning that help define the complexities of human experience but that become dangerous when substituted for that complexity. In its attempt to combine quick opinions, necessary for the process of selling images, with the development of a global culture that challenges the traditional boundaries of local cultures, American culture both promotes and offers the means to contain social unrest. Roeg's films and Thatcherist ideology both remain contradictory, as they simultaneously criticize and comply with the new world order. The films, however, expose the contradictions that Thatcherism tries to conceal through its power as myth.

Any assessment of the contribution of Roeg's films to the cinema of the Thatcherist period must acknowledge the increasing marginalization of his work. However, these subversive fables do suggest an alternative to the British realist tradition through a formal work (or play) that activates the threat of disorder but also affirms the pleasures of an unsettled spectatorship. Roeg replaces the clear-cut definitions that Thatcherism (and realism) demands with a field of tensions that encourages the spectatorial activity of "turning over the possibilities."

Although important critiques of Thatcherist ideology lie embedded within the "realist" films of directors like Stephen Frears, Richard Eyre, and David Hare, Roeg's commercial work within an American media environment has cinematic and ideological implications that need further examination, perhaps in relation to the more fantastic and experimental responses to Thatcherism in the films of Peter Greenaway and Derek Jarman. One line of approach is suggested by Lindsay Anderson, who argues that Roeg and Ken Russell were the originators of a "romantic neo-baroque" style, but Anderson feels that the emergence of this style was a sign that British cinema had "lost its way" (Hacker and Price, 55). The neglect of the complex and contradictory films directed by Nicolas Roeg during the 1980s suggests rather that British film culture may have lost its way.

Notes

1. I have chosen not to deal with *The Witches* (1989), a film about a boy who is turned into a mouse, because its fantasy functions in a much more conventional manner than in Roeg's earlier films, despite the special effects created by Frank Oz. Roeg also contributed to the compilation film *Aria* (1987), in which ten directors produced film versions of operatic arias. His resistance to making films for television ended with his adaptation of Tennessee Williams's *Sweet Bird of Youth* (1989) for NBC.

2. Roeg's practice is thus consonant with the emphasis on a "dispersed" rather than unified subjectivity in recent psychoanalytic theory based on the ideas of Jacques Lacan, and with Michel Foucault's concept of culture as a site of competing discourses (which both de Lauretis and Penman invoke in their discussions of *Bad Timing*).

3. The screenplay for *Track 29* was written by Dennis Potter, best known for his television serials such as *Pennies from Heaven* (1978) and *The Singing Detective* (1986), and the film could

equally well be analyzed in relation to Potter's response to American culture (especially his frequent use of music from the Big Band era). See Barker for a comparison of Roeg's and Potter's visions.

4. The links between Linda and the Actress are underlined by the fact that both are played by Theresa Russell, the American actress who became a star as a result of her performance in *Bad Timing*, married Roeg, and starred in most of his subsequent films.

Works Cited

Barber, Susan. 1981. *"Bad Timing/A Sensual Obsession."* *Film Quarterly*, Fall, 46-50.

Barker, Adam. 1988. "What the Detective Saw." *Monthly Film Bulletin*, July, 193-95.

Combs, Richard. 1985. "Relatively Speaking." *Monthly Film Bulletin*, August, 237-38.

———. 1986/87. "Time Away." *Sight and Sound*, Winter, 70-71.

Cook, Pam. 1987. *"Castaway."* *Monthly Film Bulletin*, February, 42-43.

de Lauretis, Teresa. 1983. "Now and Nowhere: Roeg's *Bad Timing*." *Discourse* 5 (Spring): 21-40.

Derbyshire, Ian. 1988. *Politics in Britain: From Callaghan to Thatcher*. London: Chambers.

Gow, Gordon. 1980. *"Bad Timing."* *Films and Filming*, March, 29-30.

Hacker, Jonathan, and David Price. 1991. *Take Ten: Contemporary British Directors*. Oxford: Clarendon Press.

Hall, Stuart. 1983. "The Great Moving Right Show." In *The Politics of Thatcherism*, edited by Hall and Jacques, 19-39.

Hall, Stuart, and Martin Jacques, eds. 1983. *The Politics of Thatcherism*. London: Lawrence and Wishart.

Kavanagh, David, and Anthony Selden, eds. 1989. *The Thatcher Effect*. Oxford: Clarendon Press.

Kennedy, Harlan. 1983. "Roeg: Warrior." *Film Comment*, April, 20-23.

Kettle, Martin. 1983. "The Drift to Law and Order." In *The Politics of Thatcherism*, edited by Hall and Jacques, 216-34.

Kolker, Robert Phillip. 1977. "The Open Texts of Nicolas Roeg." *Sight and Sound*, Spring, 82-84, 113.

Lanza, Joseph. 1989. *Fragile Geometry: The Films, Philosophy, and Misadventures of Nicolas Roeg*. New York: PAJ Publications.

Martin, David. 1989. "The Churches: Pink Bishops and the Iron Lady." In *The Thatcher Effect*, edited by Kavanagh and Selden, 330-41.

Milne, Tom. 1982. *"Eureka."* *Sight and Sound*, Autumn, 280-85.

Mulvey, Laura. 1975. "Visual Pleasure and Narrative Cinema." *Screen* 16 (3): 6-18.

Park, James. 1984. *Learning to Dream: The New British Cinema*. London: Faber.

Penman, Ian. 1980. *"Bad Timing*: A Codifying Love Story." *Screen* 21 (3): 107-9.

Pym, John. 1980. "Ungratified Desire: Nicolas Roeg's *Bad Timing*." *Sight and Sound*, Spring, 111-12.

Segal, Lynne. 1983. "The Heat in the Kitchen." In *The Politics of Thatcherism*, edited by Hall and Jacques, 207-15.

Waller, Nick. 1976. "Nicolas Roeg: A Sense of Wonder." *Film Criticism* 1 (2): 25-29.

Willetts, David. 1989. "The Family." In *The Thatcher Effect*, edited by Kavanagh and Selden, 262-73.

Williams, Raymond. 1975. *Television: Technology and Cultural Form*. New York: Schocken Books.

Thirteen

Insurmountable Difficulties and Moments of Ecstasy: Crossing Class, Ethnic, and Sexual Barriers in the Films of Stephen Frears

Susan Torrey Barber

> The Sixties were good at a number of things, especially at having a good time, and now, when we are having a bad time, we are inclined to read the words "too much" with a guilty awareness that the rich substance of the Sixties has been dissipated in the Eighties—and it was in the Seventies that we began to pay the price.
>
> —Robert Hewison, *Too Much: Art and Society in the Sixties, 1960-75*

Stephen Frears was virtually unknown to overseas audiences when he achieved international acclaim as director of the enormously successful *My Beautiful Laundrette* (1986), which featured a community of nouveau riche Pakistanis thriving in contemporary South London. This was one of many areas throughout Great Britain to feel the impact of the new economic policies of the Conservative Thatcher regime in the 1980s. According to Frears, *Laundrette* was his and screenwriter Hanif Kureishi's ironic salutation to the entrepreneurial spirit in the eighties that Margaret Thatcher championed, as her government transformed the postwar socialist state into a "nation" courting and supported by private capitalistic enterprise.[1]

Sammy and Rosie Get Laid (1988) represented a more acrimonious critique—Frears's and Kureishi's "declaration of war on Thatcher England"— that focused on a broad and diverse cross section of South London: blacks and whites, in addition to Pakistanis, many of them homeless and unemployed. This blighted area is seen from the viewpoint of a visiting Pakistani politician and former resident of London, one appalled by this new England and longing for the "civilized" country he fondly remembered two decades ago.

Frears's third film of the decade, *Prick Up Your Ears* (actually made in between *Laundrette* and *Sammy and Rosie* in 1987 and written by Alan Bennett), features the life of gay playwright Joe Orton and does not specifically examine the Thatcher period. Set in 1987, it covers events in the late fifties and sixties in Orton's life that can be seen as a comparative historical frame of reference. That is, the class-bound and sexually repressed society that fueled Orton's irreverent plays functions as a metaphor for the Thatcher eighties.

This essay examines these three works as reactions to and critiques of the dynamics of Thatcherism by Frears and Kureishi and Frears and Bennett, specifically with respect to race, class, and gender. All three films foreground the seemingly insurmountable difficulties—tempered by moments of ecstasy—that relationships pose when they cross class/ethnic/sexual boundaries, particularly during periods of political changes and economic upheavals. These works also chart Frears's increasing disillusionment with the Thatcher administration. As many historians note, Thatcher's revitalized England valorized capitalistic enterprise and produced a greedier, more intolerant society. Frears readily concurs: "Thatcher has divided the country between North and South, between the employed and unemployed, between the rich and poor, between the people who've got and the people who haven't" (Lindsey, 59). In order to understand this social disintegration, we must backtrack and briefly examine Thatcher's agenda for the eighties.

"See just how far we have fallen," Thatcher said shortly after her victorious entrance to Number 10 in 1979, referring to the "excesses" of the sixties and the subsequent economic downturn in the seventies. As historian Peter Jenkins commented, Thatcher labeled England as sick—morally, socially, and economically (Jenkins, 66). She put the blame squarely on the Wilson Labour government for perpetrating a welfare state that created enormous problems for England in the seventies—inflation, powerful and headstrong labor unions, crippling strikes. All this led to low productivity and no real economic growth. She linked these socialist-induced woes directly to the decline of morality during the permissive sixties: the breakdown of parental authority as well as of the nuclear family, which led to a generation of irresponsible youths who indulged themselves in too much sexual freedom. According to Jenkins, Thatcher's indictment of the sixties and seventies covered just about every aspect of British society: "crime, especially juvenile crime; violence, personal and political; industrial militancy and public disorder; flouting of the rule of law; loss of parental control, of authority generally; the decline of learning and discipline in the schools; divorce, abortion, illegitimacy, pornographic display, four letter words on television; the *decline of manners*" (Jenkins, 67-68). She attributed this "fall from grace" to the Home Office of Roy Jenkins (which liberalized the arts and granted long overdue civil liberties), "who had presided over the abolition of capital punish-

Omar (Gordon Warnecke) learns from his Uncle Nassar (Saeed Jaffrey) (joined by his mistress Rachel [Shirley Anne Field]) about the privileges capitalistic enterprise brings, in *My Beautiful Laundrette* (1986).

ment, legalization of homosexuality and abortion, the liberalization of divorce, and the abolition of theatre censorship" (Jenkins, 68).

To remedy these "setbacks," Thatcher called for a return to Victorian values, harking back to the turn of the century when "our country became great." Jenkins adds: "Her agenda could have been written on a sampler. The individual owed responsibility to self, family, firm, community, country, God in that order. Economic regeneration and moral regeneration [would] go hand in hand" (Jenkins, 67). Thus, a strong national economy would rest upon eager and enterprising individuals, its foundation a strong nuclear (read heterosexual) family.

This context is precisely Frears's and Kureishi's focus in *My Beautiful Laundrette*. As if responding to Thatcher's frequent praises of Indian and Asian shopkeepers as the new "meritocrats" (Ogden, 175), they situate and examine a community of Pakistanis that thrives in this new entrepreneurial age amid an underclass of homeless and unemployed native British, thus comparing the upside and the downside of this new economic order.

Originally immigrating to England in the postwar years and functioning as the servant/service class, Nassar (Saeed Jaffrey) and his extended family, which includes his cousin Salim (Derrick Branche) and nephew and designated heir Omar (Gordon Warnecke), have established a myriad of lucrative businesses, taking every advantage of an atmosphere conducive to private enterprise, including a series of generous tax laws. In her first budget, Thatcher reduced top bracket taxes of 83 percent on earned income and 98 percent on unearned income to a uniform 60 percent. Further, her corporate tax reform dropped the rate for businesses from 52 percent to 35 percent (Ogden, 332). All these cuts enabled businessmen such as Nassar and Salim to increase their net profit dramatically from gross earnings.

The Pakistani culture represented a new area of interest for Frears. When Kureishi showed him his screenplay for *Laundrette*, Frears had no idea that this world existed. "Nobody had ever written from that perspective before. It was astonishing because [Kureishi] got it so right. That someone could be . . . so confident about it, make the jokes, be on the inside" (Friedman, 15). Frears began his career with the "Angry Young Men" in the late fifties and the sixties: dramatists (which included Joe Orton, as well as John Osborne), novelists (Alan Sillitoe, John Wain), and filmmakers (Lindsay Anderson, Tony Richardson, Karel Reisz) obsessed with revolutionizing the arts by featuring social realism. They focused on working-class protagonists at odds with the class-bound system and positioned in their own environments: pubs, flats, factories. Frears assisted Reisz on *Morgan* (1966) and worked under Lindsay Anderson in *If* (1969). His first film was a thirty-minute short entitled "The Burning" (1967), examining the tensions among black, white, and "colored" South Africans long before it was fashionable and profitable to do so.

During the seventies and early eighties he worked primarily in television,[2] a medium, he has commented, "that gives an accurate account of what it's like to live in Britain—about men and women who go to work and lead rather desperate lives" (Friedman, 14). This explains Frears's resistence to the tradition of "Toryist" cinema when he moved into features, for he has cited "Upstairs, Downstairs" (1970-75), "Brideshead Revisited" (1981), and "Jewel in the Crown" (1984) as works that "have perpetrated myths about an England that no longer exists, while failing to illuminate British life as it is" (Lindsey, 59). Frears's attraction to the working and underclasses is consistent with his interest in the Pakistani community—another overlooked and marginalized culture.[3]

As Kureishi and Frears demonstrate in *Laundrette*, the Pakistanis now form part of the privileged class in the eighties, many holding positions of power in South London. As the new landlords, they reversed the traditional imperial/colonial hierarchy by displacing the native British. Frears dramatically demonstrates this dynamic at the film's beginning when Salim and his henchmen throw out "squatters" Johnny (Daniel Day Lewis) and Genghis (Richard Graham) from a run-down building Salim has purchased, depriving them of their only home. Salim employs Jamaicans to do his dirty work, which further fuels the hostility and resentment that the young unemployed and homeless males harbor toward both sets of immigrants and reinforces the decades of racial tension between the communities. Living on the streets, sleeping in any available shelter, and stealing to subsist, Johnny, Genghis, and their friend Moose (Stephen Marcus) aimlessly roam the streets, their actions emblematic of the expanding underclass of social and economic dropouts in the eighties, many of them teenagers and young adults without homes. These groups formed 38 percent of Britain's population during the eighties, as the unemployment rate skyrocketed, reaching a peak of 3.2 million in 1986 (Ogden, 333).

However, despite their ethnic and class differences (which go back to their days as classmates), Omar and Johnny capitalize on the Thatcher government's endorsement of private enterprise, creating professional and personal bonds by becoming shop partners and lovers. The day their remodeled and refurnished laundrette opens inaugurates a new era in British history—the establishment of private business with the blessings of the government. They call their laundrette Powders, a wry reference to its source of financing—the profits from Salim's illegal drug business. Their situation questions the morality of a government eager to support all business, legal or otherwise, for Salim's business clearly feeds on a subclass of local addicts and pushers.

The laundrette stands as a little oasis in the boarded-up, deserted neighborhood, its bright neon sign beckoning customers who eagerly flock through its doors. To celebrate, Johnny and Omar make love in the back room, defying the strong heterosexual codes and ethnic boundaries of their respective communities. Their bond, which motivates frequent hostilities from Johnny's abandoned friends, also causes raised eyebrows from members of Nassar's family, who initially look down upon Johnny. Yet they soon welcome him into their midst, providing the family he never had.

Though this relationship helps Johnny to become responsible and achieve self-worth, Omar's way of reforming Johnny is to play the boss man, reinforcing the new imperial/colonial order that privileges him. At one point, exasperated with Johnny's bouts of laziness and irresponsiblity, Omar comments, "I'm not going to be beaten down by this country. When we were at school, you and your lot kicked me all round the place. And what are you doing now? Washing my floor, and that's how I like it."

The most serious flare-up between the two communities—Genghis's and Moose's brutal attack on Salim to avenge his nearly running over Moose—becomes a crucial test for Johnny and Omar, who risk their lives by openly crossing ethnic boundaries: Johnny to save Salim from being beaten to death, Omar to save Johnny from the wrath of his own friends. Their relationship survives, suggesting not only that their bond of mutual love and devotion may bring their two communities together in a spirit of trust and collaboration, but also that they will rebuild their trashed shop and perhaps create a chain of laundrettes. Thus, this "hybrid" community built on sexual diversity benefits from the Thatcherite vision of private enterprise that serves it (Chari, 21).

Omar's and Johnny's relationship can be compared to that between Joe Orton (Gary Oldman) and Kenneth Halliwell (Alfred Molina) in *Prick Up Your Ears*. They, too, cross class and sexual boundaries to form an initially productive and fulfilling work and love relationship. Just as Omar gives Johnny the family he never had, as well as a job and self-esteem, so Halliwell offers Orton a middle-class lifestyle and literary education. Thus Orton finds a way out of his dreary, unstimulating working-class existence, for Halliwell inspires him to develop his creative potential and achieve a career as a successful writer.

However, as Bennett and Frears demonstrate, the homophobic society in the fifties and sixties in which Halliwell and Orton live suggests an increasingly conservative, insensitive, and narrow-minded establishment in the eighties, one that frowns on sexual diversity, discriminates against gays, and eventually instituted Clause 28 banning homosexual depiction in the arts.[4] As Frears himself commented, *Prick Up Your Ears* and *My Beautiful Laundrette* (and even *Sammy and Rosie Get Laid*, which features a lesbian couple) probably could not have been made after this law was passed.

Boldly challenging the sexually repressive and puritanical eighties, Frears goes beyond the romantic scenes between Omar and Johnny and prominently features Orton's heady sex life throughout *Prick Up Your Ears*, clearly intending to shake up and shock the establishment. For example, the first time that Orton and Halliwell make love, they begin to undress and kiss passionately while watching the coronation of Queen Elizabeth. Their immense enjoyment is fueled by their awareness of the watchful eyes of this highest authority in the land, who alludes to another top-ranking female, Margaret Thatcher herself. Further, Frears's creation of highly erotic atmospheres throughout the film plays out the enormous delight Orton derived from his "subversive" pleasures. (His one-night stands were frequently with men just encountered in the tube, public toilets, and cottages.) These scenes reflect what Orton's biographer John Lahr labeled his "restless, ruthless pursuit of sensation" (Lahr, 14). Frears most dramatically demonstrates this tendency when Joe visits the public toilets after he wins the *Evening Standard* award

Joe Orton (Gary Oldman) experiences increasing fame at the expense of his relationship with Kenneth Halliwell (Alfred Molina), in *Prick Up Your Ears* (1987).

for "Loot." Inside the building exists a shadowy underworld, one washed in blue-green light where figures move slowly and restlessly in and out of the shadows. Orton struts confidently into one of the stalls, casting flirtatious glances at the men. He deftly steps up to unscrew the lightbulbs, throwing the washroom into a murky sensuous darkness illuminated by glowing pools of light. As he urinates, he peeks over the next stall, beckoning the man over. The man drops down to his knees, starting to fellate Orton, who closes his eyes, smiling, as the others slowly gravitate over, their gazes suggesting a highly pleasurable trance.

As the film points out, the failure of Halliwell's and Orton's relationship, due in part to Orton's promiscuity and his intellectual outdistancing of Halliwell, succumbs to the pressures of the times. Ironically, the shunned and embittered Halliwell, who grows to resent and despise Orton, ultimately incorporates the dominant values of the period—monogamy, homophobia—into his psyche, thus appropriating the attitudes and mores of the conservative establishment figures who initially disdained Halliwell and Orton for their homosexuality. These included the prison psychiatrist, as well as the librarian who snidely categorized them as "nancies" and "shirtlifters." The film further suggests that the underlying reason Orton and Halliwell are in jail—ostensibly for defacing library books—is for their homosexuality. Thus, Halliwell functions as an agent of the establishment, ironically killing what he loved and wanted most.

The impossibility of Halliwell's and Orton's relationship in the larger social and political context suggests a fractured, self-destructive, and malaised England that contrasts with the close and potentially lasting bond between Omar and Johnny, a healthy union that bridges diverse communities. Because *Prick Up Your Ears* was made after *Laundrette*, this "regression" characterizes Frears's increasing pessimism about the impact of the Thatcher regime on private lives. In this vein, the third film, *Sammy and Rosie Get Laid*, plays out the full-blown, invasive effects of Thatcherism on British society, which breaks down along racial, class, and ethnic boundaries in the latter part of the eighties. As the opening scenes show, the country has become what Frears labeled a "social disaster" (Hunter, 30).

The small cadre of homeless youths in *Laundrette* have now increased to a larger, more beleaguered group that transcends race and class. The film's opening shot features the waste ground, suggesting the increasing rot in South London (and by implication other urban areas in England). The waste ground, a wide expanse of razed land covered with makeshift camps and abandoned cars and buses, represents the last refuge for the homeless and unemployed, ranging from children to the elderly. This scenario reflects the decline in government funding for public housing, which dropped 60 percent in the mid-eighties as the number of people living below the poverty line increased to an estimated nine million (Ogden, 333-34).

The waste ground and the surrounding tenements are preyed upon by an increasingly aggressive police force, suggesting a more militaristic state that singles out and persecutes blacks in particular. In South London, even at the beginning of the decade, unemployment among young blacks was already a serious problem. For example, in Brixton (an area in South London with a large underclass of blacks), unemployment ran close to 70 percent in 1981, providing the setting for the worst riot in England's history. When two policemen questioned a black youth, a crowd quickly formed. Soon rocks, bricks, and gasoline bombs were flying (Ogden, 173). The ensuing brawl quickly spread to the surrounding neighborhoods, lasting for three days and nights, involving a thousand policemen and some six hundred blacks. Over two hundred rioters were arrested and 120 buildings damaged, 9 completely destroyed (Ogden, 173).

In the film, a similar racial incident sparks another skirmish, when a policeman mistakes an innocent black woman for her fugitive son and kills her.

As the subsequent scenes show, a huge backlash takes place, involving black and white youths who go on a rampage through the neighborhood, setting cars afire, smashing and looting shops. As Kureishi notes, an openly racist climate still operated during the shooting of *Sammy and Rosie*, for throughout the filming of this scene, police randomly stopped blacks who were extras on the set. The production further mirrored ongoing riots in South London that were frequently covered on television.

Danny (Roland Gift), who lives in a caravan on the waste ground with his young son, most dramatically demonstrates the disenfranchisement and alienation of blacks. "No one knows the shit black people have to go through," he comments in despair and frustration, having watched his friends arrested and attacked. Thus Frears reflects the black community's sense of helplessness, as Danny comments to Rafi, "For a long time, right, I've been for nonviolence. Never gone for burning things down. I can see the attraction but not the achievement. . . . We have a kind of domestic colonialism to deal with here, because they don't allow us to run our own communities. But if a full-scale war ever breaks out, we can only lose." Throughout the film, Danny is frequently located outside events, for example, watching the riots or living in the waste ground on the edge of South London. His positioning suggests the black community's marginalization in British society. As Danny comments, his only way of centering himself is to ride the trains all day (adopting the name of one of the stations, Victoria, as his alias), as if making contact with various points in the city will center his identity and reestablish his legal residence.

The strong attraction that Danny and Rosie (Frances Barber) feel for each other, one that cuts across class and racial boundaries, has enormous potential for a mutually beneficial and fulfilling relationship. Both represent persecuted minorities in a system dominated by the white patriarchy, whose agents hover menacingly near their neighborhood: powerful landowners/developers conspiring with crooked government officials over the fate of the inhabitants of the waste ground and the surrounding area. The official comments, "You've got to invest in this area—for your sake and ours. You can do whatever you like," to which the property developer responds, "I want that open space under the motorway—*then* we can talk." Danny's and Rosie's mutual victimization strengthens their friendship; on the evening they passionately make love, Rosie sadly recalls her father's physical and verbal abuse of her, while Danny confides that the woman killed by the police raised him while his own mother was away all day at work.

Yet despite their compatibility, larger events pull them apart. Danny is literally kicked out by developers. The last time Rosie sees him, he is driving his caravan away from the waste ground, which is under siege by a huge devouring bulldozer. The film also suggests that Rosie's role as social worker will consume more and more of her time. As the number of casualties from Thatcher's economic system stack up, the underclass will expand and tax decreasing resources, including housing and welfare, especially for the elderly. For example, after traveling all the way to another part of town, Rosie arrives to find one of her indigent clients dead in his bathtub. Rosie's job suggests her attempts to resurrect Mother England's former role as caretaker welfare state in the fifties and sixties, "picking up the smashed pieces of people's lives," as she comments to her girlfriends, thus taking to heart the words of Margaret Thatcher heard in voiceover at the beginning of the film — "We've got a big job to do in the inner cities. . . . No one must slack."

The demands of Rosie's job have already spilled over into her marriage, which has become less sexual and more maternal, with her husband Sammy (Ayub Khan Din). He frequently regresses into a needy childlike state, which suggests that their relationship has become an extension of her job. "I can't always mother you, baby," she comments when a clingy Sammy urges her to stay home with him. Unlike Rosie, who dedicates her time and energy into a caretaker role, Sammy's way of dealing with the overwhelming social chaos and economic disintegration around him is to withdraw physically. Often he watches from a safe vantage point (for example, on a corner, away from the riots) muttering platitudes: "The city is a mass of fascination. . . . Rosie says these revolts are an affirmation of the human spririt." Other times he just ignores what goes on outside his flat, while indulging himself with all his material comforts. Frears illustrates this when Rosie leaves for an evening to be with her lover, and Sammy becomes all id: trying to eat a hamburger, drink a coke, snort cocaine, and masturbate all at the same time.

His attraction for his latest lover, visiting American Anna (Wendy Gazelle), suggests that she, like Rosie, functions in a maternal role for Sammy. Anna mothers him through his ambiguous feelings about his father, and Sammy even discusses his troubled marriage with her. Sammy desperately seeks to construct the family he never had, for he is estranged from his mother and barely knows his father, who left the country when he was very young. Sammy's degenerate state is initially a turn-on for Anna: she refers to him as a "couch potato" and enjoys indulging him as he lazes around her apartment. Because of Sammy's proximity to the riots, Anna links him to the excitement of the chaos. She eagerly photographs the police beatings, the burning of cars and the looting of the shops for part of her show, entitled "Images of a Decaying Europe." But she eventually tires of his passivity and

Rosie (Frances Barber) and Sammy (Ayub Khan Din), their marriage taxed by the overwhelming social and economic distress in their neighborhood, become increasingly estranged, in *Sammy and Rosie Get Laid* (1988).

indolence, literally leaving him behind as she eagerly throws herself into photographing the final destruction of the waste ground.[5]

Ironically, under an administration that extolled and valorized the nuclear family, *Sammy and Rosie* suggests the absolute breakdown of this unit under new economic pressures—a situation that was introduced in *Laundrette*. Unlike Omar, who lovingly took care of his sick and depressed father, Sammy humors and indulges Rafi primarily because of the perks he offers him—an expensive new car and luxurious home in the suburbs. Further, Sammy's alienation from his wife and his father suggests the difficulties of maintaining family ties under the pressures of the social disorder that permeates their lives, a direct result of the new economic order.

This dynamic is dramatically demonstrated throughout *Laundrette*, for Nassar's many different business interests preoccupy him and keep him away from his wife and children. In fact, his mistress Rachel (Shirley Anne Field)—*not* his homebound wife Bilquis (Charu Bala Choksi)—is the familiar presence in his garage, Omar's laundrette, or his office (where they frequently make love). Ironically, Bilquis's desperate attempt to keep her family together by using black magic to scare Rachel away only further estranges her husband. Like her mother, Tania (Rita Wolf) also tries to preserve their family unit by taunting and shaming Rachel (on the day the laundrette opens), referring to their affair as "a pretty disgusting parasitical thing." Yet Tania soon realizes that her father's double standard directly impacts her life, for he intends to marry her off to Omar—the designated heir of his fortune. Disgusted with the patriarchal lineage that capitalism favors and the sham of her home life, she simply leaves her family for a more promising life on her own.

While Nassar has the advantage of economic roots and political connections, which are clearly more important than his family ties, Rafi (Shashi Kapoor) has neither business nor family links. He remains in exile in Britain, estranged from his native country and on the run from his political enemies, ostensibly having left his second wife behind. By seeking out Alice (Claire Bloom), whom he had admired from afar thirty years ago, he hopes to find a safe haven and precious companionship in the suburbs, far away from his son's scorn and embattled neighborhood.

Both Rafi and Alice are loners (like Rafi, Alice is alienated from her son), initially drawn together by their memories of a more pleasant, civilized England in the fifties. Ironically, they romanticize this period, during which strong racial barriers prevented their friendship or marriage. Though they harken from different cultures, their mutual endorsement of establishment ideals that support the status quo solidifies their ties of affection. Both are insensitive to the larger racial/class inequities that the Thatcher administration reinforced. For example, when Rafi refers to the rioters in Sammy's neighborhood as "fools and madmen," Alice agrees, commenting "I hate their ignorant anger and lack of respect for this great land." Like Margaret Thatcher, Alice remains a product of a provincial town with no ethnic minor-

Rafi (Shashi Kapoor) and Alice (Claire Bloom) in a rare moment of intimacy, in *Sammy and Rosie Get Laid*.

ities to speak of, having had almost no personal contact with blacks or Asians (Ogden, 174). Rafi is more openly racist. Despite Danny's kind gestures toward Rafi—he functions as a guide, protector, and friend—Rafi still displays blatant prejudices. Right in front of Rosie, Rani, Vivia, and several neighbors, Rafi refers to Danny as a "street rat and bum."

Rafi's and Alice's racism is duly matched by their homophobia, for they are both openly disdainful of Rosie's lesbian friends Ranie and Vivia, whom Alice admittedly finds "unnatural and odious." This relationship also throws Rafi into a furious fit when he finds them in Rosie's bed together. Such activities enable him to conclude that the "West is decadent, sex mad and diseased," echoing Thatcher's laments of the "lost virtue" of English society (Jenkins, 67), as well as the antigay atmosphere reinforced by her administration in the eighties, and examined in *Prick Up Your Ears*. As compared with the love affair between Omar and Johnny or Orton and Halliwell, Frears gives the relationship between Rani (Meera Syal), who is Pakistani, and Vivia (Suzette Llewellyn), who is black, a minor role in *Sammy and Rosie*, suggesting that same-sex, interracial relationships are increasingly forced to the margins of society.

But ultimately, as with Danny and Rosie, Rosie and Sammy, and Sammy and Anna, the atmosphere of chaos comes between Alice and Rafi. The violence and destruction in Sammy's neighborhood reminds Rafi of the political disorder in Pakistan when a new regime inaugurated its own reign of terror. This state of affairs, foregrounded by the disfigured ghost of the political prisoner (one of many whom Rafi had tortured and/or killed) that constantly hovers around Rafi, distracts him when he is trying to become intimate with Alice. The appearance of the ghost, his face and upper body burned and lacerated, increasingly unsettles Rafi. For example, after an evening of lovemaking when Alice gently tells Rafi she wants him to stay, Rafi is so obsessed with his past as conjured up by the ghost that he declares absentmindedly, "I want to start writing my memoirs." The ghost, who initially drives Rafi's cab and follows him through the looted and burning areas, soon looks like the persecuted blacks in the area, thus becoming emblematic of their oppressed status. This explains why Rafi's relationship with Danny remains problematic, for Danny clearly reminds Rafi of his political prisoners, hence his contradictory feelings toward him. Thus, Rafi's few moments of sympathy for Danny remain tainted with distrust and condescension.

Rafi's and Alice's relationship is further strained by Rafi's chauvinism. Such an attitude is perfectly appropriate to his native culture in Pakistan, where he was a "patriarch and a little king, surrounded by servants" (as Sammy comments). Accordingly, Rafi forced the women "back into their place" by shutting all the night clubs and casinos. Yet in England, this attitude seems ridiculously callous and inappropriate. This is illustrated before Rafi spends the night with Alice, when he comments, "There's a good ten year's wear in Alice," after stroking the leg of Anna who sits next to him in Sammy's car. Alice finally comes to realize what a fool she was, waiting thirty years for Rafi, who had promised to send for her. "All I wanted was a true marriage," she tells him angrily, suggesting her increasing awareness of her need for a mutually respectful relationship and sexual equality. This new perspective functions in the larger context of her raised consciousness, a result of her conversations with Rosie's feminist friends, including Rani and Vivia, who find Rafi's sexism hateful and Alice's attitudes dated. As Vivia chides her, "You didn't have your own lives. You lived through men."

Though Rafi's suicide represents one way out of his anguish over his past, and "closes out" his age of terrorism in Pakistan, the new order there will most likely continue in an equally violent manner. This reign of terror is mirrored in England, dramatically demonstrated on the level of the ongoing racial violence in an atmosphere of class discrimination tacitly endorsed by the state. Whereas Halliwell's suicide following his murder of Orton in *Prick Up Your Ears* suggested a "disturbed" homophobic and class-bound England lashing out at itself, Rafi's suicide alludes to a more vicious and pervasive cycle, where England not only plays out its internal hostilities, but also directly impacts a postcolonial state. Thus Rafi's comment to Rosie, "We are still dominated by the West and you reproach us for using the methods you taught us," suggests that the oppressed only embodies the "values" and methods of the oppressor.

As *Sammy and Rosie* shows, the crushing pressures of Britain's economic and social upheaval render impossible heterosexual relationships that cross ethnic and class boundaries, those that have the potential to create harmony and order. Yet the film applauds a few tattered survivors: a strong group of heterosexual and lesbian females who bond together, as Rosie, Vivia, Rani, and their friends do in one of the film's final scenes. These self-appointed guardians take care of England's increasing numbers of underprivileged, while also looking out for political terrorists such as Rafi. While *My Beautiful Laundrette* demonstrated how Omar and Johnny assumed a leadership role as entrepreneurs, bringing two diverse communities together and creating a new hybrid community made stronger by the benefits of their enterprise, in *Sammy and Rosie* leaders like Rosie, Rani, and Vivia defiantly remain at odds with the businessmen who tragically destroy their communites. This pitched battle is played out when the landowners/developers, under the auspices of the government, raze the waste ground, thus destroying the fragile settlement and creating another group of homeless and alienated people. Though *Laundrette* and *Sammy and Rosie* both link sexual diversity to the preservation of communities, *Laundrette*'s optimism that enterprise can build a stronger society shifts to a bleaker message in *Sammy and Rosie*: that enterprise is obsessively self-serving.

Sammy and Rosie Get Laid culminates a progressively searing indictment of Thatcher England, aggressively questioning and critiquing the new morality of the eighties, which is dominated by the profit motive. As Frears commented, the film was intended to fully bring the government down. (It didn't, but to Frears's relief, Thatcher was voted out two years later.) Instead of creating a new economic order benefiting all British citizens, the Thatcher establishment wreaked havoc on the working class and underclasses, fracturing the country, rupturing families, and devastating communities. Only the select few who shared her vision profited and thrived.

After completing *Sammy and Rosie Get Laid*, Frears acknowledged that perhaps having run out of steam, he "really didn't have anything else to say about England right now" (Friedman, 30).[6] Nevertheless, Frears, Bennett, and Kureishi created a remarkable legacy: a formidable body of work that exposes the enormous shortcomings of an economic system that ravaged England, and boldly challenges Thatcher's era of nation building.

Notes

1. *My Beautiful Laundrette*, made on 16 mm for approximately $900,000, was completely funded by Channel Four, which was established in 1982 to fund high-quality films for local television viewers and theater audiences. *Prick Up Your Ears*, financed by Channel Four and British Zenith Films, was budgeted at $1.2 million; *Sammy and Rosie Get Laid* cost $2 million and was financed by Channel Four and the American company Cinecom.

2. Frears also made two features that played with generic conventions: *Gumshoe* (1972), a parody of the gangster and detective genres; and *The Hit* (1984), a psychological thriller mixed with the road picture that takes place in Spain. *Bloody Kids* (1979), a pre-Channel Four made-for-television feature (later shown in feature film format in the United States at the Telluride Film Festival in Colorado), focuses on the antics of mischievous youths flirting with crime. *Bloody Kids* is closer to the themes of Frears's television work.

3. The few films in the eighties to feature Indian characters showcased white actors: for example, Ben Kingsley in Richard Attenborough's *Gandhi* (1982) and Alec Guinness in David Lean's *Passage to India* (1984).

4. Clause 28 states: "A local authority shall not . . . promote homosexuality or publish material for the promotion of homosexuality . . . [or] give financial or other assistance to any person for either of the purposes referred to above" (Driscoll, 87). Driscoll further adds that "the aim of the clause is to prevent local authorities from spending their budgets on material which is held by the government to *offer homosexuality as a viable family alternative* (Driscoll, 93; emphasis mine).

5. Frears and Kureishi take a sly glance across the Atlantic at America through the character of Anna, conjuring up the warm bond between Reagan and Thatcher in the eighties. Anna suggests a power blind to its own decline during the Reagan years, conveniently ignoring and displacing its own domestic problems abroad.

6. Frears subsequently directed *Dangerous Liaisons* (1989) and *Grifters* (1990), both made outside England and financed by American companies. These films continue his fascination with power dynamics in various levels of society—the enclave of aristocrats in pre-Revolutionary France and the trio of swindlers in the latter 1950s in Los Angeles.

Works Cited

Chari, Hemelalatha. 1989. *Spectator: University of Southern California Journal of Film and Television Criticism*, Fall, 20-31.

Driscoll, Lawrence. 1990. *Spectator*, Spring, 78-95.

Friedman, Lester. 1989. Unpublished interview with Stephen Frears, June 7. Syracuse University London Center.

Hunter, Mark. 1988. *American Film*, December, 27-31.

Jenkins, Peter. 1987. *Mrs. Thatcher's Revolution: The Ending of the Socialist Era*. Cambridge: Harvard University Press.

Lahr, John. 1986. *The Orton Diaries*. New York: Harper and Row.

Lindsey, Robert. 1988. "The Dangerous Leap of Stephen Frears." *New York Times*, December 18.

Ogden, Chris. 1990. *Maggie: An Intimate Portrait of a Woman in Power*. New York: Simon and Schuster.

Fourteen

The Masochistic Fix: Gender Oppression in the Films of Terence Davies

Tony Williams

In 1983 Andrew Higson criticized a dominant tendency within critical work on British cinema that emphasized realist interpretations at the expense of examining signifying filmic mechanisms (Higson, 80-95). He faulted such readings for failing to advance beyond Christian Metz's model of the cinema as an industrial entity. Higson also condemned these interpretations for remaining solely at the level of "a sociological desire for neatness and continuity, a desire for the text to be *either* 'progressive' *or* 'reactionary,' " as well as refusing "to pay attention to the permanent and productive tensions, the play of containment and excess, in the film system" (Higson, 87). Conversely, Andy Medhurst reasserted the importance of the social text reflecting a dynamic, but not an unproblematic, historical moment. The work of independent film director Terence Davies, especially *Distant Voices, Still Lives*, represents a body of work that does attempt to unite these critical demands. His films contain nonlinear representation, contradictions, tensions, and excess, calling on the viewer to engage in an unpleasurable specularity with the narrative in a more masochistic than voyeuristic manner.

However, *Distant Voices, Still Lives* encountered critical misinterpretation. Desperate for another energetic "New Wave" emerging from a cinematically impoverished culture, British reviewer Derek Malcolm regarded Davies as a "unique voice" responsible for a "musical version of Coronation Street directed by Robert Bresson, with additional dialogue by Sigmund Freud and Tommy Handley" (Malcolm, 21). Geoff Andrew compared Davies to an Ingmar Bergman who has produced "the first realist musical" (Andrew, 16). Thomas Elsaesser associated Davies' cinematic exorcism of male childhood trauma with a recent upsurge of British films dealing with masculine subjectivity (Elsaesser, 291). American reviewer Leonard Quart noted the film's overt formal composition and its seeming neglect of cultural, historical, and psychological explanation (Quart, 42-43).[1]

The film certainly operates on a highly stylistic level, with fragmented memory, tableau-like compositions, meticulously composed photographic shots, and camera movements emphasizing the characters' physical and emotional entrapment. With the exception of one brief seaside scene, *Distant Voices* inscribes the spectator within the mental and psychological space of the family domain. Avoiding the distracting spectacular nature of exterior shots, the film allows the spectator no privileged vantage point with which to engage in a pleasurable voyeuristic gaze, thus making the text a nonchallenging fetishistic object. Instead Davies implicates the spectator in the pain and pleasure of memory. The audience experiences the present and past effects of a younger generation's traumatic childhood, the logical result of a brutal process of patriarchal gender conditioning. By presenting the viewer with the inner life of a working-class family (rather than from without as in the sixties' British New Wave), Davies avoids the pitfalls of both Hollywood escapism and British cinematic literalism. His work represents an artistic exploration of psychic trauma.

Since his first film, *Children* (1976), Davies has gradually moved away from a sixties-influenced documentary style toward an achronological, inner world of tormented personal psychobiography. However, even *Children* exhibited particular nonlinear memory traits of emotional pain that would develop further in his work. In his initial *Trilogy*, including *Madonna and Child* (1980) and *Death and Transfiguration* (1983), we chart the early years and eventual death of surrogate figure Robert Tucker. Victim of a traumatic family situation, Tucker lives a blighted life under the shadows of family morality and Catholic doctrine. He is unable to accept his gay nature, living an existence of passive misery and emotional torment. Tied too closely to his mother, his dying moments in *Death and Transfiguration* represent an imaginary transcendental union with the maternal realm. It is almost as if he is receiving an imaginary transfiguration into the false angelic costume we saw him wearing while a young boy. Tucker's final moments are ambiguous since we do not share his perceptions, but Davies' *Trilogy* is a bleak, pessimistic work leaving no fragmentary space for any alternatives.

Distant Voices, Still Lives is a more complex work. By identifying himself with the camera instead of a surrogate figure, Davies more acutely explores the familial situation, presenting explanations for its oppressive dominance and suggesting faint possibilities for individual voices to at least briefly contest the living graveyard of "still lives." Although set in the recent past, the

Young Robert Tucker's angelic predestination, in *Death and Transfiguration* (1983).

film eschews the realist devices of earlier decades of British cinema. It instead presents antirealist representations as if recognizing the ineffectiveness of traditional British cinematic discourses to combat the historical situation that has resulted in Thatcherism. Like Derek Jarman, Davies recognizes that an alternative British cinema must necessarily involve a different set of visual practices.

Funded by the independent sector, Davies must be understood as an entity implicated within that movement's discursive framework. Writing for the British Film Institute Production Board during 1977-78, Pam Cook championed the important concerns of "personal" filmmakers "with questions of point-of-view, memory and fantasy . . . the material base of film, and the possibility of creating an alternative language of film" (Cook, 276). These features certainly appeared in Davies' trilogy, which received funding from this body. But, unlike the oedipal norms of most mainstream films, Davies' cinema is one bound up with the pre-oedipal in an intense relationship with the maternal figure. Also, unlike the sadistic mainstream narratives criticized by Laura Mulvey, Davies' work has significant associations with masochism, particularly the secondary masochism resulting from a traumatic family situation destructive to both male and female. Terence Davies' films represent one answer to Mulvey's demand for a cinema based upon unpleasure rather than the typical cinematic mechanism of pleasure.

Although set in the past, *Distant Voices, Still Lives* is by no means irrelevant to the historical context of 1980s Britain. Dealing with the life of a working class thirty years before Thatcher, it is impossible to view it outside her reactionary authoritarianism. This anthology makes abundantly clear that the eighties were a decade of reaction within British society that witnessed attacks on libertarian values similar to those made in Reagan's United States. One of the chief platforms of Thatcherism was an assault on the 1960s phenomenon of "the permissive society," especially on one-parent families and gays. This resulted in ideological reemphasis on the traditional family unit. Despite increasing cuts on welfare and family allowances, Thatcherite discourses led to successful attacks on feminists, gays, minorities, and single-parent families, resulting in the increasing isolation of all those outside the family norm. Her 1980s ideological banner of "Victorian values" disavowed all criticisms of a past imperialistic system that caused considerable damage, both externally and internally, upon the British character. As Leonard Shengold has shown, several of Charles Dickens's pictures of blighted families reveal more than coincidental links between passivity and masochism that were to contaminate future generations.

As an independent work challenging patriarchal discourses, *Distant Voices, Still Lives* has significant links with feminist concepts in literature and film. Alice Jardine notes that "struggle" is a crucial component of such texts. "The *inscription* of struggle . . . whether written by a man or woman — it was this that was found to be necessary. The *inscription of struggle* — even of *pain*" (Jardine, 62). Such an inscription characterizes *Distant Voices*, which, unlike earlier 1960s "kitchen-sink" productions, is a film entirely critical of the masculine ethos behind those earlier representations. Despite its formal nature, Davies' film offers crucial insights into those insidious operations of gender conditioning that would eventually destroy the foundations of the British welfare state and lead to Thatcherite hegemony. Such hitherto neglected factors have occupied dominant positions within the British social structure. Susan Pedersen points out that "the construction of masculine identity as entailing economic rights over women and children was one of the most powerful achievements of the labour movement which understandably guarded it jealously" (Pedersen, 99). Nicky Hart notes that "gender has never been theorized as a major axiom and stratagem in any of the dominant theoretical approaches to social inequality" (Hart, 37). Davies' film provides sufficient internal evidence of gender oppression. One particular scene shows the father exploiting his family by making them chop wood in wartime Britain. While doing this the children nearly die in an air raid. When they face their father in the shelter it is Eileen he hits, not Tony. However, the working-class world of *Distant Voices* is not entirely Hart's "masculine republic" (40), since the pub also provides a space where women express solidarity in song and mutual support.[2]

Although it deals with past events, *Distant Voices, Still Lives* is firmly rooted within the historical and cultural context of the eighties.[3] As a work of fragmented memory, it has undeniable links with artistic recreations of trauma that attempt to repiece a shattered self by the use of nonlinear techniques. The family group that appears at the beginning of *Distant Voices* prior to Eileen's wedding is no mere Bresson imitation. Their frozen demeanor represents a psychic numbing, a particular traumatic symptom due to physical and/or mental abuse usually associated with gender conditioning within a nightmarish family situation. Relevant literature on traumatic phenomena reveals that Davies' cinematic treatment is no banal artistic posturing. Psychic violence has detrimental results. Negative effects usually occur well beyond the period of childhood, often resulting in "persistent thoughts about the trauma that intrude into everyday affairs; and a general dysphoria, a numbness that takes the meaning out of life and makes it hard to relate to other people. In (some) cases . . . the symptoms manifest themselves after a latency period of several years or . . . alternate with apparently asymptomatic periods that on closer inspection, turned out to be periods of denial."[4]

Whether conscious or not, Davies attempts traumatic depictions using characteristic techniques of memory fragmentation and nonlinear representation involving his audience in an unpleasurable realm. By doing this he avoids the nostalgia inherent in any work dealing with the past. Cinematic style reflects a painful content. His recreated family life does not represent cozy memories of "the good old days." To counter any deceptive familiarity endemic in realist representations of the past ("Upstairs, Downstairs," "Dr. Finlay's Casebook," "Sherlock Holmes," Ridley Scott's 1970s Hovis bread TV advertisements, etc.) that often disavow the painful circumstances of people's lives, Davies necessarily resorts to different cinematic strategies. In the opening scenes, we view the family facing us. Although the father is dead, his presence still dominates the group, since his photograph appears prominently on the wall behind them. The family faces the camera with frozen postures. Eileen thinks, "I wish me Dad were here," denying the torments he had inflicted on the family when alive. Maisie refuses such a thought. "I don't! I don't! He was a bastard and I bleeding hated him." The audience then enters her memory of past patriarchal brutality, sharing her pain and humiliation. Illustrating the secretive patterns of codependency, the family members never speak of the past. Instead memory haunts them. We often flash back and witness a traumatic family quarrel before returning to

The traumatized family (Freda Dowie, Angela Walsh, and Lorraine Ashbourne) in *Distant Voices, Still Lives* (1988).

the present in the abrupt mode of classic posttraumatic stress disorder symptoms. This occurs in the very opening of the film. We pass from Maisie's voice-over cursing her father to a memory of her brutal maltreatment, before returning to the family tableau. The audience then shares in Tony's memories of a similar past situation. Like Maisie's, they are nonlinear and fragmentary and concentrate on moments of pain, whether physical (Tony smashing his fist through a window) or mental (Tony's rejection by his numb father). His memory ends with the military police dragging him into a van and obviously beating him inside closed doors.

The work of Terence Davies thus represents an alternative to that oedipal law of cinematic articulation formulated by Raymond Bellour. Davies' films depict a masochistic realm of unpleasure rather than pleasure, a situation due to patriarchal oppression.[5] His *Trilogy* and *Distant Voices, Still Lives* illustrate psychic battlegrounds torn between potentially progressive pre-oedipal worlds and destructive oedipal prisons. Within his work, the Law of the Father is an entirely negative violent realm psychically punishing both present and future generations. However, the pre-oedipal arena is not without its problems. Although mother's presence is a comforting one for her children, her inability to oppose Tommy's brutality presents a morbid image of masochistic suffering that will scar her children's lives. Despite her gentle nature, she is a role model whose passivity under patriarchal brutality reveals to her children the negative pattern of suffering in silence. Mother comforts Tony during his scarlet fever, but the next sequence shows her powerless to intervene when Tommy refuses to let him indoors later. He is forced to seek refuge with his grandmother, who Maisie later recognizes as being just like her father.

Although the daughters and girlfriends will eventually marry, none of them appear to have an entirely satisfactory relationship with their husbands. All marriages are characterized by traits of physical brutality (mother and father), mental cruelty (Les and Jingles), passive acceptance (Eileen and Dave), and tolerable acquiescence (Maisie and George). All fall into a patriarchal snare, the result of an ideologically harmful romanticism. One sequence makes this clear. Asked why she married, mother replies, "He was nice. He was a good dancer." But, as an audience, we immediately remember earlier scenes in the film showing Tommy's initially refusing to let Maisie go dancing and forcing her to scrub a rat-infested cellar. The film then flashes back to Tommy beating his wife to the ironic accompaniment of Ella Fitzgerald's "Taking a Chance on Love." Successive shots show the battered mother passively polishing furniture, and Eileen shoveling coal in the hated cellar. We later see the daughters weeping at a film performance of one of the most perniciously romantic products of Hollywood cinema — Henry King's *Love Is a Many-Splendored Thing* (1955)!

Mother and children never speak openly of their experiences of traumatic violence. Instead, we remain privy to the truth by memory sequences that reveal the repressed brutality behind supposedly pleasurable memories. One scene pertinently illustrates this. In the pub the predominantly female community sings "Barefoot Days." Following a 180-degree panning shot we return to the past. The family prepares wood to sell in the austere wartime era. We then see the children caught in an air raid. They reach shelter just in time. It is clear that Tommy has sent them out to sell wood oblivious of their safety. Seeing his children unharmed, the hypocritically enraged paterfamilias hits Eileen. He then forces her to sing to abate the fear everyone inside feels. The scared people all join in Eileen's plaintive rendition of "Roll Out the Barrel," a communal British World War II song. This sequence reveals the buried past pain beneath a seemingly pleasurable present act. The Davies family certainly does not share in the second stanza of the song, "We'll have a barrel of fun." These are but two of many sequences showing the inextricable interrelationship of pleasure and pain within patriarchal dominance. Scenes often clash with each other, as they are chosen for their depiction of intense emotional traumatic situations rather than for any smooth, linear, chronological progression.

These masochistic scenarios are reminiscent of the more social interpretations of Wilhelm Reich and Michel Schneider rather than Freud's ahistorical, universal concepts. Unlike Freud's later formulations in *Beyond the Pleasure Principle*, masochism is better understood as a secondary[6] rather than a primary process, one caused by the family's role as an agent of social conditioning.[7] Both Reich and Anna Freud notice the rigid armor-plated bodily postures that the ego uses to defend itself against psychic attack in traumatic situations.[8] Indeed, Reich's observations uncannily parallel the opening family "portrait" in *Distant Voices*. "All masochistic characters show a specifically *awkward atactic* behavior in their manners and in their intercourse with others" (Reich, 219). However, this scene is not characteristic of others in the film exhibiting tentative opposition toward male dominance. In the pub Eileen and Micky unite in condemning Les's treatment of Jingles. Another scene shows Eileen criticizing Dave's table manners at home. Eileen also delivers a solo pub song—Harry Belafonte's "Brown-Skin Girls"—which ends in a revelation of a wife's murder of her husband, implicitly referring to Dave. Micky is the only female who can manipulate Tommy Davies so that the girls can go off dancing. Tony and Eileen utter separate threats against Father in the course of the film. What we clearly see is a hegemonic situation in which oppressed female subalterns attempt some opposition. However, despite such utopian glimpses, open revolt is clearly impossible within the film's social situation. All characters exist in a complex world of psychic and social entrapment mediated by masochistic mechanisms within the family unit.

Many psychoanalysts such as Bernhard Berliner (38-56) now agree that masochism is a fluid term covering many pathologies, not all of them necessarily sexual or perverse. Although Robert Tucker exhibits perverse masochistic practices as a result of his traumatic Catholic conditioning and repressed homosexual desires toward the father, this is not true of the family in *Distant Voices*. Instead we see a more varied depiction where each family member exhibits different tendencies. As the only male who, in father's place, gives away Eileen in the opening sequence, Tony is no Robert Tucker. The only evidence we see of self-inflicted pain is when he thrusts his hand through the window in a vain attempt to reach through to his catatonic father after going "absent without leave" during his national service. Otherwise, he is more gentle and caring than his father. But he, like Eileen, disavows the traumatic memories of patriarchal oppression. Eileen weeps on his shoulder, crying for her father, before she leaves the family for married life. Tony comforts her, choosing not to contradict her. Both are masochistic victims of childhood trauma, emotionally scarred as a result of their father's dominance during life and beyond death.[9]

As a secondary (noninstinctual) socially mediated process caused by past events, the masochistic fix affecting Davies' characters is an indissoluble result of traumatic conditioning. Jules Glenn (1984) has noted that although trauma need not be present in masochism, "not infrequently it plays a decisive role" (357). It may also result in obsessive repetitions in later adult life that represent not only attempts at mastery but also masochistic gratification. We need not pause before Freud's repetition-compulsion theory to see a definitive explanation for the cinematic construction of Davies' work. They are masochistic products of traumatic experiences repeated anew within an artistic framework. Torn between the Oedipal imperatives of honoring one's father and keenly aware of his past brutalities, the children are torn by conflicting emotions. Their loving father is a monster. They cannot admit this outside of their home, not even to themselves. Attempting in vain to forget past trauma, the repressed memories return to haunt both them and the audience in fragmented imagery. Davies' work is a form of cinematic moral masochism where fragmentation plays a special role. Writing on the links between masochism and depression, John Gedo (1984, 12) comments that moral masochism "may be viewed as nothing more than active repetition of certain subjective states that the observer would not choose to seek for himself." Phyllis Greenacre describes infantile traumatic situations that affect later life as being one of "masked repetition in which the demon [of masochism] is so constantly active that life itself is repeatedly deformed and drawn into a masochistic state of being" (298). Glenn also points out that as the child gets older and enters later adult life he "may attempt mastery by repeating or causing repetition of the traumatic event in controlled and modified form, thus causing painful experiences. He may turn his rage and/or sadism toward the perpetrator of the trauma inward and attack himself, or he may turn rage and/or sadism associated with the oral, anal, symbiotic separation experiences inward" (Glenn 1984, 384).

In the *Trilogy*, Davies uses Robert Tucker as masochistic victim. Since author is completely identified with character, he cannot really step outside the film and view from the outside. That accounts for the *Trilogy*'s bleak and pessimistic nature. In *Distant Voices*, there is no surrogate character. Instead, Davies explores through the camera, observing psychic defeats, traumatic incidents, and briefly expressed oppositional stances. This explains its more diverse nature. Unlike the *Trilogy*, Davies reveals more differential patterns of behavior, such as close female bonding, family celebration, and spontaneous singing, in addition to bleak moments. He now creates a more integrated film that is less negatively overwhelming than its predecessors. Split between several characters rather than merely one, his artistic ego can thus (following the creative axiom of Gilbert J. Rose) communicate a feeling perspective that transcends "the private dimensions of merely personal trauma" (Rose, 61).

Socially induced masochistic conditioning causes great psychic damage to its victims. Investigating usually neglected areas of environment and class in her psychoanalytic explorations, Eleanor Galenson outlines the damaging nature of aggression in the child's early life that leads to negative results in later oedipal development. Retreat into passivity has far more serious consequences for boys than girls. Galenson remarks, "The masochistic development that emerges during the oedipal phase is then inextricably bound to a basic instability in the sense of masculine identity" (195). It can also lead to a more malignant type of masochism involving perverse practices. This happens with Robert Tucker. Until Tony leaves home and marries, he is his mother's boy. After his father's death he has a warm emotional bond with her. Since he is not alone and has his sisters, he is not as psychically devastated as Tucker. The women react differently. Eileen curses her father in his presence. Yet she reluctantly returns home like a dutiful daughter when he is dying. She reveres his memory at her own wedding, masochistically repressing past traumatic events. As Galenson notes, "While the retreat to a passive maternal relationship does not endanger the sense of sexual identity of girls, the more passive nature of their object relations leads toward a permanent masochistic distortion of their relationship to the father and later to all men" (195). Concluding images in the film's first part show Eileen weeping as Dave gloats over her marital entrapment and separation from her girlfriends. All the women are caught within patriarchy in one way or another. If Eileen and Mickey escape Jingles's hellish situation, they cannot freely meet as in the past due to the hindering presence of Dave as "lord and master." Ironically, this is despite the fact that Eileen and Dave are living in her grandmother's house.

Distant Voices is thus the work of an artistic ego attempting mastery of a painful past. It is a product of cinematic fragmentary memory depicting the traditional family norm of British society with unpleasurable associations. By virtue of his visual technique, Davies forestalls the spectator's voyeuristic tendencies toward the pleasures of the cinema screen, inserting instead a more unpleasurable masochistic scenario with social consequences. Unlike earlier middle-class British New Wave directors, he depicts working-class life from within rather than without. He thus avoids those distracting external landscapes that Higson (1984, 18) describes as spectacularly creating "a huge distance between subject and object," situating "the spectator in a privileged vantage point." By fragmenting the narrative, the film avoids visual pleasure, the British anthropological Mass Observation tradition, psychological realism, and a fetishistic mode prohibiting investigation, in order to challenge the viewer to investigate a social unpleasure still relevant to British life today. Excluding any distracting "objective" historical and geographical reference in all but the most marginal sense, the film can then insert its spectator into a different mode of spectatorship, demanding interrogation rather than captivation.

Like Derek Jarman, Terence Davies as a gay director belongs to the eighties realm of the "other." Jarman highly values Davies' use of an "autobiographical cinema," recognizing his oppositional stance within contemporary independent British cinema (Jarman, 12). Davies has personally lived in the hell of a family situation. But his films do not engage in an explicit polemic. Instead, like Jarman, Davies works within the vein of an antirealist tradition calling upon the audience to enter into a self-interrogative cinematic world that is by no means irrelevant to a social context. It is thus a mistake to label Davies' technique as solipsistic or narcissistic, since it arises out of a particular historical moment within contemporary British society. Like most of the interesting works of 1980s cinema, it reacts against the attempted imposition of Thatcherite ideological norms both personally and artistically.

Victim of the past but conscious of a contemporary social responsibility, Davies organizes his painful masochistic experiences in an artistic autobiographical mode. His method parallels Gedo and Goldberg's (1973) observations concerning a hierarchical model of mental functioning involving both conscious and unconscious processes. Gedo (1983, 7) also notes that "it is no longer possible to see the artist primarily as a spinner of fantasies; he must be understood, indeed, as a specially endowed manipulator of varied perceptual elements." *Distant Voices* is thus a work of the conscious, as well as the unconscious, imagination. Emotively reacting to his past traumatic memories but not allowing himself to become overwhelmed by them, Davies' film organizes narrative and visual structures, guiding the spectator to coordinate the various fragmented memories of pleasure and unpleasure into an emotional awareness of a traumatic family situation. It thus represents a much more conscious and developed awareness of a complex situation than does the passive, pessimistic reflective nature of the *Trilogy*.

Distant Voices has also interesting links with D. W. Winnicott's idea of a transitional object or phenomenon.[10] This is an object that the child chooses as a defense against anxiety, coordinating its subjective perceptions to an external world that may (or may not) involve cruel parents and a harsh environment. Winnicott (1965, 145) states that this subjective world may be cruel as well as ideal. For our purposes, we may understand it as masochistic, involving fond memories of mother juxtaposed with ugly ones of father traumatically conditioning its recipients as well as future generations. Unlike Freud's themes, Winnicott's transitional objects have social and environmental, as well as cultural, relevance.[11] We may understand a film to be a transitional object, especially one combining subjective memory with a hierarchical mode of translating these experiences into artistic creation. There is no real objection to understanding Winnicott's ideas cinematically.[12] Arnold Modell and Philip Weisman have both applied Winnicott's transitional object toward understanding the mature creations of the adult artist.[13] Following Winnicott and Greenacre, Weisman (1971) notes that the transitional object may develop into a fetish object with either positive or negative results.[14] He states that "the characteristics of a fetish object may prevail over its feature as a created object; conversely . . . the qualities of a created object may supersede its fetishistic aspects" (Weisman 1971, 405). Greenacre also remarks that the artist may have an important capacity to organize sensory impressions with special sensitivity to rhythm and form, particularly in relationship to a "collective audience" (482). If we relate these ideas to Davies' films and the period from which they have emerged, we then see some interesting associations between artistic organization and social context that make his work more than supposedly formalist. The family is, after all, the basic unit of any society, subject to manipulation by forces both inside and outside the home. It generates human personalities equally liable to be developed or stunted by social norms. To understand its psychic operations, an interrogative, nonrealist approach is thus essential to raise consciousness.

One scene is especially noteworthy in illustrating Davies' technique in raising audience perceptions in a new materialistic cinematic manner. At the climax of *Still Lives*, the newly married Tony weeps unseen outside his mother's house. The camera remains static. We sit fixed and immobile, intruding at the specter of his grief. However, our position in the audience does not make us prurient voyeurs. Instead, we are drawn into his sadness and suffer with him. We remember his placement within a traumatic family situation. Other elements within the scene clarify the nature of his pain. Tony weeps apart from those inside. He has no one to console him as he once consoled Eileen. It is clear that Tony weeps not for his father. He realizes his impending departure from his mother, and his transition into the patriarchal realm. The scene opens after a dissolve of mother singing "For All You Mean To Me." For Tony it signifies a loss of his original pre-oedipal closeness. Tony stops weeping after someone puts on a record of "Oh, My

Papa." Will he permanently leave the pre-oedipal for the oedipal realm? We do not know. The scene of his honeymoon car departing morbidly resembles an earlier one of the military police vehicle driving away the imprisoned Tony after the futile confrontation with his father.

This is one of many key scenes in the film that exhibit an acute sense of artistic organization stressing the miserable implications of submission to patriarchy that creates masochistic victims. Eileen and Tony have suffered traumatically but cannot articulate their pain. After their respective weddings both weep, realizing their separation from a lost object. As Edwin and Constance Wood recognize, "The tearful feeling state is occasioned by the ego temporarily threatened with being inundated by complex memories and affects" (134). Ironically, Eileen weeps for a lost object that has oppressed both her and her family. She cannot create the necessary psychic space to condemn both the monster and the institution that has violated her individuality. Tony understands the implications of his forthcoming separation from mother. As Greenacre notes in her case work, "Tears come insidiously as part of a change in the individual's attitude toward his modified external reality, usually with a reciprocal change in his self-appreciation and even in his self-image. *This usually involves some degree of renunciation* and the resultant relaxation and the tears express and help along such an internal change" (251; emphasis mine). As Franco Moretti has pointed out in another context, tears also express powerlessness in the face of an irreversible direction (162). Tony will now become a husband and future father and may possibly turn into a bastion of the male order. He thus falls victim to his repressed emotions concerning his departure from the maternal realm. All characters within the film are thus past, present, and future psychic victims of an oppressive social system.

In *Distant Voices, Still Lives*, Terence Davies positions his audience in an unpleasurable masochistic dimension, uniting cinematically psychoanalytical mechanisms with relevant sociological critique. Unlike the earlier trilogy, *Distant Voices* presents us with a number of characters who represent different masochistic reactions, rather than just one solitary scapegoat such as Robert Tucker. In this way he presents images of possible alternatives (Tony, Eileen, Maisie, and Micky) in certain instances rather than just masochistically dwelling on one victim. By creatively splitting his unconscious feelings in the representation of different characters, Davies further explores psychoanalytic mechanisms of masochism among a broader section of the family unit rather than concentrating on one damned soul. His artistic technique is thus akin to those artistic methods used to master trauma noted by Gilbert J. Rose. In referring to both Greenacre and Winnicott, Rose notes the possibility for victims of trauma to use unconscious mechanisms in a creative manner. "The gifted person, while having the conventional sense of reality, is thus able to hold it in abeyance, in order to explore and concentrate full powers of integration on imaginative possibilities" (Rose, 112).

Distant Voices, Still Lives reveals this technique, displaying the creative manipulation of time witnessed in the trilogy. Davies' methodology is also akin to the schizoid personality. The latter and the creative writer share similar traits, as Rose notes: "They both treat the stuff of time and character as flexible material suitable for being shaped and molded—according to their conscious and creative or unconscious and defensive designs. . . . The author fashions fictional characters and manipulates the flow of time with flashbacks and fast-forwards according to artistic requirements. In other words, character and time are treated by both author and patient as having the quality of plasticity usually associated with *aesthetic* media" (108-9). However, despite its nondidactic quality, the semiautobiographical work of Terence Davies has undeniable social relevance. It has emerged in an era that has witnessed increasing attacks on minorities in British society. The work documents the misery that the officially sanctioned family institution has caused to human potential. Uniting the concerns of traumatic mastery and British cinematic independent film discourses, Davies remains one of the most powerful voices to have emerged from a reactionary decade in British social life.

Notes

1. For other critical observations on Davies and his work, see Barker (294); Wyeth (36-39); Floyd (295-96); Wrathall (17-18); and Williams (65-69).

2. For further evidence concerning gender oppression within the British social structure, see the detailed evidence provided by Pedersen (86-112) and Hart (19-47).

3. See Hall and Abse.

4. Quoted by Tal (1989,190). See also Lifton (153-54) and Frankl (19-21, 52) for descriptions of traumatic apathy and psychic numbing in German concentration camp victims and Hiroshima survivors.

5. For a survey of complex post-Freudian interpretations of masochism, see Loewenstein (197-234); Brenner (192-226); Glenn (672-80); Bernstein (467-86); Maleson (325-55); Grossmann (379-413); and the collection *Masochism: Current Psychoanalytic Perspectives* (1988), edited by Robert Glick and Donald Meyers.

6. In his 1915 essay, "Instincts and Their Vicissitudes," Freud originally regarded masochism as a secondary process—a view he changed in his later metapsychological explorations, "Beyond the Pleasure Principle" (1920) and "The Economic Problem of Masochism" (1924). Current psychoanalytic interpretation finds many problems with Freud's later work, especially his concepts of the "Death Instinct" and primary masochism. See, for example, Grunberger (9). As Grossman notes concerning Freud's formulation, "the term masochism, however, never did have a precise meaning or one that was generally accepted. It was a controversial term except as a literary designation for any phenomena in which sexual pleasure and physical and mental pain were associated" (Grossman, 380). Issues of superego formation and object relations, es-

pecially in regard to parental figures, are extremely important in current research. Grossman further comments, "Behavior that appears self-destructive to an observer may be organized to serve a variety of functions having to do with the regulation of unpleasurable affects, pain, and aggression. The term masochism will be most usefully and understandably applied to those activities organized by fantasies involving the obligatory combination of pain and unpleasure, or to the fantasies themselves" (409). This is especially applicable to the tormented fantasies of Robert Tucker in *Madonna and Child*.

7. Reich (1971) refutes Freud's idea of the Death Instinct and regards masochism as a secondary drive rather than an instinct in the biological sense. It is caused by the disastrous effect of social conditioning (209-18). He also points out that by turning toward the self, sadistic drives become masochistic, since the frustrated person's superego becomes a punishing agent — hence, Tony's self-destructive action in smashing his hand through the window, thus punishing himself for failing to communicate with his father in the film's opening scenes. Reich (1970,37) earlier noted that submission usually follows any rebellion against authority. Bernstein has relevant comments on female masochism that enable us to understand the social conditioning of the mother and the daughter in the film. He states, "We must beware . . . of underestimating the influence of social customs, which similarly force women into passive positions. . . . A suppression of women's aggressiveness which is prescribed for them constitutionally and imposed on them socially favors the development of powerful masochistic impulses, which succeed, as we know, in binding erotically the destructive trends which have been diverted inwards. Thus, masochism, as people say, is truly feminine" (Bernstein, 468).

8. Reich (1971), 218-19; Anna Freud, 35.

9. In the child's early life masochistic foundations may occur in a form known as protomasochism preceding the oedipal phase. Sarnoff notes that the parental image may be protosymbolically represented. Through such objects "aggression aimed at the parent can be turned upon the self" (Sarnoff, 205). Eileen's weeping for her father represents such a mechanism. Although she cursed him while he lived she now turns her former aggression against herself. Sarnoff's following observations are extremely important. "With the development of self-object differentiation, the fused libidinal and aggressive energies of the child can be perceived by the child as directed outward toward an object. Should the parent withdraw from contact or from view, the child can persist in contact with the parent through an internalized memory of the parent. This internalized image is called the introject. The aggression that had been directed toward the object accompanies the introject. It, too, is directed toward the self of the child. This produces a paradigm for the experience of self-directed aggression, called 'secondary' masochism. This becomes the basis for the patterning of relationships in which masochism involves objects. Intensification of the secondary masochistic experience by actual aggression by the parents enhances *the masochistic fantasies that will color the relationships of adult life*. As a result, tolerance for such relationships heightens. This permits people to enter similar relationships without challenge, since that which would be extraordinary for the children of parents of ordinary demeanor becomes like home cooking for the children of cruel parents" (Sarnoff, 206; emphasis mine). The application to the Davies family needs no further comment.

10. See Winnicott (1957), 182-90; (1965), 143-44; (1971), 1-26.

11. See also Winnicott's important essays "Creativity and Its Origins" and "The Location of Cultural Experience" in his 1971 collection (65-84; 95-103). In the latter essay, Winnicott notes the role of trauma in a baby's individual development, causing "a break in life's continuity, so that primitive defences now become organized to defend against a repetition of 'unthinkable anxiety' or a return of the acute confusional state that belongs to disintegration of nascent ego structure" (97). He also understands cultural experience as an extension of the transitional phenomena concept. "When one speaks of a man one speaks of him *along with* the summation of his cultural experience. The whole forms a unit" (99). The advantage of Winnicott's ideas result in avoiding Freudian individualism. Cultural experience begins in the potential space between the

individual and the environment (originally the object). If creative living is impossible because of a bad family relationship, then mastery of a traumatic situation by means of art would be impossible.

12. For one recent example, see Glass (2-13), who also cites Greenacre.

13. See Weisman (1967, 37-50; 1969; 110-23). For striking parallels of creativity to ego reaction during traumatic neuroses, see Bychowski (592-602). He comments that continuous artistic projection "presupposes a large stock of unconscious material. This is provided not only by repressed id and superego derivatives but by ego states as well. It may be said that the ego of the artist has an unusual ability for splitting off entire constellations reflected in all parts of the mental apparatus" (596).

14. For Greenacre's observations on the relationship between the transitional object and the fetish, see her essays "The Fetish and the Transitional Object" and "The Transitional Object and the Fetish: With Special Reference to the Role of Illusion" in *Emotional Growth*, vol. 1, 315-52. Davies's use of voyeuristic and fetish mechanisms is completely opposite to the usual understanding by Mulvey in regard to mainstream cinema. The director avoids the visual pleasure inherent in most forms of spectatorship and spectacle to plunge the audience into an awareness of the tragic nature of the family's emotional wasteland. It is one caused by social conditions.

Works Cited

Abse, Leo. 1989. *Margaret, Daughter of Beatrice: A Politician's Psycho-Biography of Margaret Thatcher.* London: Jonathan Cape.

Andrew, Geoff. 1988. "Home Truths." *Time Out* 946: 16.

Barker, Adam. 1988. *"Distant Voices, Still Lives." Monthly Film Bulletin* 55 (657): 293-94.

Bellour, Raymond. 1979. "Alternation, Segmentation, Hypnosis: Interview with Raymond Bellour by Janet Bergstrom." *Camera Obscura* 3/4: 71-104.

Berliner, Bernhard. 1958. "The Role of Object Relations in Moral Masochism." *Psychoanalytic Quarterly* 27: 38-56.

Bernstein, Isidore. 1983. "Masochistic Pathology and Feminine Development." *Journal of the American Psychoanalytical Association* (henceforth *JAPA*) 31: 467-86.

Brenner, Charles. 1959. "The Masochistic Character: Genesis and Treatment." *JAPA* 7: 197-226.

Bychowski, Gustav. 1951. "The Metapsychology of Artistic Creation." *Psychoanalytic Quarterly* 20: 592-602.

Cook, Pam. 1981. "The Point of Self-Expression in Avant-Garde Film." In *Theories of Authorship*, edited by John Caughie, 271-81. London: Routledge and Kegan Paul.

Elsaesser, Thomas. 1988. "Games of Love and Death or an Englishman's Guide to the Galaxy." *Monthly Film Bulletin* 55 (657): 290-93.

Floyd, Nigel. 1988. "A Pebble in the Pool and Ships Like Magic." *Monthly Film Bulletin* 55 (657): 295-96.

Frankl, Victor E. 1959. *Man's Search for Survival.* Boston: Beacon Press.

Freud, Anna. 1946. *The Ego and the Mechanisms of Defense.* Translated by Cecil Baines. New York: International Universities Press.

Freud, Sigmund. [1915] 1984. "Instincts and Their Vicissitudes." In *On Metapsychology: The Theory of Psychoanalysis.* The Pelican Freud Library, vol. 11, 105-38. London: Penguin.

_____. [1920] 1984. "Beyond the Pleasure Principle." In *Metapsychology*, vol. 11, 269-338.

_____. [1924] 1984. "The Economic Problem of Masochism." In *Metapsychology*, vol. 11, 409-26.

Galenson, Eleanor. 1988. "The Precursors of Masochism: Protomasochism." In *Masochism: Current Psychoanalytic Perspectives*, edited by Robert A. Glick and Donald I. Meyers, 189-204. Hillsdale, N.J.: Analytic Press.

Gedo, John. 1983. *Portraits of the Artist: Psychoanalysis of Creativity and Its Vicissitudes*. New York: Guildford Press.

_____. 1984. *Psychoanalysis and Its Discontents*. New York: Guildford Press.

Gedo, John, and Arnold Goldberg. 1973. *Models of the Mind: A Psychoanalytic Theory*. Chicago: University of Chicago Press.

Glass, Fred. 1990. "Totally Recalling Arnold: Sex and Violence in the New Bad Future." *Film Quarterly* 44 (1): 2-13.

Glenn, Jules. 1981. "Masochism and Narcissism in a Patient Traumatised in Childhood." *JAPA* 29 (3): 672-80.

_____. 1984. "Psychic Trauma and Masochism." *JAPA* 32 (2): 357-85.

Greenacre, Phyllis. 1971. *Emotional Growth: Psychoanalytic Studies of the Gifted and a Great Variety of Other Individuals*. 2 vols. New York: International Universities Press.

Grossmann, William I. 1986. "Notes on Masochism: A Discussion of the History and Development of a Psychoanalytic Concept." *Psychoanalytic Quarterly* 55: 379-413.

Grunberger, Bela. 1979. *Narcissism: Psychoanalytic Essays*. Translated by Joyce S. Diamanti. New York: International Universities Press.

Hall, Stuart. 1988. *The Hard Road to Renewal: The Crisis of Thatcherism*. London: Verso.

Hart, Nicky. 1989. "Gender and the Rise and Fall of Class Politics." *New Left Review* 175: 19-47.

Higson, Andrew. 1983. "Critical Theory and British Cinema." *Screen* 24 (4-5): 80-95.

_____. 1984. "Space, Place, Spectacle." *Screen* 25 (4-5): 2-21.

Jardine, Alice. 1987. "Men in Feminism: Odor di Uomo or Compagnons de Route." In *Men in Feminism*, edited by Alice Jardine and Paul Smith, 54-61. New York: Methuen.

Jarman, Derek. 1991. "The Garden of Earthly Delights—Interview." *City Limits* 483: 12-14.

Lifton, Robert Jay. 1970. *History and Human Survival*. New York: Random House.

Loewenstein, Rudolph M. 1957. "A Contribution to the Psychoanalytic Theory of Masochism." *JAPA* 5: 197-234.

Malcolm, Derek. 1988. "Voices of Experience." *Guardian*, Oct. 13, 21.

Maleson, Franklin G. 1984. "The Multiple Meanings of Masochism." *JAPA* 32 (2): 325-57.

Medhurst, Andy. 1983. " 'Victim': Text as Context." *Screen* 24 (6): 2-21.

Metz, Christian. 1982. *The Imaginary Signifier*. Translated by Celia Britton et al. Bloomington: Indiana University Press.

Modell, Arnold. 1976. "The Transitional Object and the Creative Act." *Psychoanalytic Quarterly* 39: 240-50.

Moretti, Franco. 1983. *Signs Taken for Wonders*. London: Verso.

Mulvey, Laura. 1975. "Visual Pleasure and Narrative Cinema." *Screen* 16 (3): 6-18.

Pedersen, Susan. 1989. "The Failure of Feminism in the Making of the British Welfare State." *Radical History Review* 43: 86-112.

Quart, Leonard. 1990. "*Distant Voices, Still Lives*." *Cineaste* 17 (3): 42-43.

Reich, Wilhelm. 1970. *The Mass Psychology of Fascism*. Translated by Vincent R. Carfagno. New York: Farrar, Strauss and Giroux.

_____. 1971. *Character Analysis*. 3rd rev. ed. Translated by Thomas P. Wolfe. New York: Farrar, Strauss and Giroux.

Rose, Gilbert J. 1987. *Trauma and Mastery in Life and Art*. New Haven, Conn.: Yale University Press.

Sarnoff, Charles A. 1988. "Adolescent Masochism." In *Masochism: Current Psychoanalytic Perspectives*, edited by Glick and Meyers, 205-24.

Schneider, Michel. 1975. *Neurosis and Civilization: A Marxist/Freudian Synthesis*. Translated by Michael Roboff. New York: Seabury Press.

Shengold, Leonard. 1988. *Soul Murder: The Effects of Childhood Abuse and Deprivation*. New Haven, Conn.: Yale University Press.

Tal, Kali. 1989. "Feminist Criticism and the Literature of the Vietnam Combat Generation." *Vietnam Generation* 1 (3-4): 190-201.

Weisman, Philip. 1967. "Theoretical Considerations of Ego Regression and Ego Functions in Creativity." *Psychoanalytic Quarterly* 36: 110-23.

_____. 1971. "The Artist and His Objects." *International Journal of Psychoanalysis* 42: 405.

Williams, Tony. 1990. "Terence Davies Interview." *CineACTION!* 21/22: 65-69.

Winnicott, D. W. 1957. *Mother and Child: A Primer of First Relationships*. New York: Basic Books.

_____. 1965. *The Family and Individual Development*. New York: Basic Books.

_____. 1971. *Playing and Reality*. London: Routledge and Kegan Paul.

Wood, Edwin C., and Constance C. Wood. 1984. "Tearfulness: A Psychoanalytic Interpretation." *JAPA* 32 (1): 117-36.

Wrathall, John. 1988. "Picture This." *City Limits* 367 (13): 17-18.

Wyeth, Peter. 1986. "Voices from the Past." *Stills* 25: 36-39.

Fifteen

Allegories of Thatcherism: The Films of Peter Greenaway

Michael Walsh

From the Avant-Garde to Art Cinema

Any full account of Peter Greenaway's work as an artist would have to consider his paintings, drawings, videos, and writing. In this essay, however, I will discuss only the films, which can be conveniently divided between the experimental work and the features. A filmography annotated by Greenaway for Film Comment begins with 1959, but his continuous production of experimental films dates from 1966, including *H Is for House* (1973), *Windows* (1975), *Water Wrackets* (1975), *Dear Phone* (1977), *A Walk through H* (1978), *Vertical Features Remake* (1979), and *The Falls* (1980). The features, more properly the concern of a volume whose rubric is British film under Thatcher, are *The Draughtsman's Contract* (1982), *A Zed and Two Noughts* (1985), *The Belly of an Architect* (1985), *Drowning by Numbers* (1988), and *The Cook, the Thief, His Wife, and Her Lover* (1989).

To begin with this distinction between avant-garde and feature films, between artisanal and capitalist conditions of production, is to follow a protocol introduced by David James in *Allegories of Cinema: American Film in the Sixties*, and further treated in his 1991 essay on Warhol. In the case of Greenaway, the distinction is between films funded independently and international coproductions, with the British Film Institute financing of *A Walk through H*, *The Falls*, and *The Draughtsman's Contract* marking the passage from one regime to the other. Though filmmakers who move from experimental to industrial conditions of production appear in recent film history (along with Warhol, one thinks of Cassavetes and Derek Jarman), the phenomenon is certainly unusual enough to give us pause. For that reason, and because most recent accounts of Greenaway overlook his work of the 1970s, I want to begin with his origins in the avant-garde.

According to one archaic tradition of that movement, Greenaway's move to features must be a sellout, a betrayal, and may even reveal that his earlier films were not authentically experimental. On the other hand, it is P. Adams Sitney, whose *Visionary Film* continues to define the North American avant-garde canon, who has described the influence on Greenaway of structural filmmakers like Hollis Frampton and Michael Snow. For Sitney, what Greenaway shares with these two is a dedication to Menippean satire, that is, an ironic fascination with occupational roles and habits of thought; in the features, this becomes a preoccupation with middle-class professionals (draughtsmen, zoologists, architects, coroners, and cooks) led by desire to betray or abandon their callings.

If avant-garde critical opinion is thus divided as to the two moments in Greenaway's work, it might seem tempting to have done with the problem by suggesting that the traditional opposition between experimental and commercial cinema is overly melodramatic and perhaps superannuated. However, this tactic is most enthusiastically adopted by critics intent on revalorizing the films previously considered commercial, and is historically conditioned by the comparative quiescence of the film avant-gardes and the resurgence of Hollywood spectacle in recent years. If the traditional distinction thus seems less discredited than rather weary, it seems more judicious not to abandon it but to suggest that there are limit cases in which it is erased (James says something like this about Warhol), and limit cases, like that of Greenaway, in which it seems helpful only to an extent.

For example, the idea that we may distinguish between avant-garde and industrial works on the basis of attitude to narrative seems to work for Greenaway only in some incremental fashion. The reason is that his experimental films not only involve narration but play elaborately comic games with it; *Water Wrackets* disburdens itself of an entire conquest saga, *Dear Phone* tells of numerous characters who all have the initials H. C. and wives named Zelda, and *The Falls*, with its ninety-two biographies of the victims of a "Violent Unknown Event," contains a positive excess of narrative fragments. And while the features do engage much more directly with what James calls "the grammar of entertainment cinema" (James 1991, 22), narration in those films remains partly gestural, proceeding as much according to structural principle as to the tradition of the well-made plot; the most obvious example is *Drowning by Numbers*, whose art-house audiences, instructed by the precredit sequence, delight in following the film's sequence of numbers.

Nor does it seem easy to distinguish between the two moments in Greenaway's work on the basis of favored images, themes, and conceptual systems. *Water Wrackets* introduces a love of images of the sun crisscrossed by trees and other "vertical features" that recurs everywhere in Greenaway, a love of the play of light on water that recurs in both *Drowning by Numbers* and *The Cook, the Thief, His Wife, and Her Lover*, and a deadpan fascination with the authority of BBC voice-overs that recurs in *A Zed and Two Noughts*. With its patient archaeology of the artificial lakes created by the victorious tribe or clan of Wrackets, this film also anticipates the emphasis throughout Greenaway's work on human transformations of the landscape. This emphasis is peculiarly English; the long obsession of the national culture with the countryside and the country house is the trace of a social history in which an agrarian gentry accumulated the capital for the world's first industrial revolution and then ensured both that Britain would become the first European society to economically minimize agriculture and that industry would remain subordinate to finance capital and empire. Thus, if *H Is for House* seems typical of an entire subgenre of avant-garde films that depict the immediate domestic surroundings of the filmmaker, and *Windows* seems typical of another subgenre that analogizes on the materiality of the camera, both films also participate in this peculiarity of the English by anticipating the confinement of *The Draughtsman's Contract* to the interior and grounds of a house in the country and the return of *Drowning by Numbers* to a sunstruck Suffolk.

Also inaugurated in the 1970s films is Greenaway's interest in exhaustive rehearsals of the structured materiality of every kind of signifying system; as its title indicates, *H Is For House* anticipates both *The Draughtsman's Contract* and *A Zed and Two Noughts* by giving pride of place among those systems to the alphabet. Characters too recur from film to film to film; as Greenaway's own publicity material for *Drowning by Numbers* suggests, Cissie Colpitts is mentioned in *Dear Phone* and *Vertical Features Remake*, becomes three slides of the same woman (right profile, full face, left profile) in *The Falls*, and becomes three women with the same name in *Drowning by Numbers*. Indeed, a whole essay might be written on the avidity with which Greenaway's films recycle and make intertexts of each other.

However, the fact that many of Greenaway's preoccupations first appear in his work of the 1970s does not make it impossible to distinguish between his experimental and commercial films; to paraphrase a remark of John Searle on Derrida, the fact that a distinction is not absolute does not mean that it is not a distinction at all. Most obtrusive among factors that distinguish the features is the presence of actors, with the concomitant sense of drama, motive, and psychology, however stylized and disoriented. In the experimental films, speech is typically reported; we hear about characters from a tireless, measured, bureaucratic voice-over. The features, by contrast, are populated by highly credentialed actors and often veer comically between the exigencies of structure and those of naturalistic conversation. In other words, the features are based on classically dramatic motives and tensions found only implicitly in the earlier films; *The Draughtsman's Contract* treats a struggle for sexual and social power conditioned by a crisis in symbolic paternity, *Drowning by Numbers* dramatizes the impasses of obsessional desire, and *The Cook, the Thief, His Wife, and Her Lover* depicts a brutal and adulterous love triangle.

Also more prominent in the features is Greenaway's investment in art history. This is not completely absent from the earlier work, but those films contain nothing like the profusion of paintings found in the features; William F. van Wert discovers more than a dozen direct references to art history in *The Cook, the Thief, His Wife, and Her Lover* and feels he has only begun to discuss the topic. Painting operates most plainly as a system of allusion, in which Vermeer presides over *A Zed and Two Noughts*, Brueghel over *Drowning by Numbers*, and Hals over *The Cook, the Thief, His Wife, and Her Lover*. Meanwhile, various corpses evoke Mantegna's *Dead Christ*, women in red hats evoke the (supposed) Vermeer *Girl with a Red Hat*, nude departures evoke expulsions of Adam and Eve from Paradise, and feasts evoke both last suppers and the Hals *Banquet of the Officers of the St. George Civic Guard* that looms so large in the decor of *The Cook, the Thief, His Wife, and Her Lover*.

Greenaway's use of large and familiar paintings as backdrops reminds us of Fassbinder's *The Bitter Tears of Petra von Kant* (1973), and his *tableaux vivants* call to mind Godard's *Passion* (1982), a film full of the logistical comedy involved in trying to render Rembrandt and Delacroix with live actors and animals. This combination of comparisons suggests that Greenaway's meditation on art history is a question of animation, a question of negotiating between two basics of the film image: the stillness it shares with painting and photography and the motion that decisively distinguishes it from the earlier visual arts. Noël Burch argues that the passage from the serial photography of Muybridge and Marey to the early cinema is a movement from the scientific analysis of motion to its "Frankensteinian" synthesis, a formulation that suggests a way of thinking about Greenaway's treatment of art history that passes beyond allusion and reference to link up with other aspects of his style. For example, this perspective makes it less surprising that *A Zed and Two Noughts* should imagine decay as a type of animal locomotion that had not occurred to the apparently exhaustive Muybridge; it also helps us to un-

The animate statue (Michael Feast) in *The Draughtsman's Contract* (1982).

derstand the animate statuary of *The Draughtsman's Contract*, the disturbing amputations with which Alba physically comments on the Venus de Milo in *A Zed and Two Noughts*, and the attraction of Roman statuary for the title character in *The Belly of an Architect*. The wider compass of a relationship between stillness and motion also informs Greenaway's painstakingly assembled still lives, his delight in sending clouds of mist drifting through his green landscapes, and his occasional freeze frames, as well as providing a clue as to why all the paintings, either directly presented or acted out, are premodern; cinema itself stands for and subsumes modernity.

Art Cinema under Thatcher

Finally, however, it is necessary to leave behind such formalist commentary "internal" to the texts, and to notice that Greenaway's passage from the relative deprivation of the avant-garde to the relative luxury of art cinema coincides closely with the beginning of the Thatcher period in 1979. Indeed, if we agree that the first few years of Thatcher were an uncertain transition out of Labourism, one marked by the strategic decision to postpone confrontation with the miners and rescued from likely political doom by the godsend of the Falklands, then we can map the story of Greenaway's financing quite exactly onto the historical picture. The independently funded experimental films gave way during this transitional period to British Film Institute (BFI), Arts Council, and Channel Four productions, which in turn gave way, during high Thatcherism, to Greenaway's enviable deal with the Dutch producer Kees Kasander. Such progress from economic strength to strength represents a decisive commentary on Thatcher's Anglocentric ideologemes of self-reliance; Greenaway's state-led transition to capitalist production successfully integrated with Europe reads like a textbook vindication of the "Gaullist" alternative, presented by Antony Barnett as a strategy more rational than Thatcherism (Barnett, 63).

Notice also that the two Greenaway films so far most successful with audiences (*The Draughtsman's Contract* and *The Cook, the Thief, His Wife, and Her Lover*) punctually mark the beginning and the end of the Thatcher period. These two films also parenthesize the entire history of the oldest continuously existing bourgeois state in the world, covering the ground from its establishment in the Glorious Revolution of 1688 to the present. Like my earlier remarks on the countryside and the country house, this of course refers to the interpretation of British history first elaborated by Perry Anderson and Tom Nairn in the *New Left Review* of 1964 and later taken up by many writers.

Thus Greenaway's production of the 1980s is synchronized with a Thatcherism that it parodies and refutes. Greenaway is not obviously or instinctively a political filmmaker, but he often speaks of *The Cook, the Thief, His Wife, and Her Lover* as dealing with Thatcherism. This suggests that we can see him as an allegorist whose features comment indirectly but decisively on the crisis of postimperial Britain to which Thatcherism also responds. Anderson, Nairn, and Barnett argue that the British crisis should be traced back to the Glorious Revolution; with the consolidation of the first effective challenge to the settlement of 1945, Greenaway made a film about the ancestor settlement of 1688. A few months before the end of Thatcher, if not of Thatcherism, Greenaway's greatest success to date was widely received as a critique of the consumer/casino economy of the 1980s. If these are coincidences, I will argue that they are informative and telling ones, which may be laid, like historical templates, over films that themselves so routinely impose conceptual system upon conceptual system.

Moreover, I would suggest that what Nairn (1975, 365) calls the "political emergency" of Thatcherism makes for greater urgency in historical and political reading. The crucial question of Thatcherism is whether or not it represents a real departure in British politics, and if the difficulty in answering is largely a matter of historical proximity, it seems reasonable to think that what will prove most helpful is a longer view. In what follows, then, I will work to establish the treatment of the settlement of 1688 in *The Draughts-man's Contract* as a textual and historical base-datum, and will deal with *Drowning by Numbers* and *The Cook, the Thief, His Wife, and Her Lover* as different versions of the postimperial crisis of that settlement. However, the films are not simple historical symptoms, and I will also use psychoanalysis to look at issues of gender. In terms of cultural sociology, I see Greenaway in the context of Perry Anderson's "culture in contraflow," a vision of middle-class and middle-of-the-road British intellectuals antagonized by Thatcher into moving leftward while the state has moved to the right. Terry Eagleton re-poses the key question of Thatcherism by arguing that Britain has lately seen "the most ideologically aggressive and explicit regime of living political memory, in a society which traditionally prefers its ruling values to remain implicit" (Eagleton, xi) and yet that this regime may not have decisively transformed the "vaguely social democratic values" of the British (33). One evidence of such a contradictory conjuncture is its impact on a filmmaker as natively apolitical as Greenaway.

The Draughtsman's Contract

The opening credits tell us that it is August 1694, and Talmann confirms the date with an enthusiastic comment on William of Orange, whose victory at the Battle of the Boyne helped to secure the 1689 settlement from poten-tially resurgent Catholicism and absolutism. This reference to Ireland, along with the suggestion by Sarah Talmann that Neville has "Scottish sympa-thies," reminds us that we are in the formative period of both British impe-rialism and the United Kingdom. Despite the film's emphasis on struggles for social and sexual prestige, Greenaway therefore represents a moment tend-ing toward political stabilization; little Augustus will reach maturity in the Augustan age at the beginning of the eighteenth century, and the insistence of Talmann that the boy must have a German tutor points further forward to the Hanoverian succession. The purpose of the tutor is to win Augustus over from his attraction to drawing (in one scene, we see him emulating Nev-ille on a chalkboard) and to teach him mathematics so that he can grow up to join the Royal Society. In Christopher Hill's critical account, the Royal Society indeed emphasized mathematics, along with agricultural improve-ments and "gadgetry . . . designed to entertain the Fellows," and thus failed "to contribute to the thinking which underlay the innovations of the Industrial Revolution" (Hill 1980, 64). So what is expected of the adult Augustus is a tincture of royalism (but not absolutism) and a genteel, rural amateurism (but not industrial innovation). In other words, the values of the Herbert family central to *The Draughtsman's Contract* conform precisely to those of the agrarian aristocracy that gained the upper hand in 1688 and continued to directly rule Britain until as recently as Sir Alec Douglas-Home, even if by the 1960s the continuing social power of the country gentry was finally beginning to seem anachronistic. Perry Anderson compares the situation with France and the United States, ruled by lawyers since at least the middle of the nineteenth century (Anderson 1987, 31).

Augustus will not grow up to become a draughtsman because professional work is much beneath his aristocratic social status. Indeed, membership in the gentry can make the social distinction that constitutes professionalism altogether indiscernible; for Sarah Tallman, Neville is "a paid servant contracted to my mother," as if to contract were to wage-labor or even to indenture. The point is underscored early in the film, when the flow of "ribald gossip" is interrupted by the sociological revelation that thirteen of those present are there because of a "confidence in one another's money" based on owning "a fair slice of England"; only one or two others are present on merit. Just before this, we have heard the story of a duke who casually murders his "water-mechanic," which should already alert us to the possible fate of Neville.

Talmann assumes charge of Augustus after his mother becomes a Catholic, a circumstance that reminds us that the period still thinks of its political conflicts in religious terms, and resonates historically with the birth of an heir to James II in May 1688. According to Christopher Hill, that birth was "the last straw" for the Glorious Revolutionaries, since it threatened a Catholic succession (Hill 1961, 199). When Neville mocks Sarah Talman's suggestion that a boy with a Catholic mother is effectively an orphan, Augustus is further linked with the film's crucial issue. This is not infidelity or murder but inheritance, "patrimony or the lack of it," as the Talmanns put it. Patrimony, a plainly patriarchal concept, will lead us in the direction of the film's treatment of women. At this point, however, I use the term to suggest that the dramatic motor of the film is a crisis in symbolic paternity, expressed most obviously as the departure, disappearance, and death of Mr. Herbert. This crisis lacks the direct historical extension possible in a period emerging from revolution and regicide, restoration, and redeposition. Again, however, the film depicts a finally stabilizing consensus; the world of Compton Anstey makes reference to Jacobites and colonies, but the film's severe formalities

The severe formalities of *The Draughtsman's Contract*.

emphasize the more purely symbolic aspect of Mr. Herbert's disappearance
and the struggles for power that ensue.

Lacan theorizes a crisis in symbolic paternity as a failure to properly locate the Name of the Father. He links this failure with psychosis, in which
this key signifier is missing from the Symbolic, and with mourning (at least
for a father), in which it is missing from the Real. Remembering that in
mourning a swarm of images seeks to repair the damage to the Real, while
in psychosis (for Lacan largely synonymous with paranoia) the signifiers
missing from the Symbolic return in the Real, we can gain some insights into
The Draughtsman's Contract. This is so because the film revolves around the
death of Mr. Herbert, while the attendant intrigues create a paranoid, conspiratorial maze that suspends cognitive surety. Thus Greenaway presents
us with statements that initially mislead us, behaviors whose ambiguity we
may initially recognize, actions whose meaning is altered by subsequent
events, and events whose layered meanings seem to resist definitive interpretation.

Chief among the swarm of images that seek to stand in for Mr. Herbert
are, of course, the drawings, most especially the one in which Neville plans
to place his face on the body of the usurper Talmann. With this condensation

of images of the two most powerful men in the film, Neville literalizes paternity, in marked distinction from the women in the film, for whom paternity is
a more purely symbolic principle with which one is obliged (and therefore
able) to negotiate. Other signifiers that lead lives of their own are the various
fruits, animals, and trees, along with Mr. Herbert's shirt, coat, boots, cloak,
and horse, which make a most definite return, both in the fiction's Real and in
its Imaginary (the drawings), from the moment that Mrs. Herbert lets fall
the first clue that her husband may not come home. And when Talmann remarks that Neville has "the God-like power of emptying the landscape" and
that "it is a wonder the birds still sing," we might be in the imaginative universe of Freud's case of paranoia, the Senätspresident Schreber, who was
told by the birds that God had emptied the world of all others in order to
repopulate it by procreating with him. As Sitney suggests, such a perspective is more obviously relevant to *The Falls*, which divides its ninety-two
characters between those who believe and those who disbelieve in "the responsibility of birds" for the Violent Unknown Event. In *The Draughtsman's
Contract*, such lunatic impulses seem more measured, more controlled;
nonetheless, Greenaway fills the film with figures who hope, like the para-
noiac, to take advantage of the crisis in the symbolic in order to design a
universe more in keeping with their own desires. These include Neville with
his contract, Mrs. Herbert and the two Talmanns with their various "inge-
nuities," and even Van Hoyten with his landscaping project.

Moreover, Schreber's questions of procreation and subsequent legacy are
crucial in the film, resonating not only with specific historical events but also
with what Neville calls "the place of women in English life," an issue that is
pointedly addressed at the outset. Indeed, the first line spoken in the film
concerns a Mr. Chandos, who spends more time with his garden than with
his wife. A whole string of related remarks include Mrs. Pierpoint's comment she is "not properly of the company but a part of its property," Noyes's
estimation of her exchange value as that of "two parterres and a drive of
orange trees," and Sarah Talmann's summary assessment of prevailing values as "a house, a garden, a horse, a wife, in that order." Further to this are
Mr. Herbert's cold instructions to his wife as he leaves, and the sexually abusive treatment she receives at the hands of Neville.

Yet if a wife is not as important as a horse, a house, or a garden, she is
indispensable in providing the heir who will inherit all three. To the extent
that we accept Mrs. Herbert and Mrs. Talmann's suggestions that their sexual interest in Neville lies in the hope of conceiving a child, the film's initial
protofeminism seems a stratagem, masking the women's interest in exercising the strictly limited yet pivotal power afforded to them by the way the pre-

vailing social order constructs their biology. The early remarks on sexual politics should not be simply dismissed, since these women do represent an internally oppressed fraction of their class; however, their dedication to producing even an illegitimate heir expresses their ultimate solidarity with that class. Thus we are wrong to imagine much likelihood of Neville gaining the estate by romancing Virginia Herbert; she has already exchanged her father's estate in marriage, but retains a relationship with symbolic paternity so powerful that she is determined to dispatch her husband and, if at all possible, to rewrite the Name of the Father in the shape of an heir. The more purely symbolic aspect of this desire is clear at the end of the film insofar as Mrs. Herbert is rid of all the troublesome actual men who might propose physically to support paternity; her father and husband are gone, while her potential son has yet to appear in any shape less symbolic than "the blood of the newborn" represented by the juice of the pomegranate, a figure that also suggests Mrs. Herbert's final rhetorical authority over the various men who have repeatedly equated women's bodies with fruit trees and fruit.

As a ladies' man, Neville is eager to exploit what he initially takes to be Mrs. Herbert's loneliness. In this pursuit, he deploys both the "innocence and arrogance" perceived by Sarah Talmann, the calculating cruelty depicted in his physical use of Mrs. Herbert, and the intellectual conceit conveyed in such virtuoso displays of language as his punning conversational gambit: "I am permitted to take pleasure without hindrance on her property and enjoy the maturing delights of her country garden." This last resonates once again with the country estate, which is the proprietorial hallmark of the traditional English ruling class, and with the film's particular dramatizations of the body of a woman who can neither inherit nor leave the estate but nonetheless rules it in her husband's absence.

Furthermore, Neville conceives of the sexual contract, and quickly sets about Mrs. Herbert with casual and imperious violence; the first reaction shot shows her spitting sperm and vomiting into a basin, a response compounded of her revulsion at his treatment of her and at a sexual act that cannot lead to conception. Neville draws up the first contract with Mrs. Herbert in the expectation of sadistic gratification, finds that the second contract with Mrs. Talmann has placed him in a position of sexual subordination, but is most defeated in his final effort to engage with Mrs. Herbert outside the contract. The eager sadist becomes a reluctant masochist, but is fully psychologically exposed only at the denouement. Conforming with the classical psychoanalytic picture of gender, and challenging us to say whether his conformity underscores the patriarchal or the analytic aspect of that picture, Neville returns at the end of the film to a woman he continues to imagine sadistically—attracted by Mrs. Herbert's "humiliations," he thinks of her as representing loss. Instead, he delivers himself to another contradictory image of femininity, the fatal mother of the masochist.

Significantly, the first-time viewer of the film probably identifies with Neville. Even if he does mistreat women, overestimate his potential social mobility, and strike postures of pride, Neville is certainly more sympathetic than Talmann, Noyes, and the Poulencs, whose criticisms of him as "unconventional," "impertinent," and "imprudent and provocative" help to alloy his period professionalism with the traits of a Romantic artist *avant la lettre*. By the end, however, his desire revealed as pathetically oedipal, hesitant, and genuine, he is a more conventional romantic victim, broadly comparable with the Valmont of Stephen Frears's *Les Liasions Dangereuses*. More directly, of course, with his "I am finished" and his stripped and bleeding body disposed in the frame to evoke a dead Christ, Neville is a social martyr, "a tenant farmer's son" who fondly imagines that he may outmaneuver his patron.

If any figure in the film seems to offer some relief from the rural but airless enclosure of the 1689 settlement, it is the animate statue, even though Neville at one point thinks of him as a spy or agent of Mrs. Herbert. The statue, the most obviously antinaturalistic device in the film, clarifies the basic comedy of the film's mise-en-scène; given the thoroughgoing formality of period manners and costume, for once in Greenaway it is possible to read as naturalistic the dramatic light sources, yellow-lit interiors, framings within framings, strong horizontals, tracking shots back and forth along outdoor banquet tables, and unlikely profusion of obelisks. I mention above the more general meaning of Greenaway's interest in animate statuary; here, I would notice that the statue responds exclusively to the artist, his potential apprentice, and the servant who shoos him from the gate. Perhaps this romantic conjunction of artist, child, and worker suggests a puckish possibility in the English landscape rather different from the geometry favored by Mr. Herbert and the water-mechanics of Van Hoyten.

Drowning by Numbers

The historical interval between *The Draughtsman's Contract* and *Drowning by Numbers* is long, but we are still in rural southern England, still in gardens and country houses, and still watching women dispose of disappointing husbands by water while male professionals bond with apprentices and betray their callings. And for all the historical distance of the settlement of 1689, we can still see its traces in the film's presentation of its dreamy, feckless, childish, and yet thoroughly sympathetic representative of the professional and managerial classes. In the Britain of the *New Left Review* analysis, this is the social fraction that never had a chance, that was never allowed to keep its appointment with historical destiny. Anthony Barnett restated Perry Anderson's theses of 1964 in a polemical response to Thatcher's war in the Falklands: "Historically dominated by financial capital located in the south, whose millionaires always outnumbered industrial barons, the British state was animated by those trained in an imperial rather than a domestic role, and in ledgers and in fields rather than in factories. The result has been a *marked* absence of a recognizable bourgeois political class, in any dominant sense— at once practical, realistic and—yes—businesslike" (Barnett, 53). The impasse of British history is reiterated within the analysis itself, in the comedy of a Marxism that speaks most forcefully for the bourgeoisie. The point of this for Greenaway is that such lovingly detailed depictions of the shire gentry as *The Draughtsman's Contract* and of the shire petty bourgeoisie as *Drowning by Numbers* take on a rather different significance if we think of Britain as a country in which the first of these classes has effectively compromised and subordinated the historical energy of the second.

In point of textual fact, however, that energy seems compromised and subordinated by women. If Virginia Herbert and Sarah Talmann are more interested in the physical than the artistic potency of Neville, the troika of Cissie Colpitts in *Drowning by Numbers* both echoes and outdoes them. Though in legal actuality we probaby do not agree with capital punishment for infidelity and sexual indifference, in the dramatic experience of a film we nonetheless sympathize with Cissie Colpitts 1 and 2, who drown Jake and Hardy respectively for such crimes, and perhaps even with Cissie Colpitts 3, who drowns Bellamy for conspiring against her. That third murder is rendered more ritually, and thus we are more likely to notice the echo of *The Draughtsman's Contract*; Cissie 3 has no further use for Bellamy when she is sure she is pregnant, and reveals that she married him only in order to legitimize the child. Yet a film that for a while seems cryptofeminist in a black-comic way turns more troubling when the skipping girl is killed by a car, Smut hangs himself, and the inexorable logic of the Cissies proves determined to do away with Madgett.

Of course, Greenaway is intent on a destabilization of conventional dramatic expectations, and of course he continues to make a symbolic point, perhaps most directly with the game of dead man's catch, in which gender struggle is starkly formalized—all the men lose as the undertakers bear Jake's coffin across the playing field, and they must lie down in the winding sheet as the hearse moves off into the upper right corner of the frame. Yet as this scene tends to suggest, the more pressing question in *Drowning by*

Numbers is that of the extent to which a formal principle can be considered as socially or psychologically overdetermined. In an effort to answer this question, I will begin with the hardly surprising observation that Greenaway's films contain obsessional aspects. Yet this issue has not so far been treated systematically, even if we count as symptomatic both the respectful and the reproachful comments of critics on the degree to which intellect animates the films. In what follows, then, I want to consider the obsessional aspect of *Drowning by Numbers* without crudely or arbitrarily diagnosing the text. As a first formulation, I would propose that the film makes ceremonials out of obsessional material, that it plays games with obsessional material, that it runs rings around obsessional material. To recognize that psychoanalysis thinks of games and ceremonials themselves as obsessional is an involution, but one appropriate to a film that signals a comic and detailed awareness of its own concerns.

For a first example of that awareness, we might look at two of Smut's waking ceremonials, his game of "reverse-strip jump" and the house of cards that may or may not fall before he wakes. Directly comparable with the sleep ceremonials discussed by Freud in the classic psychoanalysis of obsessional behavior, these are also quite different, even parodic; rather than a rigid sequence of obligatory observations attached to undressing and going to bed, they form a set of chance outcomes attached to getting up and getting dressed. Similarly, the film's whole catalog of invented games provide a comic perspective on what Serge Leclaire calls "death in the life of the obsessional." Games like dead man's catch and hangman's cricket, whose daylong maneuvers are abruptly terminated when a player designated the loser is delivered to the hangman and the gravedigger, remind us that all games are to some extent obsessional and that familiar games establish a quite effective distance on that fact. Freud's essay on "Obsessive Acts and Religious Practices" deals quite directly with the similarities and the differences between private and collective behavior, an issue that becomes a motif in *Drowning by Numbers*—Hardy walks away from hangman's cricket in disgust that it is not a "proper" game, Cissie Colpitts 2 remarks that Madgett plays dead man's catch as if it "meant something," and a local detective construes Madgett's marking of Smut's body with colored tape for his study of cricketing deaths as child abuse. Amusingly, Madgett himself remains capable of mystification at the obsessional behavior of others; as the athletes go by, he asks, "What's all this running for?"

Though it is not revelatory to remark on the obsessional aspect of Greenaway's films, we may still be surprised in reviewing the psychoanalytic literature to discover how much of both the anecdotal evidence and the theoretical elaborations resonate with Greenaway's work. In Leclaire's case of "Jerome," we hear of the fascination of the obsessional with both the statuary and the photographs that recur in Greenaway, of his vulnerability to sympathetic stomach pains of the kind experienced by Kracklite in *The Belly of an Architect*, and of two symptoms shared by Smut in *Drowning by Numbers* (the fantasy of a "late circumcision" and the impulse to commit suicide). In Leclaire's theoretical commentary, influenced by Lacan's revision of Freud, we learn that the obsessional devotes his life to death; he expresses the contradictions entailed in an effort to ally himself with death both by believing that he cannot die and by waiting for death, systematically temporizing with his rituals and ceremonials, his counting and collecting. According to Freud, the obsessional remains trapped in such a fix because his oedipal wish for the death of his father so consumes him that he tries, impossibly and yet insistently, to identify with death. Instead of coming to terms with the symbolic otherness of paternity, which would cause him to accept mortality, to defer genital satisfaction, and to identify with the father, he identifies with a mortality that he tries to mobilize against the father. For Jacques-Alain Miller, "while the obsessional can be friends with death, he has trouble with love" (41).

In *Drowning by Numbers*, our senior male protagonist—a coroner, a professional specialist in death and regular attendant at the funerals of men killed by women—gets nowhere in his numerous romantic pursuits. Moreover, he betrays his calling because his desire is bound up with death. He is serially attracted to the three husband-murdering Cissies and is also suspected of a passion for the corpse; Cissie 2 asks him whether he has ever molested a corpse, and he replies that he once kissed an old lady (a grandmaternal imago), and that he once had trouble bringing himself to close the eyes of a beautiful young woman, trouble, that is, in detaching himself from the gaze of life-in-death. His son, the "little ghoul," is if anything even more identified with mortality, marking the deaths of birds, animals, and humans with ceremonials involving numbers, fireworks, paint, and Polaroid photographs. While Madgett is exclusively interested in women implicated with death, Smut, remarkably, has no mother either seen or mentioned in the film; thus he cannot answer the question of "the relation of the mother to the father's word," a phrase from Lacan quoted in another study of the obsessional by Leclaire (Philo 1980b, 122). Smut tackles this issue by becoming interested in Rubens's *Samson and Delilah* and in the Bible story of the castrating woman from which it is taken, by interrogating his father on the issue of circumcision, and by attending to the skipping girl's report of her mother's opinion on the same issue. This mother is sexualized insofar as she seems to be a prostitute, and the question of her relation to the father's law is rendered at once quite literally (she is courted by a policeman) and with some subtlety (the police in *Drowning by Numbers* belong to the detective-fiction tradition that banalizes quotidian law). At the same time, Smut seals the fate of the skipping girl by challenging the word of the mother, encouraging the girl to skip on the road, and then commits suicide when the police visit him with the news of her death.

According to Freud, obsessional neurosis distinguishes itself by repressing not content but connection, retaining the disturbing material in consciousness while defeating its emotional potential by erasing the logic that binds it together. This seems applicable enough to *Drowning by Numbers*, and yet equally applicable to many intellectually puzzling films. For a more specific answer to our original question of a film so blithe and yet so somber, we turn to a point Charles Melman makes: the obsessional is not at first or of necessity troubled by his symptoms (Melman, 132). Indeed, for the bulk of the film Madgett is a cheerful, avuncular eccentric; only when rejected by the third and final Cissie does he turn to attempted rape, gorging on blackberries, and the doleful declaration that he and his son are eunuchs. This reference to a lost virility suggests the extent to which a film that at first seems to be about vengeful women is actually predicated on the abstract perceptions of the male obsessional; from Madgett's vantage, women (like the three Cissies) are imposing but interchangeable figments, others (like the Bognor brothers) are distant but conspiratorial, and the self is barred from genital achievement by its fixation on mortality. Madgett is friendly with death; putting his shoes away as the rowboat sinks, he is the unemotional obsessional to the end. The framing arithmomania and supporting taxonomies of *Drowning by Numbers* weave through a fictional experience of obsessional desire, suggesting that all of Greenaway's grids, lexicons, and encyclopedias are not simply affectless (as critics tend to say) but determinedly distanced from affect.

The Cook, the Thief, His Wife, and Her Lover

Coming to Greenaway's *succès de scandale*, we encounter most directly an allegory of Thatcherism, since this is the film he describes to Gavin Smith as dealing with "my anger and passion about the current British political situation" (Smith, 55) and to Kathy Acker as representing the impact of "an incredible vulgarian hypocrisy which slams anyone who makes radical sexual moves" (Acker, 61). Acker enlarges enthusiastically on the idea that the thief Spica represents "pure vulgarity, . . . pure . . . evil" (56), arguing that the figure of a loutish criminal upwardly mobile into restaurant ownership is an effective emblem of Thatcher's Britain. In the interview with Smith, Greenaway adds that Spica is a typical product of the new consumer economy, "a man who knows the price of everything and the value of nothing" (Smith, 55).

My account of *The Cook* will question this widely accepted view of the film. Noting that Greenaway and his two interviewers imagine politics in terms of the guild values of artists and writers (Spica's crime is "vulgarity" or lack of appreciation; Thatcher's is sexual repression), I will propose that the film is symptomatic as much as analytic of Thatcherism. Thatcherism and Greenaway both respond to the historical impasse of the British middle classes, but while Greenaway's earlier films are effectively critical of the situation, the proletarian monster central to *The Cook* suggests that this film has joined in Thatcher's vengeance on the imagined values of the lower social orders. Thus the film can be usefully compared with the more direct treatments of Thatcherism in British cinema (*My Beautiful Laundrette* [1985], *Sammy and Rosie Get Laid* [1987], *High Hopes* [1989]), and with the different type of allegory found in Dennis Potter's *The Singing Detective* (1986). These comparisons are not meant to twit Greenaway with the realist tradition he scorns, but to underscore the point that the question of Thatcherism is more likely to be answered by historical analysis than by leftist or liberal reaction. This point is sharpened by the *New Left Review* analysis of the whole history of the British state, by the remarks of Terry Eagleton quoted above, and by the various political calculations of Stuart Hall, Paul Hirst, and Bob Jessop; it is blunted by Acker, whose progressive good intentions tend to stabilize and to demonize Thatcherism.

I stress Acker's *Village Voice* account of the film because it is a good index of the simultaneously rapturous and scandalized reception of *The Cook, the Thief, His Wife, and Her Lover* by an American art-house audience well versed in imaginary contests between a cultured middle class and a brutish lumpenproletariat, but much less clear that the thief and his wife's lover are not the only possible figures of their respective class fractions. My point is not that Greenaway should set about producing positive images of the lower social strata, but that for American audiences the issue of Spica's identifying marks of class hardly exists; though the film occasions genuinely horrified reactions and even walkouts, these are prompted typically by the dog-shit smearing, vomiting, van of rotting flesh, and the like. If the film had been set in an allegorized New York, Spica might have been an African-American; such transatlantic class/race analogies are obviously imperfect, but even if the point is quite unfair, it can also be quite suggestive.

Peter Greenaway and Helen Mirren at work on *The Cook, the Thief, His Wife, and Her Lover* (1989).

Some might argue that because the figure of Spica is clearly allegorical, we should not imagine that his accent and manners refer directly to British social realities; in this view, Spica becomes a renovated version of the Brechtian idea of the entrepreneur as gangster, and is no more an affront to the working class than the Italian-Americans of the *Godfather* films. The problem with this is the exclusively downward mobility of the metaphor; capitalism is identified for dramatic purposes with the gangster, an idea of criminality that is itself capitalist. In one sense, this maneuver responds keenly to the contradictions of the system; in another, it makes it only more difficult to think beyond them. At worst, the very excesses of the gangster tend to contain the critique; the fiction serves as a counterphobic or inoculatory device, suggesting not so much that capitalism is criminal but that criminal capitalists spoil things for everyone. Alternatively, one might suggest that the figure of Spica is no more prejudicial than the representatives of the gentry and the petty bourgeoisie we have already met, that Greenaway's ironic taxonomies have moved with admirably consecutive logic through Britain's social order to arrive at the thief. Yet if Neville is naively arrogant, Mrs. Herbert coldly calculating, Madgett obsessional, and the Cissies murderous, all have sympathetic traits, in marked distinction from Spica, whose repellent characteristics are a triumph of Greenaway's impulse to catalog: he is sadistic, bullying, nagging, crude, loud, callous, self-important, sanctimonious, anti-Semitic,

The title characters in *The Cook, the Thief, His Wife, and Her Lover.*

racist, misogynist, homophobic, drunken, unlettered, and possessed of a poor French accent, all of which is only redoubled in the moments of bathos when he mourns his lack of children.

Having complicated the question of political interpretation, I want to introduce some thoughts on the stylistic values of this very striking film, beginning with the remedially exacting simplicities of its color scheme, camera movement, and articulations of space. The first of these has been widely remarked, prompted by Greenaway's own observation that the film is structured into zones corresponding to the sequence of colors in the visible spectrum (blue for the cold exterior of the parking lot, green for the productive interior of the kitchen, red for the central theater of the restaurant, blinding white for the toilets, yellow for the hospital). Less remarked but equally obtrusive is a treatment of space almost didactic in its limited number of locations, limited number of shots, and strong directional cues across cuts. The overall effect of the lateral tracking from one end to the other of the principal enclosure comprised of car park, kitchen, restaurant, and bathroom is a modernist bravura, combining with the curtains at the opening and closing of the film and such depth cues as the fan on the rear wall of the kitchen to draw attention both to the theatricality of the profilmic space and the flatness of the projected image. However, the effect is more than simply modernist. The film reminds us that we are looking at a studio space temporarily and yet thoroughly made over into a restaurant; this is linked with a 1980s economy of consumption and entertainment in which fashionably transitory restaurants actually did colonize studio-like spaces, often staying in them for a period only slightly longer than the production of a film.

The film makes this link most explicit by beginning with the finishing touch of such a speculative transformation, the installation of the neon sign that will read "Spica and Boarst." At the same time, of course, this fairly trumpets the introduction of a whole range of semiotic and symbolic issues. These include the structural imperative (the figures carried in are A and O, the first letter of the alphabet and the zero), the intertext of other Greenaway films (*A Zed and Two Noughts* begins with Z and O and with advertising signs), the continuing homage to Frampton (the *Magellan* cycle also begins with a large A), the continuing reference to art history (the thieves staggering along with the huge letters evoke the procession to Calvary), and the constellation of meanings contained in the name Spica; the anagram "aspic," for example, condenses the film's superimposition of fine food and boorishness, while its transformation into "a spic" signals the descent into ethnically stereotyped brutishness. Homophonically, and especially given the film's play with the Cockney tendency to add an "r" to a final vowel, we may even be reminded of "Mr. Speaker," the bewigged parliamentarian of the British House of Commons, who is comparable with Spica in both the atavism of his dress and his authority over speech.

Similar in elementary elegance is the film's treatment of perspective; screen width predominates with the strong horizontals of the car park, kitchen, and dining room, but is broken up by the confined spaces of assignation between the lovers. Contrasted with this is an occasional strongly marked depth of field, as at the book depository. These variations also suggest a psychological distribution of space, with Spica lording it over the banquet table at the film's center, the lovers cowering in the various enclosures to the right and left, and the book depository with its depth and distance from the restaurant serving as a haven. This distribution, in turn, supports the film's treatment of the social construction of bodily functions. Spica's ravenous vengeance on fine food includes the spoiling of special dishes served to Georgina and Michael, the company of "associates" who vomit and belch, and a declassé mother who hopes the restaurant will serve a bottle of Chianti in raffia; it further extends to his terroristic intrusions into bathroom and kitchen, including the symbolic ones that lead him to ask Georgina why she was so long and whether she has washed her hands. The last suggests a sanctimoniousness surprising in someone whose first action is to smear dog shit and piss on a victim, but Spica is a polymorphous tyrant; he rules dictatorially over the orifices, combining physical savagery ("I'll make you shit through your dick"), physical restraint ("No smoking, Georgina"), and physical possession ("that's my property") in the service of his personal authority. However, he remains (like Madgett, another banqueter) barred from genital sexuality. Thus the encounters of the lovers, confined to larders, freezers, and toilet stalls, are brutally parodied by Spica in his beating of Georgina in the car and the reported sadism of his bedroom.

The figure of symbolic paternity whose absence animates the patrician landscapes of *The Draughtsman's Contract* and whose presence is systematically depreciated in the gardens and meadows of *Drowning by Numbers* returns with shocking vengeance to the vivid interiors of *The Cook, the Thief, His Wife, and Her Lover.* This drama of the body was, of course, the aspect of the film that drew the American NC-17 rating, scandalized the more decorous of art-house patrons, and attracted larger audiences than any previous Greenaway film. In closing, I want to suggest that the film's more precise relationship with Thatcherism lies not in the politically questionable class relationships it depicts, but in the fashionable audience it constitutes and discovers; this last (the baby-boom professional and managerial class, arts and media division) was by the end of the 1980s quite familiar with sumptuary restaurants where bookish critics mingled with semicriminal entrepreneurs, and yet residually uneasy with that familiarity.

The British context of a capitalism pioneered by a patrician caste complicates the social definition of the middle classes, who failed to place their own stamp on the polity, instead merging with the gentry during the eighteenth and nineteenth centuries. Thus, *The Draughtsman's Contract* and *Drowning by Numbers* both deal with the historical dilemma of a professional stratum that is progressive but politically ineffectual. From the point of view of this fraction, Albert Spica (another problem in social definition, since he is lumpen and capitalist at once) represents a final insult and inspires a fantasy of revenge. If the social disgust of the film enlarges wildly on the moral culpability of the working-class reactionary, its political acuteness lies in mobilizing a middle-class audience that itself spent the 1980s feasting and trying to repress social questions. To be fair, Kathy Acker does recognize this last point as the basis of a liberatory potential in Greenaway. However, with the replacement of both Thatcher and Reagan by more discreet acolytes, and with the media full of superficial breast-beating about 1980s excess, the reception of the film as a critique of consumerism is another response characterized more by ideological fashion than by historical understanding.

While working on this essay, I discussed Greenaway with Tracy Biga and Paul Arthur, and Thatcherism with Krzysztof Wodicko. For guidance in art history, I am grateful to Candace Clements. For help with materials, I am grateful to David James and the Museum of Modern Art Film Study Center.

Works Cited

Acker, Kathy. 1990. "The Color of Myth: The World according to Peter Greenaway." *Village Voice*, April 17, 61-67.
Anderson, Perry. 1964. "Origins of the Present Crisis." *New Left Review* 23 (January-February).
_____. 1987. "The Figures of Descent." *New Left Review* 161 (January-February): 20-77.
_____. "A Culture In Contraflow." *New Left Review* 180, (March-April): 41-78.
Barnett, Anthony. 1982. "Iron Britannia." *New Left Review* 134 (July-August): 5-96.
Burch, Noël. 1990. *Life to Those Shadows*. Berkeley: University of California Press.
Eagleton, Terry. 1991. *Ideology: An Introduction*. London: Verso.
Freud, Sigmund. [1907] 1959. "Obsessive Actions and Religious Practices." In *Standard Edition*, vol. 11, 115-28. London: Hogarth.
_____. [1909] 1955. "Notes upon a Case of Obsessional Neurosis." In *Standard Edition*, vol. 10, 153-250. London: Hogarth.
_____. [1911] 1958. "Psychoanalytic Notes upon an Autobiographical Account of a Case of Paranoia (Dementia Paranoides)." In *Standard Edition*, vol. 12, 1-82. London: Hogarth.
Hall, Stuart. 1990. *The Hard Road to Renewal*. London: Verso.
Hill, Christopher. 1961. *The Century of Revolution: 1603-1714*. New York: Norton.
_____. 1980. *Some Intellectual Consequences of the English Revolution*. Madison: University of Wisconsin Press.
Hirst, Paul. 1989. *After Thatcher*. London: Collins.
James, David. 1989. *Allegories of Cinema: American Film in the Sixties*. Princeton, N.J.: Princeton University Press.
_____. 1991. "The Unsecret Life: A Warhol Advertisement." *October* 56 (Spring): 21-41.
Jessop, Bob, Kevin Bonnett, Simon Bromley, and Tom Ling. 1988. *Thatcherism: A Tale of Two Nations*. Cambridge, England: Polity.
Lacan, Jacques. 1981. Le Séminaire III. Les Psychoses. Paris: Seuil.
Leclaire, Serge. 1980a. "Jerome, or Death in the Life of the Obsessional." In *Returning to Freud*, edited by Schneiderman, 94-113.
_____. 1980b. "Philo, or the Obsessional and his Desire." In *Returning to Freud*, edited by Schneiderman 114-29.
Melman, Charles. 1980. "On Obsessional Neurosis." In *Returning to Freud*, edited by Schneiderman, 130-38.
Miller, Jacques-Alain. 1988. "H₂O: Suture in Obsessionality." Translated by Bruce Fink. *Lacan Study Notes* 6-9: 34-44.
Nairn, Tom. 1964. "The English Working Class." *New Left Review* 24 (March-April).
_____. 1964. "The Anatomy of the Labour Party." *New Left Review* 26 (September-October).
_____. 1979. *The Break-up of Britain*. London: New Left Books.
Schneiderman, Stuart, ed. 1980. *Returning to Freud: Clinical Psychoanalysis in the School of Lacan*. New Haven: Yale University Press.
Sitney, P. Adams. 1979. *Visionary Film*. 2nd ed. Oxford: Oxford University Press.
_____. "The Falls." *Persistence of Vision* 8: 45-51.
Smith, Gavin. 1990. "Food for Thought." (Includes Greenaway filmography.) *Film Comment* 26 (3): 54-61.

Van Wert, William F. 1990/91. Review of *The Cook, the Thief, His Wife, and Her Lover. Film Quarterly* 44 (2): 42-50.
Wills, David, and Alec McHoul. 1991. "Zoo-logics: Questions of Analysis in a Film by Peter Greenaway." *Textual Practice* 5 (1): 8-24.

Sixteen

Private Practice, Public Health: The Politics of Sickness and the Films of Derek Jarman

Chris Lippard and Guy Johnson

> There's no place like the HOME-movie.
> —Derek Jarman

> Health for me is more than being not-yet-dead. It's not something you patrol; it's something you must forget to patrol or it's not any sort of health at all.
> —Adam Mars-Jones, "Remission"

> It is vital to underline yet again that art is the spark between private lives and the public.
> —Derek Jarman

The "private function" that provides both the title and the narrative climax of Malcolm Mowbray's 1984 film set in postwar Yorkshire is ostensibly the pork dinner that Dr. Swaby (Denholm Eliot) and his allies in the town's privileged classes will throw to honor Britain's newly married royal couple.[1] The title, however, refers not only to this single event but also to a social practice and an institution just then being converted from a private to a public function. In November 1946 the newly elected Labour government passed an act of Parliament creating Britain's National Health Service (NHS)—a response to, perhaps a reward for, the trauma of the just-won war. It established that medical consultation and treatment should be free to all and that health was a public issue. *A Private Function* sets up an opposition between Swaby, the upper-class medical man, and the town chiropodist, Gilbert Chilvers (Michael Palin). We first see Swaby blithely engaged in crossing names off the list of invitees to the private function; in the adjoining room, Chilvers works diagnosing chilblains and scraping at hard skin. His work with feet— and women's feet at that—puts Chilvers on the lowest rung of the medical ladder and makes him the focus of Swaby's contemptuous annoyance: "Why we need chiropodists, I don't know: something wrong with their feet, people

278

can come to me. They'd always find a sympathetic hearing," he declares petulantly.

But in fact this is just what Swaby does not want to happen. The threat of a new public health system that allows free access to doctors and attempts to abolish the exclusive right of the privileged class to be "well treated" clearly challenges his prestigious social position. Vexed by the theft of the pig he had been fattening for consumption at the private function, Swaby lets fly at postwar British society: "Of course, practical socialism, that's what it's going to be like now . . . what's mine is yours. What a nasty piss-stained country this is. . . . It's like this new health service. Do you realize that any little poorly pillock is now going to be able to knock on my door and say I'm ill, treat me. Anybody! Me!"

Arrogant and patronizing, Dr. Swaby is the villain of the piece, a medical man who boasts of having no feelings and ridicules Chilvers for his qualms about butchering the pig. But such sentiments are not the common British perception of the medical profession. Indeed, what Swaby here predicts developed under the NHS into a system whereby general practitioners (G.P.'s) typically became family doctors dispensing prescriptions and a reliable "bedside manner." These doctors were the point at which an ill public first encountered the human face of a state system that gave the poor(ly) an equal chance at the best attention available in the land. Thus in Britain, for a whole generation, the idea of health became firmly linked to a conception of the state as a caring institution that provided for its people's physical well-being.

In the 1980s, however, the notion of private, rather than public, functions took on renewed pertinence, so it remains possible to read the analysis of social class and medical practice found in *A Private Function* as commentary on Margaret Thatcher's radically free market policies and gradual reprivatization of many of the industries taken into public ownership at the end of the war. In due course, the National Health Service, too, came up for review. Unlike other postwar nationalizations, however, the Health Service had developed the status of a consensus issue, so when the government published its white paper, "Working for Patients," at the end of January 1989, both the British Medical Association (BMA) and most of the British population—the consumers, the prospective patients—reacted adversely.[2] The queen's speech to Parliament in November 1989 announced that "a bill will be brought forward to improve the National Health Service and the management of community care."[3] At the end of June 1990, the NHS and Community Care Bill became law, offering G.P.'s the chance to manage their own budgets and hospitals the opportunity to abandon the NHS in favor of a self-governing status where they might compete for custom by offering patient

280 CHRIS LIPPARD AND GUY JOHNSON

services more attractive than those of rival institutions. In line with its advocacy of self-reliance, the Thatcher government also sought to put "the utmost importance on caring for people in their own home" (*Politics Today*, May 19, 1990, 179). At the time of writing, the post-Thatcher Tory government's major problem with the electorate seems to be that its policies are perceived to offer a diminution, not an extension of care.

Issues of health and illness have long preoccupied British filmmakers. In the fifties and sixties, for example, the hospital setting, with its potential for undressing, disturbed bodily functions, and hierarchies ripe for toppling offered the long-running series of *Carry On* films the ideal setting for their sexual innuendo and puncturing of pomposity (Johnson). Jack Gold's film version of Peter Nicholls's *The National Health* plowed the same furrow in 1973. In the Thatcher era, Lindsay Anderson, who previously dissected the British institution of the public school in *If. . .* (1968),[4] focused his attention on the hospital as an ideal microcosm of a class-riddled, self-serving society. Anderson's *Brittania Hospital* (1982) tells the story of a day in the life of a hospital on the occasion of a royal visit, a series of strikes by the support staff, and the megalomaniac head surgeon's attempted completion of a new Frankenstein-style composite man. Anderson's hospital functions as a clear allegory for a sick, deluded country, one strangled by a useless monarchy, a cruel and insensitive prime minister, and a work-shy labor force. His film uses the hospital to attach itself to the same stereotypical class markers as, say, the *Carry On* series. But though it may be as vicious a critique of Thatcherism as any in British film, *Brittania Hospital* offers little alternative space for either social progress or cinematic practice.[5]

The eighties, which began with Colin Welland's cry, as he picked up the Oscar for *Chariots of Fire* (1981), that the "British are coming,"[6] were marked by alternating declamations of the British cinema's health or sickness, and in 1985 Alexander Walker applied Anderson's title to his assessment of the state of the film industry in Britain. Walker concludes his survey of the current practices of British film production, *National Heroes*, with a section "Renaissance or Remission?" in which he speculates about whether signs of healthy life in the quality of domestic features in the first half of the decade will sufficiently outweigh the difficulties of production in the United Kingdom. His final words tend toward the pessimistic: in these years "Brittania Hospital was still open for business: but that perpetual patient, the British film industry, needed to have a lot of faith in the doctors treating it" (Walker, 272).

At the beginning of 1988 the metaphor of contagion resurfaced in the national press when Oxford historian and regular Thatcher adviser Norman Stone took Britain's sick cinema to task in the review section of the archly conservative *Sunday Times*. Stone contrasts the "sick scenes from English life" that he finds in the work of a "worthless and insulting . . . farrago of films" (*Sunday Times*, Jan. 10, 1988, pp. C1-2) with the work of Britain's cinema of quality, past (Lean, Powell, Reed, *Saturday Night and Sunday Morning*) and present (*Hope and Glory, A Passage to India*). Stone accuses the "sick," pessimistic films of a "two-dimensional ideology," lack of plot and no sense of tradition. In passing, he betrays a streak of homophobia, as, surveying the contents of his chosen few, he writes that "there is much explicit sex, a surprising amount of it homosexual and sadistic." At the head of the first page of Stone's article rests a still from Derek Jarman's *The Last of England* (1987): a hooded figure points a machine gun at a few huddled figures gathered on the side of one of London's abandoned docks. Jarman's film exemplifies all the sickness Stone finds in the cinema, and he concludes his section by acknowledging that "I do not really know what [t]his film is about and fear that its director is all dressed up with nowhere to go."

In the following week's paper, Jarman responded to Stone, arguing that, as a forty-six-year-old director, his films were, in fact, a part of British film history and tradition. He points out that two of his six films (*The Tempest* [1979] and *The Angelic Conversation* [1985] have been inspired by Shakespeare;[7] but more important, perhaps, he argues against Stone's view of Britishness—"all beefeaters and hollyhocks"—in order to defend the decay that permeates *The Last of England* as an accurate reflection of Thatcher's Britain.[8] In this essay, we choose to retain and reclaim Stone's term for Jarman's cinema: its "sickness" is a crucial part of its practice. Refusing Stone's and Thatcher's sense of a healthy Britain and a healthy film practice, Jarman attempts to "re-fuse" an active, critical, contaminated cinema of formal experimentation and social critique, one which is both intensely private and willfully public.

As Thatcher came to power in 1979, another filmic experimenter, Peter Greenaway, was completing *The Falls*, his three-hour "medical survey" of a cross section of the nineteen million people in Britain suffering from the Violent Unknown Event (VUE). His film details, in ninety-two segments, the various infections and strangely disturbed bodies of all those in the VUE directory whose names begin with the letters "F-A-L-L." Greenaway's project was an elaborate fiction, a postmodern creation of an alternate, parallel world of humans become birds, water, speakers of exotic languages, and, indeed, immortals. At the same time in New York and Los Angeles, doctors were noticing the oddity of a series of deaths in the gay population from a skin cancer, Kaposi's sarcoma—the first step toward the identification of a previously unknown and terribly violent disease: the AIDS virus. By the time *The Last of England* was released Jarman had been diagnosed as HIV-positive. The greatest threat to public health in the Thatcher decade had arrived in the body of the anti-Thatcher cinema.[9]

In 1975 Derek Jarman filmed the killing of a pig in a different setting from that of Michael Palin's. In *Sebastiane*, a group of naked Roman soldiers banished to a remote Mediterranean island spear a boar in counterpoint to the delirious ravings of one of their number, Sebastiane. He is pegged out on the sand to suffer the heat of the murderous sun, having refused the seduction of the centurion. In this film the impalement and laceration undergone by the pig points out a larger pattern of meaning, as the film's climax displays Sebastiane half flayed, tied to a pole and shot through with arrows that crucify him. The ecstasy etched onto the facial close-up evokes innumerable classical renditions of Christ's agony, and Jarman's slow-motion effects foreground both the static, pictorial nature of the composition and the filmic medium that depicts it.

Jarman's earliest and least-shown film bears some important motifs and ideas to be reconfigured in his later work. At its heart is the idea of the suffering (male) body, which we see here impaled against a pole, cut and sliced, imagining another, better place. In Jarman's films the recurrence of the body seen in various degrees of suffering is richly significant, and it may be explored in two ways: first, to understand how the suffering body grounds the narratives of the films, such that the stories told in them are never far from bodies in pain; and second, to examine how a filmmaking practice of stories shaped by suffering offers an opportunity to see the larger issues at work in the interplay of health, sexuality, and storytelling. It is across these three areas that the condition of AIDS is stretched, and within which Jarman's films articulate a personal understanding of dis-ease.

Suffering male bodies recur in Jarman's work: in *Caravaggio* (1986), the painter (Nigel Terry) is dying and stabs and is stabbed by his lover, Ranuccio (Sean Bean); *The Last of England* echoes with gunfire and shows us the execution of a young man; *War Requiem* (1989) mourns and re-images the slaughter of an entire generation of young men; in *The Garden* (1991), the male lovers are flayed and the filmmaker appears in a hospital bed. Derek Jarman carries the AIDS virus, suffers from its effects, and came close to death during the production of his films. Rather than respect a distance between the filmmaker's private life and his public text, Jarman encourages us to compare the two. This is especially clear in *Caravaggio*, the biography of the Renaissance painter celebrated for his use of a "cinematic" lighting scheme, the life story of a gay artist negotiating the patronage of the powerful while always pressed to the margins.

"I feel I have to write this book, coughing and spitting with bloody bronchitis," Jarman writes later of the notes that accompany *The Last of England* (Jarman 1987, 66). The idea of production under pressure saturates *Caravaggio*, shot on a strictly controlled budget within the confines of an old London docklands warehouse. The film begins and ends in a hospital at Porto Ercole where the painter lies dying; the sickness that seizes him involves the fetching up of his body's fluids, hawked up in spasms that rip the fabric of his otherwise delirious, still life. From the deathbed, the film builds a biography as a collection of flashbacks diluted from the paintings of Caravaggio's career, and the story flows between these reconstituted scenes as they restage the familiar paintings. Incoherence is built into the text, and it is Jarman's accompanying book that provides much-needed "plot" information. But while the film is a delirious one, driven by the ebbing life-force of the painter, a definite logic governs the narrative that can be traced back to the suffering body at its center.

Caravaggio is dying, and he endures pain of many colors. Feverish through much of the film, stabbed, afforded no other embrace than those of the people whose deaths he causes, the painter of "wounded paintings" fades out, dissolving to nothing, fighting the draining of his vital spirit with the ejaculations of remembered desire for his adolescent lover, Pasqualone. The film is pressed out from the concentrate of the paintings, mixed up from the paste of scenes, governed and grounded by a continual and regular return to the deathbed of the master painter. The film appears as a system of hallucinations geared to his desire for love and his resistance to death. It stutters between still lives, bleeding all the while the meaning that we drain off from the body of the text.

The film is a set of dissolves between paintings but is also about cuts, or slashes. Thus a particular importance is attached to Caravaggio's knife and to the stabbings in the film, the wounding and daubing of blood on flesh that match the painter's smearing paint onto canvases. This fusion of images occurs particularly at the moments when Ranuccio delivers Caravaggio a stigmata-like wound in a brawl, and in Caravaggio's betrayal of Ranuccio. In the second incident, Caravaggio looks squarely into the face of the one he has painted and loved, and delivers a final, slashing stroke.

Under the sign of suffering, the film text stands in a relation to both realism and to the visual style of Caravaggio's paintings. In reproducing the

Jerusaleme (Spencer Leigh) watches the knife fight between Caravaggio (Nigel Terry) and Ranuccio (Sean Bean), in *Caravaggio* (1986).

scenes from the painter's canon the film, rather than simply duplicating the originals, gives the sense of an entirely painted world that at certain moments nudges up against the configurations of people and props familiar from the artist's compositions. Yet the visual style is not entirely coherent: regular disturbances destabilize consistency throughout the film. Rather than disrupting a stylistic convention, Ranuccio tending his motorcycle, the Vatican financier tapping a golden calculator, and the critic seen at his typewriter become part of a visual pattern marked by instability. The effect is at the core of Jarman's work, promoting a positive sense of incoherence in which the dis-ease of the text becomes linked to the disease (and suffering) of the artist.

This sense of pleasing jarring occurs similarly on the sound track in the film, when the hubbub of an antiquated PA system and the distant sound of a steam train do not dissolve the realism of Renaissance Italy but assert a filmic region less tethered in time and space. "A-sad-reflection-of-our-time" types the critic Baglione, Marat-like in his bath, attacking Caravaggio by identifying a poisonous excess to his paintings, as if the oozings of form and reference might contaminate the body of Rome.[10] Jarman grounds the slippery realism of the film in the confined space of the dying painter: this is the operating theater of a deteriorating body and mind. The mark of this collapse is felt not only at the visual level but in relation to the narrative thrust of consecutive scenes: the clinical and mental processes of the dying man are linked to the scene-building in the text. The critic, Baglione, seated in his bathtub, shudders out invective against Caravaggio and throws himself back in blissful relief. This action is cut to Caravaggio in his death rattle, himself reclined and panting, seeking release in a remembered fantasy of ejaculation with Pasqualone. The sequence ends in the ecstatic transfer of seed and spirit into death and beyond, leaving all exhausted. Jarman's biography foregrounds the body under pressure, its products variously toxic, sexual, written, painted, and always vital.

In *The Last of England*, it is the body of England itself that is seen to be sick, and the film attempts a similarly energetic and positive diagnosis of a nation under the malaise of eight years of Thatcher government. "What proof do you need the world's curling up like an autumn leaf?" asks the narrator. More desperate and bleaker than previous work, *The Last of England* proceeds according to the vague logic of a set of situations or set pieces, shot mostly in and around the now-derelict parts of London's docklands. It is scored and over-voiced by nonsynchronous sound and the reading of verses that match a sense of destitution caught by the camera. Just as the film takes place in the realm before or after narrative sense, so it refuses the technology of 35-mm sound cinema; it is shot, instead, in Super-8, with processed, found, and home footage. The result is a wildly "personal" film that implicates Jarman as a kind of cinematic archaeologist delving into a lost past, someone seeking an irredeemable place amid the shards of contemporary ruin. "Super-8 is a documentary camera," says Jarman. "It's very close to the body" (Charity, 57). Jarman celebrates the endurance and fundamentally nostalgic quality of Super-8 in the film itself by revealing a freshly unearthed skeleton, found peering through the viewfinder of this more intimate camera.

Jarman's resistance to the terms of mainstream cinema sights him as a target for the establishment critic precisely because he declines the stories and the equipment of traditional British cinema. This refusal to work in the mainstream of cinema is crucial in relation to Jarman's situation as a gay artist, one engaged on the one hand in filmic expression and on the other in a sexual practice increasingly associated with disease and under pressure to be silent.[11] Jarman's films, inasmuch as they center around suffering and in the light of the filmmaker's own susceptibility to illness, encourage a comparison between the operations and theaters of sickness and those of cinema.

In the absence of exact medical knowledge about the disease, AIDS is necessarily discussed in terms infected by the fear of and prejudice toward the practices of those infected. In the case of gay men, attention is turned to (sexual) practices rather than to the strictly medical symptoms of the disease, and a false logic of deserved suffering is engaged. Paula Treichler refers to "an epidemic of signification," suggesting that the threat of AIDS is as much a narrative issue as a medical one (Treichler, 31-70). Watney describes the logic by which homophobia translates a medical disaster into a political process of identifying and segregating a category of people whose sickness is conceived as punishment (Watney, 71-86). Both writers imply the need to address the terms of the framework that AIDS occupies: the combination of the mystery surrounding the virus and the volatility of feeling toward groups seen as outsiders. In Pratiba Parmar's documentary film *Reframing AIDS* (1988), specific count is made of the implicit agendas that underlie the fear and confusion. The experience of AIDS delineates the degree of British society's reliance on heterosexuality and, by extension, on the family and the home. Derek Jarman's film about gay men, for whom all of these options are problematic, made at a time when government urging was to return the responsibility for health "to the community," is most interesting in its scrutiny of the home and of those people excluded from this domain.[12]

Jarman's frantic and dismembered film manically tries to recapture and refuse aspects of the past, of homes now rendered redundant and unworkable. Shots of his own childhood, lived in the quasi prisons of military housing, echo the dereliction of the abandoned housing estates, which themselves point up the destitution of a society where sick people live amid hospital wards vacant for want of funds to staff them.[13] Throughout the film there is a simmering desperation ("the ice in your glass is radioactive") that occasionally ignites into images, as in the depiction of the harassment of the new groups of nomads and dispossesseds that populate Thatcher's Britain. *The Last of England* thus suffers under a political sickness, inscribed on the body of England, on its architecture and landscape, and more directly, onto the bodies of those excluded (from health, from homes, from jobs) under a regime that would make (private) patients of us all. But it is also a beautiful film: Jarman suggests that sickness need not be shackled to images and terms of weakness and stigma, but may empower a different register of social and artistic health.

"After *The Last of England*, someone came up and said, this film tells the story of my life. Well, who was I to say that it didn't?" (Romney, 13). Where *Caravaggio* tries to tell a story under pressure, Jarman's next film abandons the attempt. This immediate lack of a clear narrative has been seen as the mark of its sickness. Jarman's remark makes it clear that a lack of coherence provides a certain democratic effect, but it also suggests a questioning of the power relations behind the idea of "traditional narrative." The frantic manner of *The Last of England* marks not only the bodies under pressure that have made and appear in it, but also suggests a similarly dis-eased, pressurized spectator. Jarman's "home movie" speaks of a disrupted homeland that repels those who seek order and coherence, but crucially vouchsafes an alternative way of making sense for those who similarly feel themselves to be "under pressure," uneasy, or subjected. *The Last of England*, then, in its "wild, orgiastic dismemberment,"[14] is not only sick but sickening. Jarman's film, made as he discovered the fragility of his own health, and most graphically describing the political and architectural dereliction of Britain, points up how the idea of sickness is used in a power struggle between the sick and the well, the strong and the excluded, as it suggests the ways in which the term can be redeployed.

Asked why he has not made a film specifically about HIV or AIDS, Jarman responded that such a film would be sentimental and that, in any case, the illness would be impossible to image. "The best thing is to be talking about it alongside the work," he argues (Romney, 13) and this he does in many newspaper interviews and as a "guest" on British radio's "In the Psychiatrist's Chair" (Jarman 1990).[15] The first film made entirely after his diagnosis, however, needs little displacement to be seen as an imaging of the AIDS crisis. *War Requiem*, a story of the deaths of some young men and the mourning that acccompanies them, is structured by the music of a gay composer and incorporates the verse of a (probably) gay victim of the war. Jarman's film provides a visual accompaniment to Benjamin Britten's *War Requiem* (first performed in Coventry cathedral in May 1962). Britten's work embraces many of the poems written at the front by Wilfred Owen during the First World War, and Jarman depicts an Owen figure (Nathaniel Parker) together with an unknown British soldier (Owen Teale) and a German (Sean Bean). All die during the film. Their stories are interwoven with those of their mourners, a function largely the province of women: the mothers of Owen and the enemy soldier (Patricia Hayes, Rohan McCullough) and a nurse (Tilda Swinton) who also seems to be Owen's sister.

Perhaps the most daring shot in the film is a nearly seven-minute, almost static, medium shot of the nurse grieving for the dead Owen. She twists and braids her hair, rocks her body back and forth, runs her hands over her face and hugs herself, expressing both despair and rapture as she responds to the mood of the music. The spectator, watching her intently private albeit highly aesthetized mourning, is held up, like the narrative, by the suspended camera. Earlier in the film, we witness Owen's own mourning after he disturbs a snowball fight between the other two soldiers, leading to their deaths in a scene that provides a reenactment of the knifing of Ranuccio by Caravaggio. In what Jarman refers to as "the moral climate of clause 28" (Jarman 1989, 34), *War Requiem* publicly offers a space for a mourning that, as Simon Watney and Douglas Crimp have argued, is not readily available to gay men in our society (Crimp 1988, 7; Watney 1987, 7-8).[16]

Just as Jarman's camera rests unflinchingly on grief, it also shows us horrific scenes of dismemberment and excruciating pain in the inserted documentary footage from near-contemporary conflicts in Afghanistan and Cambodia. Again, Jarman revives a historical narrative (of the Somme) and contaminates it with current political and social dimensions. That the AIDS virus has created war conditions in Britain is materially expressed by Jarman's filming *War Requiem* in the newly abandoned hospital at Darenth Park in Kent. Its anonymous winding corridors and ready supply of empty spaces allow Jarman, who had already spun Renaissance Italy out of a Thames-side warehouse, to stage a war in adjoining rooms. Its setting, resonant of a decline in public health facilities, continues the demand for attention to physical suffering that pervades the earlier films.

By contrast with *War Requiem*, critics quickly identified the next film, the one widely expected, as the work of a dying man, to be his last,[17] *The Garden*, as an AIDS allegory. *The Garden* continues Jarman's practice of re-fusing the home movie by setting his work at home: in and around the rocky beach garden he cultivates behind his cottage at Dungeness on the Kent coast. References to gardens are strewn through Jarman's writings and indeed his films. *Jubilee* (1977) begins in the royal gardens of Elizabeth I, to which a modern-day alternative is later offered when we see Max, a mercenary, in his garden of artificial plants. Max, concerned that all the massive weapons of destruction the world has compiled are going to waste, declares that his "idea of a perfect garden is a remembrance poppy field." *The Angelic Conversation* (1984) comes to rest finally in the garden of Montacute House where one of the lovers whom the film tracks discovers a lily pond and "sees memory in it" (Jarman 1987, 143). In *The Last of England*, the home-movie footage is mostly shot on the lawn. *War Requiem* opens with the old soldier (Lawrence Olivier) convalescing in the hospital garden; later, in flashback, his nurse remembers her past happiness sowing seeds in the company of her mother and dead brother.

The space of the garden thus accrues a set of resonances in Jarman's cinema. It is a place for the recovery of both health and memories and in *The Garden* becomes the central metaphor for another dig at British society. For Jarman one of the advantages of buying the small house in the lee of one of

Britain's oldest and best-known nuclear power plants at Dungeness appears to be the opportunity to create his own strange garden and eventual film set. Jarman's gardening, his filmmaking, and his illness are integrated in a film that is also a landscape in the tradition of the nineteenth-century English painter Turner,[18] another vision of Britain and a place for his own recuperation. Dungeness Beach serves for a new Gethsemane set by the sea in Kent, itself known as the Garden of England. The metaphorically charged concept of the garden provides fertile ground for contending with the proliferating discourse that surrounds the AIDS epidemic.

In *The Last of England* book Jarman describes the thirty plastic pots that served him as a primitive garden in London. Under constant attack from pigeons, his plants suffer but, he writes, "it doesn't stop me. Like all true gardeners I'm an optimist" (Jarman 1987, 151). It is an ill but optimistic filmmaker who sets out to displace our traditional notions of home and garden in his latest film. Even the hospital is moved onto the beach, as we see Jarman—in scenes of stunning beauty—lying on a metal-framed NHS-like bed set on the damp sands, the water lapping at its feet, while flare-carrying men and women circle him. It seems almost as if Jarman desires to imitate Caravaggio's seaside death at Porto Ercole in a magical private world totally remote from the decrepit buildings of, say, Darenth Park. *The Garden* remains an intensely personal film; despite the fact that its director's sick body allowed him perhaps less control over the final product than ever before, Jarman is more than ever present. Early on, as he ponders in his garden, we hear a woman's voice call: "Derek." He is a gardener and a cameraman, following close behind his subject with his Super-8; he is a writer slumped at his desk; and he is the bedridden, curled up body. With the director unable fully to care for the film, the film elects to care for him.

The Garden, tight with Christian imagery, features two lovers who sometimes stand in for Christ—although there is also a more conventionally coded Christ figure in robe and beard. The taunting and torture of these figures in the film forges a link between the established Christian church and the homophobia that causes so much suffering. In his *War Requiem* book Jarman writes out what might stand as a dedication to his next film: "To all those cast out, like myself, from Christendom. To my friends who are dying in a moral climate created by a church with no compassion" (Jarman 1989, 35). Using the Christian myth as a reference point, *The Garden* tracks the homophobia of British life and lays it bare. The British society that Thatcher has crafted is one that doesn't care, a garden that has not been tended, a "piss-stained" country of the small minded. Denholm Eliot's Swaby would again feel at home in a sick society where films such as Jarman's can only be

The "Christ-couple" kissed on the feet, in *The Garden* (1990).

produced under many pressures. Thus, we witness the turmoil of the film's making more fully here than before: arc lights flare and instructions are shouted as the film begins, and the whirring of the camera motor accompanies the Super-8 footage. Jarman magnifies these records of filmic surveillance by the oft-repeated shot of the revolving arm of the tracking station that overlooks his beach garden.[19] Its circular motion is picked up early in the film by twelve women, sitting at the table of a last supper, whose fingers circle the rims of their glasses; later these two movements are further elaborated by intercutting images of what looks like a carousel and of Tilda Swinton carrying a ladder in a sweep of dizzying power. Nonnarrative film, perhaps, has to circle around the issues because it pursues what *The Garden*'s voice-over calls a "journey without direction, [of] no certainty." Near the end of the film, however, we do find a direct expression of both anger and grief. A voice-over laments: "I walk in this garden holding the hands of dead friends. Old age came quickly for my generation: they died so silently. . . . I have no words. My shaking hands cannot express my fury. My sadness is all I have."

But *The Garden* also remains full of fun and hope, a film reflecting the mood of a man who fantasized himself as Thatcher's minister of horticulture, a kind of national gardener in tune with his prime minister's thinking because each hates pinks—both flower and color (Jarman 1987, 151-55). If Jarman cannot ignore the weeds in the garden of England, he is also ready to see the roses. In an interview at the end of 1990 in which he discusses his recent illness and attacks Thatcher's "starving of the NHS," Jarman continues with this praise for its workers and care-givers: "one great positive thing in all this has been the care I have received at St. Mary's [hospital] in Paddington. And the way that fortunately, I can say that nobody has stepped out of a room when I entered it, or has not shaken me by the hand. People are better than that, you see. More tolerant and more open than Mrs. Thatcher . . . would allow" (Chalmers, 18). Out of his own suffering, as out of the alternative practice of his films, Jarman conjures both sweetness and vitriol.

Refusing to be silenced by sickness, Derek Jarman's films, writings, and interviews show that sickness is a power position—that to dissolve narrative is to undermine, and so to threaten, established power. He consistently claims lineage with the great British tradition, has not stopped making his homosexual films of palliation and comfort, and continues to arouse the fury of the mainstream. Jarman makes films that, beyond suffering and sickness, bring about a fusion of the traditional and the unexamined. He writes, "Now you project your private world into the public arena and produce the flash-point: the attrition between the private and public world is the tradition you discover. . . . When everyone has taken the path we are all art and no audience " (Jarman 1987, 236). The effect is continually to reopen practices and spaces to the public, to dissolve the boundaries, to seek other homes and gardens in the name of a greater national health.

Derek Jarman's eight feature-length films are *Sebastiane* (1975), *Jubilee* (1977), *The Tempest* (1979), *The Angelic Conversation* (1985), *Caravaggio* (1986), *The Last of England* (1987), *War Requiem* (1989), and *The Garden* (1990). Of these, *Jubilee, The Angelic Conversation, Caravaggio, War Requiem,* and *The Last of England* are available on video through Mystic Fire in the United States. The best known of his shorter films are *In the Shadow of the Sun* (1980), *T.G: Psychic Rally in Heaven* (1981), and *Imagining October* (1984). He has directed several music videos, most notably for Marianne Faithful, the Smiths, and Annie Lennox, and a segment for the operatic anthology film, *Aria* (1987), produced by Don Boyd. Earlier, he was set designer for Ken Russell's *The Devils* (1971) and *Savage Messiah* (1972).

Notes

1. Princess Elizabeth, future queen, and Philip Mountbatten.

2. A white paper is published by the government and proposes upcoming legislation.

3. The queen opens each session of Parliament in the United Kingdom with a speech that lays down the general tenor of government activity over the period. The queen is herself purely a mouthpiece for the elected party's policies.

4. In Britain, "public schools" are, of course, synonymous with private schools.

5. It would be interesting to see the images that Spider (Malcolm McDowell) is taking with his miniature camera, one so small that it seems as if it might, as in arthroscopic surgery, film *within* the body and is thus more closely connected to it even than the Super-8 camera of Jarman that we discuss later.

6. For an insightful analysis of the state of the British film industry that takes off from Welland's comment, see Roddick (1982).

7. *The Angelic Conversation* includes fourteen of the sonnets.

8. Jarman's response to Stone includes the assertion that Michael Powell's *Peeping Tom* would, in its day, have made Stone's list of sick movies. Powell, who is mentioned by Stone as an example of a British "tradition of quality," has also been much praised by Jarman at various times.

9. Jarman describes the scene and his feelings on first being told that he was HIV-positive in Jarman (1987), 16-17.

10. Baglione accuses Caravaggio of "ignorance and depravity" and thus predicts the stand Stone and others later take toward the work of Jarman, Frears, and others.

11. Clause 28, a part of the 1987 Local Government Bill, read: "[A] local authority shall not a) promote homosexuality or publish material for the promotion of homosexuality; b) promote the teaching in any maintained school of the acceptability of homosexuality as a pretended family relationship by the publication of such material or otherwise; and c) give financial assistance to any person for either of the purposes referred to in paragraphs a) and b) above."

12. For a detailed analysis of issues of homelessness in *The Last of England*, see Lawrence Driscoll's piece in the *Spectator*, 10, no. 2 (1990).

13. Consider, for example, this report from David Brindle in the *Guardian Weekly* of December 30, 1990: "With an estimated 3,500 hospital beds closed to save money, the position is likely to deteriorate as health authorities struggle to balance their books in time for the government's NHS changes in April."

14. *Caravaggio.*

15. "In the Psychiatrist's Chair" is a weekly program broadcast on the BBC's Radio 4 in which celebrities discuss aspects of their lives with psychiatrist Dr. Anthony Clare. Jarman's interview was first heard on August 15, 1990.

16. Mention should be made here of Isaac Julien's narrativeless and lyrical "This Is Not an AIDS Advertisement" (1988), about which Julien says: "There needs to be a space for mourning and this tape is dedicated to those losses." This video, along with Julien's comment, is included in the package "Video against AIDS" put out by Video Data Bank. Their package also includes Pratiba Parmar's *Reframing AIDS*, a project with which Julien was also involved.

17. Happily, by the beginning of 1991, Jarman, recovered from tuberculosis and toxoplasmosis, had regained his fragile health and embarked upon a long-cherished project, filming Christopher Marlowe's *Edward II*.

18. Jarman says proudly of *The Garden*: "When did you see the landscape look like that? It looks like Turner" (Romney, 13).

19. The revolving arm of the radar repeats Jarman's use of a similar tracking apparatus in *The Angelic Conversation*. In the earlier film, however, the stop-motion effect that Jarman uses throughout breaks the circling motion into stuttering fragments.

Works Cited

Brindle, David. 1990. "NHS Waiting Lists Rise to Nearly 1 Million." *Guardian Weekly*, Dec. 30.

Chalmers, Robert. 1990. "Please God, Send Me to Hell." *Sunday Correspondent*, Nov. 18.

Charity, Tom. 1991. "Avant-gardener." *Time Out*, Jan. 3.

Crimp, Douglas, ed. 1988. *AIDS. Cultural Analysis. Cultural Activism*. Cambridge and London: MIT.

Driscoll, Lawrence. 1990. "Burroughs/Jarman: Anamorphosis, Homosexuality." *Spectator* 10 (2): 78-95.

Jarman, Derek. 1984. *Dancing Ledge*. London: Quartet.

_____. 1986. *Derek Jarman's Caravaggio*. London: Thames and Hudson.

_____. 1987. *The Last of England*. London: Constable.

_____. 1988. "Freedom Fighter for a Vision of the Truth." *Sunday Times*, Jan. 17.

_____. 1989. *War Requiem: The Film*. London and Boston: Faber and Faber.

_____. 1990. "Positive Thinking" (interview with Dr. Anthony Clare). *Listener*, Aug. 16.

Johnson, Marion. 1983. "Carry On . . . Follow That Stereotype." In *British Cinema History*, edited by James Curran and Vincent Porter, 312-27. London: Wiedenfield and Nicholson.

Mars-Jones, Adam. 1987. "Remission." *Granta* 22: 171-93. London: Penguin.

Politics Today. 1990. London: Conservative Research Dept., May. 19.

Roddick, Nick. 1982. "Breathing a Little Harder than Usual." *Sight and Sound* 51 (3): 159-63.

Romney, Jonathan. 1991. "The Garden of Earthly Delights." *City Limits*, Jan. 3.

Stone, Norman. 1988. "Through a Lens Darkly." *Sunday Times*, Jan. 10.

Treichler, Paula. 1988. "AIDS, Homophobia, and Biomedical Discourse." In *AIDS. Cultural Analysis. Cultural Activism*, edited by Douglas Crimp, 31-70. Cambridge and London: MIT.

Walker, Alexander. 1985. *National Heroes*. London: Harrap.

Watney, Simon. 1987. *Policing Desire*. Minneapolis: University of Minnesota Press.

_____. 1988. "Spectacle of AIDS." In *AIDS. Cultural Analysis. Cultural Activism*, edited by Douglas Crimp, 71-86. Cambridge and London: MIT.

Contributors

Susan Torrey Barber, assistant professor in the Communication Arts Department at Loyola Marymount University (Los Angeles), teaches film, television history, theory, and criticism. She has published articles in *Film Quarterly* and the *Spectator*. Currently, she is updating her study on the Australian film renaissance.

Mary Desjardins, assistant professor, teaches critical and cultural studies at the University of Texas (at Austin) in the Radio-Television-Film Department. She is presently working on a book about maternalism and spectatorship.

Manthia Diawara, professor, teaches film and black literature at the University of Pennsylvania. His most recent publication is *African Cinema: Politics and Culture*.

Thomas Elsaesser, chair of the department of Film and Television Studies at the University of Amsterdam, has published essays in *Screen, Sight and Sound, New German Critique, Discourse, Bianco e Nero*, and other journals. Among his recent publications are *New German Cinema: A History* and *Early Cinema: Space Frame Narrative*.

Lester Friedman, professor, teaches film at Syracuse University and humanities at SUNY, Health Science Center. Author of several books and articles on Jews in the American cinema, he is the editor of *Unspeakable Images: Ethnicity and the American Cinema* and is currently completing a book on multicultural media in the classroom.

Paul Giles, assistant professor, received his Ph.D. from Oxford in 1985. He left England in 1987 to work at Portland State University, Oregon, where he teaches modern literature and film. His writings include *Hart Crane* and *American Catholic Arts and Fictions*.

Barry K. Grant, professor of film at Brock University (Ontario, Canada), is the author of *Voyages of Discovery: The Cinema of Frederick Wiseman*, as well as editor of *Film Genre Reader* and *Planks of Reason: Essays on the Horror Film*, among other volumes. His work on film and popular music has appeared in many journals, including *Journal of Popular Film and Television, Jump Cut, Popular Music and Society*, and *CineAction!*

Andrew Higson teaches film and television studies at the University of East Anglia, England. He has published numerous articles on British cinema history in *Screen, Ideas and Production*, and *Film Criticism* and has contributed to *National Fictions*, edited by Geoff Hurd (1984), and *All Our Yesterdays*, edited by Charles Barr (1986). He is currently preparing a book on the history of British cinema and has been a member of the *Screen* editorial board.

Guy Johnson is a Ph.D. candidate in the critical studies division of the School of Cinema-Television at the University of Southern California. He has published articles in the *Spectator* and given papers at the Society for Cinema Studies conventions.

Antonia Lant, assistant professor of cinema studies at New York University, is the author of *Blackout: Reinventing Women for Wartime British Cinema* (1991) and "The Curse of the Pharaoh, or How Cinema Contracted Egyptomania," *October* 59 (Winter 1992). She is currently writing a book on orientalism and silent cinema.

Jim Leach, professor, teaches film and communications studies at Brock University (Ontario, Canada). He has published articles in *Cinema Canada, Dalhousie Review, Journal of Canadian Studies*, and *Wide Angle*. Author of *A Possible Cinema: The Films of Alain Tanner*, he is currently writing a book on Canadian filmmaker Claude Jutra.

Chris Lippard, a Ph.D. student in the University of Southern California's Film and Literature Program, has published articles in the *Spectator*. He is writing a dissertation on issues of health, illness, and medical practice in recent British cinema.

Brian McIlroy, assistant professor, teaches film studies in the Department of Theatre and Film at the University of British Columbia. His most recent book is *World Cinema 4: Ireland*. Currently, he is writing a book on British cinema from 1968 to 1990.

Leonard Quart, associate professor of cinema studies at the College of Staten Island/CUNY, is author of *American Film and Society since 1945: Revised and Expanded* and coauthor with Albert Auster of *How the War Was Remembered: Hollywood and Vietnam*. He is an editor of *Cineaste* magazine and a contributor to a wide variety of film and general magazines and newspapers, including *New York Newsday, Film Quarterly*, and *Tikkun*.

Michael Walsh, assistant professor, teaches film at the University of Hartford, where he also edits *Hartford Studies in Literature*. He has recently published essays on Chris Marker, William Burroughs, Jacques Lacan, and Jean Baudrillard, and his work has appeared in journals such as *Wide Angle, Semiotext(e), Quarterly Review of Film and Video*, and *Journal of Mind and Behavior*.

Tony Williams, associate professor of cinema studies in the Department of Cinema and Photography at Southern Illinois University (Carbondale), is coauthor of *Italian Western: Opera of Violence* and author of *Jack London: The Movies*. His publications have appeared in *Sight and Sound, Wide Angle, Science Fictions Studies, Jump Cut*, and *Inventing Vietnam*. He is currently coediting a Vietnam War filmography.

Peter Wollen, professor, is a film- and videomaker who teaches at UCLA. Author of *Sign and Meaning in the Cinema*, he codirected (with Laura Mulvey) *Riddles of the Sphinx* and *Crystal Gazing*, and directed *Friendship's Death* and *Full Cycle*. His most recent book is *Raiding the Icebox: Reflections on Twentieth-Century Culture*.

Index

Compiled by Eileen Quam and Theresa Wolner